Praises for Forgotten *an*

You have turned on all the lights for me on a fascinating trail. Now I sort of know where I have been—and why—and hope it was not all for naught!

> – W.B. Woodruff Jr., former Secretary L/35 Association,
> Decatur, Texas

Forgotten is that rare military history book which combines gripping first-person front line combat narrative with a scholar's questions as to the "why" of war, an analysis of the enemy's real motive, and how we, as a nation, should formulate national policy to best react. Author Sam Holliday, a veteran of Korea and Vietnam, is a thinking man's warrior.

> – John Ottley, COL-Infantry (Ret), USAR, Author,
> *The Seventh Deadliest Fear*

Thank you for all the information on the Korean War. Being a member of the 29th Inf and leaving Okinawa with C Co for Korea with you, it was especially interesting to me to go over the timeline from our entry to the final days. You have provided me with the answer to many times and events as they occurred.

> – David M. Williams, C Co 29th and L Co 35th,
> 1950 and 1951

Many thanks for the fine reporting of this under-reported war. Repeated miscalculations on both sides resulted in dreadful casualty totals just to maintain the status quo ante—World War I on a vastly reduced, but still tragic, scale. Your reporting reflects both the importance and unimportance of our massive technological superiority. Without our technological dominance, we clearly would have been pushed off the peninsula, and South Korea would replicate the desolation that has marked life above the parallel. And yet our technological superiority was insufficient to carry the day. Grim reading. But I was deeply moved by your reporting of small triumphs, instances of impressive courage, and costly mistakes. In short, the stuff of war.

– Jack Ives

My view, and I think that of Colonel Holliday, is that the most fundamental lesson that we should have learned from both Korea and Vietnam is that it was absolute folly for us to think that we could impose American values and an American form of government, by military means, on a foreign people in their own land. Resisting aggression is one thing, but "nation building" from the top down is quite another, especially when the "nation builder" is a foreign force. This is the message that Colonel Holliday sends. And he is right.

– William O. Miller, Rear Admiral, JAGC, US Navy (Ret), Formerly Judge Advocate General of the Navy

Being a Korean War veteran from 1951 to 1953, I have always been a strong believer of keeping our history of the Korean War alive so we veterans, who fought to keep other countries free, will never be forgotten. Now I will always have something to keep my memory alive about what I did, and where I was, in my younger days. Thanks for the work to help make sure that we old-timers are not forgotten.

– Sam Naomi, Retired SFC US Army

I am most grateful to have been included in what you have written. I am certain that future generations will read with considerable interest your detailed and documented chronology of the Korean War. My deepest respect for you prevails. Had it not been for your skillful leadership, I and many others would not be alive today. I treasure the time we had together.

– Len Becicka, Col USA (Ret)

Mere words cannot express my appreciation for your thorough research. Especially for us ol' Gravel Pounders who were there, and our war consisted of what we, as individuals, were experiencing at that particular time. Your story is enlightening and informative by giving some "reason" for how the decisions and planning were given and the resultant actions. Again, thank you. You have certainly opened a lot of eyes and "filled in the blanks" for a lot of vets across the country.

– Bill Scott

I am another veteran of the Korean War who appreciates the excellent details from the start to the armistice of this "forgotten war." Your research and detail enriched my knowledge of the war; as an aide to the C/S, Far East Command after my combat days in Korea, I gained a different perspective. Your details were more descriptive, as well as providing me particularly a fill-in from the knowledge I gained during 1952–1953.

– Phil Bardos

You will always be Captain Sam Holliday to me and others on Hill 329 (Skeleton Hill). Thank you, Sam, for your accounting of the actions in 1951 in Korea. I appreciate your efforts then and now. I've learned much I didn't know and have looked at many things that had not crossed my mind in that manner before. As you would expect, 21 May 1951 was one of the days

I shall always remember. You were a big influence on me, and I appreciate it. I think had you been in my spot you might have reacted as I did. The super aggressiveness that I exhibited probably saved lives, including my own.

– Willis Jackson DSC, PH

I hope this account will gain a life of its own for future historians and the military, not to mention the "head in the sand" politicians who elevated themselves as self-proclaimed critics and experts.

– Bill Wright

Your personal chronology of the war and your insights are invaluable. But once again, we as a country and as a military have failed to understand the true nature of war and how to prosecute it. Our civilian and military (now more a political/military leadership) has failed their country. We just don't have the quality leadership we need.

– Name Withheld

I hope you have an opportunity to teach this experience to our future military leaders, and even to political leaders. How many of our young men have died due to ineptitude and naiveté?

– Joseph B. DiBartolomeo

I could get quite dramatic and wordy in plaudits and my high regard for you and your work. I think it's far more appropriate to do it military style with the ultimate military kudo, which is just two words, but from one military guy to another, says it all. *Well done!*

– Ed West

Forgotten

Forgotten

Ideological Conflicts in Korea, Vietnam, Iraq, and Afghanistan

Sam C. Holliday

PhD, University of South Carolina, MPIA, University of Pittsburgh, BS,
United States Military Academy, Retired Colonel, US Army

BOOKLOGIX®
Alpharetta, GA

ISBN: 978-1-61005-507-9
Library of Congress Control Number: 2014911253

10 9 8 7 6 5 4 3 2   1 2 0 3 1 4

Printed in the United States of America

∞This paper meets the requirements of ANSI/NISO Z39.48-1992 (Permanence of Paper)

*To those I had the honor to serve with
in Korea and Vietnam.*

CONTENTS

AUTHOR'S NOTE

These twenty-six chapters chronicle the events that happened to me, and those who served with me, in the Korean conflict and lessons that I learned at that time. It was written fifty-eight years after the events described. Every effort has been made to record what actually happened. Yet, as in all wars, no single telling "gets it completely right." Thus it is presented as my memories and what I learned during my year in Korea. Corrections by those who were there—or by their families and friends—are welcome.

It is primarily written for my family, but I also feel that there is a need for people to know more about what happened in the Korean conflict. I would like to inform those who know nothing about that war and to give those who have anti-military preconceptions a greater appreciation of what combat is like.

It is wrong to forget the thousands of Koreans, Americans, Chinese, and others who suffered unbearably or died in Korea. We should be better than that. Those war experiences should provide some purpose or direction. If those of us who were there do not tell our story, we cannot expect anyone else to know or care about the significance of what took place in Korea or of combat in general. The future of our country depends on others being willing to do their duty when called upon as we were.

I hope this chronicle preserves something of the intensity of life so close to death, the lasting bond of combat camaraderie, the joy and lightheartedness that can be so close to horror and brutality, and the feelings of something so terrible yet so appealing combined into one. From July 1950 until July 1951, all of these were compressed into our experiences as we went up and down Korea. The strange, the familiar, the momentous, the lasting, the fleeting, the sublime, the ridiculous, and the dreadful all combined into a whole that would be difficult to match. I hope it allows many to realize why so many infantrymen and tankers refer to the agony and the ecstasy of combat.

The Korean conflict is often called the "Forgotten War." So I also hope this chronicle will encourage others to tell their experiences of this short time and small place. Is all that was learned during the first year of that conflict to be forgotten? Indeed, there is a real possibility that those experiences will fall into oblivion. If so, all of those happenings might have no real purpose. They might signify nothing. Those of us who lived through it have an obligation to prevent that. It is for us to describe what really happened and to see if we can identify some lessons to be learned.

I wrote about my experiences because of a void in what I know of my father's experiences in World War I. My father fought with an artillery battery of the Fifth Division during that war. He was wounded near St. Mihiel in September 1918, and later he was responsible for several villages in Luxembourg. Yet I know nothing more. I do not want to leave the same void for my family. For many years I had good intentions of correcting this, but I did nothing. Over the Christmas holiday of 2008, I was politely told that I had said I would record my experiences in Korea, but that I had done nothing. I was also reminded that if I did not do it soon, this project would be "overtaken by events." I promised not to let that happen. With *Up and Down Korea* I fulfilled my promise to my family, and now with *Forgotten* I have revised that effort—with an additional chapter on Vietnam and some comments about Iraq and Afghanistan—into something that I hope will be informative and also helpful in the future.

It is true that those who know combat firsthand rarely talk about it. They do not want others to think they are magnifying their own actions to satisfy their egos, and they do not want to bring back things they want to forget. Moreover, people have many other interests, and most do not want to spend their time on tales of the past by "old men who are not part of their world." Yet this does not allow an understanding of combat in general and of the critical role of the infantryman and tankers[1] in particular. The nobility and heroism of these warriors and soldiers, who are the final and essential decision makers for all of us, can easily be ignored. If this reality is ignored, the vacuum will be filled by anti-military rhetoric, which can turn a warrior into a dim-witted, uncaring brute and killer. This would destroy true patriotism. This would place all Americans in peril. Our country needs to recognize, value, praise, and reward these warriors. Americans need to select their leaders from those who have survived the emotional and intellectual trials of combat.

I want to thank all of those who have helped me develop the ideas presented here, yet they are too numerous to list. However, this book would never have been possible without the support, proofreading, and assistance of my wife Joan.

I hope that *Forgotten: Ideological Conflicts in Korea, Vietnam, Iraq, and Afghanistan* might do something to preserve the reality of combat and the importance of those who risk their lives for something greater than themselves.

---

[1] This is not to exclude artillerymen, engineers, rangers, members of the Special Forces, and others who might have engaged in face-to-face combat in a life or death struggle, but to stress that only a fraction of those in the military engage in combat—and even a smaller fraction of those living in the United States. Being in a combat area, or even supporting combat forces, is not the same thing as being in combat.

PREFACE

This chronicles the events that I remember about those I served with during the Korean conflict. I hope my memories will provide knowledge of war in general and of what happened in Korea so many years ago. I hope it will inform those who know nothing about conflict in which death is always only seconds away.

If those of us who were there do not tell our story, we can never expect others to care or learn. I have attempted to present the familiar, the momentous, the lasting, the dramatic, the lessons learned, the strange, the timeless, the sublime, the dreadful, and the human all combined into a whole that can only be found in combat.

The nobility and heroism of those sent to fight for all Americans should never be forgotten as our thoughts and actions are consumed by our personal lives and interests. If America is to remain great and strong, Americans must remain united in their recognition and praise for those warriors and soldiers who have risked their lives for something greater than themselves.

CHAPTER ONE

IDEOLOGICAL CONFLICTS

The suffering, death, heroism, courage, skill, fear, cowardice, luck, successes, and errors during war are often ignored, distorted, and forgotten, but so are the lessons that could and should have been learned. This is clearly true regarding Korea and, to a lesser extent, what took place in Vietnam.

Most people remember nothing of the Korean War. If people remember anything, it is the bold landing of the marines at Inch'on and the suffering of the marines at "frozen Chosin." Yet the myths cultivated around these two events hide more significant events during the Korean conflict. The key military battle was the holding of the Pusan perimeter, not the landing at Inch'on. Moving the Tenth Corps, including the marines, to the east coast was a strategic blunder that hindered, rather than helped, the UN effort. The important military battles in Korea were fought up and down the western part of Korea.

Just two years before the Chinese communists entered Korea, they defeated a nationalist Chinese army in northeast China. Few in the West understand why the communists won—or why the nationalists lost. This can be explained by the Oriental way of conflict as compared to the Western way of war. Also, the Chinese leaders—but not Western leaders—recognized Korea as the start

1

of post-World War II struggles to determine the world's future. To this day, Western leaders still think of the firepower and maneuvers of conventional War, or economic and political development during Peace, rather than of ideological conflict, strategic communication, and Irregular Warfare that took place in Korea along with conventional War. They forget that supreme excellence is expressed by getting what you want without killing, rather than by killing all of your enemies.

To Western leaders and most people in the West, the conflicts in Korea and Vietnam were wars during which military forces engaged in mortal conflict. They were that, but were also much more. They were ideological conflicts, in which there is a struggle over the inner compass of individuals. It is this inner compass that shapes behavior. The war aspect of these conflicts is what is expected from military history. Ideology can refer to a body of social, political, and economic doctrines and plans for establishing them. Yet in a more general sense, ideology can refer to the ideas and convictions that shape the inner compass of individuals and thus determines what is right or wrong, good or bad, virtuous or sinful in a culture. It is in this more general sense that ideological conflict is used here—which could be called a clash of cultures.[2]

Knowledge of the ideological struggle is essential today and tomorrow. Therefore, this first chapter will discuss aspects of conflict other than those associated with conventional War. In 2014, Western culture is confronted by two existential threats that are ideological conflicts: the Third Jihad and postmodern thought. These differ from the ideological conflict in Korea and Vietnam—even though there are many similarities. Even more important, success in today's, and future, conflicts can be found in lessons that should have been learned in Korea and Vietnam.

In Korea and Vietnam, the ideological conflict was primarily between collectivism and individualism. In Korea this was visible, but ignored by most Americans. In Vietnam it was obvious, but never adequately addressed by Americans. In my mind, two young Korean women symbolized the ideological struggle between communism (collectivism) and capitalism (individualism) in that country. One was a dedicated communist I met in the jail of Okchon in October of 1950. The other was the young woman in a fur coat that I met as she was fleeing a destroyed Seoul on the night of 3 January 1951. Although I know not what happened to either, it is possible to imagine that their lives mirrored the struggle between collectivism and individualism in Korea after 1951. One was willing to use all means to destroy America, and the other was willing to cooperate with America for the good of all.

In moving from past to current ideological conflicts, we see that the new problems may not be visible or obvious to most Americans. Unfortunately, there are lessons that might have been learned from Korea and Vietnam that could have produced better outcomes in Iraq and Afghanistan at much lower costs, and that can make future US foreign policies more efficient and effective.

Success in ideological conflict does not require submission to some religious doctrine, acceptance of some social-political way of life, dedication to some "group think," or loyalty to some charismatic leader. It requires an inner compass in individuals strong enough to allow them to make good decisions in times of danger, confusion, and horror. It requires a shared identity—kinship—based on long-standing myths, legends, customs, and traditions, which provide a bond stronger than personal interests and desires. It requires a way to explain the unknown and the role of humans in the universe.

Success in ideological conflict goes to those who do not freeze or flee when they face danger, but can cope with reality by making judgments that will ensure survival, commitment, growth, and satisfaction.

The Third Jihad

The current worldwide Islamist movement, known as the Third Jihad, is in an ideological struggle against Western culture. It has much in common with the ideological struggles in Korea and Vietnam between communism (collectivism) and capitalism (individualism); therefore, what happened then might be helpful in deciding what to do today, and in the future, regarding the Third Jihad.

Some might see the current struggle as a clash of civilizations, or the continuation of the fourteen-centuries-old religious conflict between cross and crescent. There is some truth to these views. However, when they are taken to the extreme and fought as conventional War, the outcome is not only costly, but also usually unsuccessful in the long run. Ideological struggles are not the symmetric conflicts with established principles, like conventional War; they have the contradictions and complexity of Warfare (which some call Irregular Warfare, or some other name). Actions in ideological conflicts should be based more on art than on science and technology. For these reasons, the ideological struggles in Korea and Vietnam provide useful guidance for any ideological conflict—including that with the Third Jihad.

The First Jihad spread from Medina in the seventh century, after Muhammad's death, under the caliphs (vice regents). It ended in 1492, when Islam was driven out of Spain. The Second Jihad started with the fall of Constantinople in 1453. The Ottoman Turks

4

then implanted Islam in the Balkans and established hegemony over the Middle East. The Second Jihad was stopped in 1682 with an unsuccessful attempt to capture Vienna, and ended in 1924. In 1979, the Third Jihad started in Iran with the Shah being overthrown by Islamists led by Ayatollah Khomeini. It was given focus in February 1998 with a *fatwa*, which declared war on America and its allies. The Third Jihad is just another effort by Islamists to establish the Great Caliphate—in which everyone is governed by "the ways of the Prophet."

The Muslim "true believers" (i.e., Islamists) are frustrated because the West is rich, technologically superior, and powerful because it is—in their eyes—materialistic and corrupt. Islamists want to weaken and destroy America and Europe. The Islamists believe they can combine the fervor of a "true belief" with piety to regain the stolen Muslim wealth. They see Americans as "infidels" that have caused ills in Muslim countries. They seek a clash of civilizations—something the US seeks to avoid.

It must be recognized that all Muslims are not Islamists, i.e. those who support the Third Jihad—even though in 2014 most Muslims will not actively oppose the Third Jihad. Modern Muslims have little interest in establishing a Great Caliphate, and they are not hateful, infantile, and irrational. Yet the West can never eliminate all Islamists, and it can only win this ideological struggle if modern Muslims, who want to live in peace with Western culture, are willing and able to neutralize most Islamists. However, this will require a transformation of Islam, similar to that which took place in Christianity after 1500—but the transformation of Islam would be much more difficult. It will require most Muslims to reject, condemn, and fight against those parts of the Qur'an that require the conversion, submission, or killing of all nonbelievers.

The Islamists cannot be neutralized if the policies of the West start with the naive notion that money and rhetoric can win minds, hearts, and stomachs and thus turn modern Muslims against the Islamists. All ideological struggles are a test of wills. Economic, military, or legal means rarely change the inner compass of individuals, yet it is the inner compass that establishes and maintains wills. The inner compasses determine what a person considers good or bad, right or wrong, and virtuous or evil.

The leaders of the Third Jihad recognized the frustration engendered when people give up their traditional cultures for dreams of Western culture. The gap between what they observe in Europe and America and what they observe in their own countries obliges them to blame the West for all of their ills—even as they long for the material benefits of the West. Moreover, there is always a gap between expectations and reality. The leaders of the Third Jihad motivate Islamists through manipulation of such feelings.

The erosion strategy of the Islamists is based on success and failure in Warfare; it is protracted conflict. Yet it differs from past "wars of national liberation" and typical guerrilla operations during War. The members of the Third Jihad throughout the world have no single leader, no center of gravity, limited state sponsorship, and are not restricted by conflicts within Islam. They lack pyramidal hierarchies of control; their organizational networks are flatter. The Islamists do not seek success through War (symmetric conflict between military forces), but through erosion of their enemy's will and uniting and motivating their followers. For them, nonviolent means are as important as violent means.

This erosion strategy relies on Americans being impatient and seeking a swift victory with their technological superiority and the application of overwhelming force. It also relies on using the idealistic, compassionate, humane ideals of Westerners to weaken and destroy Western culture. The Islamists know that without a swift victory, Americans often lose their will when influenced by a postmodern media and antiwar activists, stressing casualties, costs, and misdeeds. They know that many Westerners do not want to recognize that evil exists.

Islamists seek to protect people from worldly temptations so that there will be no obstacles for them to submit to Allah. Their goals were expressed in a 2002 *Letter to the American People* as follows:

"What are we calling you to do, and what do we want from you?

"The first thing, we are calling you to Islam…the religion of Jihad is the way of Allah so that Allah's Word and religion reign supreme…

"The second thing, we are calling on you to stop your oppression, lies, immorality, and debauchery."

In other words, all totalitarian ideologies have clear, direct commands regarding legal, social, and political matters, usually masquerading as a religion. For Muslim true believers (Islamists) there is a battle between infidels (nonbelievers) and the true faith (Islam). Shari'a, like fascism and communism, wants a specific ideology to dominate all aspects of society. They all have a founder, a mythology, a sacred book, and a sociopolitical ideology. They cannot accept the idea of individuals with free will or of individuals with many different convictions living together in a climate of order and satisfaction. They do not recognize the foundations of Judeo-Christian religion as understood by the Founders: God's love, personal responsibility for behavior, and individual redemption. Collectives of both the right and the left demand submission to the "chosen" leaders.

Does Islam itself require all Muslims to be Islamists? If so, a clash of civilizations is inevitable. The destruction, suffering, and death which would result would make all previous wars pale in comparison. Therefore, our efforts should weaken the Islamists through separating them from the modern Muslims that accept pluralism. While our strategy must attempt to eliminate Islamists, it must also seek alliance with modern Muslims that respect pluralism and want better lives—freedom, equality, self-determination, representative government, and the pursuit of happiness—rather than spiritual purity in the eyes of Allah. However, we must always be aware of *taqiyah,* which is religiously sanctioned deception to protect or promote Islam; *taqiyah* is not only moral, it is admirable because it comes from the Qur'an and experiences of Muhammad himself.

The Islamists have infiltrated the governments of many Islamic countries, particularly in the security forces, as they attempt to weaken or destroy secular leadership. Also, the Islamists have attempted to gain international support from, and build support in, all non-Islamic countries. The Islamists are aided by support they receive in Europe and America from the elites, intellectuals, and academics. Many of these "useful idiots" opposed military action in Afghanistan and Iraq from the start. Some became distressed by doubts resulting from casualties, costs, and the treatment of prisoners. Islamists draw strength from Westerners that oppose military action or have gone "wobbly" in this test of wills.

The strategy of the Islamists seeks the five goals of the Third Jihad:

1. To remove US influence from the Middle East and to increase their supporters in the United States and Europe.

2. To have all international relations conducted through the United Nations, thus paralyzing effective action by the United States.

3. To control the oil in the Middle East, and then use that control to weaken the economic power of the United States.

4. To eliminate Israel.

5. To create a Great Caliphate.

If the Islamists can achieve the first three of these five goals, the threat to the US and Europe would be just as great as the threats during World War II and the Cold War.

The penetration by the Third Jihad into the US and our allies must be stopped. This is only possible if our actions are not restricted because some consider Islam a religion rather than what it is—an ideology. It is the aggressive, intolerant, and all-inclusive nature of this ideology that motivates the Islamists and prevents Islam from being accepted as a religion under our Constitution. Of course, any Muslim who accepts those who do not believe in Allah as equals and does not expect others to submit to Islam is welcome into our community of freedom and liberty for ALL. Otherwise, we must defend ourselves from the intolerant Qur'an, Shari'a, and the dicta of Muhammad. The fact that *taqiyah* allows Islamists to lie in furtherance of their faith makes it impossible for it to be recognized as a religion in keeping with American principles and ideals.

Modernism versus Postmodernism (Progressivism)

Currently there is another ideological struggle similar to those in Korea and Vietnam between communism (collectivism) and capitalism (individualism). This struggle is between progressivism (postmodernism) and Western culture as it evolved after 1500 (modernism). Thus, in 2014, there are two ideologies (Shari'a of the right and postmodernism of the left) which are challenging the principles and ideals that created traditional Western culture.

Although this ideological struggle between modernism and postmodernism started during World War I, it took off in the counterculture movement of the 1960s and can now be observed in most aspects of European and American life. This struggle is between progressives, who want to replace the concepts, institutions, roles, rules, and standards of modernism, and those that want to continue the evolution of modernism. Postmodernists (progressives) think they know how to achieve progress toward a better world. Today's modernists believe that the "progress" offered by the postmodernists is actually decline and decay. They do not want to return to 1914, but they do want a continuation of the equilibrium between belief, nationalism, patriotism, and science that produced modernism.

Modernism refers to the progressive economic and administrative rationalization and differentiation of societies that evolved in Europe from 1500 to 1914. The fundamental aspects of modernism (belief, national identity, patriotism, and science) are means developed during this period to achieve order and prevent chaos. Modernism evolved from Hebrew-Christian, Greco-Roman, and

Germanic roots and the striking cultural growth during the European Renaissance. The ensuing three-hundred-year struggle between belief (accepted thoughts) and science resulted in significant advances in both science and theology. Islam has never gone through this transformation.

From 1650 until 1914, there was a struggle between belief and science during which Western culture, and modernism, evolved. Change was commonplace. Some "answers" repeatedly proved to be no solution at all, while the dignity and creativity of the individual grew rapidly. By 1850 that struggle had profoundly weakened the influence of religion on shared civic virtues, and for some, science became a secular God.

After 1850, modernism continued to evolve as long as it maintained the golden mean (i.e., equilibrium among its four fundamentals).

1. **Belief** provided individuals with the free will and inner strength to control their behavior, to be creative, to enjoy freedom, to have self-esteem, and to be responsible for their actions. Belief provided an inner compass for making judgments. It prevented the individual from being subordinated to either the state or nation.

2. **National identity** provided a community (nation) with a sense of kinship and a unique intellectual, creative, technological, and artistic culture.

3. **Patriotism** supported the structure for a state of political unity, a representative polity, and economic success.

4. **The scientific method** established an objective means for uncovering falsehoods.

Modernism flourished when these four fundamentals were all vibrant and in equilibrium. However, whenever one would dominate the others, the evolution of modernism would be slowed or cut short. It is the evolution of this balance that current modernists want to preserve.

What is postmodernism? It includes all efforts to deconstruct the concepts, institutions, roles, rules, and standards associated with traditional Western culture. It often stresses subjectivity and claims that objectivity is an illusion (created by "dead, white, Western men") used to maintain patriarchal societies and to oppress females, the disadvantaged, and people in less developed countries. Postmodernism is at the heart of most antiwar movements.

Since the 1960s, it has resulted in a cultural struggle within Western civilization, and has affected the lives of all Americans and Europeans. Belief, national identity, and patriotism were prime targets of postmodernists. Although postmodernists accept the scientific method, they stress feelings and emotions rather than facts and reason.

Postmodernism visualizes "progress" toward a new ideal postmodern culture that is nonjudgmental, nondiscriminatory, in which disagreements are resolved by debate and compromise—but never by the use of force. In 2014, postmodern thought shapes the views of most of the intellectuals, academics, and the media in Europe and America.

The Unknown War

The Korean War was, and remains to this day, the Unknown War. The Vietnam War took place after television news came into its own. The Korean War was reported in newsprint and had little emotional impact on the American people. One author aptly noted how unappreciated the Korean War is by the fact that in 2004 a library in Florida had eighty-eight books on Vietnam and only four on Korea. The three best-known movies about the Korean War are: *The Bridges at Toko-Ri* (1954) based on an antiwar novel by James Michener. *The Manchurian Candidate* (1962) tells of an American prisoner of war brainwashed by the Chinese who turns into an assassin. *M*A*S*H* was a comedy about a mobile surgical hospital in the Korean War. However, it came out in 1970 and was actually an antiwar movie designed to influence opinion about the Vietnam War. Therefore, much of the importance of Korea and Vietnam is now unknown—the ideological conflicts have been forgotten.

Lessons from Korea and Vietnam about Ideological Conflict

As both Korea and Vietnam show, neither legal nor military means alone produce a climate of order and satisfaction. Legal means are appropriate and effective during peace. Military means are appropriate and effective during War. Both legal means and military means are useful during ideological struggles, yet they are not sufficient; policies and means that are appropriate and effective in Warfare are needed. Ideological conflict and strategic communication are important during Peace and War and also Warfare.

For success in the two current ideological struggles (against the Third Jihad and postmodern thought), there must be policies and means appropriate for Warfare (Irregular Warfare): (1) to achieve and maintain stability at the least possible cost, (2) to develop the inner compass of individuals so they have strong wills and can make sound judgments, and (3) to neutralize Islamists and progressives. Hopefully, the needed policies and means can be found in lessons from Korea and Vietnam, and they can be used as guides in the future. It is the goal of this book to provide such guides. History is not merely the recording of economic, political, cultural, and military currents at work. Gifted and determined individuals can show that we are not pawns moved by forces beyond our control.

What took place in Korea in 1950 and 1951 should have altered the way the US views conflict and cooperation—but it did not. Most looked at the tactical operations in Korea and saw evidence that technological and firepower superiority were the way to military victory. Some were impressed by the daring amphibious maneuver that landed the marines at Inch'on, but ignored the fact this was of little importance as MacArthur's goal was the capture of Seoul rather than trapping and destroying the North Korean Army in the south. Few recognize that the suffering at Chosin was not only unnecessary, but the outcome of ignorance and hubris.

---

[2] When cultures clash, their conflict and cooperation can take many forms and go by many names. Ideological conflict to shape the inner compass of individuals, including strategic communication, is always a critical part of those clashes during War, Warfare, and Peace. Warfare, or Irregular Warfare, is neither Peace nor War, and it goes by many names. Warfare is protracted conflict by non-state individuals, groups, and movements using all means possible to weaken or overthrow those in authority.

CHAPTER TWO

AMBUSHED

27 July 1950

We lose sight of the truck as it turns the corner. *BOOM*. Black smoke. *Rat-tat-tat*. Machine gun fire comes from the opposite bank of the river. We jump from the jeep into the ditches. Then the bullets start to hit our jeep. This is my first experience of combat. It is 27 July 1950. It is a clear, warm, sunny afternoon in south central Korea near Anui.

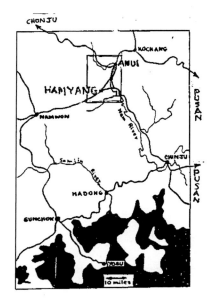

In 1950, I am a twenty-four-year-old First Lieutenant in the US Army. I grew up in Texas, and graduated from West Point in 1948. After graduation, I went to Fort Leavenworth and Fort Benning for additional training. In September 1949, I was assigned to the Twenty-Ninth Infantry Regiment on Okinawa.

I was in one of the two infantry battalions that arrived in Korea from Okinawa on 24 July 1950—a month after the North Koreans attacked. On 27 July 1950, we are in the Hamyang area, eighty-five miles west of Pusan. This area is the focal point of two routes toward Pusan. A third route to Pusan swings through Hadong and Chinju.

At Headquarters, First Battalion, Twenty-Ninth Infantry Regiment

I am the intelligence officer (S-2) for the battalion sent to the small village of Sanggun-iang. B Company is sent to Anui to relieve a unit there, I am sent to Hamyang to contact the ROK (Republic of Korea) unit there, and LT Iwanczyk is sent to contact the US unit north of us.[3]

After I return from Hamyang I am worried. Two of the men I sent with B Company to check on the situation in Anui have not returned. LT Dearoff, the executive officer of the Heavy Weapons Company, reports that he heard heavy gunfire from the direction of Anui on his return from there. He left Anui as B Company started to take over positions at Anui from A Company, Nineteenth Infantry.[4] LT Iwanczyk, who had been sent north with two jeeps, has not returned.

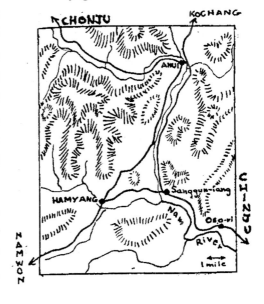

I tell LTC Wesley C. Wilson, our battalion commander, I want to go to Anui to see the situation.

The colonel is a forty-year-old, 1929 graduate of West Point. He has the calm, deliberate manner more typical of a Midwest business-man, with a few extra pounds more than a charismatic combat commander. His time in China had not only given him knowledge of the Orient and its people, but he had learned much about the Chinese way of thinking. This green, unprepared battalion was lucky to have him as its "Old Man."

Ambushed

LT Frank Iwanczyk, the assistant S-3 (operations), rushes in just as I am about to leave the battalion headquarters. He tells us of being ambushed near Anui, eight miles north of the battalion headquarters. Frank is a good-looking, polished gentleman of twenty-two from New Orleans. He was married the week before he shipped out to Okinawa. He had expected his wife to join him there, but the Korean War changed that. In fact, Iwanczyk did not see his wife until 1953, as the Chinese captured him in November 1950.

LT Iwanczyk had stopped at the crossroads across the river from Anui to talk briefly with some members of B Company who were waiting to take over positions in Anui. After checking his map, he started toward Kochang ten miles to the northeast. Due to the heavy dust, he followed the first jeep by well over 100 yards.

After going only a mile from the crossroads, the lead jeep received machine gun fire from a hut at the turn in the road. The driver lost control. The jeep plowed off the road. All four men in the jeep were either killed or badly wounded by the initial blast. Their bodies fell from the jeep into a rice paddy at the side of the road. The second jeep stopped, and the men jumped into ditches.

After three or four minutes of silence, eight North Korean soldiers came toward the jeeps from near the hut. As they passed the first jeep, they shot those who were still alive. When they were within fifty yards of the second jeep, they started to run and shout. PVT Sidney D. Talley stood up in the ditch and fired his Ml rifle at the charging men—the first time he had fired the weapon since it was issued to him in Okinawa two weeks earlier. He killed two of the enemy, and the others stopped. Seeing his chance, PVT William C. Stauffer scrambled onto the road and turned the jeep around. The other two fired at the enemy while jumping into the jeep. Driving as fast as possible, they stopped briefly at the crossroad opposite Anui to shout what had happened to them. Then they drove back to Sanggun-iang where LT Iwanczyk told us what had happened.

Colonel Wilson immediately tells me I can go to Anui.

"Be careful, Sam," is my only instruction. I stop briefly with LT Boyd K. Alderdice at an outpost of A Company. They have no additional information. We go very slowly as I have no desire to

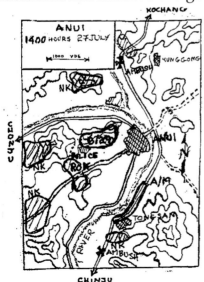

run into an ambush like Iwanczyk. At each turn in the road, we stop the jeep and two of us walk around the curve. After a few curves, I decide it would be best if we walk all the time. With Private Woddie L. Tharp in the jeep to our rear, the three of us walk toward Anui. It is a clear, dry, hot day. There are rice paddies near the river. Trees cover the knolls, and in the distance there are hills. Other

18

than the hills, it is not unlike walking on an unpaved road in rural North Carolina near Fort Bragg. We see no one.

We have walked a mile or so when we see a cloud of dust on the road to our rear. It is a ¾-ton truck with twelve South Korean policemen. After much hand waving, pointing, and nodding, we gather they are also going to Anui. I have Tharp pull our jeep over to the side of the road to let them pass. The truck spins its wheels and tears off.

The four of us follow at a comfortable distance. The Nam River is to our left. We see the truck turn a corner and lose sight of it. *BOOM*. Black smoke comes from where the truck had gone. Then machine gun fire from the woods on the other side of the river. Rifle fire joins in.

By the time the bullets hit our jeep, no one is in it. PVT Tharp and PVT Kenneth H. Miller are in the ditch on the river side of the road. CPL James D. Gausnell and I are on the other side. He is armed with a Browning automatic rifle (or BAR for short) and has two bandoliers of ammunition.

"Are you all right over there?" I shout to Tharp and Miller.

"Yes, sir, we're both okay."

"Can you see where the fire is coming from?"

"No, sir, but I think the machine guns are across the river in those trees."

"I see one!" Miller shouts. He fires.

"Did'ya get him?" Gausnell asks.

"Don't know. Can't see a thing in those trees. I think I did." The firing slows. Our jeep is full of holes.

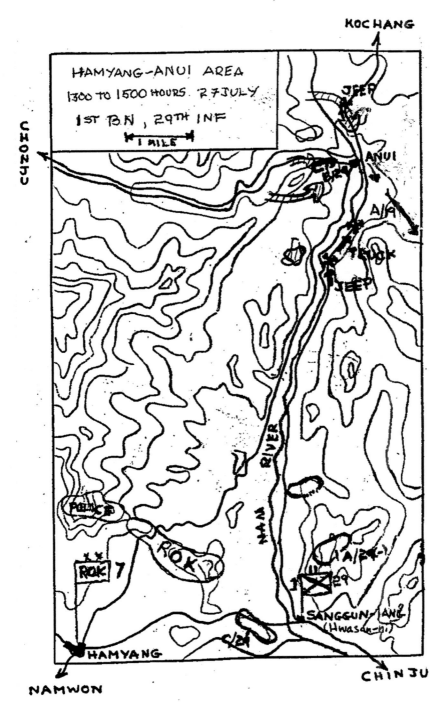

"All right, let's move back," I call. In their ditch, Miller and Tharp start crawling. We have just started on our side when there is a burst of bullets and Gausnell cries, "I'm hit!" He falls back in the ditch and holds his chest.

"How bad is it?" I ask.

"Don't know," he answers in a low voice. I rip open his fatigue jacket, which exposes a blood-covered chest. I tear open my first aid packet and place the gauzed bandage over the wound.

"Let me have the BAR," I say as I lift the weapon from his hands. Then I take the ammunition from around his neck and slip it over mine. One of the bandoliers has been torn and a magazine split by a bullet.

"Can you move by yourself?"

"Yes, sir."

"Start moving then. I'll cover you." With one hand to his chest, Gausnell starts to crawl in the muddy ditch. I place the automatic rifle in a position to fire down the road. Bullets hit the jeep and whizz over my head, hitting the bank. Other bullets skip off the road and over Gausnell. He keeps crawling in the ditch.

Where are those bullets coming from? There is no movement in the green foliage on the other side of the river, only the sound of several machine guns. Then quiet. What appears to be a thin white line of smoke rises slowly above a bush. I aim carefully at that bush and squeeze the trigger. Dust kicks up as the bullets from the BAR dig up the ground beneath the bush. I fire again and slip back into the ditch to load another magazine. I fire again and again. Everything is silent now. I look down the ditch.

Gausnell has passed a small concrete bridge over a small stream, and is among some abandoned huts some 200 yards from me. I start to crawl down the ditch. There is no firing. I can hear nothing except the splash of the muddy water in the ditch. I reach the small stream and bridge, and glance back. I see nothing. Then I start to run in a half crouch to the huts. As I emerge from the huts, I can see four men walking down the road ahead of me. One is holding his chest. One is a South Korean policeman—the sole survivor of the truck.

I start to trot toward them. I suddenly realize I am very tired, but continue to trot. By the time I reach them, we have passed completely out of the area where we were ambushed.

We continue walking. About halfway back to the battalion, we meet a jeep that carries us the rest of the way to Sanggun-iang. We stop briefly at the A Company outpost, and I tell LT Alderdice and LT Jim A. Blakeslee what happened.

At the battalion headquarters, I sit down and drink from my canteen. I think, *So that is what combat is like. We are lucky to be alive.*

I will start another trip to Anui within a few hours. This time it will be on the west side of the Nam River, with twelve men.

---

[3] The Thirty-Fourth Regiment, Twenty-Fourth Division is at Kochang on the road north east of Anui.

[4] B Company, Twenty-Ninth Regiment is sent to Anui, with men from the Heavy Weapons Company, to relieve A Company, Nineteenth Regiment, Twenty-Fourth Division.

CHAPTER THREE

ATTEMPTS TO CONTACT B COMPANY

27–28 July 1950

Also on 27 July 1950

We do not know what had happened to the 180 men of B Company and thirty-five men of the Heavy Weapons Company who had gone to Anui in trucks at 1300 on 27 July, before the two ambushes. We do know that some South Korean police and about 100 men of the Seventh ROK Division are in Anui. We think there has been an attack on Anui. We know that Anui is on a main route from the west to Pusan. Since we have heard nothing, LTC Wilson decides to send a patrol to Anui to tell our men there to withdraw to Sanggun-iang. He asks me to take that patrol.

I am to take the patrol through the Seventh ROK Division lines on the west side of the river, and then follow the road from Hamyang to Anui. Earlier that day, I had made contact with the commanding officer of the Seventh ROK Division (Colonel Min Ki Sik) in Hamyang; he spoke excellent English and had studied at Fort Benning. The twelve men in my patrol come from C

Company, commanded by Captain McDaniels. The leader of these men is SFC Lamon Marshall Day, a thirty-one-year-old who had been in the 501st Parachute Battalion, Seventeenth Airborne Division during World War II. He is a short, square-jawed man in good shape, with a firm waist and muscular arms and legs. He has brown hair and blue eyes. Curiosity and the call of adventure had caused him to enlist in the army in 1940 to become a paratrooper. My patrol will be the third attempt to reach Anui from Hamyang.

First and Second Attempts, 27 July 1950

The first attempt to reach Anui on the night of 27–28 July is by the Seventh ROK Division. The plan is for a regiment (now reduced to only 180 men) to attack up the road toward Anui from Hamyang as soon as it is dark.

They load into four old school buses that the Seventh ROK Division had picked up in their retreat from the 38th Parallel, and rattle off into the moonlight. The buses drive as fast as possible up the road until the lead bus is fired on. The Koreans pile out of the buses and attempt to envelop the enemy position. After an hour of fighting in the dark shadows of the wooded hills, the ROK troops return to their lines north of Hamyang.

We eat some rice balls and have some hot tea, and I move the patrol to the northern outpost of the division. There, we wait for first light on 28 July so we can move toward Anui.

A second attempt on the road from Hamyang to Anui on the night of 27–28 July is by the reconnaissance company of the Twenty-Fourth Division. It is dark after they drive up from Chinju. They get less than halfway to Anui before receiving fire from captured American .50-caliber machine guns. The reconnaissance patrol has no casualties; they return to our battalion headquarters at Sanggun-iang and then head back to Chinju.

We do not know our men in Anui had started to withdraw at 1900 hours on 27 July, or that they had fought their way through that burning town until midnight. Those in the ROK Division headquarters are both excited and worried. They do not know what has happened in Anui, but they know it is not good.

Battle of Hamyang, 28 July 1950

My patrol is the third attempt the night of 27–28 July to reach Anui, but we are caught up in the middle of the Battle of Hamyang.

The North Korean Fourth Division that had captured Anui turns south on 28 July to link up at Chinju with the Sixth NK Division moving on Chinju from Hadong. The result is the Battle of Hamyang. West of the Nam River, the Seventh ROK Division blocks the road to Hamyang with two defensive lines. The inexperienced troops are in the first line, on a low ridge four miles north of Hamyang. My patrol spends the night just behind that line. The veterans are in the second line, three miles from Hamyang. Two hundred South Korean Marines are in reserve. To the left, west, on a high hill mass are outposts manned by South Korean police.

At first light on 28 July, just as I am preparing to move the patrol toward Anui, two seemingly endless columns of mustard-brown uniformed men appear in the distance on the road from Anui. They move like giant worms toward the ROK positions. East of the river a smaller column moves down the road toward A Company. I know I am not going to take my patrol forward, so I move it back to where the South Korean Marines are in reserve. I then join the ROK Division commander with his command group to observe the battle. With my binoculars, I can see much of the battle. They know they are being attacked by the Fourth NK Division, which had a string of victories since it crossed the 38th Parallel on 25 June 1950—including the defeat of the US Twenty-Fourth Division at Taejon.

With scattered rifle shots from the first line of the South Koreans, the columns vanish. For more than an hour the North Koreans send patrols toward the defenders' line, only to withdraw as soon as they draw fire. Then mortar shells start to fall among the defenders. A wave of men advance against the first line of South Koreans—they break and run toward the second defensive line.

At the same time, the soldiers of A Company, on the east side of the Nam River, use their rifles and machine guns to beat back enemy attacks by what is at least a battalion. They use up all of the 4.2 white phosphorus rounds during the initial attack. The enemy fires at them with rifles, machine guns, and mortars. However, the company lives up to its motto, "Always Available and Able," as the enemy cannot get close enough to make an assault on their positions.

The ROK veterans in the second line start to fire on those retreating from the first line. Many stop and fire back at the North Koreans. Soon, the mile between the two defensive lines becomes a jumbled, confused melee. But the second line holds firm. On the hill mass to the west, the North Koreans now launch an attack directly toward Hamyang. The South Korean Police outposts on that ridge crumble.

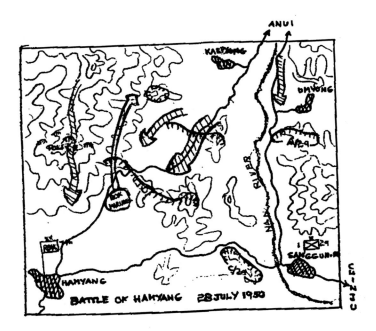

COL Min Ki Sik, the Seventh ROK Division commander (later the commanding general, Fifth ROK Division), orders his reserve, the South Korean Marine unit, forward. They move through low hills between the main attack and the secondary attack against the police outposts. I see this as an opportunity to learn what had happened to our men in Anui. I have my patrol follow the marines. This counterattack advances a half-mile beyond the initial first defensive line and sets up on a knob, which had been prepared in advance as a defensive position. From there it is possible to fire into the flank and rear of the main attack of the North Koreans. My men join in this firing at targets of opportunity. I realize there is no chance of our patrol moving toward Anui.

With firing on its rear and flank, the main attack toward Hamyang is stopped. The North Koreans move against our positions on the knob, but this only gives us more targets. For several hours there is an exchange of rifle and machine gun fire. And every now and then a mortar is fired.

While the melee is raging on the west side of the river, east of the river there are several more attacks against A Company, and a unit attempts to envelop the company's right flank. LT Jim Blakeslee, the executive officer of the company, organizes soldiers from the company headquarters and the mortar platoon, and moves them to a position from which they can fire on the enveloping force. Somehow, CPT Becicka and LT Blakeslee are able to instill in these green soldiers the qualities usually found in men who have been through many battles. A Company's actions on 27 July 1950 are arguably the first non-loss defense by any American unit in the Korean War.

In the early afternoon, I hear some horns from the direction of the enemy. "What does that mean? Are they going to assault us?" SFC Day asks me.

"I'm not sure. They use horns to give commands in battle. But I don't know their signals."

Are they going to launch an overwhelming charge on our knob? The answer comes as I notice the enemy fire diminishing.

Through my binoculars, I notice small groups moving back. They are withdrawing! This is followed by a withdrawal of those on the high hill mass to the west. Finally, I see a column of mustard-brown uniformed men on the road going north toward Anui. This battle is over.

By dusk, all of the North Koreans are gone, and with this defeat the Fourth NK Division gives up the attempt to link up with the Sixth NK Division at Chinju. Later, we learn that it turned toward Kochang to pursue the Thirty-Fourth and Twenty-First Regiments of the Twenty-Fourth Division.

As the Sun Sets on 28 July 1950

From prisoners, I learn of the defeat at Anui on the 27 July. I also learned that some of our men in Anui had crossed the Nam River and fled into the hills. With this information, I take the patrol back to C Company and go to the battalion headquarters at Sangguniang. Just before dark, we receive a report that an enemy unit is moving along back trails in an effort to block the road back to Chinju—the first of a series of withdrawals is started after dark on 28 July.

We also get word that the Third Battalion, which had come to Korea from Okinawa with us, had been destroyed at Hadong Pass on 27 July, but we know nothing about how it happened.

Strategic Importance of the Battle of Hamyang

The strategic significance of the Battle of Hamyang has been overlooked. It should not be forgotten. The Fourth North Korean Division reported this battle as a "minor engagement." Few Americans have ever heard of it. However, after this battle, the Fourth North Korean Division went east toward Taegu, rather than joining the Sixth North Korean Division at Chinju for a drive to Pusan. These two divisions plus the Eighty-Third Motorcycle Regiment could have turned the flank of the Eighth Army and ended the Korean War. Alone, the Sixth NK Division was unable to advance to Masan and then Pusan before US reinforcements arrived.

Without success in the Battle of Hamyang there would have been no success at the Pusan Perimeter and no Inch'on Landing. There would have only been a Dunkirk-like withdrawal to Japan. In combat, small overlooked battles often determine the outcome of larger well-known battles—as did the Battle of Hamyang on 28 July 1950.

Now this chronicle will return to the events prior to 27 July 1950 to describe the start of the war and the preparation of the two battalions of the Twenty-Ninth Infantry Regiment on Okinawa.

CHAPTER FOUR

START OF THE KOREAN WAR

25 June–24 July 1950

The North Korean People's Army (NKPA) began their attack across the 38th Parallel at 0400 on Sunday, 25 June 1950, with 135,000 soldiers. Based on excellent intelligence, the NKPA knew the exact location of the ROK Army units and sent superior forces against each. The ROK had 98,000 soldiers. Only one regiment of each of the four ROK Divisions (First, Seventh, Sixth, and Eighth) guarding the border occupied preplanned defensive positions. The other regiments were in their barracks ten to forty miles south of the 38th Parallel.

First Two Weeks

The main NKPA attack was down the Ch'orwon Valley toward Uijongbu, the gateway to Seoul. At two p.m. on 25 June, New York time, the United Nations Security Council convened an emergency meeting and adopted a resolution calling for all members to give South Korea assistance. The Security Council only approved it because the Soviet Union was not there to prevent action on the "Korean question." Shortly after six p.m. the resolution was released. American influence in Asia was now at stake. President Truman ordered General MacArthur, commanding general of the far east command, to take the necessary action including sending a survey party to determine the situation. At 1900 hours, 27 June, MacArthur's survey party landed at Suwon Airfield, fifteen miles south of Seoul. This started events that resulted in the commitment of US ground troops. In New York, on 27 June, the United Nations recommended that members "furnish assistance to the Republic of Korea as may be necessary to repel the armed attack." By 30 June, President Truman authorized the use of US combat troops in Korea.

At 0800 on 26 June the Fourth North Korean Division, led by a column of forty tanks, attacked Uijongbu. President Syngman Rhee ordered the police to execute members of the Bodo League and the South Korean Workers Party. The number actually executed has been disputed ever since. There was no effective force to defend Seoul at the end of 26 June. By 28 June, Seoul had been taken, and the ROK Army in the Seoul area had been destroyed. In Seoul, the soldiers of the Third NK Division and the secret police had killed hundreds—maybe thousands—of South Korean police, politicians, capitalists, teachers, government officials, and others designated "enemy of the people" by the South Korean communists.

In western Korea, a disorganized rabble of 22,000 soldiers remained south of the Han River. The best of the ROK Army had been lost north of the Han. The Fourth North Korean Division was past Suwon ten days after the start of the war. Seven months later (26 January 1951), I would enter Suwon, when that walled city was recaptured for the second time. In the mountains of central Korea and on the east coast, ROK units made orderly withdrawals. The US Korean Military Advisory Group (KMAG) was partially responsible for the defeat of the ROK Army. The US and Syngman Rhee did not agree on the purpose of the ROK Army. Rhee wanted to use it to unify Korea. The US did not. MacArthur had little interest in Korea. Therefore, KMAG provided no tanks, no heavy artillery, and no fighter-bombers. The ROK Army was given leftover, worn-out World War II weapons. In keeping with US doctrine, the ROK Army was road-bound and did not appreciate the tactics used successfully against the nationalists during the Chinese Civil War.

In contrast, the NKPA was well equipped and well trained by the Soviet Union. A third of the NKPA, and most of its officers, had served in the Chinese Army. Kim Il-sung was determined to liberate the southern part of his country "from the American imperialists and their lackeys."

The roads south of the Han were clogged with refugees: men, women, children, and oxen. The ROK Army struggled to get organized and was no match for the confident NKPA with its T-34 tanks. The soldiers of the NKPA knew whom they were to fight: white foreigners, imperialists, and their puppets—the capitalists, oppressors in the south. They had already won the ideological conflict.

Task Force Smith, 440 soldiers of the Twenty-Fourth Division, loaded on C-54s to fly to Korea. They knew neither the country nor the enemy they would face; they were not disciplined, hardened fighters. Many of the officers were veterans of World War II, but most of the men were immature teenagers. Because of budgets cuts, units in Japan were at reduced strength and had none of the newer weapons; therefore units sent to Korea were patched together at the last minute. They were not a fighting force to which war and dying were to be expected. Yet 33,629 did die in Korea and another 103,284 were wounded.

Few of us at the lower levels had any awareness of how past decisions at the highest level would affect our lives. Budget cuts had created a hollow army. As Cabell Phillips of *The New York Times* noted, it was not fat being cut but muscle and bone. The emphasis was on Europe. Secretary of State Dean Acheson had failed to include South Korea in America's defense perimeter. The big one had been won, and it was now back to peace.

First US Combat

On 5 July 1950, the first US combat unit in Korea was dug in along the main highway south of Suwon and about twenty-two miles south of Seoul. This was Task Force Smith, the two under strength infantry companies with the support of a battery of light artillery. LT Philip Day and LT Jack Doody, two close friends of mine of over six years, were in Task Force Smith.

That morning thirty-four North Korean tanks came down the road from Suwon. Antitank mines would have stopped them, but the task force had no such mines. Recoilless rifles were fired at the tanks, but the rounds just burst against the T-34s, causing the tanks to turn their .85-mm cannons and 7.62 coaxial machine guns on the dug-in defenders. The 2.36-inch rocket launchers did no damage to the tanks which passed through TF Smith and headed for Osan. One hour later the Fourth North Korean Division attacked. LTC Charles B. Smith gave the order to withdraw in the early afternoon. The next morning (6 July) LTC Smith had just over 200 men left. In small groups, they moved south of Osan to P'yong'aek, thirty-six miles from Seoul. Survivors straggled in for several days. Task

Force Smith had delayed the North Koreans for about seven hours, but at a cost of one hundred and fifty lives.

The closest units of the Twenty-Fourth Division[5] were dug in astride the road on low hills two miles north of P'yong'aek, which was north of Ch'onan. Survivors of Task Force Smith told them of the disaster north of Osan. Attempting to prevent envelopment, foxholes were spread out and filled with water. It was foggy. There were no antitank mines, no artillery support, no close air support.

Tanks and large numbers of brown-uniformed North Korean soldiers moved toward the defenders. Terror grabbed the unprepared soldiers; many did not fire and cohesion was lost. They fled or were killed. The Americans withdrew to prevent annihilation. For hours the disoriented straggled into Ch'onan. Throughout the night, the Americans tried to reorganize so that they could halt the advance of the Fourth North Korean Division.

During the night of 6–7 July, some of the tanks that had gone through Task Force Smith on 5 July arrived outside of Ch'onan — they had gone thirty-six miles in thirty-six hours. The enemy infiltrated Ch'onan. As the Fourth North Korean Division prepared to attack Ch'onan, the Americans withdrew to the Kum River. The roads were clogged with peasants, merchants, and South Korean soldiers streaming south.

During 9 and 10 July, a US regiment withdrew to a ridge northwest of Choch'iwon where it fought off enemy probes. The sky cleared; air strikes and artillery punished the Third North Korean Division, delaying its advance by three days. B-26s, F-80s, and F-82s struck a column of tanks and trucks in one of the largest kills of the war. After this, North Korean tanks and vehicles were concealed during the day and only moved at night.

On 12 July, 2,000 North Koreans drove the Americans back to the Kum River by 1500. The Third North Korean Division began attacks against the units of the Twenty-Fourth Division on a horseshoe bend of the Kum River. Three of the four light tanks were destroyed. At 1600, the withdrawal across the Kum River was completed with stragglers coming in for the next five hours. The Twenty-First Regiment had been reduced to only 325 men.

On 14 July, the Nineteenth Regiment held the main crossing places over the Kum River. The river is 200 yards wide, has six-foot embankments, and a depth of six to ten feet. The enemy attacked at 0600, and by 1100 the Americans had readjusted their position. Air strikes failed to prevent a buildup of tanks and artillery on the other side of the Kum River. The enemy crossed the river and moved around defenders. Four hundred North Korean soldiers attacked and overran a field artillery unit two miles to the rear. At the end of the day, there were wide breaches in the Kum River defense. At best, this was going to be a delaying action since morale was not good. But holding the Kum River and Taejon as long as possible was all that GEN Walker had asked. Would those on the Kum River have the military skills, discipline, and inner strength to do maximum damage to the enemy, keep their unit integrity, minimize their casualties, and withdraw orderly?

During the early morning darkness of 16 July, North Korean firepower punished the Nineteenth Regiment on the south side of the Kum River. For the next three hours, the enemy poured across the river and then moved through gaps to seek "soft targets" in the rear. Many of those on the river held their positions. Communication broke down. At dawn, artillery and other units in rear areas were under attack; this would continue for the rest of the day. Air support, which was to come at dawn, never came. A counterattack at 0900 drove some of the enemy back across the river. After fighting all morning, the Americans thought they could hold on. Yet, those North Korean soldiers in the rear areas had won the battle.

The North Koreans established a roadblock on the main supply route (MSR) three miles behind the front lines. Those nearest the roadblock were unable to break it; the road was clogged with vehicles. Many enemy soldiers in the rear were wearing the white robes of farmers. It was hot. The Americans were not in good physical condition; they could not climb the hills. The enemy moved off-road with ease.

At 1300, units on the Kum River were ordered to withdraw. All afternoon those withdrawing were under attack, and the enemy roadblock controlled over a mile of the MSR. Many left the road and attempted to escape over the hills. Some made it, but the North Koreans *murdered* many. Throughout the night, soldiers streamed into Taejon. Of the 3,401 men defending the Kum River, 650 were lost.

Battle of Taejon

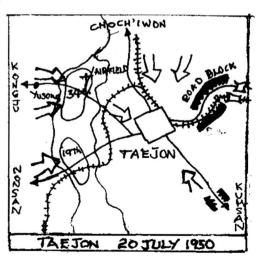

At 0720 on 19 July, North Korean aircraft bombed and strafed Taejon. The US Air Force bombed enemy concentrations. The battle for Taejon began at 1000 with contact southwest of Taejon. Then the Fourth North Korean Division attacked from the west. Artillery exchanged fire in the afternoon. After dark there was some movement of US vehicles to the rear, and the Third North Korean Division moved into positions northwest of Taejon. At 2000 enemy tanks were heard. Before midnight a roadblock was found six miles southeast of Taejon. That meant that the North Koreans had surrounded Taejon.

GEN Walker told GEN Dean he needed to hold Taejon for two days so that the First Cavalry and the Twenty-Fifth Divisions could stop the enemy's drive to Taegu. Those newly arrived divisions were improving defensive positions west of Taegu and twenty-five miles southeast of Taejon.

At 0400 on 20 July, tanks and infantry of the Fourth North Korean Division attacked from the west and moved to the Taejon airport. Shortly thereafter, the defenders on the southwest were attacked. Just before daybreak, the Nineteenth Regiment started withdrawing from its battle position west of Taejon.

At daylight, tanks with soldiers on them entered Taejon from northwest. They went to the center of the city and unloaded the soldiers. On this day, ten tanks were destroyed with 3.5-inch bazookas, two by artillery fire. The air force knocked out five tanks before they got to Taejon. At noon, the enemy to the northwest started to move forward. The Third North Korean Division joined in the attack. By then the enemy had been able to get to the rear of the city. There was a roadblock two miles east of the city on the road to Taegu, extending a mile to two tunnels.

At noon, the situation did not seem alarming to the American commanders. The tanks had not caused panic, and most units had held their positions. Orders were given to withdraw; however, since messengers had to be used, some messages were never received. A lack of communication and a lack of information of the enemy's location doomed the Twenty-Fourth Division. Enemy soldiers disguised in the white clothing of farmers were inside Taejon. Individuals were fighting each other all over the city. Trucks were burning. Snipers were firing. There was confusion. At 1600 the withdrawal started. That afternoon, an enemy force moved toward Taejon from the southeast.

Some American units fought and then fell back, only to be cut to pieces. Other units disintegrated and then soldiers in small groups attempted to get away. Many units and individuals took wrong turns. Some American units kept their cohesion and attempted to withdraw. At 1700, GEN Dean ordered a general withdrawal. There was chaos at the roadblock east of Taejon. While this was going on, the understrength Twenty-First Regiment held its position undisturbed only four miles east of Taejon, but when a North Korean regiment moved against them, they withdrew. After dark, an effort was made to break the roadblock from the eastern side. It failed.

In the battle of Taejon, the Twenty-Fourth Division was defeated by the same tactics used by the North Koreans as they crossed the 38th Parallel on 25 June. The North Koreans would make the initial assault directly at the defenders; this was to be a secondary attack to pin the defenders in place. Then the main attack would be envelopments around the flanks or an inundation, in which self-contained units would move through gaps in the defenders' positions to seek "soft targets" and to establish roadblocks in the rear. The North Koreans considered the taking of Taejon a great victory.

Of the 3,933 engaged in the Battle of Taejon, 48 were known KIAs, 228 known WIAs, and 874 missing and assumed to be KIAs or POWs. The CG of Twenty-Fourth Division, GEN Dean, wandered thirty-five days in the hills. He was captured and remained a POW until 1953. The Twenty-Fourth Division was not prepared for combat, and the leaders relied on materiel and firepower superiority rather than on superiority of military skills. These deficiencies were to be seen many times.

Lesson Learned: US Military Failures

Americans would repeat the failures of the Twenty-Fourth Division again and again:

- They were road bound;
- They did not recognize that the initial attack was usually a secondary attack while the main attack was an envelopment;
- They relied on an MSR (main supply route) rather than having self-sufficient units;
- They did not understand the maneuver of inundation (they only thought of penetration and envelopment);
- They did not patrol enough;
- They had poor intelligence;
- They did not recognize how the enemy used civilians; and
- They were unprepared for an enemy who had no respect for the "civilized rules of war" as expressed in the Geneva Conventions.

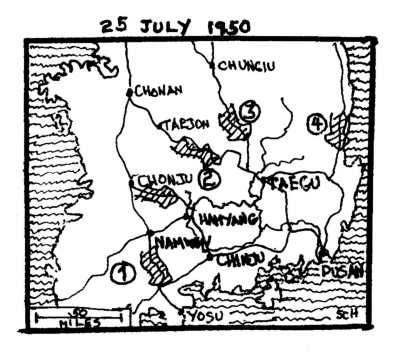

(1) Sixth NK Division and Eighty-Third Motorcycle Regiment sweep through southwest Korea—opposed only by police—and turn toward Chinju. (2) Fourth NK Division moves from Chonju toward Hamyang. After capturing Taejon, the Third NK Division and Second NK Division advance on Yongdong against US Twenty-Fifth Division and US First Cavalry Division. (3) Eighteenth, Thirteenth, and First NK Divisions push South Korean Forces back toward Taegu. (4) South Korean forces make a delaying attack on the east coast.

By 22 July, the First Cavalry and the Twenty-Fifth Divisions were deployed west of the Naktong River on either side of the corridor from Taejon to Taegu, where they confronted the Third and Second North Korean Divisions. Yongdong was lost on 25 July. The Americans withdrew because the enemy repeatedly moved through gaps between units to establish roadblocks in the rear of their defensive positions. The remains of the US Twenty-Fourth Division[6] were fighting, delaying actions against the Fourth North Korean Division south of Taejon. The Sixth North Korean Division and the Eighty-Third Motorcycle Regiment had swept around the southwestern part of the peninsula, meeting only resistance from South Korean police, and by 22 July they had turned east toward Pusan.

On 29 July, GEN Walker issued his "stand or die" order. Many had been doing just that, but the road-bound US units were being bypassed and damaged more in their rear than by attacks to their front. Yet Walker's demand of a tenacious defense was to become more meaningful in a few days as the Pusan Perimeter began to take shape.

The Twenty-Ninth Infantry on Okinawa

On Okinawa, we listened with interest to the news from Korea. Even though we knew it would affect our future, it all seemed unreal. We could not understand how the North Koreans could crush Americans again and again. Yet it was more like a vivid war novel than something that was actually happening. It was with this feeling of disbelief that I stood at the entrance of a small tent one hot afternoon in the first week of July 1950.

We were in the "field" for the first time. Our companies were spread out in a bivouac area just outside our barrack area. Our situation was much like the boy who wanted to take a camping trip in the woods, yet settles for a tent in his backyard. I had gone over to the large squad tent, which was the command post of the Second

Battalion. Just as I was about to leave, LTC Edwards called me over to his small tent.

I saluted. He came right to the point, "I've gotten word that we're going to have to send some men to Korea, and I'd like to know how you feel about it in case I have to pick some to go. Do you want to go or not?"

While I generally look ahead so I will be prepared to act in any situation, this one caught me flat! I did not know what to say. After only a blink of the eyes, I just said: "I'm a professional soldier, and it is my duty to fight wherever needed by my country. Right now that seems to be Korea. I sat out the last war while many others did the fighting; now it is my turn. If some officers have to go from the Twenty-Ninth, I should be one of them."

The colonel thanked me and said he just wanted to know how I felt. I have never thought that my answer had anything to do with what happened. I'm sure I would have gone to Korea in any case. However, from that moment on, the Korean War became more than news bulletins.

Lesson Learned: The Importance of the Inner Compass

I have often wondered: Where did my answer come from? It wasn't the result of thought. It must have come from something within me. But where did I get that inner compass?

It is our inner compass that guides us in making judgments between good and bad, right and wrong, and virtue and evil. We get our inner compass from Sacred Authority (that which cannot be ignored or denied). If we rely only on Secular Authority (the rules, regulations, and laws of government), our behavior is determined by external factors. Therefore, it is best to keep Secular Authority and Sacred Authority in balance so that both guide our behavior. This is what ideological conflict is all about: How is sacred authority created and maintained? What is the importance of Eros?

---

[5] The Twenty-First was the first regiment of the Twenty-Fourth Division sent to Korea, and it was followed by the Thirty-Fourth Regiment and the Nineteenth Regiment.

[6] Nineteenth, Twenty-First, and Thirty-Fourth Regiments.

CHAPTER FIVE

THE TWENTY-NINTH
GOES TO KOREA

14–27 July 1950

On 14 July 1950, the Twenty-Ninth Infantry Regiment on Okinawa was ordered to send two battalions to Korea. The First and Third Battalions were selected. The Second Battalion and the other companies of the Twenty-Ninth Regiment were stripped of most of their personnel. Men and equipment were transferred from all over the island to the two battalions being sent to Korea. I went from Cannon Company to the First Battalion, where I became the S-2 (intelligence officer).

These were days of turmoil and confusion. Personnel were assigned jobs, equipment was issued, and everything on the company supply books was packed for shipping—even tropical pith helmets. However, no time was devoted to firing weapons or even the most basic unit combat training. Members of platoons barely knew each other's names, much less have time to develop a feeling of brotherhood. Unfit and unprepared, they were heading into the unknown.

En Route to Korea

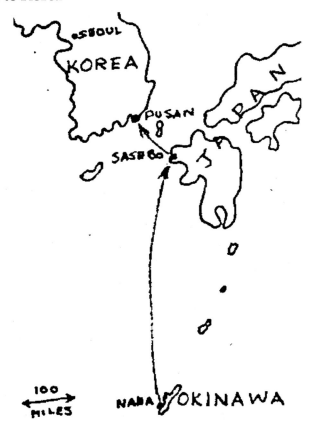

On 21 July, these two battalions loaded on the *Taka Saga Maru* at Naha, Okinawa, with four hundred replacements—freshly arrived from the USA and marched straight from their troopship to the *Taka Saga Maru*. It rained throughout the loading. It was hot, wet, dark, and dreary—very appropriate for what was ahead. Over half of the men in these battalions had been with their unit for less than a week; most had never fired their weapon; the mortars had not been test-fired and had no high-explosive rounds. These were infantry battalions in name only.

Five of us on the ship had been together for six years: Jim Blakeslee, Don McGraw, Tenny Ross, Dick Warren, and myself. During the next year all of us would be wounded, and two killed.

We were told we would go to Japan for six weeks for tactical training and to get our equipment in shape. Only then would we be sent to Korea. Although this would not be enough time to actually prepare these battalions for combat, we needed any time we could get. We were also told we would be assigned to regiments already in combat. That way we would get the support we needed but lacked as separate battalions.

The *Taka Saga Maru* did stop in Sasebo, Japan, but we did not get off for any training. About halfway to Pusan, the escort destroyers dropped several depth charges at a submarine, but we made the trip with little difficulty except for the hot, overcrowded conditions on the ship.

En route, we were told we would have two weeks of tactical training in Korea before we joined the Twenty-Fifth Division to become the third battalions of the Twenty-Seventh and Thirty-Fifth Regiments. We never got that training, but several weeks later we did become the third battalions of those regiments.

On 24 July, we arrived at Pusan, Korea, and the battalions unloaded. We wondered where we would go for the two weeks of training we were expecting. We spent one night in Pusan.

As the map on the next page shows, by 25 July, Pusan was already the target of the North Koreans. Two of the five drives were from the west. Who knew this? Someone made the decision to send these two untrained battalions to face these two drives by experienced, battle-tested North Koreans.

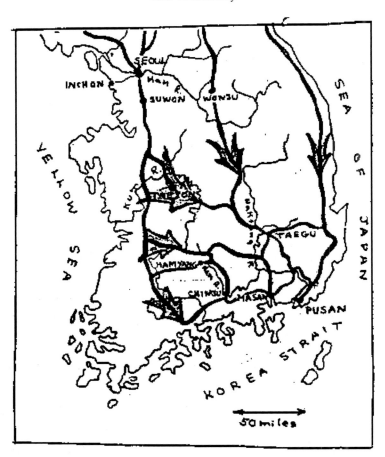

A Tragic Change

A message at 1550 hours on 24 July from the commanding general, Eighth Army, to the Twenty-Fourth Division said in part:

DESIRE YOU MOVE TWENTY NINETEENTH RCT TO VICINITY OF CHINJU SOONEST. FIRST AND THIRD BATTALIONS OF TWENTY-NINTH INFANTRY REGIMENT TO BE ATTACHED TO TWENTY-FOURTH DIVISION UPON ARRIVAL IN VICINITY OF CHINJU.

Lesson Learned: Staffs Should Deal with Reality, not Abstractions

Did the Eighth Army think there was a Twenty-Ninth Regimental Combat Team? Was it not known that we were only two separate, untrained battalions without any logistical or fire support? Or was the Eighth Army only concerned with getting bodies west of Pusan? Or was it that the Eighth Army entirely missed North Korea's intentions? In *The Coldest Winter: America and the Korean War*, David Halberstam is very critical of the quality of the officers at both Eighth Army Headquarters and MacArthur's headquarters in Tokyo.

In order to comply with the message from Eighth Army, we left Pusan shortly after daylight on 25 July. The vehicles and a few of the soldiers went by road, but a train was packed with most of the men and their personal equipment. This was exactly one month after the Korean War had started.

I rode in the cab of the train's engine with my carbine in hand. My job? I was to see that the train kept moving in case we were ambushed. I ate coal dust. I burned from the heat of the engine for the whole trip. We stopped briefly in Masan to shift cars. We arrived in Chinju in the afternoon of 25 July. Although we did not know it, we had passed by Chungam-ni Pass where the Sixth NK Division would be defeated eight days later (2 August 1950) for the first time after it crossed the 38th Parallel.

Lesson Learned: Poor Intelligence is Very Costly

We had no idea that on 25 July, the Sixth North Korean Division was less than thirty miles west of Chinju. Nor did we know that the Fourth North Korean Division was moving toward Anui.

Did the Eighth Army not know where these enemy divisions were located? Or did they know and just not send that information down to those at the point of the spear? During the next year, I was to learn that intelligence on the location and movement of major enemy units was inadequate at best and usually just plain wrong.

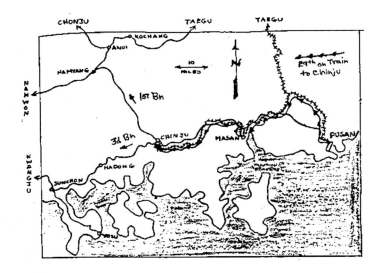

Poor intelligence and the road-bound nature of the American forces were two of the main causes of US failures in Korea during 1950. Of course, the other main cause was a lack of preparedness.

Orders from the Nineteenth Infantry Regiment

Commander of the Nineteenth Regiment, Twenty-Fourth Division (COL Dennis Moore), gives both new battalions their orders in Chinju. I am the S-2 of the First Battalion, so I ask for a report of the enemy situation. We are told that there are reports of some North Koreans using motorcycles and small trucks to attack police stations at Choju, Kwangji, Namwon, and Suchon.[7]

"They can move very fast, but we do not know their strength or where their larger combat units are located. We have received no reports of tanks, like those that attacked Taejon," they tell us.

Then COL Moore goes on, "You can be sure that any enemy we find will be attacked by swarms of carrier-based aircraft. But you should also realize that many of the locals support the communists, and the North Koreans have been known to dress up as local farmers.

"The overall intelligence estimate is that the major North Korean drive will be from Taejon toward Taegu, and any attack from the west toward Pusan will be a secondary effort. So we do not expect any major attacks here for several weeks."

I ask: "Why then have we been rushed to Chinju?"

"Oh, that's because the Nineteenth and Thirty-Fourth Regiments are to be removed from contact and moved closer to Pusan, so they could reorganize and prepare to defend Pusan."

However, we face reality two days later—on 27 July. The initial actions against the two battalions of the Twenty-Ninth Regiment reveal that the North Koreans are already engaged in major drives toward Pusan from the west. We are provided no intelligence on either the Fourth North Korean Division or the Sixth North Korean Division. Did anyone have valid intelligence that was withheld on these two divisions driving toward Pusan from the west? Or was intelligence so poor that no one knew where these divisions were? I never learn the answer to those questions.

The two battalions of the Twenty-Ninth Regiment are to be the US units blocking the advance toward Pusan from the west. The Third Battalion is to move to Hadong (twenty-two miles west of Chinju) to destroy any guerrillas in that area and then hold Hadong. It leaves Chinju just after midnight on 26 July.

The First Battalion, Twenty-Ninth Regiment is to relieve the First Battalion, Nineteenth Regiment in the Hamyang area (thirty-four to forty-two miles northwest of Chinju) and block the roads from the west.

Having convinced Colonel Wilson I know how to read a map, I lead the First Battalion convoy on the morning of 27 July 1950, from Chinju to the Hamyang area.

Initial Actions of First Battalion, Twenty-Ninth Regiment

The First Battalion, Twenty-Ninth Regiment arrive at Sanggun-iang (just after noon of 27 July) to relieve all elements of the First Battalion, Nineteenth Regiment, including a company at Anui, eight miles to the north, blocking the road west from Chonju. The battalion commander tells us there are some guerrillas near Anui, but nothing else. He is very proud of his men in Anui. He considers them wise in the ways of combat after having fought the North Koreans for several weeks.

"Just this morning we spotted twenty of the guerrillas on a hill west of our positions. We fired on them, and the bastards ran like rabbits.

"We did get a report of three enemy trucks a few miles west of Anui—if you care to believe it. The Koreans tells us those stories all the time. If we believed them, we would be chasing shadows night and day."

We are also told that the Thirty-Fourth Regiment is at Kochang, ten miles northeast of Anui, and that there are remnants of the Seventh ROK at Hamyang five miles west of Sanggun-iang.

B Company, with thirty-five men from the Heavy Weapons Company, leave Sanggun-iang in a truck convoy for Anui. Those in Anui are to use the same trucks to go back to Chinju.

The artillery battery with the battalion leave for Chinju. We have no artillery, no armor, and no tactical air controller. We do have one platoon of 4.2 mortars; however, that platoon has only twenty-two rounds of white phosphorus shells. There is also none of the logistical support normally provided by higher headquarters. We have no reliable communication with anyone. We are all alone, thirty-four miles in front of the nearest US forces at Chinju.

On 27 July 1950, there are two ambushes near Anui, the battle at Anui, and three attempts to reach Anui. For several days, we do not know what took place at Anui on 27 July. However, from those who made it out, we learn more about that battle.

At 1330 on 27 July, the enemy starts to fire on B Company; at the same time, the trucks are stopped by a roadblock on the road south of Anui. At 1525 hours, the ROK troops withdraw from Anui as 300 North Korean soldiers advance toward B Company from the southwest.

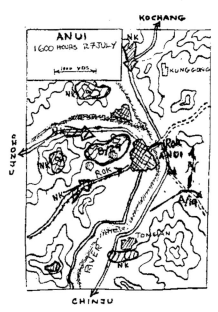

By 1600 only twelve South Korean policemen remained on the left flank of B Company. At the same time, another 200 North Korean soldiers advanced down the main road from Chinju to attack B Company, and a large column was seen coming from the north, down the road to Kochang.

Orders were given to withdraw to a hill across the Nam River from Anui at 1900 hours. From then until midnight, there was fighting throughout the burning town of Anui. The survivors had to walk several days through the hills fighting skirmishes with enemy patrols. Half of the men from the First Battalion sent to Anui never returned.

Initial Actions of Third Battalion, Twenty-Ninth Infantry Regiment

We learned how the Third Battalion, Twenty-Ninth Regiment was destroyed on 27 July. In Chinju on 25 July, Battalion Commander LTC Harold W. Mott met some ROK soldiers, including General Chae, the former chief of staff of the ROK Army. They explained how bad conditions were in Hadong and why that city was so vital for the defense of Pusan. They offered to help in any way possible. At the same time, I talked with two of my friends in the Third Battalion that had been with me on Okinawa: Dick Warren and Tenny Ross. We discussed what combat might be like and wished each other good luck.

The battalion left Chinju at 0100 hours on the morning of 26 July. Colonel Moore, the regimental commander, had expected the battalion to move into Hadong at dawn. But at daylight they were only halfway to Hadong. Mott attempted to get the orders changed from taking and holding Hadong to establishing a blocking position on the Hadong-Chinju road. Moore insisted that the battalion carry out the original orders.

On the afternoon of 26 July, the battalion moved to within three miles of Hadong, just east of Hadong Pass. It went into defensive positions for the night. The next morning, a company was sent up to secure Hadong Pass, and the command group followed in order to look down at Hadong in the valley as they planned how to move on that city. A group of enemy soldiers coming up to the pass from Hadong were told to halt by General Chae. Immediately, machine gun fire killed several in the command group (including General Chae) and wounded most of the others. Mortar shells began to fall on the pass. Then North Korean soldiers charged from many directions and attempted to block the road back to Chinju. The battalion had been trapped.

The fight continued all morning, but the battalion command group, many officers, and many experienced NCOs had been lost. Command of the battalion went to Captain George Sharra. The green troops started to run away. This inexperienced and unprepared unit soon collapsed. By 1530, Captain Sharra had assembled those who could move and staggered back to Chinju.

The North Koreans took about one hundred prisoners on 27 July, but when the area was recaptured, remains of the bodies of about a third of the battalion were found in the rice paddies and along the river. Many of those who had fled were killed, those who had been wounded were killed, and some of those captured were killed. Those who did survive were able to hold together as squads and platoons. All recoilless rifles, mortars, machine guns, communication equipment, and most of the rifles were lost. Four company commanders were killed. There was little left of the Third Battalion when it arrived back in Chinju on 28 July, and there would be even less to leave Chinju. The battalion was not effective until it was reorganized as the Third Battalion, Twenty-Seventh Regiment several weeks later.

Those captured had their hands tied behind their back and were taken to a house for interrogation. There is no record of what took place, but those that did live were very lucky.

A master sergeant who had fought in World War II in the Third Division through Italy, into southern France, and then into Germany was one of the first to be questioned.

He was asked, "What unit, and when you come to Korea?"

He gave his name, rank, and serial number.

"I say, what unit, and when you come to Korea?"

Again the sergeant gave his name, rank, and serial number.

The interrogator spoke in Korean to the guards. They took him outside, shot him in the back of the head, and dumped his body in a rice paddy.

Another sergeant was brought in and asked, "You capitalist come here to exploit Korean people?"

"I don't know anything about such things," was his reply.

The interrogator got very angry. "Why you lie? We know you come our country to help running dogs?"

"I don't know anything about all that stuff."

The interrogator spoke in Korean to the guards. They took the American outside. *Bang!* Another lifeless body was dumped in a rice paddy.

An eighteen-year-old boy from Arkansas went in the house.

"What unit, and when you come to Korea?"

"Third Battalion, Twenty-Ninth Regiment. Two days ago."

"Why you soldier who like to kill Koreans?"

"I don't like to kill anyone."

"Then why you in army and come Korea?"

"I was going to Japan, but the boat went to Okinawa. Then they put me on another boat, and it came here."

"Why you go to Japan?"

"Well, I had never been outside of Arkansas, and this recruiter told me how things were in Japan and about all of the geisha girls there. I thought I would like to spend some time in Japan, so I signed up."

"I no believe you. I no fool," he says in English, and then he spoke to the guards in Korean.

Another American body was dumped in a rice paddy to decay in the water and heat, and for the bones to be cleaned by scavengers.

This continued for several hours, but a few of the prisoners were taken to the jail in Hadong.

It was a long time before we learned of many of the horrors which took place at Hadong Pass—and many more will never be known. LT Richard L. Warren had been with me in Cannon Company, on Okinawa, and I had talked with him in Chinju on 25 July a few hours before the Third Battalion left for Hadong. Dick never came back. Anytime I met someone who was at Hadong Pass, I would ask if they knew what happened to Dick. Was he killed? Was he captured and murdered? Where was his body?

The remains of Dick lay somewhere among the bodies of the men of the Third Battalion who were killed near Hadong. There, death takes the form of the rancid smell of rotting human flesh that few Americans know. Dick had been a friend and comrade for six years, yet as much as I tried, I never learned what happened to him.

As is so often the case in combat, the only memories are those soldiers instinctively know: the threads that weave combat camaraderie.

Tenny Ross, who was also with the Third Battalion on this fateful day, did survive.

Lesson Learned: The Importance of Leadership

Did the leaders of the Eighth Army, Twenty-Fourth Division, and Nineteenth Regiment know that these battalions were unprepared for the missions they were given? Were these battalions given appropriate support? Or did higher headquarters just not care what might happen to them? Any military professional should have known that only experienced battalion combat teams, with adequate fire support, should have been assigned such missions.

If good leadership means good judgment, the leadership of those who sent the two battalions of the Twenty-Ninth Regiment into combat was tragically bad. If good leadership means developing adequate intelligence on enemy threats, the leadership of those who sent these units into combat was tragically bad.

Lesson Learned: Much Can be Learned from the Action in Korea

Neither the brutality of the North Koreans nor the sacrifices and heroism of those who fought were ever recognized by the American people. It was never seen as a crusade against evil to protect our country like World War II, nor as a topic of heated debate like Vietnam. The soldiers who fought in Korea were often ignored. It just happened and was soon forgotten.

This lack of knowledge is the greatest tragedy. In the thousands of lives lost, and even more thousands of bodies damaged, there are lessons to be learned. If they had been learned, many other lives and bodies might have been saved in Vietnam, Iran, the Balkans, Iraq, and Afghanistan. What are those lessons that should have been learned? They are the ones I learned during the first year of the fighting in Korea. Yes, this is primarily a chronicle written for my family, but I would be negligent if I did not attempt to pass on what I learned.

In Korea there was both a political struggle to determine who governs what territory and an ideological struggle to determine who is right or wrong and what is good or bad. From 1946 to 1961, the political struggle was between socialism and capitalism and a clash between two versions of authoritarian and oppressive rule—that of the left (North Korea under Kim) and of the right (South Korea under Rhee).

In Korea after 1961, there was an ideological struggle between collectivism and individualism. However, in South Korea the ultimate goals were freedom, accountability, and limited government, even while their survival depended on achieving security through tarnished means. Events after 1961 illustrate the two forms of stability. One (North Korea) is achieved through the authoritarian and oppressive rule by a centralized authority. The other (South Korea) is achieved through a climate of order and satisfaction based on a common identity, shared values, and decentralized authority in matters of personal behavior yet centralization on economic and overall policy matters. South Korea achieved stability through equilibrium rather than stability through oppressive uniformity.

Thus, Korea was both a conventional War to defeat the armed forces of an enemy state and achieve victory, and Warfare with protracted ideological and communication struggles. It is during Warfare that the inner compass of individuals is shaped, a common identity is created, and a climate of order and satisfaction is realized. Unfortunately, most people saw only conventional War in Korea. As military history, there is much to be learned about strategy, tactics, firepower, and maneuvers from the Korean conflict. Yet the ideological and communication struggles offer more that is useful today and tomorrow in the struggles against the Third Jihad and postmodern thought.

The First Battalion, Twenty-Ninth Regiment, which had fought the Battle of Hamyang on 28 July 1950, was just as green and inexperienced as the Third Battalion, Twenty-Ninth Regiment. Yet thanks to Colonel Wilson, the actions of the battalion, and specifically its withdrawal to Chungam-ni and the Pusan Perimeter, had different outcomes. The Battle of Hamyang was on 28 July, and then we made a series of withdrawals back to the Pusan Perimeter.

Of the some 1,500 men in these two battalions who arrived in Korea on 24 July 1950, 618 were casualties three days later—most known dead or MIA who were never heard from again. Few military units in history have suffered such losses. There are many lessons to be learned from the lack of training, lack of time together, rapid deployment, poor intelligence provided, and lack of support for these two battalions. No one should ever be sent into combat as unprepared as these two battalions. Yet much can be learned about the differences between warriors, soldiers, supporters, and MINOs (military in name only), about the importance of the inner compass of individuals, and about the Oriental way of conflict.

---

[7] Cities west and northwest of Chinju.

CHAPTER SIX

WITHDRAWAL
TO CHUNGAM-NI

28 July–1 August 1950

On 28 July, after I get back to the headquarters of the First Battalion, Twenty-Ninth Regiment at Sanggun-iang, LTC Wesley C. Wilson calls a meeting to discuss our situation. We know none of our people remain in Anui. We know our sister battalion has been destroyed near Hadong. During that meeting, we receive a report that the enemy is moving on trails to cut the road to Chinju. At the end of the meeting, Colonel Wilson summarizes his plans like this:

> There are two things we must do. First, prevent them from cutting the road behind us. Second, deceive them so they will not have a full day to prepare an attack. Wherever we are during daylight, plan to withdraw to a new position after dark.

The First Three Days: 28, 29, 30 July 1950

After dark on 28 July, the First Battalion marches seven miles from Sanggun-iang to positions two miles south of Oso-ri. Thus begins a withdrawal to prevent the battalion from being destroyed by the enemy south of us near Chinju or the enemy north of us (which the South Koreans had identified as the Fourth North Korean Division). Advance parties from each of the companies are assigned positions near Oso-ri during the afternoon of 28 July. These advance parties select exactly where each platoon will go after dark and prepare to guide their platoons into those positions. This is difficult because it is necessary to keep "lights out."

The elements of the Seventh ROK Division in the Hamyang area withdraw through our positions. Enemy patrols are observed throughout the next day (29 July). When will they attack? When will they infiltrate men to block the road behind us? A few men from B Company, who had taken trails through the hills, come in, and we learn some of the details of the defeat at Anui on the evening of 27 July. They report many enemy patrols north of us.

I tell LTC Wilson: "The enemy is in the outskirts of Chinju, so I don't think we'll ever make it through there. The only alternative is a trail to Massang and then on to Uiryong. However, they took Kochang yesterday. They should be well on their way to Hyopchong. If they go down to Massang, we will have no way out."

LTC Wilson looks at the map and agrees and tells us to plan to take all of our vehicles to Uiryong. I send some of my men to check out that route. He has me select the positions we are to use each night during the withdrawal because I could visualize the shape of the ground from the outdated, unclear, black-and-white topographical maps we are using.

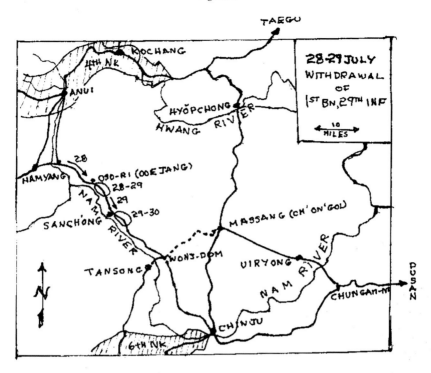

The Japanese had prepared these maps before World War II; they have the names of locations in Japanese and/or Korean characters—which no one can read. I am able to tell locations by the shape of the terrain revealed by the spacing of contour lines. Even this is very difficult because the maps are not clear. Names in Western letters are overprinted on the maps we received in August. Yet this is not much help because the phonic translations are poor, and the names are often not those currently used. Even good map readers find these maps an enigma.

After dark on 29 July, we withdraw again. I go with the advance party to select a defensive position for each company. The positions I select for the night of 29 July are near the town of Sanch'ong, which is about five miles closer to Chinju. On 29 July, we are in our new positions near Sanch'ong before 2200 hours.

On the morning of 30 July, we learn that the enemy had attacked, just before midnight of 29 July, the position we had occupied south of Oso-ri until it was dark.

A Company, reinforced by some local police, prepares defensive positions south of Sanch'ong on 30 July. The rest of the battalion go into positions three and a half miles closer to Chinju near Wonj-dom—as ordered by the commanding officer of the Nineteenth Regiment on 29 July. By then, regiment headquarters must have known that the enemy in southwest Korea was not just local communist sympathizers fighting as guerrillas and a few North Koreans on motorcycles. They probably had even identified the unit moving toward Chinju as the Sixth North Korean Division. But we were never given any such intelligence. I am, however, getting some information from the South Koreans.

I decide to send one of my men from Wonj-dom toward Chinju to see if we can find any enemy moving toward us. I selected CPL George R. Jackson back in Okinawa because he says he likes to spend days and nights in the mountains near his home in eastern Tennessee hunting. He grew up on a farm and is a highly skilled woodsman. He is tall, thin, and soft-spoken. I tell him to go toward Chinju but to stay off roads, away from people, and to just look for any enemy. As soon as he sees any moving toward us, he is to return to Wonj-dom and tell me what he has seen.

Coping with Chaos, Fate, and Death

During 28–31 July, as we withdrew, there was time for the men to reflect on what they had experienced since arriving in Korea. Chaos, fate, and death are things warriors and soldiers have always faced, but they are new for most of these men during their first combat. They must learn to cope with combat quickly if they are to be fighters capable of killing with skill and determination. If they do not, they will be mental casualties for months—if not for the rest of their lives. Training, discipline, and combat camaraderie maintain effective fighters—these overcome chaos, fear, and death. Yet the old adage "Good sex makes good fighters" should not be slighted. After the fatigue, horror, uncertainty, and ever-present death they had experienced, their inner compass, plus unity (the original meaning of Eros), had to prevent the mental deterioration of combat fatigue—that, since Vietnam, is often classified as Post-Traumatic Stress Disorder (PTSD).

Successful warriors have always taken attractive females for their own after they killed any male rivals. Those who had occupied Germany and Japan after World War II had such memories.[8] Their tales seemed to be just what the soldiers of the Twenty-Ninth Regiment needed at this time in order to cope with death.

SGT Mikolinski gives graphic descriptions of all of the girls he got for a Hershey Bar as he moved through Europe with the Third Army. Others who had been in Europe would tell their own tales of sexual memories. But they failed to mention the suffering, horror, chaos, and death these women had experienced which made them so willing. SGT "Pinky" Sisson describes his year with the lovely, warm Ingrid whose home was destroyed by American bombs and whose husband was killed by the Soviets. After so many German men had been killed in combat, during the first years of occupation American soldiers enjoyed the fruits of victory, and now in Korea they remembered those times.

CPL Kessler tells of the many Japanese girls who cost twenty-five dollars, or less, for a full night. Each would take him up some narrow street to a house with paper sliding doors. There she would remove all of the pieces of her traditional Japanese clothing, fold them, and pile them neatly on the straw mats that covered the floor. As the final piece came off, it revealed the body and small breasts of a young girl. She would put on a robe, give him one, and together they would go for a hot bath followed by cold water from a wooden bucket. Then back to their room with its soft pillows for the night. Those who had spent time in Japan would often add their own interesting details to Kessler's story. Tony Wall remembered the Japanese girl who cleaned his room and washed his clothes. Her face and hands had been badly scarred in the fire bombing of Tokyo. She thought she was so ugly no man would ever again be interested in her. When Wall suggested that they might have sex, she was more than willing. She would thank him after each time they were together since it proved to her that she was still a desirable woman. Then there were the American women who came to Japan during the first years of occupation who were more than willing to use sex to compete for young soldiers.

These tales might not have been able to counter the fear of death as well as actual sex, and some might have stretched the truth, yet under the circumstances, they were able to hold off the specter of death seeking to gain control of the minds of these men. If South Korean girls had been available, they might have provided new memories—and no doubt some of the female refugees moving along the roads with us did.

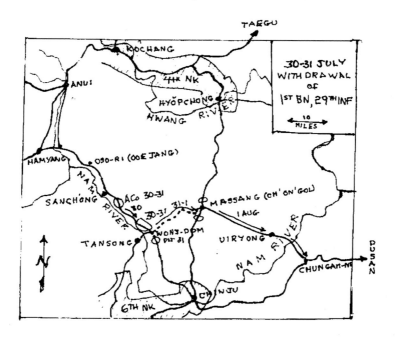

30–31 July 1950

Most of those in the battalion think we will withdraw to Chinju where the headquarters of the Nineteenth Regiment is located. The blocking position at Wonj-dom only makes sense if Chinju is to be defended. But to me, withdrawal through Chinju seems unlikely, so I look for other routes. The map shows a trail from Wonj-dom to Massang. The order, received on 29 July, requiring us to set up a blocking position near Wonj-dom is the last communication we have directly with the Nineteenth Regiment until 1 August.

We are receiving no supplies from the Nineteenth Regiment, to which we are attached. The First Battalion has even left its P&A (Pioneer and Ammunition) Platoon with the regimental headquarters in Chinju to facilitate the battalion getting the needed supplies. The S-4 instructed all companies to conserve their ammo and to get food from the locals. Most enjoyed tasty meals of chicken "Go Hung" and fruit.[9]

On 30 July, more men from B Company join us, as well as two from the Thirty-Fourth Regiment. This was the first we know of the defeat of that regiment at Kochang on 29 July. I look at the map and immediately go to LTC Wilson. I think we need to move quickly.

The Escape Trail: 31 July–1 September 1950

During the morning of 31 July, A Company observes enemy patrols around their position near Sanch'ong. By withdrawing after dark, we get the enemy off balance and thus hinder their ability to attack. During the afternoon of 31 July, we learn that the Nineteenth Regiment had withdrawn from Chinju early on 30 July. The South Koreans tell us, "Some Americans were left to defend Chinju." We know this means Chinju is lost; we will have to withdraw through Massang and Uiryong. After all, the North Koreans that destroyed the Third Battalion at Hadong Pass are already at Chinju. At this point, we had heard nothing from the Nineteenth Regiment for over twenty-four hours. LTC Wilson orders all of our vehicles moved to Uiryong.

MAJ Arnold, the executive officer, a thirty-five-year-old career officer with World War II experience, is sent with the vehicles on the route through Massang to Uiryong. There is no road between Wonj-dom and Massang; there is only a walking trail. The lack of tracks tells us no vehicles, other than maybe motorcycles, have used the trail. Certainly trucks have not used it. With the effort of a few men, and all the Koreans he can round up, MAJ Arnold is able to improve the trail just enough. Also, he establishes roadblocks north and south of Massang to hinder any enemy attempting to stop our withdrawal. Finally, our vehicles—except for one truck that breaks through an improvised bridge on the trail—reach Chungam-ni safely.

One platoon from A Company is placed in a blocking position south of Wonj-dom to prevent the enemy from stopping the withdrawal by moving up from Chinju. I tell the platoon leader that I have sent CPL Jackson toward Chinju to look for any enemy moving toward us and that he should come back to their position soon.

After dark on 31 July, our battalion starts a march along the same route traveled by MAJ Arnold with the vehicles. Two messages are dropped from a small aircraft telling of the defeat at Chinju on 30 July and giving instructions to withdraw. One is dropped on the battalion command post before the march starts and the other on the A Company platoon near Wonj-dom. After the march starts, there is to be no halt until the critical crossroad near Wonj-dom is passed. CPL Jackson has not returned when the last unit passes Wonj-dom. I assume he has been captured or killed. I know the South Koreans still hold Massang, so our goal is to get everyone past Massang as soon as possible. I also know the Fourth North Korean Division has just captured Hyopchong, but they have not turned south toward Massang. Nor has anything moved north from Chinju toward Massang; they are going east toward Pusan. Therefore, as the battalion nears the crossroad at Massang, during the early hours of 1 August, the men are given a few hours of sleep.

We are marching again before daylight. Just after we start, we meet some trucks MAJ Arnold has sent. They are able to take some of the men to Chungam-ni. The rest of the men march on past Massang, and then stop to await the return of the trucks.

On the Wrong End of Airpower

At early morning twilight of 1 August, I decide to wait for A Company which is bringing up the rear after having picked up its platoon at Wonj-dom. LT Louis Carapolis, the S-1 (adjutant), drives up in his jeep. Lou is a Californian, but the antithesis of the happy-go-lucky, beach-loving surfer. He is serious and thoughtful, and at times sardonic; he always has his pipe. He could easily be a college professor. I consider him experienced, wise, and old—after all, he is almost thirty.

We decide to drive back down the trail to meet A Company. Just as we start, we see two fighters overhead. Knowing they are ours, I think nothing about it. Lou says, "I don't think they know we are friendlies." Their action soon makes me realize they are looking for targets.

One turns to dive at us. I can see only a circle and two lines out to each side. I expect bullets. The driver and I jump into the ditch, and we get as low as we can. Lou has another idea. He shouts, "Where are the panels?" He pulls a panel from the back seat and opens it. After one pass, the plane turns, wiggles its wing, and flies away. I look up from the ditch with a sigh of relief.

Days later, I learn that during our withdrawal Navy Task Force 77 had been attacking convoys, troop concentrations, and bridges in an effort to stop the Sixth North Korean Division.

Unfortunately, the enemy had moved faster than the navy expected. Nevertheless, there is now hope that our air superiority will begin to take its toll on the enemy. Shortly after the airpower up-close incident, we meet A Company. I walk on with them. Lou takes some of the men in the worst shape in his jeep. We meet the trucks just past Massang and ride through Uiryong to Chungam-ni. As we cross the Nam River, hundreds of refugees are also crossing.

The Fall of Chinju: 29–31 July 1950

In Chungam-ni, we are able to learn something of the rapid departure of the Nineteenth Regiment from Chinju. Some of those left behind to "defend" that city did straggle into Chungam-ni, but many never left Chinju. The Sixth North Korean Division took very few prisoners. Graphic descriptions of the killing that took place in Chinju on 30 and 31 July match those we were hearing from the survivors of the destruction of the Third Battalion at Hadong Pass on 27 July.

The capture of Chinju started at 1000 hours on 29 July. That night, they cut all roads around Chinju. The morning of 30 July brought new attacks, and the Nineteenth Regiment retreated to the east bank. The "defense" of Chinju was left to anyone that remained plus 700 replacements that had just arrived but had not yet been assigned to units. Needless to say, this collection of bodies was not a combat unit. Snipers were firing on all Americans remaining in Chinju after 1400 on 30 July.

By nightfall of 30 July, the enemy had infiltrated into Chinju and was moving tanks into the city. The final assault began at dawn 31 July, and by 1000 hours no one was even attempting to stop the North Koreans. Any Americans that had been captured, wounded, or had not escaped were killed. These stories did not give us confidence in the leadership of the Nineteenth Regiment, which was especially worrying since we knew they would be giving us orders because we were still attached to them.

In the Village of Chungam-ni

Little did we know that the next day (2 August) we would meet the Sixth North Korean Division head on, and it would be the first time that division would be defeated since it crossed the 38th parallel on 25 June.

But on 1 August, we were just happy to have escaped the fate of so many of those we had left Okinawa with on 21 July — just ten days ago. We had one day to rest and resupply. We are told we will make a reconnaissance in force through Chungam-ni Pass, but that we are just to be following the tanks. That did not sound bad at all. However, this reconnaissance in force turned into the deadly first battle of Chungam-ni Pass.

---

[8] The names used to illustrate the concept of Eros and its relationship to sex, death, and combat camaraderie are fictitious. Eros is used in its original meaning—unity—rather than with the sexual connotations of Schopenhauer and Freud or the religious interpretations of the Middle Ages. The Greeks from 2,000 to 600 BC had three primordial gods: Earth (nature and living things), Chaos (conflict, disaster, tragedy, and hate), and Eros (unity, cooperation, and love). Eros and Chaos engaged in endless struggles to control and use Earth. Eros was the power capable of uniting people in a common bond. In *Phaedrus* Plato represented Eros as a charioteer trying to control two horses, one passion and the other togetherness. Kant saw Eros as the power to release a person from the prison of the self. Thus the Ethos of Eros is an accurate name for that which generates combat camaraderie.

[9] "Go Hung" is what GIs called stew made by the Koreans, Japanese, Chinese, etc.

CHAPTER SEVEN

FIRST BATTLE OF CHUNGAM-NI PASS

2 August 1950

A low pass four miles southwest of Chungam-ni plays a critical role in the defense of Pusan. Several battles are fought there in order to stop the North Koreans.

The Naktong River is the anchor of the last stand in Korea. Where the Nam and Naktong Rivers join they turn east, providing an opening south of the Nam from Chinju. The Sixth North Korean Division is ordered to drive south of the Nam through Masan to Pusan. If the Fourth North Korean Division had also attacked toward Pusan, those two divisions would outflank the Eighth Army. However, the Battle of Hamyang (on 28 July) had prevented this. A month later, on 1 September 1950, the Seventh North Korean Division did attack across the Nam River from Uiryong, but the opportunity for a victory by the end of July had been lost.

The Plan for the First Battle of Chungam-ni Pass

The first battle of Chungam-ni Pass (which is also called "The Notch") halts the victorious Sixth North Korean Division. Members of the Twenty-Ninth Regiment are the main fighters in the battle of 2 August 1950.

Plans for US operations west of Masan call for reconnaissance in force by two task forces using tanks. A task force of the Twenty-Ninth Regiment is to move through to the Chungam-ni Pass along the north road toward Chinju. The "Wolfhound" Task Force is to move from Chindong-ni along the south road toward Chinju.

All did not go as planned for either task force. After early morning success, two of the tanks of the "Wolfhound" Task Force are knocked out, and the road behind it is cut by enemy units which infiltrated the hills around Chindong-ni during the night.

That task force has to fight all day to get back to Chindong-ni. The Twenty-Ninth Task Force never gets past Chungam-ni Pass.

Preparation for a Reconnaissance in Force

On the evening of 1 August, after we arrive in the town of Chungam-ni, we are told we will be making a reconnaissance the next morning. I then make the rounds, talking with the people of the Nineteenth Regiment to get information on the enemy.

"They are out there; they've left Chinju. We don't know where they have gone. When we pulled back from Chinju, they sent patrols against us every night."

The most recent information comes just before dark: "Three trucks are near the lake west of the pass. Division told us that there has been traffic on the south road toward Chindong-ni. It looks like they will attack Masan along that road." Not much, but more than we had received when we were sent to the Hamyang-Anui area after we first arrived.

Starting at EMT (early morning twilight) on 2 August, the Twenty-Ninth Task Force is organized in Chungam-ni. The tanks and armored cars of the Eighty-Ninth Tank Battalion are in the lead with soldiers from C Company riding on them. The rest of our battalion is in 2½-ton trucks full of soldiers standing up. There is a lot of milling around as the trucks match up with soldiers.

I walk up to where the men of C Company are loading on the tanks and armored cars. It was the first time I had seen SFC Lamon Day since we had been together in the Battle of Hamyang on 28 July. He is climbing up on the second tank, and I ask him how he feels.

"Great, this is better than walking or being packed like sardines in those trucks. Sir, what do you think we will find?"

I reply, "Some North Koreans, but we are going to have surprise and tanks on our side this time. We should be able to take care of things."

I go back to see Colonel Wilson in his jeep. "I think I'll place my jeep right after the C Company trucks. I can evaluate the situation, and if there is any action, I can give you a call to let you know the situation."

"Good idea," he replies. We then talk about what we might find. Both of us have heard the same reports from the Nineteenth and have no reason to think this would be anything other than a very routine reconnaissance.

"With those tanks up front, they probably won't even raise their heads," I offer. "They have not seen US tanks before. Maybe our people won't even have to get out of their trucks."

"After our walk to get here, our men will like that." He looks at me, adding, "Do you want a drink?" It is warm. A little water would be great, so I take his canteen. However, it is not water. I choke on a swig of bourbon. I guess the colonel was having a little fun with me.

I place my jeep after the trucks carrying C Company and before the trucks with B Company. I have my driver, another soldier, Lieutenant Kim (my South Korean interpreter), and Kim's "boy" (as Kim called the soldier with him). The column leaves Chungam-ni and moves without incident the four miles to Chungam-ni Pass.

Initial Attacks on Nineteenth Regiment in Chungam-ni Pass

We have no idea that those holding Chungam-ni Pass have been under attack for several hours. The Nineteenth Regiment occupies the right side of the pass, and what is left of our Third Battalion is on the left side. All of these units have less than half of their authorized strength.[10]

During the night, men of A Company—including the company commander—had been bayoneted while they were sleeping. The company had failed to climb all of the way up the high peak on the right side of the pass. The North Koreans, as they climbed up to secure the high ground in advance of an early morning attack, came upon them sleeping.

At dawn, other defenders of the pass heard communist marching songs from the North Koreans coming up the road. They were the soldiers of the Sixth North Korean Division. Their commander, GEN Dang Hu San, had told them, "Comrades, the enemy is demoralized. The liberation of Chinju and Masan means the final battle to cut their windpipe." When the defenders fired, the head of the enemy column stopped and fanned out into the woods on either side of the road. But those following continued to come up the road. The Twenty-Ninth Task Force knows none of this as it comes up from Chungam-ni to the top of the pass.

Surprise in the Pass

A few yards short of the crest of the pass, Lieutenant Colonel Robert Rhea (commanding officer, First Battalion, Nineteenth Regiment) is waving and shouting, "It's clear to the lake." There is a small lake in the valley floor. It is now 0830.

Fifty yards down from the crest of the pass, the lead tank meets the enemy. The tanks move slowly down the crooked road.

BOOM, WHMMP. They are firing point-blank at those coming up. Then their machine guns: *Rat, tat, tat.* Then the big gun: *BOOM, WHMMP.*

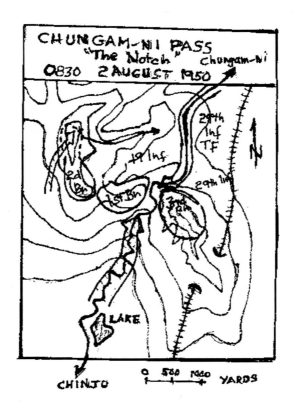

Machine guns, mortars, ammunitions, wounded, and dead men are left in the ditches. North Koreans scamper into the woods on either side of the road. The soldiers of C Company, who had been riding on the tanks and the M-8s, jump off to take cover in the ditches and culverts or go into the woods.

My jeep moves slowly down the road; it is like watching a very graphic movie as I look into the ditches. Men in mustard-colored uniforms are half-dead, dead, and blown to bits by the tanks' guns and machine guns; men are tangled among their weapons. Some are moving and moaning. Is this real?

Also in the ditches are groups of our soldiers. The tanks' guns leave a pungent odor. My mind just cannot register it as being real—but it is. *BOOM, WHMMP*. The tanks continue to move down toward the lake.

Then a larger *BOOM*. Halfway to the lake, an antitank shell hits the lead tank. A hole is torn through its steel. The burning M-4 tank blocks the road. One of the crew members runs up the hill naked except for pieces of his burning clothing. This stops the column.

By this time, all of the men on the tanks and armored cars not killed or wounded have jumped off and are taking cover in the ditches. However, the North Koreans are on the hillside above them. SGT Day and the men with him come under intense fire but fight back, killing many of the enemy. A blast from a machine gun hits Day in the neck and chest. He feels no pain, but falls back into the ditch. He can't move his arms or legs. He tries to shout, "Medic," but can't get any air into his lungs. He knows he is dying and thinks of his five-year-old son back in Columbus, Georgia, with his ex-wife. Time seems to slow down. He can only see white. Damnit. He could have killed many more of those damn gooks, but it is the end.

Chaos and Death

All of C Company and some of B Company are over the crest of the pass, but some of the soldiers are still in the trucks—those killed or wounded. There is a melee which will last several hours.

When the truck in front of my jeep is hit, all of us jump into the ditch. The ditch is full of dead and half-dead North Koreans.

Some are moaning, but they don't bother us. I place my two men facing down the road. Lieutenant Kim, his "boy," and myself face up the road. I then realize that Kim and his young soldier are in great danger since their uniforms might cause our soldiers to think they are North Koreans.

Some of the soldiers from C Company come crawling up the ditch; their eyes are full of fear.

I shout: "Get back to your company." They move back.

There is a lot of firing going on around us, but it is impossible to tell who is shooting at whom. The North Koreans in the ditch with us are still moaning. I try to use my radio but reach no one. I sit back in the ditch—knowing full well that we aren't going to change the situation. I remember that concentration on how to survive is the best antidote to anxiety.

Two more of the tanks are damaged, as are most of the M-8s. The trucks stand on the road—some are burning, and all have bodies of Americans. I crawl down the ditch over and around tangled bodies, some of which are Americans, and I pass a burning truck. It is a confusing, dangerous, surreal scene. I scramble for any cover possible from the North Koreans above us on the side of the hill. All around, Americans and North Koreans are shooting at each other—or trying to hide.

I look into a culvert and see some mustard-colored uniforms huddled together. I can hear rifle shots and the blasts of grenades in all directions, but can see little of the melee. However, I do see some soldiers of C Company stop an assault by a group of the enemy. One North Korean soldier falls back, his hand reaching for an arm that is hanging limp and covered with red-black blood. A bullet rips through the chest of the man next to him, and a bullet blasts a hole in the throat of a third man. I hear voices moving down the road from the pass crest toward us. I recognize it as English, although I cannot tell what they are saying. Then I see their American uniforms. It is B Company coming down to make contact with C Company. I recognize Captain John C. Hughes. Knowing that my rear is secure, I decide to move down the road to join C Company.

The five of us reach a small ravine where some twenty-five soldiers are together. They are working their way up a ravine to higher ground. I decide we should join them, since we are of no use in the melee all around us. However, we have to run across an open area that exposes us to enemy fire. About every sixth soldier is hit.

To protect LT Kim and his young soldier, I have one of my men go with each of them. The first two get through safely. When the young South Korean soldier tries, he is hit but crawls to safety. I run through the open area. The soldier's leg is broken, and he has a chest wound. We take turns carrying him up the hill. We finally reach the defensive positions at the top of the ridge. I take the young soldier over to a safe spot and lay him down. In a few minutes, he is dead.

The Rest of the Battle

I am suddenly very tired. There are a lot of people standing around on the road east of the pass. Most are "lookers" and know nothing. I walk around trying to learn what had been going on while I was in the chaos on the other side of the pass. I question anyone who can provide me any bit of information. I am not interested in small talk with the onlookers.

I learn that just prior to the lead tank passing through the pass, the right flank company—which had lost many of its men to bayonets during the night—abandoned the highest peak on the right overlooking the pass. This makes the whole pass vulnerable. The enemy moved to the top of the peak after the company of the Nineteenth Regiment had fled. A Company, Twenty-Ninth Regiment is sent to secure the right flank of the pass. Captain Becicka and LT Blakeslee lead the company in a fight to retake the peak. After heavy fighting, A Company drives the enemy off. However, the right flank is too large for A Company to secure. Also, after a few hours, LT Alderdice and his platoon are pulled from the company and told to clear the road down from the crest to uncover the tanks.

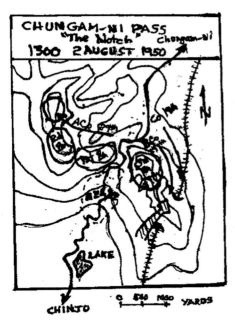

Just before noon, the North Koreans attempt to envelop the left flank of the ridge. From noon until 1400 hours, the left flank is fired on from three directions. The melee continues for several hours along the road below the crest of the pass and in the wooded slopes on either side of the road.

Also, the enemy attempts to use a railroad tunnel south of our left flank positions to get to our rear. I suddenly realize this is the same railroad we had used on 25 July to go from Pusan to Chinju. While the fighting is taking place on the left side of the pass, the fighting along the road southwest of the pass is diminishing, and a platoon of A Company is moving down the road from the pass, clearing out the last enemy resistance. LT

82

Alderdice moves his platoon down both sides of the road and ignores the dead and wounded—both American and North Korean—in the ditches. They are to be taken care of by others. The platoon has several firefights, but is able to overcome all opposition. They reach the lead tank at 1500.

Soon after that, the North Koreans realize they have been beaten and start to withdraw toward the lake. Although the fighting stops at Chungam-ni Pass, on the south road, the Sixth North Korean Division is still trying to reach Masan through Chindong-ni and the Twenty-Seventh Task Force.

During August, the North Koreans come back several times to attack those holding Chungam-ni Pass.

Reflection on the Battle

The *Times* reporter said this about the soldiers who fought the First Battle at Chungam-ni Pass:

> *After the fighting GIs had found, in the pockets of dead Korean Reds, all too many reminders that the Reds, for their part, had looted the American dead. One GI said wryly: "Every time I hit one of those bastards, I get a fresh package of Lucky Strikes."*
>
> *They spoke of the dead with a casualness that seemed callous. "Too bad about the sergeant," two boys said as they watched stretcher-bearers carry the blanketed form of their platoon sergeant downhill.*

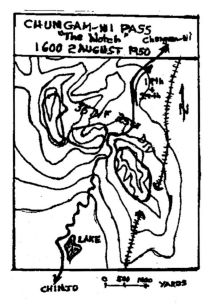

By 1600 hours, the battle is over. Following hours of chaos and noise, the quiet seems strange. The wounded and groaning are now gone. The sides of the road down to the lake are still full of twisted bodies, burned vehicles, and abandoned equipment. The wrenching pain and death of this battle can never be unlived, but it taught all of those in it lessons that will save many lives in the future. It is our duty to build on this experience. We have to make it a stepping-stone. We have to get past the mistakes made, to neither dwell on errors nor to blame others. We cannot waste our time and energy in faultfinding. It is our duty to be better prepared for whatever the future might hold. Soldiers grow through experience; if they meet combat with honor and courage, they become warriors. If they accept it as a duty, they will remain soldiers. If they lack the inner compass to handle such stress, they will become casualties of combat fatigue. We learned that the greatest weakness lies in giving up; the way to succeed is always to try just one more time.

Combat has always fascinated humans—no doubt the legacy of evolution's survival of the fittest. It is a life-altering experience. It provides fascinating moments of awe, chaos, and horror. Most soldiers yearn for such excitement, and it remains the most vivid part of their lives. Warriors are drawn under its spell. Yet some individuals only endured combat and cannot forget its trauma. Reflection is rare during combat, but it is impossible to escape later.

Few know why they return again and again to the unusual, threatening sights and sounds of those days.

The Sixth North Korean Division, with so many victories to remember, including the destruction of the battalion that came to Korea with us, is now defeated for the first time since they crossed the 38th Parallel on 25 June 1950.

Before dark on 2 August 1950, all of the units that had fought the First Battle of Chungam-ni Pass are relieved by elements of the Thirty-Fifth Regiment, Twenty-Fifth Division. Several days later, we begin to operate as a battalion of the Thirty-Fifth Regiment, and the Third Battalion begins to operate as a battalion of the Twenty-Seventh Regiment. Later, both will become part of the Twenty-Fifth Division.[11] We have no idea what to expect from being part of the Thirty-Fifth Regiment or how that might differ from our attachment to the Nineteenth Regiment.

---

[10] Chungam-ni Pass is on the north road to Chinju, four miles from the town of Chungam-ni. On the ridge northwest (the right for the defenders) is a peak which dominates the pass. On the night of 1–2 August, the Nineteenth Regiment defends the northwest (right) part of that ridge. The lower part of the ridge southeast (left of the pass) is defended by what is left of Third Battalion, Twenty-Ninth Regiment. In the valley west of Chungam-ni Pass, there is a small lake.

[11] First Battalion, Twenty-Ninth Infantry becomes the Third Battalion, Thirty-Fifth Infantry, Twenty-Fifth Division, and the Third Battalion, Twenty-Ninth Infantry becomes the Third Battalion, Twenty-Seventh Regiment, Twenty-Fifth Division.

CHAPTER EIGHT

THE PUSAN PERIMETER

2–29 August 1950

A new defensive line along the Naktong River—to establish the Pusan Perimeter—is not possible if Masan is captured. This is why the drives by the North Koreans from the west are so critical. The 2 August attack by the Sixth North Korean Division on Chungam-ni Pass is not their only effort. The attack continues further south through Chindong-ni.

North Korean soldiers infiltrate all around Chindong-ni during the night of 2–3 August. On the morning of 3 August, they attack the command post of the Twenty-Seventh Regiment. By the end of the day, they withdraw. A rapid drive toward Pusan from the west, which could have ended the war, has been stopped. This gives the Americans a chance to organize their "last stand." Premier Kim Il-sung's aim of uniting all of Korea under his rule by 1 August has vanished.

Establishing the Perimeter: 3–7 August 1950

Forty-three days after the first combat by US forces in Korea, the battlefield for a "last stand" is established in a 5,000-square-mile area around Pusan. The Naktong River is the anchor because the Eighth Army decides to defend sixty-five miles of that river. But the Naktong turns east above Masan, making an attack from Chinju, south of the Nam River, inviting. The US Twenty-Fifth Division is to defend this approach.

The twenty miles the Twenty-Fifth Division has to defend requires units to be far apart. Even with such wide frontage, observation, communication, air power, and artillery give the Americans superiority during the daytime. However, the separation of units allows the North Koreans to infiltrate between positions at night. They use this to great advantage.

The American leadership does not understand the basic maneuver of inundation. Focused on conventional War as conducted by Europeans, US military doctrine considers only the maneuvers of penetration and envelopment. It ignores a very old maneuver (i.e., one that flows past strong points in the form of self-contained units to strike any weakness discovered). Therefore, US commanders stumble when confronted with an enemy that uses this maneuver. Also at this time, American GIs are not skillful night fighters; often they fall asleep in their foxholes, and there are no night patrols to infiltrate enemy locations. At times during darkness, they engage in one-sided firefights, as soldiers shoot at shadows or sounds.

We go into reserve following the battle in Chungam-ni Pass as the battalion is reorganized and trained. On 5 August, I had a very happy surprise. CPL George Jackson, who I had sent on a patrol during our withdrawal, walked into the battalion command post. On 30 July, I had told him to go toward Chinju from the outpost south at Wonj-dom to find out if any enemy were moving toward us. He explained:

"Sir, on the day I left you, I went a long way before I saw any of them. And they weren't moving toward us. They were just sitting around. So I decided to stay hidden in the hills to see if any more came along. I stayed there for two nights, and on the third day—the first of August—I started back. When I got back to where you had been, the outpost was gone. You had told me where you were going, so I just started walking—mostly at night because now many enemy soldiers were all around. I finally crossed this big river and found some GIs. So here I am."

Lesson Learned: "Pacifist's Fallacy" and Ideological Conflict

During 3–7 August, we get reports of action by other units of the Thirty-Fifth Regiment. The North Koreans make nightly probes at Chungam-ni Pass. Too frequently, the enemy creeps up on a foxhole and shoots a sleeping GI. The high peak on the right flank was a frequent target. One incident there influenced my thinking about the "Pacifist's Fallacy" and ideological conflict.

Instead of the North Korean night fighters shooting a soldier they found, this time they pulled him out of his foxhole, bound his hands behind his back, and tortured him for several hours. The whole company heard his screams, and many recognized his voice. He was killed before dawn. On reaching his body, his platoon leader found many deep cuts in his flesh and one eye missing. He had been castrated. This was just one of many such events during our first days in Korea.

Perhaps this was just a case of sadism, but more likely it was designed to have a psychological impact on others. The

Chinese—and Koreans—have long considered defeating your enemy without fighting to be supreme excellence. This is not only true at the strategic level, but it is true for all levels. This requires the weakening of the will of an opponent. In contrast with the Western way of war, the Oriental way of conflict is based not on firepower and destruction but on erosion of the will of your enemy. Fear is one of the ways an opponent's will is eroded.

What is torture? Torture is action that causes permanent physical damage to a person from an attempt to compel compliance, to influence others, or from sadism. To think that if you are peaceful and compassionate, others will be the same is the Pacifist's Fallacy. There are evil people in this world. There are those who use fear as a tactic in order to weaken the will of an opponent.

Today this fallacy can be observed in the actions of those who consider Islam a peaceful religion. There are a few Muslims who consider the inner jihad the only legitimate teaching of Islam. For those Muslims, Islam is indeed a religion of peace. For them, Islam is a struggle by an individual to free himself from the baser instincts; it is a religion of personal salvation, redemption, and peace. However, most Muslims believe in Shari'a, the outer jihad, and an authoritarian legal and political ideology. These are the Islamists or "true believers" who support the Third Jihad. For them, lying to nonbelievers is not only acceptable, it is expected, according to *taqiyah*. For them, "do unto others as you would have others do unto you" is only a deception to neutralize nonbelievers. To consider Shari'a a religion deserving protection under the US Constitution would be a fallacy of the highest order. Most Muslims believe to some extent in the outer jihad as taught by

Muhammad, which requires all nonbelievers to submit or be killed. They might not engage in violent activity, but they will not openly oppose those who do.

In Korea, I saw evidence of what "true believers" will do to those who do not accept their ideology. Today the Islamists use fear to weaken the will of their opponents just as the North Koreans did. Yet there are many who do not recognize there are evil people in the world and think that if they are compassionate, caring, and do no harm, their enemies will do the same in return. This is the fallacy of many who are unable to modify their attitudes and convictions about what is good, right, and virtuous during Peace to what is appropriate during War and Warfare.[12] Then their peacetime attitudes and convictions become dangerous, harmful, and dysfunctional. Then, without knowledge of real torture, they will call appropriate and necessary interrogation techniques torture. Then, doing the harder right rather than the easier wrong takes on a whole new meaning. Then, honor, which requires a person to do what is right even when it goes against desires, career interests, orders, and even life, is far more than not telling a lie. Then an honorable soldier might have to choose reprimand, and even disgrace, when obedience is incompatible with honor.

During August 1950 what I observed made it clear to me that War, Warfare, and Peace are distinctive and different conditions that require their own attitudes, convictions, strategies, tactics, organizations, processes, and procedures. War is a battle between states, Warfare is revolution, and Peace is cooperation.

Lesson Learned: Torture

Is it compassionate to do unto others as you would have others do unto you? This is a teaching of many religions. However, unless all of those involved share moral and ethical convictions, it is naive to think that others will do unto you as you do unto them. In such situations, you will probably become the victim of your own compassion before others change their ways.

Politicians, lawyers, and human rights activists have given us several definitions of torture. But these are only expressions of how they would like things to be. These definitions are idealized visions of what some think civilized conduct should be; they are an expression of the utopian goal of universal "rule of law." They fail to realistically describe torture. Real torture is action that causes permanent physical damage to a person from an attempt to compel compliance, to influence others, or from sadism. Anything else is no more than a technique to collect information.

Too often those with unrealistic views of torture confuse aggressive interrogation techniques and torture. Those with experience in interrogation should make the decisions on which techniques are effective and which are not. Politicians, lawyers, and human rights activists should never be allowed to determine which interrogation techniques are appropriate. To do this will result in unnecessary deaths and an inability to obtain necessary information. What is appropriate should be determined by those experienced in the use of interrogation techniques.

Those who dream of a utopian world of love, peace, and harmony often do not understand real torture. Torture, for them, is a horror to be avoided, ignored, and outlawed. They refuse to recognize that torture has long been one aspect of the human condition that has often been used by evil ones to achieve some goals or desire. It is necessary to distinguish interrogation to save lives from the actions of evil ones. Pacifists are unable to distinguish between information collection techniques, which do no permanent physical harm, and real torture, which causes permanent physical harm—and death.

Task Force Kean: 7–13 August 1950

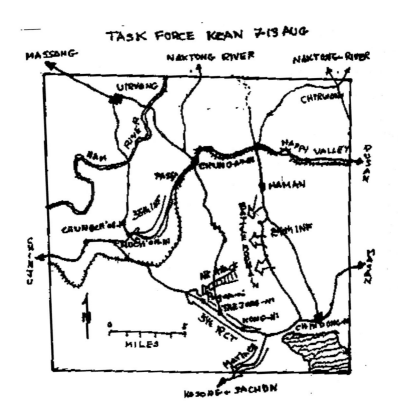

Map of 9 August 1950:

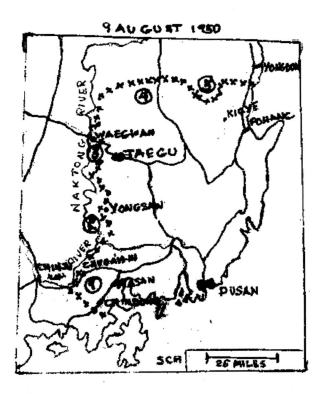

(1) Task Force Kean is making the first major offensive by UN forces. (2) Nine thousand enemy cross the Naktong River into the Twenty-Fourth Division's area. The Second Division moves in to back up the Twenty-Fourth Division. (3) A two-week battle between the First Cavalry Division and the Third NK Division starts with a crossing of the Naktong River. Seventieth Tank Battalion is attached to First Cavalry Division. (4) NKPA advances two miles against ROK forces. (5) Twelfth NK Division crosses mountains to join Fifth NK Division in attacking Third ROK Division.

The commander of the Twenty-Fifth Division (MG William B. Kean) is given responsibility for the first major UN offensive of the Korean War. He commands four regiments. The Thirty-Fifth Regiment is to attack along the north road from Chungam-ni Pass. The Fifth Regimental Combat Team (RCT) is to attack along the middle road from Chindong-ni to meet the Thirty-Fifth Regiment at Much'on-ni. The Fifth Marine Brigade is to attack on the southern road from Chindong-ni. The Twenty-Fourth "Deuce Fo" Regiment is in reserve and is to secure the area behind the three attacking regiments. The final phase is to be a drive to Chinju.

The first days of the offensive do not go as planned. The Sixth North Korean Division had moved several thousand troops into the Sobuk-Sun hill mass near Haman. For good reason it becomes known as "Battle Mountain." It is a mining site, and the mine entrances are ready-made bunkers. It is very hot—often over 100 degrees; many of the soldiers are taken out of action by heat exhaustion. On 7 August, the North Koreans hold positions around Chindong-ni.

On 7 August, the Thirty-Fifth Regiment is able to fight its way to Much'on-ni but is told to halt because the enemy still holds positions near Chindong-ni and Battle Mountain. The Twenty-Fourth Regiment will fight on Battle Mountain until 13 August. On the southern route, the Fifth Marine Brigade has little opposition and is able to reach its objectives by 9 August and send forces toward Chinju.

The center is a problem. On 10 and 11 August the Fifth RCT (Regimental Combat Team) finally takes it first objective, but it is strung out on the road for miles. On the morning of 12 August, the North Koreans assault the 555th Field Artillery with great success in what is now known as "Bloody Gulch." Several attempts are made to retake Bloody Gulch without success. When the marines reach the hill overlooking the artillery's position, they can only see enemy troops. The artillery does not exist. Later we learned that many of these artillerymen had been captured, tortured, and murdered. On 13 August, Task Force Kean is ordered to return all units to their original positions. The Fifth RCT withdrew through the Thirty-Fifth Regiment at Chungam-ni Pass. The 555th Field Artillery had to be completely rebuilt. The marines leave to prepare for the landings at Inch'on, which will take place on 15 September.

The good news is that Task Force Kean has blocked the advance of the Sixth North Korean Division toward Pusan.

During this time, I have a very sad personal experience. On 9 August, I am on a hill watching, with my binoculars, a unit of the Thirty-Fifth cross a small bridge several miles away. I see a tank crush the bridge and slip over on its side. Several hours later, I hear that the tank had crushed a lieutenant as he attempted to guide the tank over the bridge. I think no more about it until the next day when I learn that the lieutenant was Marty Nelson. Marty was not only a classmate at West Point, but we had been in the same company. Joan (who I married in 1951) and I had often double dated with Marty and Ginger—who married on graduation. Any death is tragic, and I have seen many, but those who are close always hurt the most.

Organization of the Pusan Perimeter: 13–22 August 1950

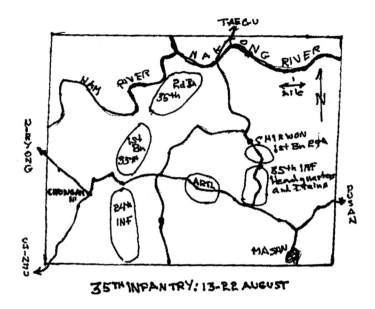

35TH INFANTRY: 13-22 AUGUST

The Thirty-Fifth Regiment holds ten miles of the Pusan Perimeter from the junction of the Nam and Naktong Rivers to Battle Mountain. This includes the main roads from Chinju and Uiryong to Pusan. The Second Battalion overlooks the Nam and Naktong Rivers. The First Battalion is several miles east of the Nam River and one mile east of the town of Chungam-ni.

The Twenty-Fourth "Deuce Fo" Regiment, south of the Thirty-Fifth Regiment, is still fighting the enemy on Battle Mountain, and north of the Naktong are the Twenty-Fourth Division and the First Marine Brigade.

Our battalion is in reserve, near the regimental command post and logistical support units, during 13–22 August. The battalion headquarters is in a temple. These eleven days are used to relearn, reequip, and prepare for what we know is ahead. Here Major

Robert L. Woolfolk takes command from Lieutenant Colonel Wilson, and the First Battalion, Twenty-Ninth Regiment is renamed the Third Battalion, Thirty-Fifth "Cacti" Infantry Regiment, Twenty-Fifth "Tropic Lightning" Division. The Third Battalion, Twenty-Ninth Regiment becomes the Third Battalion, Twenty-Seventh Regiment. The Twenty-Fifth Division had been in Japan before coming to Korea, but it only had two battalions in the Thirty-Fifth and Twenty-Seventh regiments. The Twenty-Fourth Regiment had three battalions. For many years, it was stationed in Hawaii and had long been the primary army division in the Pacific—hence the name Tropic Lightning.

The Pusan perimeter is organized by US officers competent in the tactics and logistics of conventional War as the result of World War II experience, but few have knowledge of a wider view of conflict and cooperation. There is little interest in how ideological conflict, strategic communication, civic virtue, Eros, and national spirit can affect the outcome of the struggle in Korea.

Many acts of heroism, much hardship, suffering, and death took place from 5 July to 13 August 1950, yet overall the combat performance of the US Army ranged from poor to mediocre. Nevertheless, reports from Korea and Washington and a sense of national pride successfully hid this reality and spun each retreat as a triumph against overwhelming odds. This deception did give comfort to the survivors, nurturing illusions of combat skills, which in time would improve effectiveness in the conventional War aspects of the Korean conflict. Yet the deception would prevent the truths about Warfare and ideological conflict from being learned, and this would come back to haunt US efforts in Vietnam, the Balkans, Afghanistan, and Iraq.

Kim Il-sung had promised to bring all of Korea under communist rule by 15 August.

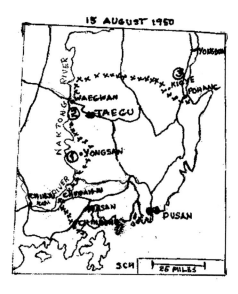

(#1 on this map) In the "Naktong Bulge" the Fourth NK Division attacks towards Yongsan. The Twenty-Fourth Division is fully committed. Clouds prevent a planned air strike. It is raining. Second Division attacks to remove the enemy from a hill complex in the Twenty-Fourth Division area. Heavy fighting continues. First Marine Brigade is attached to Twenty-Fourth Division. Fourth NK Division has suffered greatly in the ten days of fighting; from attrition and exhaustion it is much weaker and no longer able to hold the "Naktong Bulge." (#2 on map above) At 0520, over five hundred NK soldiers cross the Naktong River and attack Seventh Cavalry Regiment a mile from the river. More enemy cross the river after daylight. By dark the enemy has been driven back across the river. It is estimated that 1,500 of those who crossed are killed. Shortly before midnight, NKs use an underwater bridge to make a similar crossing in the First ROK Division's sector, but turn south (toward Waegwan) to attack the

Fifth Cavalry Regiment. (#3 on map) Third ROK Division
is surrounded by Twelfth NK and Fifth NK Divisions.

The Koreans

Koreans of all ages move through our area with a few pitiful
possessions, going they know not where, seeking food and
shelter. There are shattered families, and many see no future
other than suffering, fear, and death—and wonder why they have
been caught in such evil times.

I know little about the Koreans or Korean history when the war
started. So I attempt to learn as much as I can. In a few months I
know more about the Koreans than most Americans, but my
knowledge is still very limited. This is a great weakness since
ideological conflict depends on accurate knowledge of the beliefs,
values, convictions, and attitudes of those involved.

I learn that the Koreans have a history of harsh treatment, both
from their own rulers and the Japanese after 1910. Yet they have a
history full of notable memories and a desire to preserve their
culture. There are many refugees. Although thin, Koreans carry very
heavy loads. The women balance large bundles on their heads. The
men use a back frame to carry 160- to 200-pound loads.

I heard that the Korean language is more closely related to
Finnish, Hungarian, and Turkish than to either Chinese or
Japanese—but I was never able to confirm this. Most Koreans read
Japanese and usually write in Chinese characters. Many are
Presbyterian, and those usually speak some English. They have a
long Buddhist tradition, and their temples were a good place to
rest. Yet Buddhism is not the dominant force it was from 372 to
1392. At its peak, Buddhism was a sociopolitical ideology that
overruled courts, led revolutions, and supplied the ruling elite.

Some of the men wore Western shirts and pants, but most of the peasants wore distinctive white cotton shirts over baggy trousers. The women wore long skirts, usually white, with a waistband. Most wore a white blouse with long sleeves, but women with babies wore a half blouse, which exposed the lower part of the breasts. Most Americans are unable to distinguish Koreans from either the Japanese or Chinese.

Korean life is simple: no sewing machines, no washing machines, and no refrigerators. Each village had a deep well full of cool water. In the fields, there were watermelons, which on a hot summer day are a welcome delight. However, it came at a price. The smell of night soil—human excrement—used to fertilize the fields could not be escaped. This combined with the fruity smell of the Korean staple *kimchi*—a highly spiced cabbage dish—gives the landscape a distinctive fragrance. In summer, it is impossible to get away from the putrid stink.

Most farmhouses have walls of mortared stone more than a foot thick and a roof of thatch. The floors are packed mud over vents that carry hot air in the winter. Heat from a fire pit under one side of the house is vented to the opposite side of the house, creating a central heating system superior to a fireplace at one side of a room or an open fire pit in the center of a room. Earthen crocks hold food to be stored throughout the year. Everyone sleeps on thin mats laid directly on the floor. Washing is a never-ending task. Most Koreans have faith in fortune-tellers, palmists, and astrologers.

None of this information is necessary, but it is interesting and keeps me aware of my environment. Most importantly, it takes my mind away from thoughts of future horror—in the future I will have enough dangers and opportunities. To avoid combat fatigue it is necessary to keep your mind active, to think of the positive, and to eliminate the negative.

Paul

After my lieutenant interpreter went back to the ROK Army, I am sent a young civilian to interview.

"What would you like me to call you?" I ask.

"My Christian name is Paul."

"That is appropriate," I respond. "He was a fighter and a man of action when he was your age—before his revelation on the road to Damascus."

"I am not that Paul. I believe in the peaceful teachings of Jesus. I'm not as aggressive as Paul." This Paul is an intelligent, thoughtful, cheerful, and sincere nineteen-year-old. He is a dedicated Christian, a product of the Korean Presbyterian Church. He sees all killings as a sin and thinks all war is evil. He wants peace and harmony.

"Why are you willing to be an interpreter for the American military?" I ask.

"The communists are Godless. I want all of my countrymen to have the opportunity to learn of the salvation that Jesus has given us. I do not want Korea to be a Godless country. I hope the Americans can prevent this."

"But you know we will be killing those Koreans who are communists?"

"I know that, but I will not. I will not be carrying a weapon, and I will kill no one."

"Okay. That is up to you. I will never ask you to do anything your Christian convictions tell you not to do. All that I ask is that you give me accurate translations. We will always try to protect you, but this is a dangerous world, and you might have to protect yourself someday."

Then I go on, "Paul, I am also a Christian, and I also hate war. Probably I'm not as good a Christian as you since I am a sheepdog." He says nothing, but his face tells me he does not understand my analogy.

"As I see it, there are wolves in this world. They are evil and cause conflict and war. There are also many sheep who desire peace and a happy life. But the sheep cannot ensure peace, since the wolves destroy them. It is the sheepdogs which ensure peace, for they keep the wolves at bay."

"I guess I'm a sheep," Paul responds.

Thus starts our relationship which is meaningful for both of us.

"Happy Valley"

The night probes against the First and Second Battalions become more intense. It is clear that the enemy is moving through the gaps between units. Therefore, a major repositioning of the Thirty-Fifth Regiment is made.

A ROK (Republic of Korea) company is placed between the First and Second Battalions. L Company (formerly C Company) is attached to the First Battalion and given responsibility for the main road. I Company (formerly A Company) and K Company (formerly B Company) take up positions on either side of the main road but two miles behind the forward defensive positions. Headquarters Company of the Third Battalion, Thirty-Fifth Regiment (former Headquarters Company of the First Battalion, Twenty-Ninth) joins the artillery along the road in what becomes known as "Happy Valley."

The main road and railroad from Chinju to Masan, and then on to Pusan, ran through this valley east of Chungam-ni. It starts at the junction with the road to Haman. To the north of this valley is the Sanin-Myon hill mass. We called it Happy Valley because we are not fighting—and dying. We lost no one since the battle of Chungam-ni Pass on 2 August—we hope this will continue. However, the firing of the artillery at all hours is a loud reminder that beyond our valley all is not happy.

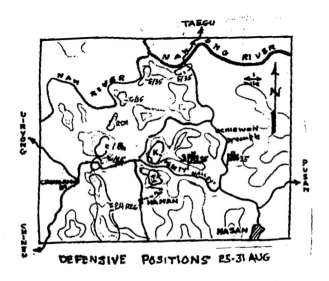

DEFENSIVE POSITIONS 25-31 AUG

By this time, the battalion has become "battle hardened." Sergeants and lieutenants practice "tough love." They expect no nonsense and they allow none, and soldiers know the importance of self-discipline. Dead and decaying bodies are no longer a novelty. Everyone knows that anyone they see might provide information to the enemy, and know when in doubt to shoot to kill.

We know there will be more attempts to take Pusan and that there will be a major assault in our sector. We have intelligence that the enemy has infiltrated between front line units and are in the hills all around us. We do not know how many there are, or which of the civilians are their agents.

Pine and alder cover these hills. While it is not difficult to walk in these woods since the slopes are not great and the undergrowth is not thick, the visibility is limited. Patrols should have been sent into these hills to determine exactly who is there. But Americans prefer to stick to the roads; they do not yet understand the importance of patrolling. Nor have they made night their friend.

The frontline units and outposts are often probed at night. On the roads, some vehicles are attacked, some small isolated units in the rear are attacked, but company size combat units are not.

At dusk, we can sit on the steps of the schoolhouse in which we are living to look across a peaceful, beautiful, restful landscape. It is still dry and hot but not like it had been during the Task Force Kean operations. Only a few Koreans remain in the valley, and they usually stay indoors. The artillery for the whole area is located in the valley with us, and the roar of the howitzers echoes throughout each night. Yet it is still a happy and relaxed period compared to what we had experienced during our first two weeks in Korea.

One morning I receive word that the First Battalion had been probed several times during the night. Since our L Company is attached to that battalion, I thought I should go up to find out what had really happened. I ask Major Woolfolk if I can go.

He says, "No, I need you here."

The First Battalion is just over two miles up the road. I know the trip will take about half an hour. I really am not doing anything. Thinking perhaps he really didn't mean it, I go back a short while later and ask again.

"I told you no."

I am annoyed by what I consider the denial of a most reasonable request. I call my driver, Tharp. Together we go to a nearby stream and take a swim. I clear my mind—I guess it is a form of meditation. I enjoy the water and the hot sun. It is much like San Antonio in June. We must have spent almost two hours swimming and washing our clothes.

When I return to the command post, I have only entered the door when Major Woolfolk casually glances over my way and asks, "How are things up front?"

"I don't know, sir."

He looks straight at me. In a stern voice, he says, "What do you mean you don't know?"

"I can't know, sir, because I didn't go up to the front. I went swimming."

"Why didn't you go?"

"Because you told me not to, sir."

He then went back to whatever he had been doing. Nothing more was ever said. From that time on, however, he relied more on me.

This valley will certainly not be a happy place during 1–3 September, when the Thirty-Fifth Regiment will earn a Presidential Unit Citation for the defense of this critical sector of the Pusan perimeter.

Warriors, Soldiers, and Supporters

In Korea, the army needed men who were hardened warriors, not garrison soldiers. It needed leaders who were warriors, soldiers—and some supporters. It did not need those who have a weak, flexible, ill-defined, morally relativistic inner compass (i.e., a lack of willpower that would cause them to vacillate, reconsider, compromise, and be under great stress when they had to make life or death decisions in the heat of battle).

Hostile fire causes warriors and soldiers to focus their thoughts and to speed up their actions. On the other hand, hostile fire causes many to lose their focus, and it tests their will. Warriors and soldiers think clearly and act quickly to cope with danger; some people freeze and are only able to flee from danger. Warriors and soldiers are dormant and quiet until they hear the trumpet, then they go into action. They do not hesitate, have doubts, or do what is politically correct and serves their personal self-interest. Warriors and soldiers are able to cope with ideological conflict much better than some people since each has an inner compass based on absolutes.

For battle-hardened men, bluntness and a jovial manner is looked upon as sincerity and strength, while carefully chosen words and haughtiness are seen as signs of a faint-hearted MINO (military in name only) who will lose his head at the sound of hostile fire. Warriors and soldiers are masculine and aggressive; to them, gentler, feminine, emotions are a sign of weakness.

In combat, the leader must be able to master his emotions and constantly think of what might come next. The future might present situations that will turn him, and those he leads, into dust. But the leader cannot allow this reality to paralyze him or dominate his actions; he must make rapid judgments about how best to accomplish his mission and to take care of his men.

The key to success in combat is that the men have confidence in their leaders and in what they are doing. This bond has three components:

1. Leaders never ask their men to do anything they are unwilling, or unable, to do themselves,

2. Leaders always tell the truth, and

3. Leaders share hardships, dangers, and comforts with their men.

Successful leaders are not politically correct; they have an inner compass which allows them to make difficult decisions quickly. *Being deeply respected by his men gives a leader strength, while loving his men deeply gives the leader courage.*

---

[12] War is conflict between the acknowledged armed forces of states, each attempting to destroy the symmetrical armed forces of the other. Success in War is victory for one side and defeat for the other. Warfare is protracted asymmetrical conflict between sovereign states and insurgents willing to use all means to weaken or overthrow those in authority. Success in Warfare is Peace (i.e., a climate of order and satisfaction in which no one is willing to use force to achieve political ends).

CHAPTER NINE

THE TWENTY-FIFTH DIVISION WINS

29 August–15 September 1950

Despite two months of air attacks seeking to deteriorate the supply of the North Korean Army, ammunition, food, guns, tanks, and replacements are still getting to enemy units facing the Pusan perimeter in the end of August. Much of the movement to the south is done at night. The ROK (Republic of Korea) Army has been rebuilt to ninety-one thousand men and it is no longer the rabble of twenty-two thousand it had been two months earlier south of the Han. Espionage has been reduced by greater security consciousness and by a policy of shooting anyone moving around military units at night. However, this also has some very tragic consequences: the killing of our soldiers and innocent civilians. We are glad the news reporters did not use this in their dispatches.

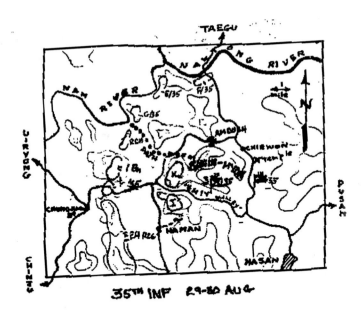

Enemy Infiltration

On 29 August, I notice the fields on both sides of the road I am traveling are crushed. I am en route from K Company to regimental headquarters. The crushed fields create a path about six feet wide. Looking west, I can follow the path only a few hundred yards, but in my mind I can see where it goes: it passes between the ROK Company and G Company. Looking east, the path goes toward the Sanin-Myon hill mass in the middle of the Thirty-Fifth Regiment's area. There can only be one explanation: a large number of enemy troops had infiltrated to our rear during the night. Of course, I have no way of knowing why. Are they going to establish roadblocks? Are they going to attack our supply units? Are they part of a future offensive by the North Koreans? Nor do I know how many of the enemy walked that path during the night.

I go on to the regimental CP (command post). I tell the S-2 what I have seen and express my concern. He thanks me but expresses no interest in checking it out. I tell others, but I can generate no concern or even get someone to go with me to look at the path.

I return to the Third Battalion CP. On two overlays, I draw three big red circles over the Sanin-Myon hill mass in the center of the regimental area. I write in red inside these circles the numbers 1,000, 500, and 300. I post one on  the map at the battalion and send the other up to regimental headquarters. I then go outside, look around at the beautiful scenery, pick up a paperback, and start to read. About two hours later, Major Woolfolk comes over and says angrily: "What the hell do you think you are doing? Regiment just called me and wants to know where we got this information about all of the enemy around here."

"Oh, those numbers? That's just my estimate of the enemy situation."

"I see, but where did you get the information?"

I tell him about the path I had seen. He left without saying a word.

On the next day (30 August), my analysis is partially confirmed. A group of cooks are ambushed while bringing hot food from the trains[13] area, near the regimental CP, to one of the companies. This took place on the road I had used several times the previous day. Two of the cooks escape but hear the screams of those being tortured. They get to the nearest American unit and tell what happened. A relief team is sent, but by the time they reach the ambush site, the North Koreans have gone—only the dead remain. I arrive ten minutes after the relief team, but before the bodies are moved. Their hands are tied behind them. They are all shot in the back of the head. Some have their tongues cut out. Others have their feet chopped off. The head cook has been castrated, and his testicles stuffed in his mouth.

The Attack to Breakthrough to Pusan: 1 September 1950

At the end of August, the commander of the Inmun Gun (North Korean People's Army) General Kim Chaik launches the largest offensive ever conducted by the North Koreans. By then, all "front line" infantry companies have spent several weeks organizing their positions; in the last few days of August, they know the major attack toward Pusan will be directly at them. Sweat-covered soldiers naked to the waist dig foxholes in the sandy clay soil and fill sand bags. Foxholes are deeper, gun emplacements are ready, and mortars are zeroed in on likely enemy attack routes. Each of the platoons has been repeatedly visited to check crossfire of machine guns and BARs. Procedures for engaging enemy targets have been reviewed. Also the importance of fire discipline has been stressed so as to preserve ammunition and to prevent disclosure of positions.

The Initial Attack

Now comes the attack. Soon after dark on 31 August, the enemy begins probing with small arms fire. As the night progresses, the probes intensify. Enemy rifle, automatic weapons, and mortar fire hit at all front line companies. After midnight, two divisions attack in the sector of the Twenty-Fifth Division in an attempt to reach Pusan. At least three North Korean battalions are already miles behind the front defensive positions of the Twenty-Fifth Division when this attack begins on 31

August. The Seventh North Korean Division crosses the Nam River, using underwater fords, a mile in front of the ROK Company attached to the Thirty-Fifth Regiment.

At the same time, the Sixth North Korean Division moves up to the vicinity of Chungam-ni. The initial assault by that division is against F Company, Twenty-Fourth Regiment just south of L Company, Thirty-Fifth Regiment.[14] This is quickly followed by attacks just north of the main road against the First Battalion to which L Company is attached. This attack reaches the front line rifle companies before midnight. For several hours, hundreds of the North Korean soldiers are killed in front of these defensive positions, both by the infantrymen and artillery.

In the front line rifle companies, the men are told: "Hold your fire. Three-round bursts max. The ammo you have is all you are going to get. Make each shot count. If you run out, you are going to have to fight with your bayonet. There will be no bugging out. Do you understand?"

Flares provide a brief canopy of light with which to view surroundings. Throughout the early morning hours of 1 September, the sky is filled with tracers, phosphorus rounds, and mortar explosions. The warriors and soldiers of the Thirty-Fifth Regiment fight gallantly. There are enemies everywhere looking for an opportunity to kill. No one protects the flanks of anyone; each unit has to protect itself. Most of those in the front line rifle companies are tired and weary young men with limited battle experience; however, they hold their positions like the best of infantry throughout history. They know this is a fight for survival since there are no reinforcements to send forward to give them help and no place to go. Air support is not provided during these night hours. Many of those in the supporting units become warriors and soldiers that night.

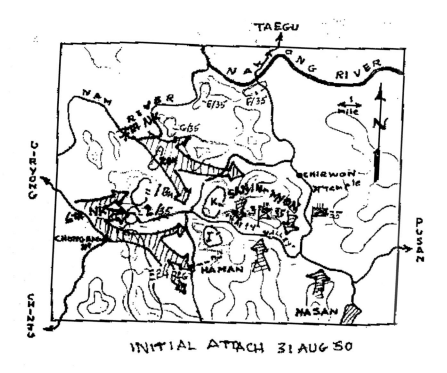

INITIAL ATTACH 31 AUG 50

Each squad in all front line rifle companies has its own battle. Many teenagers look out of their foxholes through barbed wire at North Korean soldiers moving toward them. Each tries to stop breathing. Each remembers: "Hold your fire." Each hears his buddy next to him swallow. "Come on in, you bastards!"

The lieutenant shouts: "Fire, fire, fire." North Koreans tumble forward onto the wire. Others drop down. A few crawl forward. More firing, and the attack stops—some crawl back. But there will be another attack soon. More voices and more sounds of movement. When will there be the next rush? The riflemen slide down into their foxholes and check their ammunition. For several hours, hundreds of the North Korean soldiers are killed in front of the Thirty-Fifth Regiment.

By 0400 (1 September) the ROK Company has fled to the rear, and the soldiers of the Seventh North Korean Division are flowing through their abandoned positions. This results in G Company, just north of the penetration, being surrounded. Just prior to dawn, the enemy halts their attacks and conceals their positions.

By daylight on 1 September, the attack by the Sixth North Korean Division has reached Haman and I Company, Thirty-Fifth (formally A Company, Twenty-Ninth Regiment) on a hill overlooking that town. The enemy pours through the positions abandoned by the Twenty-Fourth Regiment. Bullets dig up the ground in front of I Company. The platoon leaders report that the enemy is advancing on their position. Mortar fire breaks up these attacks, but the enemy keeps coming. There are enemy bodies in front of all of the rifle companies. At dawn, US tanks counterattack through the fog to contain the enemy.

The penetration is just as bad on the left flank of the Thirty-Fifth Regiment when some of the Twenty-Fourth Regiment breaks and streams to the rear. The North Koreans move through the abandoned positions. This made the First Battalion an island in a sea of enemies, with I Company and K Company becoming the "front lines."

The command post of the Third Battalion is never actually assaulted on the first night. Yet we have foxholes around the schoolhouse facing in all directions. I place my men north of the schoolhouse facing some woods. I go back and forth between the battalion CP and my men in their foxholes. Whenever the artillery near us fires, there is a tremendous roar, and red streaks of light flash into the air. After midnight we see many dark figures moving—we shoot at them, and they fire back.

At 0300 hours, we see some movement in the woods. I wait—the seconds pass slowly. I want to burn off the adrenaline in my blood. Breathing quietly, I wait. Moving figures emerge out of the darkness. I do not think they know we are waiting, but they are moving slowly toward the schoolhouse. "Fire," I shout. Some of the figures fall, and others stop, as if in disbelief. We fire again. The figures disappear in the darkness. The bodies left do not move. There is silence broken by the roar from the artillery close by, and the rumble from the other artillery of Happy Valley. No other North Koreans approach the schoolhouse before dawn. Yet fighting is intense throughout Happy Valley and as far as ten miles east of us near Masan and toward Pusan. Many units in the rear areas are overrun, and many die in violent hand-to-hand fighting.

After the Initial Attack

From midnight on 1 September until the end of 4 September there are firefights—with both North Korean soldiers and their local guerrilla supporters—throughout the regimental area. The term "front lines" has little meaning during these days and nights. The artillery in Happy Valley is assaulted by troops that come down from the Sanin-Myon hill mass. Artillerymen are usually behind the front and do not engage in up close and personal firefights. But this is not true on the first two days of September 1950. The North Koreans are fighting throughout the regimental area. Two artillery units in Happy Valley are overrun. The gunners pulled their firing lanyards to provide fire support to the "front line" over a mile away; at the same time, they are throwing hand grenades and shooting at those only yards away.

The Second Battalion, Thirty-Fifth Infantry holds its positions during 1 and 2 September. Further north, on the other side of the Naktong River, the Second Division is fighting to stop advances miles east of the Naktong River, which will continue until 5 September.

By daylight (morning of 1 September), members of the Twenty-Fourth Regiment and ROK soldiers are pouring past our CP in Happy Valley. The enemy control Haman and most of the area forward of the defensive positions of I Company and K Companies,[15] except the islands actually occupied by the First and Second Battalions.

All of the front line companies of the Thirty-Fifth Regiment hold their positions during the first night (1 September). The light of day reveals the bodies, torn clothing, and abandoned equipment in front of the rifle companies. It is time to buoy up spirits, for there will surely be determined fights during the coming nights. Tank/infantry teams of the Twenty-Seventh Regiment and the Thirty-Fifth Regiment counterattack through the morning fog to contain the enemy that had flowed through penetrations of the Twenty-Fourth Regiment and ROK positions during the night. All day, companies attempt to resupply their ammunition, restore and improve their defenses, and get ready for another attack on the night of 1–2 September.

North of the Thirty-Fifth Regiment, on the other side of the Naktong River, the Second Division is fighting a desperate battle to stop advances miles east of the Naktong River.

Bugging Out of the Twenty-Fourth Regiment

During the morning of 1 September, Twenty-Fourth Regiment and ROK soldiers are pouring past our CP in Happy Valley.

Some forty men from the Twenty-Fourth Regiment come down the road. Some have their rifles, but others have nothing. There is a lieutenant with them. Captain Lester J. Brown[16] walks over to the road with several of our men. He tells those fleeing to halt and says: "Lieutenant, get these men together and have them set up a roadblock back there until we can get you back to your unit." He points to a group of houses on the edge of our position.

"I ain't going back. They're right behind us."

"Lieutenant, there is no place to go. We have to stop them here."

"Not me," the lieutenant replies in a matter-of-fact manner. The men are now gathered around the two. The lieutenant turns to continue down the road. Brown pulls his .45 from its holster, points it at the road next to the lieutenant's boots, and pulls the trigger. The sound seems much louder than normal. The bullet kicks up some stones and flies off to the side.

The lieutenant turns his head to look back with scorn at Brown and then deliberately starts to walk away. Brown wonders if he should fire another warning round.

He points his pistol at the lieutenant. He pulls the trigger. The recoil knocks his hand back. The lieutenant falls in the middle of the road, tries to rise, and then falls back with his arms dangling beside his body.

The men from the "Deuce Fo" stare at the lieutenant's body. Brown spots a sergeant, a six-foot-two black man in his early thirties. "Sergeant, these men are now under your command. Take them back to those houses and set up a roadblock. Don't let anyone—Americans, South Koreans, or North Koreans—pass you. Do you understand?"

Brown then turns calmly to our men. "Cover them as they set up the roadblock. If anyone does not go with the sergeant, shoot them."

He walks over to the sergeant. "I'll see that you get a Bronze Star if you pull this off."

"Yes, Captain. Will do."

The sergeant touches his right hand to his forehead in a sloppy movement. It wasn't a proper salute, but it did show respect. For a moment, his eyes meet the steely glare of Captain Brown.

"Carry on, Sergeant."

During Daylight on 1 September 1950

I Company and K Company, with tank support, spend all day of 1 September clearing out the area between their positions and the positions held by the First and Second Battalions. Before dark on 1 September, K Company takes over the old ROK Company position, and the Headquarters Company, Third Battalion in Happy Valley move to the old K Company position—here it is surrounded by North Koreans that have moved past the "front lines."

On 1 September, the First Battalion, Twenty-Seventh Regiment, with extensive use of aircraft from the carriers *Valley Forge* and *Philippine Sea*, counterattack to retake the positions lost by the Twenty-Fourth Regiment. They drive the enemy out of Haman, and by noon on 2 September regain all lost positions.

North of the Naktong on 31 August and 1 September 1950

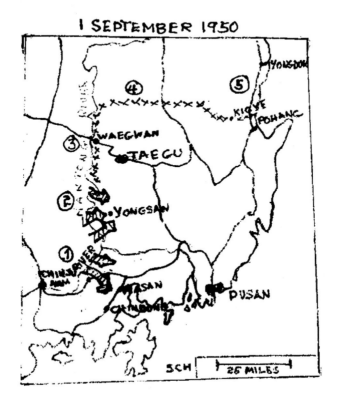

(1) Twenty-Fifth Division south of the Naktong is attacked by Sixth and Seventh North Korean Divisions. (2) In the center of the Pusan Perimeter, the Second, Fourth, and Ninth North Korean Divisions make seventeen attacks across the Naktong River. Tenth North Korean Division prepares to follow. (3) Near Taegu, the First, Third, and Thirteenth North Korean Divisions hold their positions. First Cavalry Division moves forward but is stalled. (4) Along the northern side of the Pusan perimeter, the Fifth, Eighth, Twelfth, and Fifteenth North Korean Divisions hold their positions, as do the ROK Divisions.

In the center of the Pusan perimeter, four North Korean Divisions attack across the Naktong River. At 2030 hours on 31 August, thousands of troops come down to the river and cross. The Second Division is divided; the Twenty-Third and Thirty-Eighth Regiments and the artillery in the north are separated from the division headquarters and the Ninth Regiment in the south. The fighting is relentless, cruel, primitive, and fierce—more than matching that by the Japanese in World War II. Isolated companies are left on hills overlooking the Naktong, and some units withdraw to new positions. The Ninth North Korean Division, with tanks and artillery, advance eight miles to Yongsan; the Fourth North Korean Division follows.

Near Taegu, three North Korean Divisions hold their positions. First Cavalry Division moves forward but is stalled. Along the northern side of the Pusan perimeter, four North Korean Divisions hold their positions, as do the ROK Divisions. Air force, marine and navy fighters and air force bombers range over the fluid battlefield, shooting any enemy found.

Thus ends the first day of the decisive battle of the Korean War.

Continuation of the Battle to Capture Pusan: 2 and 3 September 1950

During the night of 1–2 September, the North Koreans send more troops through the gap between the First and Second Battalions of the Thirty-Fifth Regiment and continue the attacks on G and E Companies. The enemy attempts to dislodge G Company for thirty-eight hours. As the division commander said: "If those men had not held the high ground, the breach in our line would have been widened, and the enemy could have poured through in a flanking move to threaten our entire front."

On 2 and 3 September, the enemy already in the rear area attack the closest units, including the Sixty-Fourth Field Artillery in Happy Valley. Americans in all branches (engineers, ordnance, transportation, quartermaster, signal, etc.) find themselves engaged in the close combat usually associated with infantrymen.

On 2 September, Colonel Henry G. Fisher, commander of the Thirty-Fifth Regiment, comes to our positions and compares the dead in the paddies in front of the defensive positions of the Thirty-Fifth Regiment to the slaughter he had seen of the Germans at Falaise Gap during World War II. He then tells us, "I never intended to withdraw. There was no place to go." This was true for most units. There were assaults and hand-to-hand fighting throughout the regimental area, but there are also unseen snipers killing our soldiers—particularly officers.

By the evening of 3 September, most enemy units have been removed from the area of the Thirty-Fifth Regiment, but the Twenty-Fourth Regiment to our south is still having trouble near Haman.

A 155-mm howitzer, known as the "Little Professor," is moved up into the defensive area of one of our rifle companies. This is to allow its eleven-mile range to reach deep into the enemy's rear. Although we do not know it at the time, the North Koreans have moved their Fifth Division up to support the attacks in our area. All of this fighting provided a large number of prisoners. I noted a change in those captured.

Many of those who had infiltrated to our rear areas before 1 September (and local guerrillas) are still active. Some of the enemy fighters are women; in fact, on 3 September, it is a woman who murdered four members of a radio relay station surprised by a group of local guerrillas. They tied up the Americans, looked through the station, and then the woman shot all four.

On 4 September, the briefing officer said that the Twenty-Fifth Division had killed or wounded at least 12,000 of the enemy since 31 August. The Thirty-Fifth Regiment is awarded the Presidential Unit Citation for what it did on 1–3 September 1950.

Attacks toward Taegu, 2–12 September 1950

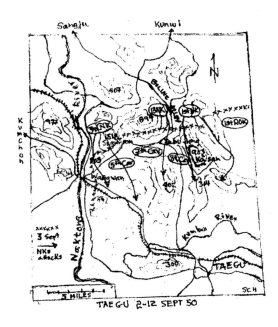

TAEGU 2-12 SEPT 50

The Third North Korean Division advances three and a half miles against the First Cavalry Division from north of Waegwan toward Taegu. Thirteenth North Korean Division reaches Kasan (an ancient oblong-shaped walled fortress) north of Taegu. Kasan is captured the next day. During the night, the First Cavalry Division withdraws toward Taegu. It is wet and foggy. General Walker considers a general withdrawal of the Eighth Army and does move his headquarters closer to Pusan.

The marines and Second Division attack, causing the enemy to flee back toward the Naktong. Artillery kills many North Koreans. The advancing infantry meets little resistance, but there are many bodies and much abandoned equipment. The sky is clear, the air is warm, but the mud makes movement difficult. By 1500, the soldiers reach the high ground known as Cloverleaf Hill. At nightfall, they go into defensive positions.

In Pyongyang, Zhai Junwa, the Chinese emissary, tells Kim Il-sung there is a stalemate in the Pusan area that North Korea alone cannot overcome. Kim replies that his great offensive has just started, and it will soon break the deadlock, and then he states: "We estimate that presently a US counterattack is not possible."

On 11 September, the fighting north of Taegu, by the First Cavalry and First ROK Divisions, is intense and confusing, as there is no clear "front line." There is fear of a breakthrough to the blocking position of Third Battalion, Seventh Cavalry Regiment. The Eighth Engineer Battalion, fighting as infantry, holds a bridge across the Kumho River. An attack by Third Battalion, Eighth Cavalry Regiment fails, while Thirteenth North Korean Division advances to a hill mass with steep slopes that commands the Taegu Valley.

Performance of the Twenty-Fourth Regiment

The Twenty-Fourth Regiment did not perform well. It was composed of all colored (as black people were called then) soldiers; it collapsed on the night of 31 August. General Kean had the Twenty-Seventh Regiment retake the ridge, which was then given back to what remained of the Twenty-Fourth Regiment. Also, a company from the Fifth Regiment is brought in to round up stragglers every night and take them back to their units in the morning. On 9 September, General Kean recommends the immediate removal of the Twenty-Fourth Regiment from combat and that the men be transferred as replacements to other units, with the officers and NCOs being the cadre for a new regiment. He states: "The Twenty-Fourth Infantry has demonstrated in combat that it is untrustworthy and incapable of carrying out missions expected of an infantry regiment."

General Walker does not act on this recommendation. Washington does not want to admit that an all-black regiment did not fight well. Soon there are several studies that claimed that the whole problem is racism in the army and that full integration must be accomplished as soon as possible.

On 14 September, the Sixth North Korean Division again attempted to gain control of Battle Mountain.

The next morning, Task Force Woolfolk is formed to remove the enemy from Battle Mountain.[17]

All day the three infantry companies move up the mountain against stiff resistance, but they have limited success. A Company, Twenty-Seventh Regiment does make it to the top of one ridge of Battle Mountain and sets up a defensive position. Almost immediately, they are attacked. All afternoon they beat off the enemy, but toward dark, their ammunition is running low, and they have many casualties.

I am on the radio when the company commander calls to explain the situation, which ends with: "I do not think we can hold off another attack. I can hear them forming up now. I think we need to pull back from this ridge to a small knob down the slope. That way I can make sure my wounded will not be captured."

Of course, we all know what the North Koreans do to Americans they capture. I step over to Major Woolfolk. I hear rifle shots of the enemy attack, and on the radio, I hear the company commander.

"We've got to get out of here. If I don't get my wounded out now, they are all going to be killed!" he shouts frantically. I turn and look at Major Woolfolk.

"What do you want me to tell him?" I ask.

"I'm not going to be a butcher just to save my own neck." Then he adds: "Get them back!"

For this, he is relieved of his command of the task force, and we go back to the battalion. It is renamed Task Force Blair, for the new commander, Major Melvin R. Blair.

The fight for Battle Mountain continues, but Task Force Blair is never able to hold the highest ridge. The task force is finally withdrawn. Nevertheless, the enemy on Battle Mountain is never able to move. They just stay in the mine tunnels and threaten no one. They are ignored.

Lesson Learned: Command

Command requires both courage and judgment. It requires someone with the inner compass to be able to do the right rather than the self-serving wrong. All good commanders think of both the mission and their men; to accomplish one at the expense of the other is to fail. Good commanders have the judgment to know how to be faithful to both. Anyone can be given the authority to send men to their death, but only a select few are good commanders.

Success in the Battle of the Pusan Perimeter, which is the decisive battle in Korea, is largely the achievement of General Walton "Johnnie" Walker and those who fought with him. He is a skillful, energetic, fearless commander. With many poorly prepared troops against a capable, fierce opponent, he patches together units, shifts forces, and skillfully uses his advantages of mobility and firepower. They fight and die. Together they prevent a North Korean march to Pusan. Walker demonstrates the balancing of thought and action so essential for success in combat. Those who fight with him do their best. He is a thinking soldier, and they are gallant warriors and soldiers.

Unknown to us, the marines land at Inch'on on 15 September. At dawn, British and American cruisers fire on NK gun emplacements in the Inch'on port as Operation Chromite. At 0630 the Third Battalion, Fifth Marines land on Wolman-do Island without resistance. Late in the afternoon, the marines take the seawalls of Inch'on against scattered resistance. Unfortunately, some of the casualties are from naval gunfire. By midnight, most of the key objectives are captured.

This is MacArthur's greatest success in Korea. Landing at Inch'on is unconventional, unpredictable, and audacious. He wanted to use naval superiority to avoid ground combat where harsh terrain can offset technology. He goes against the opinions of the navy and the joint chiefs. At Inch'on, he gambles and wins. Yet this is not the decisive battle of the Korean War—that had been the holding of the Pusan perimeter until this invasion could take place.

Four days after the landing at Inch'on (19 September) we will counterattack from the Pusan perimeter; that attack will take us back to Chinju and beyond. Here we will learn what the North Koreans had done after they gained control, and in time we will learn something about ideological conflict.

---

[13] The regimental logistical support, supply, and maintenance units.

[14] Which had formally been C Company, Twenty-Ninth Infantry Regiment.

[15] Formally A and B Companies, Twenty-Ninth Infantry Regiment.

[16] This is a fictitious name.

[17] For this task force Major Woolfolk used the Heavy Weapons and Headquarters companies of the Third Battalion, Thirty-Fifth Regiment; A Company, Twenty-Seventh Regiment; I Company, Thirty-Fifth Regiment; and a company of combat engineers, which was now fighting as infantry.

CHAPTER TEN

THE LULL
BETWEEN THE STORMS

15–21 September 1950

After the dramatic struggles of the first two weeks of September, there are a few days of relative calm before we move up and down Korea. However, reports from other units about treatment of American wounded and prisoners are most disturbing.

It becomes clear that the atrocities committed by the North Korean People's Army and their local communist supporters, which we had observed, are typical of what had been done after they invaded South Korea. Americans had been repeatedly tortured and killed in the most barbaric ways. This must have been intentional—as a tactic which they thought would break our will—since so many different units reported such barbarism.

Politically Correct View of Torture

One of the tragedies of this Forgotten War is that real torture and wanton killing of political opponents, which the North

Koreans did again and again, has been forgotten—and worse yet that some lump this barbarism together with legitimate, and necessary, aggressive interrogation techniques. This is not to overlook similar acts by South Koreans, but to recognize what actually occurred and to challenge the moral equivalence some make.

The elevation of compassion, understanding, and tolerance above principle, dedication, and aggressiveness is the cardinal sign of the decline and decay of any group. Yet also is the absence of an inner compass, which allows individuals to distinguish barbarism from self-preservation, torture from interrogation, and sadism from heroism.

Beacon in the Night

Normally we would place our battalion headquarters in a building. The Headquarters Company CO (Captain Donald McGraw) would find a temple, school, or house a short distance behind the rifle companies. But after we moved out of Happy Valley on 1 September, we are actually in a defensive position just like a rifle company. There are no buildings. We are using a tent for the battalion command post (CP). It sits on the back side of a small knob surrounded by Headquarters Company and a tank platoon.

From 1 September until 20 September, everyone knows there are enemy patrols and stragglers outside our defensive positions. At night, they move about. Sometimes they seek to avoid contact; sometimes they are seeking someone to kill. Having the enemy all around us each night results in tank-led sweeps each morning.

I have grown to like and admire Major Woolfolk. He is not friendly or gregarious—he is always the battalion commander. He is a knowledgeable, hardworking, political, intense, manipulative, up-tight military professional soldier. I do not consider him a warrior. In my opinion, he would be more suited for the staff of a larger headquarters than as a combat commander. But you always know where you stand with him and what he expects from you. He is one of the types of officers the military must have: knowledgeable, trustworthy, honest, dedicated, and capable.

One night we are in the CP tent talking, joking around, and telling stories. There is no activity; therefore, all we had to do is answer the phone as the negative reports are called in. There is a lot of laughter.

Captain Don McGraw comes through the tent door flap: "Thanks for the help."

"For what?"

"It's dark as a cave out there," he replies. "I went out to relieve myself, but on the return, I could not see the tent. But I sure heard you!"

"So the blackout is working?"

"It sure is. Not a speck of light. But Sam's laugh was a homing beacon—direct to the tent."

We all have a laugh. Then back to our bull session.

In about ten minutes, the major comes in, sits down, and turns to me: "Holliday, you are going to have to quit that laughing or stay out of this tent at night—it is dangerous. Every North Korean within two miles will be down on us."

From then on, I tried to subdue my laughter—no doubt with limited success since my two nicknames are Smilin' Sam and

Laughing Boy. But I did my best, since I did not want to jeopardize the safety of the battalion.

Warriors, Professional Soldiers, and Supporters

The military needs professional soldiers, and the military needs warriors—it also needs many in uniform who see no combat but do jobs to support those in combat. It makes no difference how someone looks and talks before the danger and confusion of combat. Combat makes the thinking and actions of warriors and soldiers clear, direct, and effective. It freezes the minds of some and prevents them from acting—they only want to escape; these MINOs (military in name only) lose it at the sound of hostile fire. Those in supporting units normally do not live with ever-present death, but when they do, they become warriors, soldiers, or MINOs. Warriors and soldiers think clearly under stress. Even though supporters often are not in combat, they do contribute to making a large, complex, technology-laden organization function effectively—they perform logistics, communication, and supporting activities that are essential for success. Warriors and soldiers think it is better to die fighting than to die running away; they do the killing and dying. A few supporters are the pacifists, Hamlets, and the self-centered, politically correct MINOs who scheme and manipulate. Most supporters are just competent technicians.

Eros and Death

Genesis 2–7 says God turned dust into humans with the "breath of life." However, exactly how humans got a soul has always been a mystery. Nevertheless, it is the inner compass of individuals that gives humans the ability to either obey the orders of instinct and the flesh (in common with all mammals), or to struggle against such dictates in keeping with the life-giving force of Eros. Eros is everything that seeks to protect and preserve life. Prior to the fifth century BC, the Greeks considered Eros the force that united people. It is possible that evolution has placed deep in the mysterious human mind imagination, commitment, and belonging as the essence of the highest form of life. And it is just possible that Eros is the door to such life since it is a union-seeking fulfillment. If so, Eros is the key to survival—and critical to the warrior spirit.

Although often noted, the reason for the connection of both lust and Eros with death remains unknown. We do know that death is the end of sex. And we know that sexual union is the start of all life. This is dramatically illustrated by the female praying mantis who bites off the head of the male while they are having sex; his death throes make fertilization more certain. Then the female eats the male to provide food for her offspring. Some spiders do the same. Instinct is the urge found in all organic life to restore. It is true that instinct controls the actions of insects, while all mammals have a complex brain with which to make decisions about unexpected circumstances. Among mammals, only humans have the free will that allows them to behave in accordance with Eros. Even the most primitive humans had the human passions of compassion, jealousy, generosity, anger, belief, caring, hate, and sympathy. Human behavior is real, active, and creative, which are qualities lacking in all instinct-controlled insects and most mammals. Yet it is not unreasonable to wonder if all creatures—including humans— might not retain some of the basic instincts. It is often said that men and women behave differently because they are not "hardwired" the same—could that be evidence of instinct?

Anyone who has ever been around soldiers knows they think about women and sex much of the time. Soldiers often find any female appealing, and many women are attracted to a military uniform. This passion seems to be stronger in War and Warfare than in Peace. Perhaps this is because the isolation, loneliness, fear, and danger soldiers experience can be eased by thoughts of women and sex. Or perhaps this passion is an instinct humans retain so they want to reproduce when so many of their species are being destroyed.

In combat this passion takes two forms: sex and Eros. Sex is nothing more than an outlet and relief in a physical sense. Most soldiers in combat place sex in the same category as the needs of eating and drinking, which relieve hunger and thirst. Sex alone is a way to relieve a need. The taking of a woman becomes much like the conquest of an enemy. Any woman will do. This attitude is no doubt associated with the violent, capricious, impersonal nature of combat. Yet these same men would have very different attitudes about sex at home during Peace—as would antiwar activists, pacifists, and humanists who have never experienced combat.

It is the other form of this "love"—Eros—which seeks unity and to preserve.[18] Eros and sex can combine into a love affair of tenderness, charm, and beauty, even though it might last only a few days or weeks. The two believe they are brought together in such awful times for a reason, thus perceiving their relationship as stronger than military regulations, country, religion, race, custom, or tradition. Both tend to give the other attributes of tenderness or virtue, which are most likely fantasy. The threats of danger, separation, deprivation, and death intensify the bliss of having found each other—a union of mutual affection they want to preserve.

Then Eros can stand alone without sex. Eros holds off the destruction of life and limb during War and Warfare. Self-preservation during violent battles cannot be done alone. Thus men give up their lives in battle, acting against the instinct of self-preservation, in order to preserve something more important than self. Reason cannot explain this. The best examples of it are combat camaraderie and a soldier's caring more for the lives of his comrades than his own. In a broader sense, Eros can cause a person to identify with those of a large group, community, nation, or all humans, preventing cruelty, sadism, killing without purpose, and pleasure killing.

While the frequency of sex and Eros within armed forces has been well documented in history and literature, there has been little interest in how these passions affect combat effectiveness. Warriors have always been very masculine, macho, and gung-ho. While there are many tasks that women can perform in armed forces—and women can probably do some better than men—combat is not one of them. The issue that needs to be addressed is: What will the introduction of women into the military do to combat effectiveness?

Soldiers of the North Korean Army

I notice a change in the soldiers of the Inmun Gun (North Korean People's Army) we capture after the 1 September attacks. Those captured at the first battle of Chungam-ni Pass had fought all of the way down from North Korea. They were either North Koreans or Korean-extraction veterans of the Chinese communist forces that were returned to North Korea in June 1950. They were well-trained, experienced, disciplined soldiers.

Many of those we capture after the attacks of 1 September are conscripts. They lack the training, skills, or equipment of those who had crossed the 38th Parallel on 25 June. Many of the conscripts had been idealistic young men when they joined the army; they wanted to unite Korea under a socialist regime. They wanted equality and social justice more than freedom. They expected the government to take from the rich and to give to the poor. They thought in terms of a collective rather in terms of the individual. But the reality of combat had changed all of that.

They had been seeking a redeemer to give them protection from economic, social, and psychological distress. For them Kim Il-sung had been a mirror, a channel, a voice, and the very depth of the Korean soul. They thought he offered absolution from the sin of being Korean—who both Japanese and Chinese considered inferior. Of course, there is no reason or logic behind such feelings. Those who came from South Korea had wanted to rid their country of the wealthy landowners and the corrupt politicians controlled by foreigners. But their experience with violence, barbarity, and wonton killing had caused second thoughts. By the time of their capture, most realized that their idealism had turned them into cannon fodder, and their capture is a welcome escape. Their ideological dedication had vanished.

The local guerrillas are cut from the same cloth, yet they have not yet realized how the communist utopia is being used to manipulate them. These guerrillas, about a fourth of which are women, are still political activists. They had done whatever they could to advance the communist ideology and to destroy the Republic of Korea; most still thought their guerrilla activities were just another means for advancing a noble cause. Perhaps it had been the prolonged fighting of the North Korean Divisions contrasted with the swift action of the guerrillas that made the difference.

Lesson Learned: The Heart of Ideological Conflict

How can you build a nation of free, independent humans with people like this? I noticed similarities in the psychology of these willing Oriental pawns of the political "left" and those of Western pawns of the political "right" under Hitler and Mussolini. Why did they seek a utopia through a centralized government and give to the state their ultimate loyalty? Why were the inner compasses of these people of the "left" and the "right" so similar and so in contrast with those of most Americans? Was there any hope for a republic with limited governmental powers with people like this? Why were they motivated by emotions and feelings while ignoring facts and reason? I only had questions. It would be many years before I had any answers. Yet the answers are at the heart of ideological conflict.

Failure to Understand Inundation

Although the Thirty-Fifth Regiment had been successful in defending its portion of the Pusan perimeter on 1–3 September, the losses of many US units throughout 1950 reflected a lack of understanding of a basic maneuver used by the North Koreans.

The enemy would rarely attempt a penetration. The initial attack was usually a secondary attack. They would probe to find any weak spots and gaps. Then they would move around the flanks or move through any gaps. At the same time, they would establish roadblocks to the rear of the unit being attacked. Most of their damage to US units was done during withdrawal rather than during the initial attack. Since inundation was not taught in US military schools, it was necessary to learn by experience—often at a very heavy cost.

Before and during World War I, this maneuver was called "infiltration"; however, infiltration lost any meaning as a form of maneuver. Infiltration became only the method used by individuals or groups to move undetected through enemy positions.

Inundation is something different. Inundation is a form of offensive maneuver launched simultaneously against enemy positions. It flows past strong points in the form of self-contained units to strike any weakness discovered. It can be contrasted with penetration (the main attack seeks to rupture) and envelopment (the main attack is against a flank).

I raised this issue in 1963 with "Inundation: A basic maneuver that shouldn't be ignored" (*Army*, Vol. 13, No. 6, January 1963, pages 29–32).

MANEUVERS

PENETRATION

ENVELOPMENT by flank

ENVELOPMENT by air mobility or infiltration

INUNDATION as main attack

INUNDATION as secondary attack

No doubt, the performance of US forces in Korea would have been much better if inundation had been understood. Unfortunately, to this day it is not taught in US military schools. However, many of our potential enemies around the world understand the maneuver of inundation—and use it often off the military battlefield in their ideological struggles against traditional Western culture in their erosion strategy.

One-Way Information

Everyone's view of what should be is shaped by personal experience. Therefore, my views of the intelligence failures in Korea are no doubt shaped by the fact I was a battalion S-2. "Where you stand depends on where you sit." Nevertheless, in less than a month as a battalion S-2 I had seen much evidence of one-way information. And for the rest of my time in Korea, I would see more evidence of the same.

The staffs of large headquarters are very concerned about getting as much information as they can. Correctly, they know the more information they get, the better their intelligence on the enemy is likely to be. However, they have few incentives for pushing information down. Also, they rely too much on what they receive from above. Their primary concern is to provide intelligence to their commander. This means that those at the point of the spear know very little about the enemy situation beyond their immediate environment.

It would be equally dysfunctional to attempt to push all information down, since that would result in overload at the lower levels. It is a question of judgment. And good command depends on good judgment more than anything else. Nevertheless, it is essential that information about movement of major enemy forces be pushed down to those who will have to face that enemy.

As unprepared as the two battalions of the Twenty-Ninth Regiment were on their arrival in Korea, it is clear that many of their casualties could have been prevented—and the Eighth Army would have had combat-ready units sooner—with more accurate intelligence. It is impossible for those at the lowest level to generate such intelligence. Much of it must be pushed down. Also, it is critical that false information not be pushed down from higher headquarters.

Inch'on Aftermath: 15–18 September 1950

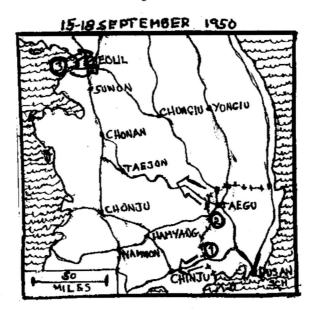

On 15 September 1950 the US X Corps conducted Operation Chromite, a landing on the west coast at Inch'on—the port of Seoul. However, we did not move up Korea until 21 September.

Within twenty-four hours of the US First Marine Division and US Army Seventh Division landing at Inch'on, they had moved far enough to prevent artillery fire on the port area (#3 on map). On 26 September, the First Marine Division was in the center of Seoul, and the Seventh Division had cut the supply routes of the North Korean People's Army south of Seoul. This was to fundamentally change the Korean War.

The Eighth Army plans an offensive to coincide with the landing at Inch'on. The plan is simple: a main attack to penetrate along the Taegu-Taejon-Suwon route (#2 on map) plus an envelopment around the left flank through Chinju (#1 on map). On 16 September, the Eighth Army starts the main attack toward Taejon. There is a heavy rain, and the skies are murky. The Fifth RCT moves toward Waegwan. A Company, Seventieth Tank Battalion is to break through the enemy lines but is stopped by a minefield south of Waegwan that damages seventeen tanks. After the sky clears, air strikes are made. Then the Second Division moves towards the Naktong River. But the penetration of the enemy for the main attack fails.

By 18 September, there is fighting everywhere around the Pusan perimeter as units probe to determine the location of the enemy. There are many losses in desperate, seesaw battles. The Fifth RCT attacks east of Naktong River near Waegwan, where the Third North Korean Division is defending. The First Cavalry Division has heavy casualties but little progress in its attacks near the walled fortress of Kasan. Also, there is heavy fighting for hills three miles east of Waegwan. However, the First Battalion, Seventh Cavalry Regiment pushes ahead to find disabled T34 tanks, dead oxen, artillery, ammunition, and other military equipment. An attack by the Eighth Cavalry Regiment is stopped by the Thirteenth North Korean Division. Across the Naktong, forty-two B-29s bomb west and northwest of Waegwan but apparently without damage to the enemy. The Second Division crosses the Naktong River, but the enemy is making a fight of it.

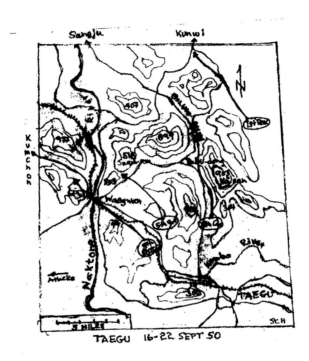

TAEGU 16-22 SEPT 50

The Breakout: 19–21 September 1950

The advance north from the Pusan perimeter moves toward Taejon on 19 September. By 20 September, the Inmun Gun is in full retreat. A senior colonel in full dress uniform, the chief of staff of the Thirteenth North Korean Division, walks into a village held by the Eighth Cavalry Regiment to surrender. His division is falling apart. However, in captivity he will cause damage greater than he did in the military conflict. In May 1952 in a POW camp, he organizes a revolt and captures the camp commander. Then he contributes to the ideological struggle by accusing the US of "torturing and mistreating prisoners." This becomes a major theme in the media—and lives on to this day as a tool of both postmodernists and members of the Third Jihad as they attempt to weaken America.

In the center, the Twenty-Fourth Division crosses the Naktong River in assault boats and engages the enemy on the west side of the river.

With the success of the main attack, it is time for the envelopment maneuver around the left flank. On 21 September, the Twenty-Fifth Division returns to Chungam-ni Pass where the Sixth North Korean Division had first been stopped on 2 August.

It is a relief to escape the constant concern that anytime you are out of a company defensive position you might have to face an enemy with a gun who wants to kill you. We anticipate seeing some of the places we had been during our first days in Korea. But none of us are prepared for what we learn about what the communists did when they controlled much of South Korea.

Near Seoul on 21 September the marines cross the Han River and move to the outskirts of the capital of the Republic of Korea and to the edge of Yongdungpo south of the Han. The Seventh Division moves into the hills south of Seoul and goes south through the walled city of Suwon to a position three miles south of that city. During the night of 21–22 September there are several fights south of Suwon with North Korean soldiers and tanks.

---

[18] The concept of Eros takes its name from the son of the Greek god of war (Ares) and his mistress (Aphrodite). Eros is often translated as "love" and is used for all forms of love. Moreover, the followers of Freud use it to mean sexual passion. However, here it is used in its original meaning (i.e., unity). Prior to 500 BC, the Greeks had three primordial gods: Earth (nature and living things), Chaos (conflict, disaster, tragedy, and hate), and Eros (unity, co-operation, and love). Eros and Chaos engaged in endless struggles to control and use Earth. Eros was the power capable of uniting people in a common bond during these struggles. Therefore, Eros is the most appropriate word to use for the bond of brotherhood found in combat.

CHAPTER ELEVEN

UP FROM THE PUSAN PERIMETER

22–25 September 1950

On 22 September, the Thirty-Fifth Regiment pushes from Chungam-ni Pass toward Chinju against scattered resistance until it reaches the vicinity of Chungchon.

After receiving fire from the hills west of that town, L Company attacks the enemy on that hill. Then K Company advances up the road but meets stiff resistance from its right as the road twists up to the crest of the pass.

On the night of 22 September, L Company goes into positions on the hills just above Chungchon. K Company takes up positions before the pass. I Company is east of the road. Just before dark, Major Woolfolk and I are walking up the road to see what is happening with K Company.

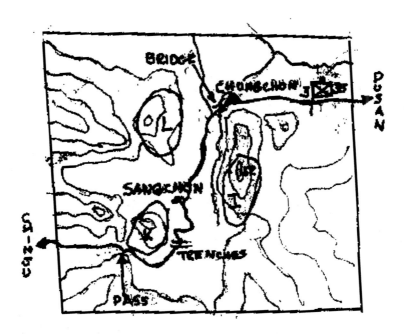

ZZING. ZZING.

From somewhere a sniper shoots at us. He misses, but his bullets come too close for comfort. It is a common practice for the North Koreans to identify officers and to kill them. I had learned to do whatever I could to blend in with others so that it would not be obvious that I am an officer. This is why I did not wear the insignia of my rank.

The next morning (23 September), the companies report no enemy. K Company does report two enemy anti-tank trenches across the road. Tharp drives me up to look at those trenches. The bridge over a small stream at Chungchon is destroyed, so it is necessary to use a ford bypass. There is little water in the stream, so this is not a problem.

I walk around the trenches and decide a few men with shovels can make it suitable for trucks.

General Gavin's Visit

I drive back to the command post, again having to use the ford bypass. I tell CPL Jackson—whom I have learned to value after he walked back when I had sent him scouting alone during our withdrawal—and another man from my intelligence section and three men from the P&A (Pioneer and Ammunition) Platoon to go back to the trenches. I had planned to go with them, but was told Major General James Gavin who is visiting from Washington wants to talk with me. The men get some shovels. I explain to CPL Jackson what needs to be done and tell Tharp, my driver, to take the five men to the trenches in my jeep. As they leave, they are jammed into the jeep with Jackson's long legs hanging over the right rear wheel.

General Gavin is in clean-pressed fatigues and shiny jump boots. He is ramrod straight and physically fit. His stars are bright. He is carrying an M-1 rifle. He asks about our men and about the enemy. He asks how I thought the war is going. He asks me about Colonel Wilson, our first battalion commander, who is his West Point classmate. I cannot detect any specific interest; he just seems to want to know the situation. Of course, I know of him as a highly decorated, charismatic commander of the Eighty-Second Airborne during World War II, and I know the joint chiefs of staff sent him to Korea as an observer. These things are never mentioned. It is simply a friendly discussion about what is going on.

I have just finished talking with General Gavin when I am told: "A jeep hit a big mine. It was blown all over the place. A captain has been killed."

"Where did it happen?" I ask.

"Up at the destroyed bridge."

A few moments later, I get another report that it was my jeep—I had sent it back to the trenches. But who is the captain?

I had seen my jeep leave. Tharp was driving, one of my men was in the front seat where I usually sat, three were in the back seat—Jackson had his legs hanging over the side—and one man was riding on the right front fender. They took the same route I had taken twice.

I immediately went to find out what had happened. As the jeep was going through the bypass, the right rear wheel detonated a mine. From the size of the explosion, it must have been several mines on top of each other. It was clearly intended to stop a tank. The whole rear of the jeep is pulverized. Jackson's legs are found seventy feet away. Large parts of the jeep are found all around the site. Of the six men in the jeep, only two are not killed, and both of them are critically injured. One is Tharp, my driver, and the other is the man on the front fender. The man in my seat is dead. But who is the captain?

The two wounded are evacuated, and the bodies of the other four are identified. They are the men I had sent. The report about a captain being killed came from the fact a cap with captain's bars on it had been found at the scene. I got my cap back, but not some wonderful men. I had two caps. I kept the one with my captain's bars on it in the jeep to be used only when necessary.

Tharp is the only one of the two wounded who ever came back to the battalion. He had spent several months in a hospital in Japan. After his return, I observed that his back had not completely healed. Sometime later I also learned from others in the intelligence section that he had been offered a limited duty job in Japan driving an ambulance, but he had turned it down so that he could come back to be with me.

I immediately arranged for him to be sent back to Japan on a limited duty status.

Back to Chinju: 24–25 September 1950

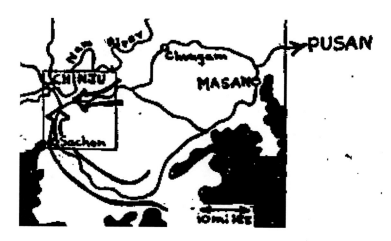

On 24 September 1950, a task force of the Twenty-Fifth Division sweeps up from the south with their tanks while the Second and Third Battalions of the Thirty-Fifth Infantry push through the last hills on the road to Chinju. At dusk on 24 September, we reach a hill from which we can see the Nam River. In the distance, we can faintly make out the city of Chinju.

After dark, we receive word that the tanks of the task force should be at a crossroads a couple of miles in front of us. Major Woolfolk decides to send a patrol to that crossroad to make contact.

"I'd like to take that patrol," I offer.

"Why?"

"I'd like to find out what is up there. I think we need to know how we are going to cross the river. Surely the bridge is destroyed, and this is a pretty big river. No fords are shown on the map. No one at regiment can give me information about crossings, and I doubt that division knows anything. Maybe I can find out something if I go up there."

"Okay. Take about fifteen men from Item."

I meet the men on the road. Master Sergeant Frederick is in charge. The night is clear and crisp; there is a bright moon which turns everything into black and white shadows. We are in two columns on each side of the road. There are five to ten yards between men. We walk briskly down the road.

After about twenty minutes, I notice a group of men walking on a road to our left which angles into our road. The two roads meet in about 100 yards. Others see them at the same time. Our whole patrol stops. I wave my hand for them to get down. The patrol vanishes into the darkness. I note some thatch-covered houses near the road. Some of the men take up firing positions next to these houses; others are in the ditches on either side of the road.

Those on the other road continue. In the moonlight, their movement is visible. I think there are about fifty. Are they Americans or North Koreans? I cannot tell, but I can think of no reason Americans would be on that road. They come closer. They apparently have not seen us.

I send two men forward toward where the two roads join: "Challenge them when they get close." The two men move closer to the road junction.

"HALT!"

The unknown column stops.

"Who goes there?" No answer. The men in the column turn and start to trot away. That is all I need.

"FIRE!" I shout. Hardly had the words left my mouth before there is an explosion of rifle shots. The flashes from the rifle barrels light up the road. We fire for less than a minute, but when we finish, there is no movement on the other road. I do not hear any cries of pain. But they are gone.

"Get the men back on the road," I tell Frederick. Then we are off again. Finally I see the outline of a tank ahead of us.

"Take it easy. They will not know who we are," I tell the men at the head of our patrol. I stop the patrol and have them get off the road.

"Go closer. Call out to them in English. They might be trigger-happy. Let them know we are friendly," I tell two of the men. After the tankers halt them, the two men are told there are mines just in front of the tanks. I go up and talk with the tankers.

"What kind of mines?" I ask.

"Don't know; that looks like ours. Ya know, those that blow up tanks."

"Are there any antipersonnel mines among them?" I ask.

"Don't know. We've gotten h'ar after dark. Ain't check 'em yet."

I tell Frederick to hold the patrol where it is and I'd check things out. As I move up, I can see a pattern of hastily dug-in antitank mines. There is nothing to indicate there are any antipersonnel mines among them. Since the antitank mines had been placed there in a hurry, the odds are they had not had time to put in any antipersonnel mines. But you never know.

I pick out two rows of antitank mines and look for wires. The moonlight makes things clear, but it would still be easy to miss a wire. I take each step with caution. I look carefully. "Will the next step set off something?" It seems like a very long time for me to walk those ten yards. Then I am through.

I tell Frederick to bring the patrol on. I know the path I had taken is okay. I show it to Frederick and tell him to make sure each man follows that path.

I leave the patrol on the road and go to the task force command post. It is in the back of a truck. I explain our situation and get any information I can. They do not know if the river can be crossed or not. I decide to go to an outpost on a cliff over-looking the river.

I have to go through another stretch of road where there are no friendly troops. Moving down the road there are thatch-roofed houses on each side. A flicker of light comes now and then from the doors, telling us that people are inside. Every 200 yards, I stop to scan the road ahead; I get through it with no problem. Later I learn enemy patrols have been active all night along this stretch of road. I am having an incredible string of good luck. Will it last?

At the outpost, I question the men at length about what they have seen. They mention they have seen some civilians wading across the river a few hundred yards downstream. They say there are a few huts on the riverbank there. I walk down to the huts and find a few Koreans still there. They are asleep. I have Paul, my interpreter, wake them up, and then we sit down to talk about the river.

"Can you cross the river? Where? How deep is it now? Is the river bed hard?" I got some answers, but I push them for more details.

"It depends," is the most common answer. "Sometimes you can cross. Sometimes you can't. It all depends on how high the water is."

I go down to the river. I get close enough to see a rough line of water in the moonlight. The rest of the water is smooth. Moreover, the last weeks have been very dry, so the river is probably lower than normal. I feel sure that it can be forded. I return to the task force CP.

I make arrangements for a wire to be strung back to our CP. We make our way back without incident, except that we do not have enough wire to go the whole distance. It is necessary to run a line from our CP back to where the wire ended.

After my return, Lieutenant Reed Suddeby takes a patrol from K Company along the same route I had taken. They continue on past the task force to the bridge across the Nam into Chinju. The bridge is destroyed as I had assumed. His patrol holds the near side of the bridge site until daylight when the task force takes over those positions. The Third Battalion crosses the

Nam at the ford I had found. Chinju is ours by noon on 25 September. When we leave Chinju on 27 September to move up Korea, the conflict is in a new phase.

Combat Fatigue and Eros During War and Warfare

Psychologists and psychiatrists have never been able to adequately explain the connection of Eros and death, even though it often appears in history and literature. I thought about the connection. We do know that after death there is no Eros. If there is an absence of Eros during combat, the fear of death takes control of the mind—and such uncontrolled stress can result in mental disability. Death is the ultimate symbol of impotence—the lack of life—and Eros is a way to counter this inner dread. Sex does prove vitality; it shows individuals they are alive. Together, sex and Eros are able to preserve a clear, strong, purposeful mind under the most stressful of situations. They can reduce the opportunities for combat fatigue.[19]

Physical acts of sex alone are not able to counter the fear of death. They can only release tension. Countering the fear of death requires the human quality of imagination, commitment, and belonging. It requires the seeking of fulfillment and collective self-preservation, such as the union of a male and a female—or combat camaraderie. Lust and relief alone are not sufficient—there must also be Eros. The mysterious way that Eros protects the psyche of warriors and soldiers during War and Warfare can take many forms; I decided these needed to be better understood.

In Peace, youth think they are immortal; they dismiss death as something that happens to others—they can minimize death because it is passive, and their lives are active. Yet in War, warriors and soldiers must face the reality of death. The sight of bodies in unnatural positions or a human torn apart or burned beyond recognition cannot be ignored. Since Warfare is protracted asymmetrical conflict, death is less apparent than in War. Yet in Warfare, death can come quickly at any time. In Warfare, individuals think they can prevent death with knowledge, caution, and skill—but this is often untrue. During both War and Warfare, anyone who does not care for those fighting with him, his "brothers," will be overcome by fear and the specter of death; he will become a mindless body—a self-preserving coward. For him, death becomes an all-encompassing, relentless presence and void. On the other hand, someone who through Eros has a bond with his "brothers" can find death a willing sacrifice he makes out of love; in that case, death is seen as an event in his being and a way to prove his worth. He becomes a fearless warrior capable of heroic deeds and is able to escape the overwhelming stress that produces combat fatigue. Warriors and soldiers require an inner compass capable of handling death as a natural part of life, allowing them to cope with the most awful, gruesome, arbitrary, senseless, and chaotic of conditions. This should be called the Ethos of Eros. It helps to have a curiosity about the possibility of a transformation of life beyond death.

Unfortunately, there has been little attention on preventing combat fatigue; instead it has been on soldiers after they have returned to civilian life. Since Vietnam, psychologists and psychiatrists have classified many veterans as "mentally ill" with layers of debilitating psychological wounds because they have difficulties in adjusting. The veterans are said to have the mental illness of post-traumatic stress disorder (PTSD). They have survival guilt, are impatient, and are unable to understand the carelessness, lack of order, negligence, laxity, selfishness, and animosity they see around them. Yet these symptoms are only an accurate reflection of how Peace differs from the reality of War and Warfare. Instead of focusing on the "mental illness" of veterans, attention should be on how to maintain healthy functioning minds in chaotic and stressful situations where death is always near—such as during War and Warfare.

It is suggested that the answer to combat fatigue might be in a more accurate understanding of the connection between Eros and death. And that answer might be the acceptance of how War and Warfare differ from Peace, rather than seeing that which is appropriate for Peace as the desired norm with conditions of War and Warfare being untoward aberrations. It is a mistake to think that anyone having trouble coping with how War and Warfare differ from Peace has a mental disorder. The inner compass of those diagnosed with PTSD just might not have been strong enough to cope with the reality of War and Warfare because of the Ethos of Eros. Veterans might even have a better understanding of human conditions than those "treating" them for PTSD. And the solution to combat fatigue might not be in post-combat treatment of a "mental illness," but in pre-combat training and an appreciation of the qualities of warriors and soldiers. There is a critical need to analyze combat fatigue with the aim of improving combat effectiveness—rather than just the treatment of a mental disorder. The goal should be to develop through moral absolutes a strong inner compass in individuals so they have the resilience to cope with the stress of combat.

Rapid decisions in combat are particularly difficult for a person with a weak inner compass filled with doubt, uncertainty, self-deception, and a lack of moral absolutes. For them, self-interest, self-preservation, and instinct tend to take over. But even people with strong inner compasses react differently in combat. Making difficult decisions does not bother the warrior who is careless about life, because he seeks adventure in experiences and sees combat as an exciting and dangerous game. The professional soldier is able to handle such decisions because he sees death as a normal part of life, his attitudes are governed by fate, and he believes courage and duty are worthy ideals. A person of deep religious convictions sees death as the end in a struggle and the opening to a better life. The romantic's desire to feel the pulse of life can cloud the reality of combat. In each case, it is a strong inner compass based on absolutes that allows the individual to cope with the excessive stress of making repeated decisions in combat. They all have the resilience to quickly overcome trauma that makes others victims of combat fatigue (i.e., Ethos of Eros).

To explain combat fatigue as the result of cowardice, as was often done in the past, is an oversimplification. During World War II, General Patton wanted to shoot "malingering cowards," and in Sicily he slapped two soldiers suffering from combat fatigue. Previously, 1.75 million men had avoided service for mental reasons. Over 36,000 were convicted of "evading hazardous duty by dishonorable means"—many no doubt from various forms of mental trauma. That all deserters are not cowards is illustrated by PFC Wayne Powers. In December 1944, Powers deserted to avoid combat and to be with a French girl. Fourteen years and five children later, he was found guilty of desertion. Many others served bravely but then "lost their minds." Many men who were strong mentally and physically had nervous breakdowns after "reaching their limit." On the other hand, it cannot be denied that many use mental reasons to avoid danger and to receive benefits. The mental health profession has not been able to hit the correct balance between these extremes. Therefore, fairness and combat effectiveness require the mental health profession to hold each individual responsible for his actions by including cowardice as a significant factor. At the same time, it recognizes that some men are indeed casualties of combat fatigue. Mental health and PTSD must not be a way cowards avoid combat and place others in danger.

While mental illness receives a great deal of attention, it is mostly on diagnosis and treatment. There is woefully little effort to determine how to prevent combat fatigue. The mental health profession has a vested interest in making PTSD a "disease to be treated by professionals"—and some cases no doubt will take many years of treatment to overcome the effects of combat fatigue. Yet an understanding of the causes of combat fatigue and of the need for an inner compass molded by firm absolutes is more important. In most cases, camaraderie, training, discipline, and Eros can prevent combat fatigue; they can always reduce its severity. They can counter the weakness of a flexible, ill-defined, morally relativistic inner compass that causes a person to doubt, vacillate, reconsider, compromise, and be under great stress when difficult decisions must be made in combat. While in the past combat fatigue was surely too often dismissed as cowardliness, now the mental health profession appears to have gone too far in the opposite direction.

---

[19] Combat fatigue is as old as conflict, but it has gone by many names—the most common is cowardice. In World War I, it was called "shell shock." In World War II, it was called "battle fatigue" and "combat neurosis," and after Vietnam, it has been called Post-Traumatic Stress Disorder—or PTSD. Combat fatigue is the most accurate term, but PTSD better fits in the concerns and interests of mental health professionals.

CHAPTER TWELVE

UP TO TAEJON

25 September–3 October 1950

After crossing the Nam River, the Third Battalion is initially in the southeastern part of the city, but in the afternoon of 25 September, it relieves the Second Battalion on the hills overlooking Chinju from the east. The companies are assigned their defensive positions, and they prepare for the night.

An Incident on Chinju Hill

About an hour before dark, I see "Honcho," the South Korean interpreter of one of the companies, walk by the battalion command post with three prisoners. Their hands are tied; they have tattered uniforms and downcast faces. Thinking he is bringing them to me for interrogation, I call to him:

"Honcho, I'm over here."

"Yes, sir, how you this evening?" he answers, but he continues with the prisoners.

"Where are you taking them?" I ask.

"To village."

"To the village? Wait a minute." He stops, and the prisoners stop.

I continue: "What for?"

"To kill them," he answers in a matter-of-fact tone.

I am stunned, but I manage to ask: "Who told you to?"

"Captain," he replies.

I question him. I want to know exactly what was said, when it was said, and why. He stuck to his story that the captain had told him to take them into Chinju, to find someone who had a relative killed by the North Koreans, and to give the prisoners to that person so the "score could be settled."

"Just give them to me, Honcho. I'll take care of everything."

I take the prisoners. Honcho leaves. I turn the three prisoners over to my men to be processed in the normal manner.

The captain is a good friend. He is a colorful, aggressive, macho man who is loved by his soldiers; he is able to get the maximum from them; he is a warrior. He is a take-charge kind of guy. Some consider him egotistic. He is courageous and brave. We had enjoyed many good times together at the officers' club in Okinawa. We had gone to glider school in Japan together and had managed to spend an extra week in Tokyo. He is someone I feel I can always trust, and we had been through a lot together since we arrived in Korea on 24 July.

I decide to go down to see the captain and check this out personally.

I find him in his company area. I say: "Why did you send Honcho to kill those prisoners?"

His eyes narrow, his lips tighten, and he angrily snaps at me: "I didn't!"

I realize I have made a mistake by not getting him alone before I said anything. But it is now too late. I will never get to the truth—whatever it might be. I take comfort in knowing that the only people who never make mistakes are those who never do anything.

"No f—— staff weenie is going to come down to my company and talk to me that way. I run this company, and I'll do what I damn well please!"

"You sure as hell won't go around killing prisoners as long as I can prevent it."

My words are equal to his in passion and tone. Other heated words pass between us as he makes the point that he has yet to receive any worthwhile intelligence from me, etc. I add a few unkind words about murderers.

I tell no one about this incident. We never discuss it again. After several days, the incident seems to have been forgotten. Yet we never are as close as we had been. While people might forgive you for what you say, and they might even forget what you do, they are unlikely to forget how you make them feel.

After Korea, we did not see each other for twenty years. One day in Vietnam, again in the Twenty-Fifth Division but then as full colonels not captains, we did meet and were able to hug each other as long-lost brothers.

What the North Koreans Did

We move through Namwon, Chinju, Iri, and Nonsan to Taejon. As we liberate cities, towns, and villages in southwest

Korea, it becomes clear what the North Koreans did when they took control. They had come as conquerors prepared to eliminate the republican form of government and to replace it with a socialist collective under a supreme ruler. For them, this was an ideological conflict as much as it was a conventional War.

The communists had established a fifth column and networks of supporters throughout South Korea long before the North Korean People's Army crossed the 38th Parallel. As soon as they gained control of any location, the former officials were jailed, and local members of their fifth column were installed as a new government. It made no difference that most of the people were anti-communist; the communists quickly assumed control. Then they moved against the wealthy in the name of equality and social justice. Many moneylenders and wealthy landowners were executed as soon as they were identified. Those who had worked for Americans were executed. There were no trials—the word of members of the fifth column was enough. They had no plan to convert people to communism; rather, the plan was to eliminate anyone who could not readily be assimilated into a socialist collective. Their fifth column identified religious leaders, teachers, lawyers, and intellectuals that they consider hostile to communism as "enemies of the people."

The new government at all levels then collected the "enemies of the people" and led them to mass graves, hands bound, wired to each other. They were shot. This was all done for a purpose.

This is a form of conflict that most Americans did not understand. This is not War with overwhelming firepower being used to destroy "their" armed forces.

Lesson Learned: North Korean Cruelty

If we have found the wanton killings isolated, it might be concluded they were the actions of a few cruel, sadistic, or undisciplined individuals. However, we noted the same pattern in every village and town we liberated. These killings were planned. This was the elimination of those who might block the communists from the consolidation of power. They killed anyone they could never trust. The communists were just being efficient. This was the easiest, quickest, and cheapest way to achieve centralized authority.

Those targeted are capitalists, landowners, government employees, policemen, those who worked for Americans, and their families. The victims were required to dig their own graves before being shot in the back of the head. Often those doing the killing were teenage girls. Some victims were tortured before they were killed. It was not always clear why they were tortured. Their hands and feet would be tied, and then fingers, ears, lips, or flesh would be cut off. Women and girls were often raped. Often the young men were not killed but were sent off to the North Korean Army. They were confined until they were sent forward with only a pointed stick in the first wave of an assault.

The other aspect of the communists' plan is to gain the support of the disadvantaged. They constantly claim to be the defender of peasants as a collective whole and that they will bring social justice to all Koreans. They will take from the rich and give to the poor. They were careful to pay the poor any time they required food or lodging. Being an individual is to be eliminated; centralized authority by some revered person is the only solution.

This is ideological conflict.

Koreans have always known harsh rule, so what the North Koreans offered is just more of the same. A union of sovereign individuals with limits on government is a strange, alien idea. It is easy for them to understand a totalitarian state governing a united Korea, with equality for all, as a utopia worth working and dying for. Many Koreans saw this as true democracy—as contrasted with the false democracy preached by the Americans.

Taegu to Osan by TF 777

At dawn on 26 September, artillery shells start to fall on the enemy positions north of Taegu. The artillery flashes are less visible as daylight arrives, but the ZOOM of shells passing overhead continues. Lieutenant Robert Baker, the tank platoon leader, raises his hand over his head and makes a "wind it up" signal. The engines of the Sherman M4A3E8, with 76-mm gun, roar. At 1130, Task Force 777 starts north toward Osan to link up with the Seventh Division (#2 on map on next page). The tank platoon from C Company, Seventieth Heavy Tank Battalion, leads the Seventh Cavalry Regiment toward Osan 106 miles away. There are many fights as TF 777 speeds north, with many lives lost, which would never be recorded in history or even known. Then there is that which is known but is forgotten.

Ahead of the task force, planes attack any enemy sighted. For miles, there are only cheering villagers. At Ch'onan they find enemy soldiers. Not knowing which way to go in Ch'onan, LT Baker asks a North Korean soldier on guard, "Osan?" The soldier points, then recognizes the tank commander as an American and runs away. The tanks move on toward Osan. Groups of North Korean soldiers just watch the column speed by.

Along the road, there are many fires. Some are from firefights with the Seventh Cavalry Regiment, but the North Koreans also set buildings on fire as they retreated. There are smoldering T-34 tanks taken out by F4U Corsairs from carriers. But there are many fights, with many lives lost, which will never be recorded in the history books.

With luck, the three lead tanks of TF 777 arrive at Osan at 2226 on 26 September after traveling the 106 miles. Within a few hours after contact with the Seventh Division, there is a tank battle with what is left of the North Korean 105th Armored Division. In this battle, several T-34 and two American tanks are destroyed. The rest of TF 777 arrives in Osan the next day (27 September).

Capture of Seoul

The marines finally reach the center of Seoul on 26 September (#1 on map above). They raise the American flag. The English writer Reginald Thompson describes the destruction of Seoul like this: "...the tearing noise of dive bombers blasting right ahead, and the livid flashes of the tank guns, the harsh fierce crackle of blazing wooden buildings, the telegraph and high tension poles collapsing in an utter chaos of wires..."

MacArthur issues a communiqué that Seoul is free, yet there will be two more days of heavy fighting in that city. The JCS sends MacArthur a directive "to use no non-Korean forces in the provinces bordering on the Soviet Union or along the Manchurian frontier."

Back to Where It All Started

Led by the Eighty-Ninth Tank Battalion, we return to Hamyang on 27 September (#4 on map on previous page). I go over to see LTC Welborn G. Dolvin to let him know that I had been up the road he was going to travel. He is delighted to talk with someone who actually knows the terrain.

On the road from Chinju to Hamyang we meet no real resistance. There are a few mines. We catch up with some enemies fleeing north, but most of them are only on the roads at night. There are far more flag-waving civilians. Probably many of those waving are North Korean soldiers who have slipped into civilian clothes as they head home. By the time we reach Namwon, only the flag wavers remain. In Namwon, we free eighty Americans from the local jail. Although the North Korean military does not keep prisoners, they have turned a few over to the locals to keep in their jails.

At Iri we stop for a break. We hear that the First Cavalry Division has linked up with the Seventh Division south of Suwon. Many of the North Korean stragglers have fled into the Chiri-san mountain mass, which has been a stronghold of communists for years. Later we are to learn that over 3,000 soldiers of the Sixth North Korean and Seventh North Korean Divisions, our old nemeses from the Pusan perimeter, had taken refuge in these mountains. UN forces are close to the 38th Parallel.

When we reach Taejon, I pass by trenches where the bodies of over 600 South Korean civilians and police are laid out. All had been murdered. The stench of death is overpowering. People are moving among the bodies, with their noses covered, to identify relatives. I am told thirty-five bodies of Americans are among the dead.

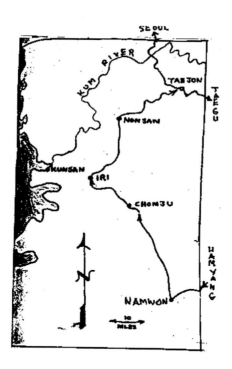

Lesson Learned: What is conflict that is neither Peace nor War?

War is conflict between the acknowledged armed forces of states, each attempting to destroy the armed forces of the other. Success in War is victory for one side and defeat for the other.

Warfare is protracted asymmetrical conflict between sovereign states and insurgents willing to use all means to weaken or overthrow those in authority. Success in Warfare is Peace (i.e., a climate of order and satisfaction in which no one is willing to use force to achieve political ends).

The number killed in Taejon is larger than those killed in smaller towns and villages, and we heard that many thousands of bodies had been found in Seoul. What we had seen is not War as defined by the Geneva Conventions; it is not even Civil War; it is not Peace enforced by the rule of law. This is ideological conflict (i.e., Warfare), which is neither War nor Peace; this is conflict of a type and an intensity of hatred that Americans found difficult to understand. While such ideological conflicts have been common in the past, it is difficult for Americans to understand because of their preconceptions about progress and civilization.

First, for the past three hundred years, Westerners have thought War should be conducted as conflict between the armed forces of states in the name of national interests.

Second, civilization requires human beings to be compassionate, fair, loving, and to "do unto others as you would have others do unto you."

Third, progress means individuals have rights that grant freedom of thought, speech, and religion, and individuals should be able to enjoy life, liberty, and the pursuit of happiness.

Fourth, Americans are repulsed by the brutality and killing associated with ideological conflict.

Fifth, Americans dream of victories where there are no deaths, injuries, or mistakes—in short, war without human costs. This is a very appealing fantasy. However, history tells us that human conflict and cooperation never fundamentally change with regard to human suffering.

Such American preconceptions are difficult to reconcile with what I had experienced. Perhaps this is because cultures have different tolerances for brutality at the personal level. But I know it is foolhardy to ignore reality. Warfare, ideological conflict, strategic communication, and common identity are challenges: What are the lessons to be learned from my experience? What is Warfare, and how is success achieved in ideological conflict, strategic communication to shape the inner compass of individuals, and struggles to strengthen or weaken common identities of "we" and "they"?

CHAPTER THIRTEEN

OKCHON AND HAMCH'ANG

3–21 October 1950

Our next mission is to capture stragglers and to defeat local guerrillas who control many of the mountains south and east of Taejon. Here I am able to talk with young people who want to kill me. Here I will again have to come to grips with ideological conflict and how the inner compass of each individual is formed.

On 1 October, General MacArthur demands the surrender of North Korea. Kim Il-sung does not reply.

On 2 October, South Korean troops cross the 38th Parallel on the east coast near Yangyang.

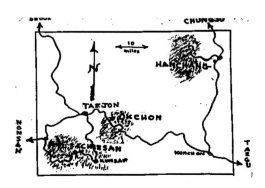

As the battle lines move north, the Twenty-Fifth Division remains in the vicinity of Taejon to "mop up stragglers." The Third Battalion, Thirty-Fifth Regiment is initially sent to the Okchon area and then to the mountains west of Hamch'ang. Finally, the battalion is sent to the Chinsan-Kunsan area to fight "guerrillas" in a mountainous region which had long been a communist stronghold.

Capturing the Enemy near Okchon

In Okchon, we attempt to capture soldiers who are trying to find their way back north after fighting around the Pusan perimeter. They are moving in small groups. After two weeks in the hills, these soldiers of the North Korean People's Army are weary and hungry. While near Okchon, the Third Battalion is credited with the capture of 1,374 enemy soldiers during a six-day period. We capture more than we can handle. However, our first days were not fruitful.

At first, our patrols wander over the hills searching, but they see none of the hundreds of North Korean soldiers that the South Koreans report. I conclude that the enemy spot our patrols and merely hide in the brush. They wait until our patrol passes. Not only are these soldiers hungry and weary, but they are defeated and dejected. Their aim is to get home—not to fight. Many might also be disillusioned with the utopian goals of communism.

We know many of the North Korean soldiers are wearing civilian clothing. How are our soldiers to tell the difference between those South Koreans living in the area from those who had been in the North Korean army? I decide we have to get the support of the locals. So, I turned to the police chief who had just returned to Okchon. At this time, the chief of police is also acting mayor of the city of Okchon and acting governor of the district. He agrees with me.

"Good. Whatever you say, Captain. We work together. I send people with you. What we do? When we start?"

I tell him I didn't think it would do much good to send his people with our patrols. I have another plan: "I want you to send some people out in civilian clothes. No uniforms. If they meet any strangers in the hills, just tell them Americans are crazy! They give food to everyone. They even give the communists rice and cigarettes. Anyone that does that must be crazy!" The police chief/mayor/governor thinks it is a good idea. We discuss some other details.

"Never suggest that they surrender," I say. I do not want the North Koreans to lose *face*. "Just offer to show them where they can get rice, other good things to eat, and cigarettes."

In a few days, we fill all the jails, and our soldiers are very happy they do not have to walk for hours through the hills. I wish our soldiers knew how to conduct surveillance without being seen, but there is no time for them to learn such skills. They are infantrymen trained to shoot and conditioned to kill or be killed.

At least three thousand stragglers from the Sixth and Seventh North Korean Divisions, plus two thousand from other divisions, have attempted to move through the Twenty-Fifth Division's area while we were there. It is good to know that our battalion has captured far more than anyone else.

Local Young Communists

While we are interested in capturing North Korean soldiers, I learn that the police chief is more interested in getting those who had helped the North Koreans while they occupied his district. They had identified former officials, rich landowners, and political supporters of the Republic of Korea. They had helped run governmental affairs for the North Koreans. He has thirty-two of them in the Okchon jail, eleven of which are women. He asks if I would like to talk with them.

I find them to be very different from the soldier stragglers. I have no way of knowing if they had done the things the police chief claims. They might just be his political opponents. However, I do get a good feel for who they are—dedicated communists. They are well-educated and young—eighteen to twenty-six. They hate Americans and think we are preventing a united Korea of, by, and for the Koreans. They understand the ideals expressed in our Declaration of Independence but do not think we want others to enjoy them. They want to know why we are killing people we do not know. They believe in socialism. They think capitalism exploits the poor for the benefit of the rich. They think socialism is fair and just because people are neither rich nor poor. They have not considered whether socialism will really work or not. They do not like me. They want to know why I am in Korea. They want to unite Korea under communism and think America is preventing that noble goal.

I find that we have some things in common. We both want the best for the Korean people. They claim to value the principles advocated by our founders. I am dedicated to what I think is right, and so are they.

Yet they hate America—and me by extension. They would kill me if they could.

After several hours of talking with them directly or through my interpreter Paul, I thank the police chief and start to leave. He asks me directly in English: "You want to take her?" He points to one of the younger women. Although she has been a prisoner for several days and is obviously not at her best, she is still very lovely.

I smile and say: "No thanks." I turn to leave.

He follows and says, "Maybe I give the women to your soldiers? They do what they like." I know that the police chief speaks English, but I pull my interpreter Paul over to me, get face-to-face with the police chief, and say: "I do not want any Americans to touch any of these women. Translate. I want you to protect all of the prisoners. Translate. If you do not," I pull my .45 out of its holster, "I will come over here and shoot you. Translate."

"Oh yes, Captain. Don't you worry! I take good care of them."

I turn and leave.

The Role of Ideology and Political Spin

Americans think of politics as debating different views of economic, social, and political issues, with such debates being resolved peacefully through elections to determine who will govern. Then Americans think laws, which are fair and just, will maintain order and resolve disputes impartially. This view is appropriate during Peace. However, my observations of what took place among Koreans did not match this American ideal. Why? I concluded that struggles for power in Korea were shaped by ideology. In Korea, there is neither Peace nor War—this is an ideological conflict being fought with all means. In such a situation, the only solution is to neutralize (convert, confine, or kill) those who do not agree with your ideology (i.e., your belief regarding what is right or wrong, what is good or bad, and what is virtuous or evil).

Many progressives, academics, and human rights lawyers have said South Korean police were just as ruthless and brutal as the North Koreans. They claim that the rule of law was often ignored while anyone called a "communist" was beaten and tortured—or executed—by South Korean Police. And from the documentation provided, we must conclude that some such things took place. Just as in Vietnam, we know that the My Lai massacre did occur and that in Iraq, US military police guards did stupid things in Abu Ghraib prison. But we also know that these were isolated events that do not represent the heroic, compassionate, and honorable things that hundreds of thousands did in Vietnam or Iraq. Yet the truth seems always to be overshadowed by the words anti-military zealots use to excite.

During my time in Korea, I never knew of any ruthless or brutal actions by the South Korean Police. However, there are always those who consider themselves morally superior because they oppose War. Stories of brutality always shake Western sensibilities and receive undue attention.

I can say with certainty that whatever the South Korean police might have done, their actions were never on the scale of the North Koreans in either numbers or brutality. Let us recognize the truth and not be swayed by dreams of a utopia without violence. Let us realize that decline and decay is the outcome whenever military virtues are no longer valued. One of the keys to success is to have realism replace idealism.

The Night Visitor

I return to my room from the Okchon jail. As I undress, I think about the day, and then I lie down for a good night's sleep.

There is a knock on the door. The door slowly opens, and the young girl the police chief had offered walks in. She is now in the traditional Korean-style blouse and skirt, and she has added some makeup. She looks lovely.

"May I come in?" This is a double surprise. First, that she is in the room. Second, that she speaks English—which she had not done while being questioned in the jail.

"How did you get here?" he asks.

"The police chief asked me if I wanted to visit you. I said I did. So he brought me here."

She walks over to his bed and sits down. They talk about this and that. Then she says: "Do you mind if I get more comfortable?" He does not answer.

She takes off her blouse and skirt. She has on only a flimsy, very short slip. He can see that she wears nothing else. Her small breasts and the black hair below her waist are clearly visible. She walks slowly back to the bed.

Although young, she soon demonstrates that she knows how to please a man. With her motions and soft sounds, she even suggests that she is enjoying great pleasure. He certainly is. Then he falls back exhausted. She curls up beside him but listens to his breathing. When she is satisfied that he is asleep, her eyes turn cold.

She gets up from the bed, walks over to the chair, and picks up his Colt .45. Then she returns to the bed. She points it at his head, looks at him, and smiles. Then she pulls the trigger.

I wake up. The room is empty. My Colt .45 is still on the chair where I had placed it.

Back in the jail, an eighteen-year-old girl is sitting in the corner of a cell. She looks just as she had during the questioning, except she now seems sad. "If I only had been more appealing, perhaps I could have killed him," she thinks. After all, she had been denied an opportunity to kill an American officer.

Hamch'ang

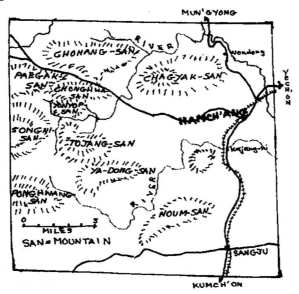

We next move into the mountains to the west of Hamch'ang. Here we have the same job as before, but with none of the previous success.

In many ways, our time in the mountains west of Hamch'ang is much better than in Okchon. It is more scenic. We attempt to use the same techniques that had proven to be so successful in

Okchon, but capture very few of the enemy. It is primarily a good break. The food is the best we have had since we left Okinawa. We repair and replace our vehicles and equipment; we also get some new personnel.

Major James Lee takes command of the battalion. He is a large, friendly, energetic, but cautious man who can be mistaken for a former Penn State linebacker.

Without radios or newspapers, we really do not know much of what is going on outside of our battalion. We do not really know even what the rest of those in Korea are doing, except we know that others are also attempting to capture the stragglers going north. We do know American and South Korean forces are moving through North Korea toward the Yalu River—and China. However, we have no idea of what units are where or what they are doing. We know nothing of the debates between MacArthur and Washington on how to conduct the war. And we certainly have no idea of what is going on in Peking or Washington.

This is the first time Chief Warrant Officer Harold L. Sims is with us in the CP. He usually supervises our administrative and supply activities in the "trains" where all of the logistics for the battalions and regiment are located. He is old compared to most of us—he is a forty-two-year-old career soldier who enlisted in 1929 from Nebraska. With limited facilities, he did his best to support all of the battalion. He is an example of the supporters that are essential for success in combat, and there are many more like him in the rear areas.

Reflection on Behavior

Near Hamch'ang I have time to reflect. There is a small shrine (myo) on the side of the mountain above the battalion command post. It is only a short walk away. It is isolated but has a beautiful view of the mountains; it is most tranquil at early morning twilight. There is a beautiful sunrise as the sun slowly appears from behind the mountains. Often the clouds hang low in the morning air, and I never see anyone when I am there. The slopes are dark green with shadows; there is fog hanging low in the valleys. It might have been southwestern Virginia late in the summer. I also return as the sun sinks behind the mountains to illuminate the clouds. Then there are far-away sounds in the still air. Yet I know that hidden in all of this beauty there are those who want nothing more than to kill me. At the same time, the vastness of the sky and landscape render any individual insignificant. This overwhelming spectacle makes me feel small.

Korean Myo (Shrine)

Yet I know the inner compass of each individual is more powerful than the majesty of nature that surrounds me.

Here I am able to reflect on what I have observed during the past three months. For an infantryman, behavior in combat is raw and naked without most of the games, deceit, obfuscation, and camouflage of civil society.

In this shrine, I come to some conclusions about behavior and develop a conceptual framework that allows me to better understand human actions—regardless of time, place, or culture. My view starts with the pursuit of happiness and the flight from fear but is also built on the opposites of action and thinking. I do not know if it will be of benefit to others—and I do not care. It allows me to quickly evaluate the significance of what someone does—or does not do.

War and Warfare have periods of boredom, dullness, and routine as does Peace, but these periods are compressed between anticipation, movement, strangeness, change, helplessness, excitement, cruelty, danger, praying, capriciousness, violence, powerlessness, meaninglessness, and fear in lightning succession. Such rapid compression of different emotions creates surges of energy and stirs thoughts of potentialities. People are reduced to their essence: they live in the present; their inner compass is exposed; their inhibitions are weakened—they are revealed as heroes, cowards, saints, animals, warriors, soldiers, and MINOs.

The strong inner compass needed for success in conflict—be it in War, Warfare, or Peace—might be called willpower. Yet it differs from nineteenth century willpower, which required conformity with rational and moral cultural rules. Nineteenth century willpower attempted to repress any irrational tendencies or untoward behavior. In contrast, the inner compass of an individual includes instincts, urges, fears, and drives as well as customs and traditions. Sacred Authority establishes cultural norms and shapes the inner compass of individuals by telling that person what life is and what behavior is correct, good, honorable, noble, admirable, and worthy of praise. This is at the core of ideological conflict.

Warriors and soldiers feel responsible for their actions. In the past, willpower made warriors honest, brave, and courageous. A strong inner compass does the same. Without a firm inner compass, individuals lack the ability to make rapid, decisive decisions—they become flotsam moved by determinism. Of course, taking anything to the extreme, as warriors often do, is likely to produce a bad outcome. Thus the behavior of the professional soldier is not determined by nineteenth century willpower—"Where there is a will there is a way"—nor by passivity—"Willpower is only an illusion." The challenge for the military professional is to combine free will, personal responsibility, duty, and discipline—to have sacred authority and secular authority equally strong but parts of a dynamic whole. Combat requires both warriors and soldiers who take orders and have a sense of duty, yet are imaginative, thinking, self-motivated individuals who want to be all they can be—and to do all they can do.

Cooperation/conflict describes reaching out—interaction with others. It is a way of molding, forming, relating to others, and trying to get a response; it describes "we–they" relationships that use power to influence "them" and to be influenced by "them." While cooperation/conflict always interacts within a dynamic whole, conflict with "others" dominates during the rise, or building stages, of any polity while cooperation with "others" dominates during the fall, or decline stages.

Warriors reflect the attitude that "I am the captain of my fate." Yet a person who is indeed the master of his fate is unlikely to cooperate or to use Eros to preserve. Conflict alone will rarely bring success. Therefore, successful soldiers hear others and cooperate in order to be creative and to adjust rapidly to changing situations. They know how to combine cooperation and conflict. Warriors tend to set "we" against "they" during the building of any polity, yet long-term survival requires soldiers who know when to "turn the other cheek" and when to fight to the end.

Both warriors and soldiers care for their "brothers" — those who face death with them. If they did not care, they would only be animals. This is illustrated by an ancient Greek parable about a dispute between Jupiter and Care over a clay figure. The resolution has Jupiter, since he had given the figure its spirit, getting its spirit back at death. But Care, having shaped this creature from dirt, gets to name it "homo" and to possess it as long as it lives.[20] Caring for your "brothers" brings duty, honor, and Eros together since the person acts upon his caring with courage, duty, and honor—his is not the empty abstract sentimentality that pacifists and humanitarians profess.

Lesson Learned: Human Behavior

To me, it seems that all of the human behavior I had observed since I came to Korea is the result of either happiness or fear. Both are powerful motivators, yet the pursuit of happiness is the more complex. The brutal and horrifying actions of the North Koreans made fear real and personal. It clarifies the Pacifist's Fallacy. Also, the trauma of combat triggers a struggle in the mind with fear. Yet it is the various ways that people pursue happiness that I found more interesting.

Flight from fear is not complex. It involves a direct struggle in the mind. You either overcome fear, or it overcomes you. For everyone this struggle takes place in the here and now, but for some it continues. Those who win this struggle are considered courageous; those who lose are considered cowards. For some the struggle also lasts after the trauma of combat. For a few, who are unprepared for the reality of killing or being killed, the struggle with fear caused by combat lasts a lifetime. The outcome is dependent on both the training received and each individual's inner strength.

Having specific goals is the greatest obstacle in the pursuit of happiness, yet having specific goals is also essential to the realization of happiness. This is why I found it so complex. Too often, individuals set goals that can be defined in terms of fame, fortune, status, and rectitude. The pursuit of such goals can bring happiness; in fact, if you have no such goals, you will probably never achieve happiness. Nevertheless, such goals can also be the cause of great unhappiness, because they can rarely be achieved. Any time any level of fame, fortune, status, or rectitude is reached, there is another, higher level. Therefore, each individual must learn to be thankful, content, and happy with whatever level of fame, fortune, status, or rectitude they have achieved through his or her own efforts—in the pursuit of his or her bliss. Since this distinction is a very fine line, the most difficult aspect of the pursuit of happiness is finding the appropriate balance.

For individuals to be responsible for their behavior, they must at times reflect on why they behave as they do. If an individual is to be happy in the long run, he or she needs to be aware of the advantages and disadvantages of the different ways to pursue happiness. Too often, an individual finds happiness or protection from threats through a specific behavior and will then keep repeating that behavior without realizing that he or she can achieve happiness through other behaviors. When this repetitive behavior is linked with dreams and desires, the result is addiction. Also, it is easy for an individual to believe that his or her way of achieving happiness is in some way superior to how others achieve happiness—this results in a "true believer." All "true believers" are extremists who have difficulty accepting those who do not think or act as they do.

The bottom line is that attempts to achieve happiness or escape fear will have negative outcomes when carried to the extreme.

The same relationship exists for another aspect of behavior: the two opposites, action and thinking. Both are good behaviors, yet when either is taken to the extreme, the outcomes are usually bad.

Action is necessary to achieve goals. Reputations are made through action. Action can result in either success or failure, and it is this fact that produces a high—and thus action is the most visible form of behavior. But happiness through action is short lived. It lasts no longer than the action. Happiness from action is only possible when there is stress—the higher the stress, the greater the exhilaration.

However, action alone can produce great unhappiness, and when carried to the extreme, it leads to endless conflict and self-destruction.

Most behavior is related to experience, not to thinking. We do what we have been taught to do, or have learned from experience, or in accordance with "common sense"—which is learning used to advance self-interest. However, if a person is to do the harder right rather than the easier wrong, that person must think. Thinking starts with ideas, but thinking itself is the processing, dissecting, refining, and original application of those ideas. Ideas can come from listening or viewing, but new ideas usually come from reading. Thinking can be done in the mind alone, but usually it takes place during writing.

Thinking provides openings to creativity, yet it is orderly, brooding, and lacks emotion. Therefore, thinking taken to the extreme results in extinction through isolation and atrophy.

For me, all of these aspects of behavior (pursuit of happiness, flight from fear, action versus thinking) were neatly combined in duty, honor, and country.

The same truth is illustrated by the Christian view of sin. After all, each of the recognized seven deadly sins is something good taken to the extreme:

- Commitment to something of value becomes **Anger** (rage, wrath).

- Self-esteem becomes **Pride** (hubris, vanity, and self-love).

- Appreciation of quality becomes **Greed** (acquisition of wealth, hoarding, theft, and robbery).

- Working to be the best you can be becomes **Envy** (desire of others' status, abilities, and goods).

- Eros becomes **Lust** (excessive thoughts and seeking of pleasures of the body).

- Calmness, or the absence of zeal, becomes **Sloth** (apathy, laziness, and depression).

- Appreciation of food and drink becomes **Gluttony** (overindulgence and overconsumption).

As many have observed, War brings out the best and worst in humans. I think this is also true for Warfare (often called Irregular Warfare).[21] Much of the mask in behavior is stripped away. Thus I think what I learned from June 1950 to June 1951 would be difficult, if not impossible, to learn during peaceful times.

Trouble in Chinsan

Everything suggests an early end to the fighting, and we expect to be out of Korea by Christmas. However, we keep getting reports of "guerrillas" south of Chinsan. These "guerrillas" are really communist insurgents who have been fighting the government ever since 1945. They want to unite Korea under socialism and see the weakening of the "American lackeys" in Seoul as the way to achieve that goal. Finally, we get orders to move to Chinsan and are given a search and destroy mission. My time for reflection is replaced by the reality of Warfare.

---

[20] Parable in Martin Heidegger, *Being and Time*, 1962, p. 242.

[21] Warfare has been given many different names because more people think of conflict/co-operation in terms of the War and Peace dichotomy, and it does not fit within either War or Peace. The most common term is Irregular Warfare, yet in the past the following have been used: revolution, unconventional war, internal war, subversive war, intrastate war, rebellion, insurrection, wars of national liberation, civil war, and guerrilla war. Each of these names has several definitions. These names overlap in meaning. Therefore, it seems best to use the one word, Warfare, for all of them.

CHAPTER FOURTEEN

CHINSAN-KUNSAN AREA

21–31 October 1950

In the Chinsan-Kunsan area, we face a much greater challenge than we had in Okchon or Hamch'ang. There we had been trying to capture soldiers who had been defeated and were trying to escape. In the mountains south of Chinsan, we face insurgents who have been active long before the North Koreans invaded the south. Here, our enemy is armed and organized local Communists. They know the terrain; they are dedicated and ruthless. Fighting here in the mountains, with narrow, winding roads, the insurgents— usually referred to as guerrillas—have a "home court" advantage. Here, I would learn about the violent side of Warfare.[22]

Terror and Torture as Tactics

Two trenches are found across a road west of Chinsan. The insurgents have dug them to stop our vehicles from going into an area that has long been a Communist stronghold. The Pioneer and Ammunition (P&A) Platoon—which is the battalion's engineer and ammunition supply unit—plus a couple of squads of riflemen are sent in trucks to fill in the trenches. I think we should also send some men from the intelligence section to check out the area. I send my jeep with Sergeant Gausnell in charge, Paul (my interpreter), a driver, and one other soldier. I consider this a routine task that does not require me.

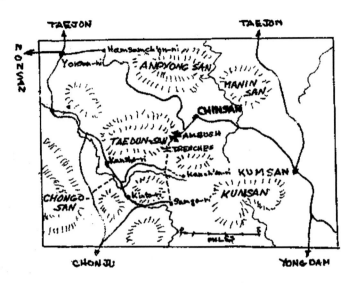

Gausnell had been with me on our first day of combat (27 July) with a BAR and had received a chest wound. Fortunately, a BAR magazine in a bandoleer he had around his neck took the bullet. His wound was large but not deep since the bullet was never able to enter his chest—the magazine had dug into his chest. After some stitches and a few weeks of bandages, he was completely recovered. He has proved to be a reliable and capable leader. I had him promoted to sergeant. I put him in charge this time just as I have done many times during the past two months. If I had not been busy with other things I, not Gausnell, would have been in the front seat of that jeep.

Paul, a young Presbyterian who became my interpreter after Lieutenant Kim, who was with me at the First Battle of Chungam-ni Pass (2 August), went to a South Korean division which was being reorganized. Paul is a dedicated Christian and a pacifist. He considers all killing sinful and thinks all war is evil. He dislikes all things military—as he has known them before the war. His ideal is a world of peace and love based on the teaching of Jesus. However, he thinks the Communists are a greater evil than war and soldiers, and he knows of the many atrocities they have committed after they took over parts of South Korea. As a patriot, he is therefore willing to work with me as an interpreter. For some reason Paul does not consider me one of the soldiers that he dislikes in general. He is comfortable working with me, and in fact, he respects me as somewhat of a father figure.

The road repair team never reaches the trenches. Some insurgents are dug in on either side of the road waiting for them. At a curve in the road, before the trenches, the lead truck with the P&A soldiers stops because of an obstacle in the road. Then the other vehicles stop. Immediately, all of the vehicles come under fire from both sides of the road. They have no radio contact, so the first word of the ambush comes from several men who escaped and walked back.

I go with the rescue force. We find the trucks burning, but no enemy. We also find the bodies of those ambushed. Each body has the shoes removed and has at least two wounds—one always through the back of the head at close range. The bodies of my two soldiers and my interpreter Paul are found together. But Gausnell's body is not there.

For several days, we send patrols out to try to find SGT Gausnell, or at least his body. We never find either. Since we cannot use the interrogation techniques necessary to get the information we need from the villagers, we are never able to achieve justice.

In our search, we do find several human fingers that have been cut off at the first knuckle. We do find a Korean man swinging from a tree with a rope around his neck. He has had his big toe cut off and a message pinned to his chest. The message is written in blood, no doubt from his own toe. The message is in Korean, and the characters are not clear, but as best we can determine, it gives the man's name and address. Then it says he is an enemy of the people, and he is being killed as an example of what will happen to anyone who does not support the Communists' efforts to give power to the people.

Paul's Brother

A few days later, I am told: "Paul's brother is here to pick up his body." I wish I could avoid having to face someone with such a loss, but I know I have to meet with him to share our common grief and perhaps help him get through this tragedy. I walk over to where he is standing.

"I'm Captain Holliday, Paul was…"

"I know who you are. Paul told me all about you."

"I want you to know how sorry…"

"Sorry?" There is sarcasm in his voice and both sadness and anger in his face. "You are a soldier, you enjoy war, Paul's death means nothing to you. No matter what you say, you do not understand love and have no desire for peace. You killed Paul. You will go on killing more, just like soldiers always do."

I am not sure how to reply, but I say: "Paul was killed by the Communists and their ideology."

"Yes, yes, I know. It is always like that. Paul would not have been here to be killed if we lived the love and peace Jesus teaches—and if you had never come to Korea." We continue to talk, but whatever I say is no more than a leaf falling in a forest.

I know he is going through the stages of grieving. I am too. But his is more intense than mine. He has lost part of himself: his beloved brother, who was such a fine young man with so much potential. Also, as a professional soldier I am better able to handle it, as he has suggested. However, I know that the raw emotions, doubts, and anger will be with him a very long time—probably his whole life. I know he will have:

- Guilt: Why did I not stop Paul from becoming an interpreter for the Americans?
- Disbelief: Why did the Lord take him?
- Remorse: That our memories of Paul will in time fade.
- Hope: That in God's plan we will meet again.

Fate and the Constraints of Compassion

I ask myself: Why was it not my body, rather than the body of Gausnell, that was never found? Was it fate? Was it the hand of God? Was it just luck? I never find satisfactory answers to these questions.

Also, this incident reminds me that the Pacifist's Fallacy (i.e., to think that if you are peaceful and compassionate, others will be the same) is no protection against evil. Paul, with all of his pure and noble thoughts, was murdered just like the others.

Our patrols find nothing, and no one admits they have seen anything or knows who might have staged the ambush. Of course, the insurgents are from these very villages. Everyone in the villages knows who they are. What should be done? How can we get them to tell the truth? We ask questions. We look for weapons. We look for any evidence that might connect someone to the ambush. We find nothing.

In the days of Rome, the legionnaires would have started killing the villagers until someone told them who murdered our soldiers and where they could be found. Legionnaires would have kept killing people until they had tracked down and killed those who ambushed their soldiers. However, in Korea we were operating under constraints of compassion established by those who have never experienced combat. Yet these constraints prevent actions that have been effective in the past. But which is right and which is wrong? Which is good and which is bad? Should laws for Peace apply during Warfare?

Throughout history, many other great powers, during their rise, handled such situations much the same as the Roman legionnaires. However, once they stop rising and accept the Pacifist's Fallacy, there is erosion of ruthlessness in the military.

These constraints of compassion are followed by decay and decline.

Also throughout history, we can find the rise and fall of great powers. During their rise, the citizens share moral confidence and certainty; there is no hesitation about doing whatever is necessary. They are decisive and ruthless. As great powers fall, many factions have their own interests. Unity and purpose are lost. There are many individuals with torments and uncertainties as they search for equality, fairness, compassion, and justice. During the decline stages, the constraints of "civilized rules" are imposed on the military, and within the military, there are politically correct enforcers to ensure compliance. As a result, the military is no longer hard, ruthless, and strong, but it becomes soft, sophisticated, and weak. This is one aspect of ideological conflict.

Insurgents Attack Chinsan

The Third Battalion remains in Chinsan to neutralize the insurgents, but they seem to be doing a better job of making us look ineffective. Our patrols wander around the hills finding nothing, only to be ambushed by those that vanish as fast as they appear.

COL Fisher, the regimental commander, comes down from Taejon to ensure that we find no more enemies. He feels that the war is all but over, and he thinks it best for us to manage to leave the insurgents alone. Then they will leave us alone, and that will speed our return to Japan. We brief the colonel on the situation in our area. He then gives his orders:

"Lee, (MAJ James Lee is our battalion commander) I want you to sweep the area for several days, but I do not want you to find any Communists. Just send patrols to all those areas where we have had contact, but make sure they don't get into any firefights. I want to see reports that you have found no enemy. The South Koreans are going to have to take care of these people after we leave."

"Yes, sir." His orders are recognition that conventional War fighting forces and tactics are ineffective against insurgents. COL Fisher decides to spend the night with us.

Around the battalion command post is a rifle company, a battery of field artillery, and our headquarters company. The command post is in a schoolhouse with the artillery outside in the schoolyard. Just for extra protection, I Company comes in to occupy some hills around the town.

After dark a platoon of half-tracks with multiple .50-caliber machine guns arrive. Two of the half-tracks are on the main road to the south—leading to the stronghold of the insurgents. Feeling very safe, we go to sleep.

I am awakened by rifle fire. Before I get to the window, the hills erupt. Rifles. Bazookas. Men shouting. Then the .50-calibers on the half-tracks open up. It is a cornucopia of sounds and flashes.

COL Fisher rushes in: "Lee, what the hell is going on?"

Knowing no more than any of us, MAJ Lee replies: "I think we're getting attacked, sir. I'll check right away!"

"Attacked? What stupid bastard would attack all the people we've got? Now get out there and stop those men. They're trigger-happy. You would think this was their first combat." Firing continues for at least fifteen minutes. Finally it begins to die down. Reports start to come in. About sixty insurgents had taken over one of the unoccupied hills and fired down into the town. Our troops on either side returned fire. At the same time, another group of about forty insurgents attempted to capture the police station. The police station had been burned several days earlier, but it still has a rock tower from which a machine gun can sweep the whole town. The thick stone walls still stand above the ashes of the destroyed building. It seems the attackers did not know the half-tracks blocked their path to the station.

MAJ Lee reports to the colonel what we had learned. The colonel is not happy. I say to MAJ Lee, "I sure hope we find some bodies out there in the morning."

"So do I," he replies.

The artillery is firing. Every few minutes, they fire a volley, and the whole school building shakes. Dirt falls from the roof. I am sure that the insurgents will not attack again that night, so I curl up on the floor and go back to sleep.

The next morning, we do find some bodies and a lot of blood. This, I am sure, did not make COL Fisher happy, but at least we are off the hook. While we are out looking at the bodies, MAJ Lee says: "Sam, how can you go to sleep after all of that? There you were, snoring away as if you were home in your own bed. On the other side of the windows, four howitzers could have awoken the dead. You never missed a beat."

I reply, "I do not know. Just lucky, I guess." But I know that I have some mind-body thing that allows me to shut down whenever I know that I can. It might be for a few minutes or a few hours. But in combat, it comes in handy. Unfortunately, many of those with us do not have that ability.

We make a few sweeps as COL Fisher had ordered. The reports from up north make it clear that the war is not ending.

We are soon sent north, and the insurgents remain in control of the Chinsan-Kunsan area.

Meanwhile Up North

On 21 October, we learn that the First Cavalry Division and the ROK First Division has captured Pyongyang, the capital of North Korea. At a ceremony, the two hundred men of F Company, Fifth Cavalry Regiment are the honor guard. Those who had arrived in Korea ninety-six days earlier with the company are asked to step forward. Only five men do, and three of them had been wounded.

We hear that US airborne troops drop north of Pyongyang on 20 October and free some POWs. Caught between the 187th Airborne Regiment and the British Twenty-Seventh Brigade, the North Korean rear guard[23] is practically destroyed (805 KIA and 681 POW). We also learn that of 150 American POWs who left Pyongyang by train on 18 October, only 21 are not killed after the airborne landing. After that, more bodies are discovered.

The Seventh Cavalry Regiment moves to take Chinnanpo, the port city for Pyongyang. When they arrive, they find this sign: "You are riding on Horseshit Street courtesy of the 24th Division Artillery." From the southwest side of a river, North Korean soldiers are seen leaving Chinnanpo by boat. So a few artillerymen of the Twenty-Fourth Division get a boat and go over to the city to post their sign on the east gate to welcome the cavalrymen.

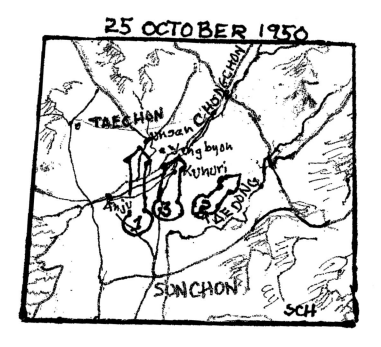

On 25 October, from Anju north of Pyongyang near the west coast, the First ROK Division (1) moves to a town called Unsan, north of the Ch'ongch'on River. Just over a mile northeast of Unsan, the lead tank is attacked, and the first Chinese soldier is captured in Korea. All night fighting continues around Unsan. Twenty-Fourth Division crosses the Ch'ongch'on River.[24] ROK Eighth Division (2) moves up the Taedong River, and the ROK Sixth Division (3) moves up Ch'ongch'on River.

On the east coast, the First Marine Division makes an administrative landing at Wonsan, which had been captured by the Third ROK Division on 10 October. The landing is delayed until the navy can sweep the harbor of 2,000 mines. The Seventh

Division is also scheduled to land at Wonsan but is diverted to Iwon.

MacArthur removes all restrictions on the use of UN ground forces south of the border. JCS informs MacArthur that the removal of all restrictions is not in accord with the policy guidance given him. MacArthur replies that lifting the restriction is a matter of military necessity.

On 26 October, we hear the ROK troops are getting close to the Yalu River. But we also learn that a ROK regiment had been attacked by 7,000 Chinese troops near Unsan. This was the first I had ever heard of Unsan; I found it on a map. It is seventy miles from Pyongyang and north of the Ch'ongch'on River. The Eighth Army estimated that in northwest Korea there were two Chinese divisions. The optimism we had about the war ending soon vanishes. MacArthur claims only a few Chinese have crossed the Yalu. He says this is symbolic support rather than a military force capable of preventing a victory by the UN.

Those of us at the lower level in Korea have no knowledge of the massive troop movements in China toward the Korean border during October. Of course, we have no idea that the Nationalist Chinese on Taiwan, who had excellent intelligence sources in China, have been telling Washington that the Communist Chinese will enter Korea if American and South Korean forces got near the Yalu. We were also not aware of the debates between MacArthur, in Tokyo, and Washington. We did not know that during the first months of the war MacArthur had considered the possibility of Chinese forces coming to the aid of North Korea, but after the breakout from the Pusan perimeter, he thought this was less likely.

On 31 October, the First Marine Division is sent toward the Changjin (Chosin) Reservoir to relieve ROK units northeast of

Hamhung. This would have been appropriate if reaching the Yalu was the only goal. But it is a costly strategic blunder because it places X Corps too far north to move against the flank of any Chinese that move down the center of Korea via the Taedong River corridor.

---

[22] Warfare, or Irregular Warfare, goes by many names. It is protracted conflict between non-state actors using all means possible to weaken or overthrow those in authority. It is neither Peace nor War.

[23] 239th Regiment

[24] Also on 25 October, the Twenty-Seventh British Brigade leads the move west on the main road to Manchuria. In the center of Korea, the Eighth ROK Division reaches Tokch'on. The Sixth ROK Division captures two trains carrying eight tanks and fifty boxcars of ammunition, and at Huich'on it captures twenty tanks needing only minor repairs. Both the Eighth and Sixth ROK Division are in the mountains, with very high snow-covered peaks north of them.

CHAPTER FIFTEEN

UP TO NORTH KOREA

1–19 November 1950

The first Chinese prisoner is captured on 25 October 1950. We have just received orders for our movement to Japan. The Chinese launch a major offensive in the Unsan area. Our orders to Japan are cancelled. By 6 November, the Americans and South Koreans have withdrawn and are establishing a defensive position along the Ch'ongch'on River. We receive orders to move.

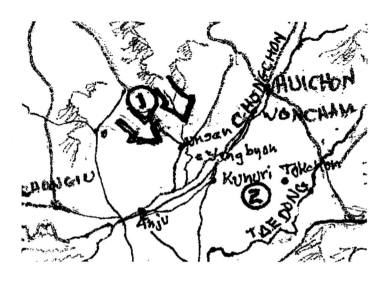

On 1 November near Unsan, two Chinese Divisions (#1 on map on previous page) move to attack the First Cavalry Division and First ROK Division. By noon, there is a roadblock six miles south of Unsan. During the day, several civilians say there are many Chinese in the area; they report columns of enemy troops moving forward in the late afternoon. An air strike destroys twenty-one vehicles nine miles from Unsan. At dusk, artillery fires on columns moving toward Unsan.

The assaults by the Chinese start at 2230 on 1 November, with the strongest assault against the Eighth Cavalry Regiment. By midnight, violent assaults are flaring against all frontline units, and there are also attacks in the rear areas. There are bugles and whistles. There is chaos, confusion, and death for the rest of the night. LT W. C. Hill said: "I thought I was dreaming when I heard a bugle sounding taps and the beat of horses' hooves in the distance. Then, as though they came out of a burst of smoke, shadowy figures started shooting and bayoneting everybody they could find." By daylight on 2 November, pockets of men from both the First Cavalry and First ROK Divisions have set up defenses. The Fifth Cavalry Regiment attempts to break through to those at Unsan, but fails. Just before dusk, a plane drops a message into the positions of the Third Battalion, Eighth Cavalry Regiment ordering it to withdraw under cover of darkness.

For three more days and nights, fierce fighting continues near Unsan; some soldiers of the Third Battalion, Eighth Cavalry are able to crawl out, but the wounded remain behind. The Eighth Cavalry Regiment loses most of its equipment. Casualties are high; for example, only two hundred of the eight hundred men in Third Battalion, Eighth Cavalry Regiment make it out. On 22 November, the Chinese will set some of those captured free to "tell their comrades" of the humane treatment received.

Seventh and Eighth ROK Divisions are beaten and withdraw from their defensive positions between Yongbyon and Tokch'on, and the Chinese take a mountain that dominates Kunu-ri (#2 on map on page 203). It is very confusing. It is raining and cold. The roads are muddy. ROK soldiers are retreating, and some Chinese soldiers, in ROK uniforms, are among them. Also, some Americans are wearing Korean clothing they have acquired.

On the east coast, the marines run into roadblocks on the road northwest of Hamhung as they climb up to the Chosin Reservoir. Seventh Division fights a bitter battle in the snowy mountains eighty miles north of Hamhung.

The Chinese have proven themselves to be well-trained, disciplined, tough, and vicious fighters who charge enemy positions without regard to casualties and move unseen through gaps to attack communication, command, and supply units in the rear. By 6 November the Americans and South Koreans have withdrawn and are establishing a defensive position along the Ch'ongch'on River.

On 7 November, there is the largest air battle in Korea as F-51 Mustang fighters engage Soviet-built fighters. On the ground, the Chinese break contact and melt away, leaving only observation posts.

The Trip to Kaesong

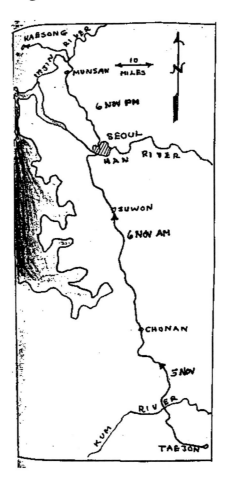

We receive orders to move. We leave Taejon, and by daylight on 6 November, we have reached Chonan, and then we end up in Kaesong that evening.

Halfway through the morning, as we approached Suwon, I see my driver blinking his eyes. I feel I had better replace him at the wheel. It is less than half an hour later that I fall asleep and drive the jeep into a ditch. Two of the men are hurt badly enough to be sent back to the hospital. For the rest of the trip, we have to stop every fifteen minutes to fill the radiator with water.

We drive through Seoul during the afternoon of 6 November. We arrive in Kaesong just before dark and move into some Quonset huts south of town. There I learn that Tenny Ross had been killed that same day. A sniper shot Tenny while he was traveling in his jeep. There are now only three (Don, Jim, and myself) of five of us who had been together since 1944. Today, battlefield medical care has improved so much that Tenny probably would have survived such a wound.

The mission of the Twenty-Fifth Division is to clean out all armed opposition south of Pyongyang. We are to find and destroy active elements of the North Korean People's Army and to neutralize any guerrilla activities by local Communists. We identify elements of the Second, Fourth, Sixth, and Seventh North Korean Divisions—all of which we have fought in South Korea.

The soldiers who made it back to North Korea are now attacking supply trains, ambushing our patrols, and causing many who oppose the North Korean regime to flee their homes. Those soldiers set the town of Kapyong ablaze, causing more than eight thousand residents to flee. On 9 November, seven of fourteen soldiers from the Twenty-Fifth Division are killed when a patrol is ambushed; all have been shot in the head (i.e., murdered after they are captured). Although never stated, I think we are the strategic reserve for the west portion of the Eighth Army with an additional mission of keeping open the main supply route (MSR) from Seoul to Pyongyang.

It is now getting cold, and everything is brown. It is cloudy, and we rarely see the sun. There is no rain and no snow. It is dry, dusty, and cold. No longer do we have the varied terrain we had been in the first two months or the lovely green mountains west of

Hamch'ang. Now it is just flat and brown. The farmers live in houses of mud bricks and thatched roofs. The towns are a mixture of concrete and wood one-story buildings with tile roofs. A dark, somber, forbidding feeling is in the air.

Housekeeping

We are now in winter clothing with synthetic fur caps, scarves, gloves, and sweaters. Later we would be very thankful for this, but since we wear the same clothes all the time and take no baths, we are all magnets for lice—and assorted other bugs. So from time to time we get a visit from some medical corpsmen who examines us for lice—which they usually find. Then DDT for everyone.

One day we are told some dentists are coming and everyone will have their teeth examined. It is not what we expected. There is none of the equipment of a dentist's office. There are three young men with only a few weeks of dental training after they entered the army. Out in the open, each one sets up two folding chairs facing each other; next to them is a small folding table—what might be called a TV tray—with a few instruments and some cards.

The men line up and rapidly go through the procedure. There is no dental work done. Perhaps something is identified for future dental work, but mainly they are recording where the fillings are and their shape.

It does not take long to realize what this is all about. They are making records so that if in the future some unidentified skull is found they will be able to identify the body. It is just another reality check.

We do make use of local housing. In the warm weather, it is often more comfortable to sleep in the open rather than in a building. We would use a schoolhouse or office building in a village for the battalion command post, but often we preferred the outside. However, as it turns cold that is less attractive. We try to include houses within our defensive positions. The farmhouses have dirt floors over a hot air system. There is a fire pit on one side of the house, but the heating system is designed so that the vents would take the hot air under the floor to come out the other side of the house. In cold weather this is very inviting.

There is one problem. The enemy identify the houses they think the Americans will use and then place some form of explosives under the floor. In the middle of the night, there might be an explosion. We learn to look carefully at the hot air vents before settling in for a night's sleep.

These heating systems have another advantage. The same fire that heats the house can be used to heat water. With that, we can have sponge baths, which are better than using the icy streams. No doubt there are Japanese-style bathhouses in the cities, but I never spend any time in any city. The army does have quartermaster bath units, but I never saw one while in Korea. The quartermaster does provide clothing exchanges, and this was always a happy event.

Encounter with the Turks

Our battalion is conducting search and destroy operations northeast of Kaesong. As normal, one afternoon we select where we will spend the night. This time battalion headquarters is close to a small village. The rifle companies are on the surrounding hills. We have just begun setting up our defensive perimeter when we get a message from regiment that a Turkish battalion will arrive before dark to relieve us in place. We have heard of the Turkish Brigade's arrival in Korea but have never seen them.

Night comes, but no Turks. We tighten our defensives, black out all lights, and settle down for the night.

One of the companies flashes a message to us: "There is a column of lights coming toward us."

Then we see it. A long column of bright lights as far as you could see. They roar through our blacked-out positions and come to a stop in the little village next to us. As they halt, it seems every truck bumps into the one in front of it.

Captain Fraser, the solid, conscious, capable regimental assistant S-3 storms in. "Here are your God damn jerks. Take 'em!" With a scowl on his face, he goes over to the stove to warm himself without another word. Finally I go over to him. Trying to defuse his anger with a little humor, I say: "How come you were so lucky to get some Turkish delight?"

"I guess someone hates me." He then goes on to explain what had happened after he had been told to escort the Turkish battalion down to us.

"They were to be ready to move at 1600. I was just to show them how to get here. So I got there a little early. I expected them to be in their trucks ready to go. What the hell do you think I saw: a whole bunch of happy Turks sitting around, gnawing on loaves of bread, talking, wrestling, and sleeping. The trucks were everywhere. I couldn't find anyone who would do anything.

"The damn officers said the sergeants would take care of everything. And the sergeants said they could not speak English. I spent an hour trying to get anyone to get the battalion on the trucks. I finally said to hell with it and sat down. My job was just to guide them.

"By 1800—I expected to have them to you by then—the trucks were lined up, but the men were still milling around. Then I went around trying to get the men on the trucks. Some would get on, and then jump off. At last, the officers came out and got into their jeeps. The men jumped on the trucks, and we were off. It was now dark, so we had to use lights. I sure hope they can fight, but they look like a mob to me."

"Well, how was the trip over here?" I asked.

"Hell. I was leading the way. We had gone a little over a mile when I looked back. The Turks had stopped. I have no idea why. But in the headlights I could see them jump off of their trucks. They started to search. Unfortunately, this was at a horseshoe curve in the road. It was not long before some from the end of the column were shooting at some from the front. It took them several minutes of shouting back and forth before they stopped. I thought they were going to kill each other."

I laugh, but Fraser doesn't think it is funny.

"And that wasn't the end of it. Just then an old Korean man happened to pass by with a cart full of his stuff. My guess is he was moving during the night to somewhere he thought he would be safe. The Turks decided to search him. In the cold, this guy was stripped. Each piece of his clothing was examined. The cart was next. Each item was removed and thrown on the ground. By the time the cart was empty, the column was ready to move on. The Turks jumped back on their trucks. The poor man was left standing with all of his things on the ground."

After the Turks arrive, we assure them that we control all of the surrounding hills. They will be safe in the village, and we ask them to unload their weapons and quietly go to sleep for the remainder of the night.

The Turks do not go to sleep and waste no time in making themselves at home in the village. First they build fires. Our blackout was pointless. Next there are female screams from all over the village. Finally the squawks of chickens fill the night air.

When morning finally arrives, I take stock of the situation. All of the women and girls are leaving. There is nary a live chicken to be found—only feathers, heads, and feet. We are very thankful that no one has been shot during the night. Only one house has burned down—the Turks made the fire a bit too large.

With much delight, we leave the Turks as soon as we can after daylight. On our way back to Kaesong, we follow the same route used by the Turks. At most sharp curves, we find a truck in the ditch. Nearby there would be several happy Turks around a fire. They wave to us, and we wave back.

Thus ends our first encounter with the Turks.

Chinese Appraisal of US Military

After their contact in early November 1950, the Chinese made their appraisal of the US military:

Their firing instruments are highly powerful. Their artillery is very active. Aircraft strafing and bombing of our transportation is a great hazard. Their transportation system is great. Their infantry rate of fire is great and the long range of fire is still greater.

When cut off from the rear they abandon all of their heavy weapons. Their infantrymen are weak, afraid to die, and haven't the courage to attack or defend. They depend on their planes, tanks, and artillery. They are afraid of our firepower. They will cringe when, if on the advance, they hear firing. They are afraid to advance farther.

They specialize in day fighting. They are not familiar with night fighting or hand-to-hand combat. If defeated, they have no orderly formation. Without the use of their mortars, they become completely lost, dazed, and demoralized. When surrounded they do nothing. They are afraid when the rear is cut off. When transportation comes to a standstill, the infantry loses the will to fight.

The Importance of Strategic Communication during Ideological Conflict

There is optimism at MacArthur's headquarters by 15 November. Unwelcome facts are ignored. MacArthur assures the JCS that "complete victory is possible, and it would be fatal to abandon the original plan to destroy all resisting armed forces in North Korea." MacArthur is thinking in terms of "victory" in a conventional War, rather than stability on the Korean peninsula with a strong independent Republic of Korea and a weak Communist state confined to the northern mountains.

Records made public in the 1970s reveal that the Chinese leaders in 1950 did not want to fight the Americans; they wanted a resolution of the Korean situation that provided a buffer along the Manchurian border. They also wanted American forces withdrawn from Korea, since they thought they could, in due course, work out relations to their advantage with any Korean government. Primarily, they wanted to turn their attention to rebuilding China.

The messages sent through Indian Ambassador K. M. Panikkar to the UN, US, and to Tokyo were ignored because he was considered to be a typical Indian leftist intellectual. Washington and Tokyo thought his messages were just insincere diplomatic maneuvers. In July 1950, Prime Minister Zhou Enlai told Panikkar that China would not enter the Korean War. However, after the Inch'on landing, the view in Beijing changed; Panikkar heard many ominous warnings. On 2 October, Zhou Enlai told Panikkar that China would intervene in force if the UN crossed the 38th Parallel. Panikkar duly reported all of this, but it was largely ignored.

Also, the complete withdrawal of Chinese forces on 7 November 1950 following the 1–6 November battle at Unsan was intended to communicate the same message. However, neither Washington nor MacArthur understood this attack and withdrawal as such a message. It was one of the costs of not understanding the Oriental way of ideological conflict.

Chinese forces in North Korea are deployed in accordance with the Chinese concept of mobile defense designed to defeat a superior force. The goal is not to hold defensive positions but to destroy opposing forces in brief actions. The underlying strategy is to invite attack: fight a delaying action while allowing the attacking force to penetrate deep, then, at a point of Chinese choice, counterattack suddenly when the opposing force is ill prepared.

The Chinese deploy their major forces behind screening units; therefore, the UN forces encounter only outposts after 7 November. Showing little awareness of the adversary's doctrine, MacArthur assumes the Chinese have withdrawn into defensive positions close to the Yalu River. Moreover, he incorrectly interprets this deep, voluntary withdrawal as Chinese weakness.

The planning and decision making for the UN forces reflect very limited knowledge of the strategies and tactics used by the Chinese throughout their civil war that ended in 1949. Also, the focus on conventional War is difficult to understand since ideological conflict is so central to the thinking of the Chinese and Koreans.

Why were the Communist leaders willing to confront the US armed forces? The US had just defeated Germany and Japan and ended that war with the nuclear bomb. Clearly nuclear weapons had changed conventional War as much as the stirrup, the crossbow, gunpowder, and the machine gun. Yet, the Chinese were willing to challenge the US. It was obvious that they had a means of conflict they considered superior to nuclear weapons. Mao had said: "If they use their bomb, we will use our hand grenade."

What was their hand grenade? Mao never said, but it is clear that Mao had in mind strategic communication and ideological commitment. The Chinese leaders thought they could influence, and perhaps control, the US decision-making process. They knew that throughout history the enemy's decision-making process had always been a prime target. And they did not think that the US was very good at the strategic communication aspect of ideological conflict, because the US had to consider the views of its public—which wanted a swift victory. It turned out the Chinese leaders were correct, for they were able to cause US leaders to make decisions that ensured a stalemate.

In the winter of 1950, Chinese soldiers were motivated by a sense of participation in building a new central kingdom that offered a brighter future to replace the old China of tyrannical landlords, corruption, and foreign exploitation. For them, Mao and Communism were the way to this new utopia. Many were mature men with extensive military experience that had been fighting for an ideology since their teens. The UN soldiers lacked any such ideological motivation. Years later this same need for ideological motivation was neglected in Vietnam, the Balkans, Iraq, Afghanistan, the Middle East, and Africa with the Western way of war's focus on technological superiority, firepower, and maneuvers. Yet final success in all conflict goes to those who can keep their will strong while they weaken the will of their enemy.

Back to the War

Our situation would soon become much more serious and frightening as we moved north of the Ch'ongch'on River and confronted the Chinese near Unsan.

CHAPTER SIXTEEN

ANOTHER WAR

20–27 November 1950

We move north again. In Korean cosmology, north is associated with winter and the "Divine Warriors." We know we will confront winter, but who will be revealed as the "Divine Warriors"—them or us? The countryside is barren, bleak, and brown. The air is brisk and cold. I see very few people.

On 20 November, we drive through the North Korean capital of Pyongyang—a dull, dingy, empty city of gray concrete. We are tired from the long drive. Finally, near Sunchon, military police direct us to where we are scheduled to spend the night. But it is now the early hours of the morning.

It is not until the middle of the morning that the whole battalion arrives. Some of the trucks had run out of gas. We spend the next two days getting "battle ready" and attempting to learn as much as we can about what we might be doing. We will be attacking toward Unsan, where the Chinese had first attacked the First Cavalry Division on 1 November.

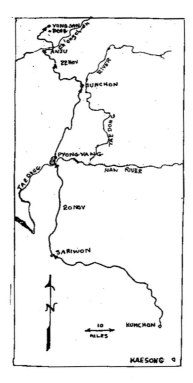

On 22 November, we move up to Anju, cross the Ch'ongch'on River, and relieve the Nineteenth Regiment, Twenty-Fourth Division in the vicinity of the two villages with similar names (Yongsan-dong and Yongyon-dong) south of Unsan—where the Chinese had badly mauled the First ROK Division (25–30 October) and the First Cavalry Division (1–5 November). On the east coast, several divisions of experienced soldiers of the CCF[25] Third Field Army are waiting in the mountains around the Changjin (Chosin) Reservoir.[26] In fourteen nights of marching, these new divisions came from the Yalu River over the mountains. They had left their artillery, tanks, and heavy vehicles behind. Carrying their rifles, mortars, and machine guns, they pushed across the icy mountains unseen. They are some of the hardiest soldiers in the world. They have a saying: "Two legs can be better than four wheels."

Sung Shih-Iun, a forty-year-old who has spent his whole life leading men into battle for the Communists, commands these divisions. He is brave, stubborn, and quick-tempered. Sung knows exactly what units he faces and where they are. Also, because he has studied the Americans, he has a good idea of where they will go and what they will do. He knows that a massive attack awaits the Eighth Army.

On the other hand, the Americans only know there are Chinese in the mountains; they know little about who they are, where they are, or what they will do. They have lost contact with the enemy. They discount accurate information obtained from captured privates; they did not know that in order to motivate their troops, those of lower rank are treated as equals and that the Communist political commissars often give lectures to everyone about future plans. When the two task forces from Seventh Division are attached to the First Marine Division, they are given no intelligence regarding any enemy on the east side of the reservoir. Seventh Marine Regiment advances slowly on the west side of the Changjin (Chosin) Reservoir, which is on a high, cold plateau. Fifth Marine Regiment is still on the east side of the reservoir. The two battalion task forces from the Seventh Division attached to the First Marine Division request winter clothing like that of the marines (i.e., arctic parkas and warming tents). They are told to requisition their own needs through army channels.

After Giving Thanks

For Thanksgiving Day, we have a full turkey dinner, literally from soup to nuts. We are only sixty miles from the Yalu River and Manchuria. On everyone's lips is, "We'll be home for Christmas!" We are sure that the final drive to the Yalu is about to start.

On that Thanksgiving, I also receive a letter from my father. He tells me that he and Uncle Bob have contacted people in Washington about getting me ordered back to some post in the States or to Europe. He says they all agree that I have seen enough combat, and he is certain that he can work things out. However, he says he does not want to do anything on this until he knows how I feel. After reading his letter, I put it in the pocket of my field jacket.

We know the First ROK (Republic of Korea) Division and the First Cavalry Division had been badly mauled at Unsan when the Chinese entered the war on 1 November. But we think that was only because the Chinese had surprised them. Also, it is reported that the Chinese forces are only volunteers sent at the last minute to show China's support for another Communist country. Higher headquarters says the Chinese are not prepared for a direct confrontation with the United States. Besides, the whole Eighth Army will advance to the Yalu River rather than just a couple of divisions—as had been attempted earlier.

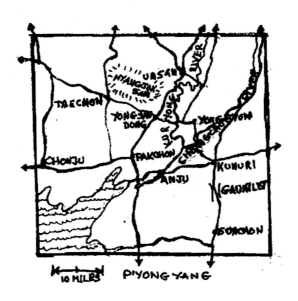

Is it too much to expect that higher headquarters, after a month to analyze information, has gotten the intelligence correct? All reports we receive indicate that after a face-saving fight, the Chinese will pull back beyond the Yalu, and that this final push will bring the war to a close. We know nothing of the debates going on between MacArthur and Washington, nor what the Nationalist Chinese on Taiwan were telling the United States from their sources.

Our Attack Toward Unsan

The day after Thanksgiving, 24 November 1950, we start the attack toward Unsan. Just before this attack, I make what I consider the most serious intelligence error I made in Korea as an S-2 (intelligence officer). Reflecting the optimism of the reports from higher headquarters, I issue an inaccurate intelligence estimate. I state that the enemy will most likely put up only rear guard fights as it retreats to the Yalu.

At this time, I did not have enough knowledge of international relations or of the Chinese to make my own evaluation of the overall situation. Therefore, I accepted what I received from higher headquarters. After I studied international relations and Chinese history, I realized that a miscalculation had been made. To advance toward the Yalu without assurance that the Chinese would not intervene displayed not only poor strategic judgment, but a failure to accurately evaluate the situation and a lack of knowledge of the Oriental way of fighting. The Chinese had prepared a trap, and we were the prey.

Some writers have stated that the movement to the Yalu River was not a strategic error, but a planned strategic move to prevent Communist China from becoming a member of the United

Nations and from being accepted as a world power. Also, such writers often suggest this move was planned to cause the US to be militarized so that it would be able to control the less-developed parts of the world and to use the resources of others to maintain the American empire.

I think the answer is far less Machiavellian. I think the answer is to be found in MacArthur's conviction that he was more intelligent and knew more than anyone else, and the fact he was a risk taker. Also, he thought he understood the Chinese better than he did. MacArthur was an old soldier with a long distinguished career dealing with conventional War that few could match. To him the only satisfactory end of the Korean War was the destruction of the North Korean armed forces. He could not accept stability with protracted conflict as success. He wanted to avoid a long, costly stalemate. He wanted victory.

Another possibility is that MacArthur gambled boldly and lost. When he learned that the Chinese were massing troops north of the Yalu River, he ordered ninety B-29s to destroy all of the Yalu bridges. This attack was aborted on orders from the State Department. If that mission had been completed, the Chinese move south of the Yalu would have been difficult. Did MacArthur think the Chinese were bluffing? Did he think they would send only token troops south? Did he want to show that he was a better strategic thinker than Washington? We will never know for sure MacArthur's thoughts when he ordered the advance of 24 November 1950, but his actions were those of a conventional War commander seeing victory.

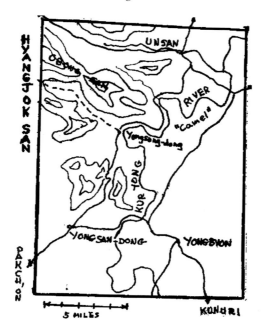

However, the part of my estimate based on my own analysis of our immediate area was correct. I had not only gathered information from the South Korean military and civilians, but I had studied the maps of the area and what the Chinese had done in the Unsan area on 1–3 November.

I state that the enemy will probably counterattack our left flank, between the First ROK Division and the Twenty-Fifth Division. I include a sketch indicating exactly where I expect the strongest enemy attack to come: from the Hyangjok-San area driving toward Yongsong-dong on the Kur Yong River. I say they would try to trap any units near Unsan. This turns out to be correct.[27]

On the first day of our attack (24 November), the Twenty-Fifth Division advances four miles toward Unsan with no enemy contact. The lead element on the east side of the Kur Yong River is Task Force Dolvin. The Thirty-Fifth Regiment is on the west side of the Kur Yong River. At the end of the second day (25 November), the Thirty-Fifth Regiment is on the ridge overlooking Unsan, and a rifle platoon gets to a small bridge just south of Unsan. All lead elements are past the camel head bend in the Kur Yong River.

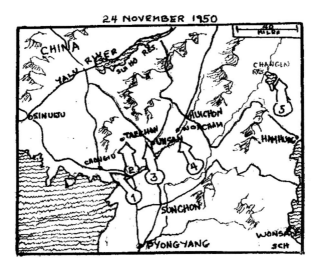

(1) US Twenty-Fourth Division (2) ROK First Division (3) US Twenty-Fifth Division moves seven miles toward Unsan. (4) US Second Division and ROK Sixth, Seventh, and Eighth Divisions (5) Marines and Seventh Division

Where to Position the Third Battalion?

The Third Battalion is in reserve and has been given no specific instruction except to be prepared to move through the other battalions after Unsan has been taken. I am convinced that we need to go into a defensive position facing west in the pass toward Hyangjok-San and south of Obong-San. To establish a position in that pass would require two companies to move two and a half miles west of the road to Unsan. Some think this would cause those two companies unnecessary effort and delay things after Unsan is taken. They favor placing all of our battalion in the valley closer to the regimental headquarters.

I think it is essential to defend that pass, and I make my case as best I can with LTC Lee, our battalion commander, and at regimental headquarters for several days before Thanksgiving. I argue that the enemy could drive down the valley to the river at Yongsong-dong (where regimental headquarters is to be located) and trap much of the regiment, which would be north of that toward Unsan.

However, on 24 November, I pick up some additional arguments. There are very few people in the villages along the road to Unsan, but several tell me that large numbers of Chinese had been there until the night of 23–24 November. Indeed, I found evidence that many Chinese soldiers have been there. More disturbing, when I check places along the road suitable for roadblocks, I find fresh machine gun emplacements and foxholes. This tells me that the Chinese plan to return to these positions at some point.

I do not know if it is my arguments or something else that prevailed. Nevertheless, with nothing better for our battalion to do, on 25 November it is decided that at least one company will guard the pass through Hyangjok Mountain (i.e., facing west toward the First ROK Division). I select the location for K Company, and they take their position before dusk. I do not believe the pass would have been defended if I had not repeatedly argued that a counterattack there was likely. It is fortunate that a company is in that pass.

In the late afternoon of 25 November, reports come in that the First ROK Division, to the west, has been attacked. Also we hear that Task Force Dolvin opposite Unsan, on the eastern side of the Kur Yong River, has been attacked. Our lead units overlooking Unsan have still only seen a few people on ridgelines. Throughout the night of 25–26 November, there are countless struggles by all front line units, one of the more notable being by Task Force Dolvin near Unsan on the right bank of the Kur-Yong River. That night "many Chinese" hit the lead elements of the Task Force: E Company, Twenty-Seventh Regiment, and the Ranger Company. A bitter battle lasts all night on 25–26 November. The Ranger Company with that task force is finally overwhelmed in a hand-to-hand fight in the sixth Chinese assault. Of fifty-one rangers and nine KATUSAs at the start of these assaults, only twenty-one rangers and eight KATUSAs are fit for duty the following day. During this night, LT Ralph Puckett earns the first of his two DSCs and the first of his five Purple Hearts.

25–27 November

On the night of 25–26 November, an enemy patrol creeps into K Company's position and captures several of our soldiers.

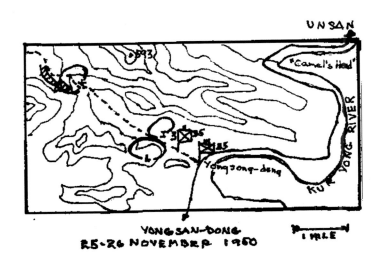

YONG SAN-DONG
25-26 NOVEMBER 1950

226

During 26 November, we move L Company into the left (south) side of the pass, and K Company takes over the right (north) side. I Company takes a position on the mountain north of the pass. The other two battalions of the Thirty-Fifth Regiment pull back to better defensive positions south of the camel head bend in the Kur Yong River. They still have not contacted any Chinese, although they have seen several of their patrols.

At about 2100 hours, I note a fire on the very top of a hill behind us. Why is there a fire? There is no reason for our people, or any of the locals, to be up there. It is not where someone might have started a fire by accident. Why that fire? I am not sure, but I can think of only one reason. The Chinese started it so their troops have something to use as a guide during the night. I call our companies and regiment and tell them to expect a major attack during the night and to be sure that the artillery is prepared to deliver defensive fire in front of K and L Companies.

I am asked, "Why do you think there is going to be a major attack tonight?"

"Because of the fire on the hill behind us," is my answer. I'm sure many did not think that was much of a reason to think there was going to be an attack.

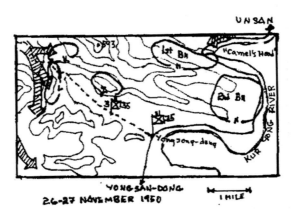

On the night of 26–27 November, the Chinese Communist Forces XIII Army Group do launch their major attack against all ROK and US forces in the west with more than 150,000 men. Task Force Dolvin and other units of the Twenty-Fifth Division, east of the Kur Yong River, receive attack after attack. The First ROK Division to our west is torn apart—we didn't know how badly until 28 November.

The ROK First Division—always considered one of the South Korean's best—is driven out of Taech'on and retreats to the Ch'ongch'on River. Then there are no South Koreans to our left— only Chinese.

L and K Companies, in the pass, are repeatedly attacked throughout the night. Fortunately, the artillery is able to bring fire on groups of attackers as they move up. But there is still plenty of close combat. The soldiers in those two companies do many brave deeds that night. They hold the pass; the Chinese are unable to drive to Yongsong-dong and are unable to get to the roadblocks they had prepared. They do not close the trap. The enemy does, however, flow around the southern (left) flank of L Company.

As soon as there is daylight, the enemy goes into hiding. Yet many pieces of paper marked "Safe Conduct Pass" are scattered along the roads. I pick up one and stick it in my pocket.

Early in the morning, we are told the regiment will withdraw. The regimental headquarters moves back seven miles from Yongsong-dong to Yongsan-dong, and the First Battalion takes up positions northwest of that town. In the afternoon, the Second Battalion pulls back to a ridgeline, on the east side of the road, two miles south of Yongsong-dong. Finally, after 1600 hours our battalion pulls back to positions in line with the Second Battalion, on the west side of the road. I Company is actually on the road, L is to go into position west of I Company, and K Company is to go to a small hill farther to the west. However, K does not reach its positions until it is dark.

While our companies were moving back, I stay in the valley west of Yongsong-dong to see if I can spot any enemy. If I can, I might be able to predict the attack, which I am sure will come during the night. I hide my jeep in some huts fifty yards east of me and tell my men to cover me and to be on the lookout for any enemy attempting to get behind us. They are to be prepared to get away as fast as possible if any Chinese approach. I am confident that I can spot any movement. While I recognize the danger of snipers, I think the distance to the hills is so great that there is little chance they will be able to hit me.

I know that we are at least two miles closer to the Chinese than our new positions for the night. As I look through my field glasses, I see no movement. There is no sunshine, the hills are solid green, and the fields are brown. There is a weird silence—no sounds of humans, animals, wind, or water. The valley is covered with empty fields, and as it gets closer to Yongsong-dong, it widens. For five hours, I move around looking for signs of the hundreds of enemy I'm sure are in those hills and the thousands I'm sure are on the other side of those hills. I see nothing. I hear no sound of troop movement and not even the whistles, horns, or music they use to communicate. Nevertheless, I am sure thousands of Chinese will emerge during the coming night. It is a very strange five hours that we remain alone in that valley. When darkness approaches, I decide it is unwise to stay. I walk back to the jeep, and we drive to the CP of the Third Battalion, which is now in a pass a mile behind the rifle companies. This pass, which became known as "The Pass of No Return," is where the Third Battalion, Thirty-Fifth Regiment became the lost battalion.

27 and 28 November

After dark on 27 November, I notice a new fire on the top of the hill on the east side of the pass in which the battalion CP is located. We are in for more night attacks. By midnight, all units are engaged. The Second Battalion and I Company receive attacks from the north straight down the road.

By mistake, L Company has taken up a position on a small knoll in front and to the left of I Company. Shortly after midnight, L Company is surrounded and is being attacked from all directions. K Company, to the far left (west), only has patrol contact. We receive word that the First Battalion is under heavy attack by Chinese that have broken through the First ROK Division near Yongsan-dong; also, the regimental command post in Yongsan-dong is being attacked. Early in the morning of 28 November (0200 hours), we get word to withdraw in coordination with the Second Battalion.

All of the trucks of the Third Battalion have been sent back during the afternoon of 27 November, so that is done. K Company is told to come back to the pass, and L Company is told to break out of their encirclement and to also come to the pass. There is no contact with K Company for two days, until 29 November, when most of that company reaches the walled city of Yongbyon. By 0330 hours, most of the survivors of L Company have joined I Company on the road.

Colonel Lee and I go down to the Second Battalion command post to make arrangements for the withdrawal. Since the Second Battalion failed to send their vehicles out on 27 November, it is agreed that they will get them out as fast as possible. The two battalions are then to march out before daylight.

But the vehicles take too long, and it is almost early morning twilight (EMT) when they reach the pass. Some of the vehicles do make it out; however, as the column moves down from the pass toward Yongsan-dong, machine gun fire opens up from both sides of the road. Then some rockets. Several of the trucks are set on fire. In the twilight, the fires light up the scene. Vehicles clog the road, and men are running, firing, and hiding. All the time the Chinese are firing from their emplacements on both sides of the road. This three-hundred-yard roadblock certainly had been prepared before 24 November.

Attempts to Get Past the Roadblock

Since the tanks are attached to the Second Battalion and it is their vehicles that are on the road, it is decided that they should attack directly down the road to clear the roadblock. At the same time, the Third Battalion will attack the hill above the roadblock to the west. When the roadblock has been neutralized, the Second Battalion is to suppress any enemy fire and allow the Third Battalion to move through. Due to the clogged condition of the road, confusion, and the poor light of the early morning, it is after daylight before the attack gets under way.

The tanks push destroyed vehicles off of the road and neutralize all enemy fire. Riflemen of the Second Battalion move behind the tanks, attempting to neutralize anyone firing at them. The Chinese start to pick off the men of the Second Battalion. Many of them are killed outright or wounded to never make it out of the roadblock—including PFC Roosevelt "Jack" Clark and PFC Ernest Fuqua, whose remains are not identified until 2012.

At the same time, LT Boyd K. Alderdice and Captain Becicka of I Company move up the hill on the west side of the roadblock. Near the top they meet well dug-in enemy—in positions prepared many weeks before. Two men are hit by the first fire and die on that hill. A base of fire is established with the platoon sergeant in charge, while Alderdice and Becicka take the rest of the platoon around the right flank to get behind the enemy that had fired on them. As they get close, there is another burst of fire from another position.

Alderdice calls out "Oh no!" and falls to the ground. He never moves again. Two others are killed. Their bodies are not recovered. Three more are wounded.

The company commander Captain Leonard Becicka, a military police officer serving his required year with a combat branch, realizes infantry soldiers cannot overcome such well-prepared positions. Leonard is a calm, dedicated professional who is highly trusted and respected by not only the men in his company, but by anyone who has spent any time with him. He reports that without fire support, riflemen cannot take the top of that hill. If an assault is ordered, it would result in unusually high casualties because there is at least a company dug in on the top of the hill with crossfires in all directions.

It is known that Chinese units are closing in rapidly from the north after the Second Battalion and I Company have left their positions. It is impossible to advance to the south except with very heavy casualties. Enemy troops have been seen advancing toward our position in the pass from the west. A platoon of I Company is sent to defend the west side of the pass. Men from many units are crowded together in the pass. Enemy fire into the pass would surely cause panic.

By 0900 hours, all of the Second Battalion has passed through the roadblock, and we expect them to set up at the far (south) end of the three hundred yards in which the enemy has emplacements. The plan is for them to do what they can to keep the road open for us. To our surprise, we see them moving on over the hills and out of sight.

A feeling of disappointment sweeps over me. I know this is a preplanned roadblock. We could have bypassed it if the trucks of the Second Battalion had been sent to the rear the previous afternoon when we sent ours back and if that battalion had reached the pass before daylight as planned. What should be done now?

What To Do?

Everyone is excited in the battalion command group. There are heated debates about what to do.

- Should we attack the west hill, where Alderdice and his men had been killed?
- Should we attack the east hill where the signal fire had been?
- Should we try to fight our way down the road through the roadblock?
- Of course, we had the "Safe Conduct" passes, and we understand that the Chinese follow the Geneva Conventions better than the North Koreans.

I do not like any of these alternatives. I have another idea. But can I sell it? Can I pull it off?

Also, at some point, I will have to answer my father's letter. An answer will be unnecessary if I don't make it out.

---

[25] Chinese Communist Forces.

[26] They replace the CCF 124th Division, which moves to the Taedong River corridor.

[27] Yongsan-dong and Yongsong-dong are on the west side of the Kur-Yong River, with Yong-song-dong being halfway between Yongsan-dong and Unsan. Yongbyon is on the east side of the Kur Yong River, six miles from Yongsan-dong. These locations are very important during 25–29 November 1950.

CHAPTER SEVENTEEN

THE LOST BATTALION

28 November 1950

The press reports that a battalion of the Twenty-Fifth Division is "cut off on Monday and Tuesday and encircled by Reds." This could have been some other battalion, but this item probably is from a reporter who heard discussions about the Third Battalion, Thirty-Fifth Regiment being surrounded in the pass between Yongsan-dong and Unsan. We have no radio contact with either regiment or division. Later we are told that we have been written off as a "lost battalion."

The Pass of No Return

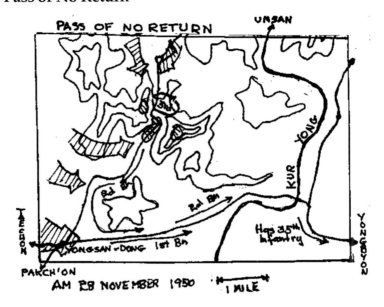

Meanwhile (see map on previous page) attacks that started on 25 November against the Twenty-Fifth Division near Unsan and the First ROK Division near Taech'on continue. The attack down the Ch'ongch'on valley against the Second Division continues. There are frontal assaults against the front line companies, but other Chinese units pass through gaps to attack units in the rear. Twenty-Ninth British and Turkish Brigades are ordered forward. As the Chinese drive down the Taedong River valley, all of the South Korean divisions on the right flank of the Eighth Army fold and move at least ten miles south to Tokch'on. The Turkish Brigade is sent to Tokch'on to protect the right flank of the Second Division. Two task forces of the Seventh Division relieve the Fifth Marine Regiment on the eastern side of the Changjin (Chosin) Reservoir. Most of the First Marine Division is still near Hangaru-ri, but units of the Seventh Marine Regiment are moving slowly up the western side of the reservoir toward Yudam-ni.

There is actually a collection of men from many units crowded together in the Pass of No Return: all of I Company, those of L Company who had broken out of the encirclement during the night, those of Headquarters Company who had not gone out with the vehicles, and some men from the Second Battalion who had been separated from their units during the night. The Chinese are advancing on this pocket of some four hundred men crowded together in a pass between two hills north of Yongsan-dong. This collection certainly is not organized to defend its position. It is little more than a formless mob with soldiers milling around. Some officers are able to hold their men together. In such situations, discipline can overcome bodily sensations that call for fear and flight with a hundred insistent voices. Yet an appeal to the inner compass of those who have experienced combat can produce heroic action. Some are weak, and others are strong; some think only of themselves, and others think of those with them; some are paralyzed into inaction or go wobbly, and others make decisive decisions and move with zeal.

I am able to contact the field artillery by radio. On Okinawa I had been the executive officer of Cannon Company, Twenty-Ninth Regiment (the last such unit in the army) that had 105-mm howitzers and was the only artillery on Okinawa. I try to adjust fire in order to provide the cover needed to get past the roadblock. I have no success. Only a few rounds come in, and they are so scattered, adjustment is impossible. I decide the artillery will do more damage than good.

It is now obvious that swift action is needed. It makes no difference what we do. If we do nothing, we are soon going to be dead or prisoners. It is going to be minutes before Chinese riflemen start firing directly on us. If that happens, all control will be lost. There will be panic.

It is decided that we should move through the roadblock as fast as possible. L Company is to lead the way, and I Company is given the job of holding off the enemy until all the other men have cleared the roadblock. I watch as L Company starts down toward the roadblock; I happen to feel the letter from my father in the pocket of my field jacket. It is still unanswered.

Just then, one of the radio operators shouts: "I've got Lieutenant Smith!" Smith commands the platoon of the Eighty-Ninth Tank Battalion attached to the Second Battalion.

I tell the radio operator: "I'll speak to him." I take the radio.

"Smith, Captain Holliday here. We need you to come back."

"Can do."

"Just come back to where you can fire into the roadblock area. Shoot wherever you think there might be a machine gun."

"Roger, out."

The tanks come back and set up south of the three-hundred-yard area held by the enemy on either side of the road. This makes it possible for many of those in the L and Headquarters Companies to get out.

Groups of men make a dash through the roadblock area, firing at any enemy they can see. Some make it, and some do not. Whenever a Chinese machine gun opens up, the tanks fire at it. The machine guns are in well-prepared dugouts, with riflemen in foxholes around them, so only a direct hit knocks them out. They are positioned to fire on the road. The tank fire, at least, limits the effectiveness of the Chinese.

A Better Way

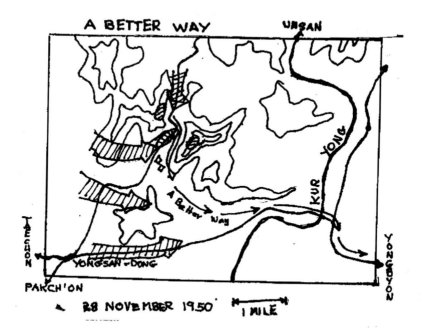

I decide there is a better way which would reduce our casualties. I know that the Chinese are dug in on the tops of the hills on either side of the roadblock and that three hundred yards of the road is in their firing zone. But the sides of the hills are covered with trees, so someone could move through those woods without being seen—or at least without being seen clearly. Only the command group and the rear guard (I Company) remain in the Pass of No Return.

I go over to LTC Lee, the battalion commander, and say: "I think we can get more men out if we go out on the side of that hill," I point to the east hill, "rather than attacking through the roadblock."

"It'll be defended. A single file can be ambushed and can't fight back," he answers.

239

"True, but it's the best way to get these men out. If we don't move right now, they are going to be either dead or prisoners. I'll lead the way."

Thus starts a single file of the remnant of the "lost battalion."

I pick a path a little higher than halfway up the hill. I do not think the Chinese on the top of the hill will be able to see us there, and I think those in the roadblock area will not be looking up that high. I know that I might run into some Chinese, since they might have outposts on the hillside as Colonel Lee suggested. I start walking with my carbine ready and with the men in my intelligence section directly behind me. Sergeant Graham moves up to just a few feet behind me. All of them have their M-1s ready. There is some rifle fire down at the roadblock. Every now and then I hear the *BOOM, SWISH, WHUMMP* of a tank firing.

No one in the column behind me says a word. It is all very peaceful. Just a walk in the woods. But I keep looking ahead. We could be ambushed at any moment. I know if I can get past the three hundred yards of the roadblock, it will be all clear. I keep looking down through the trees at the burnt-out vehicles in the ditches on the side of the road. There are still a few men trying to run through the roadblock and occasionally a rifle shot. But it really does not seem like we are in combat. There is a dreamlike quality to all of it. But I know it could turn violent in a second. I can hear the crunch of leaves under my boots. Finally, when I look at the road, I see that I have passed the roadblock area! I turn to look at Graham and smile. He smiles back and comes up next to me.

"Sergeant, it wasn't very smart of you to get so close to me," I say with a smile.

"Yes, sir, I know that."

"If we had run into anything, both of us would have been killed."

"I know that."

After a few minutes walking together, I ask, "Why did you do it?"

"Well, sir, as I see it, the odds are that neither of us is going to get out of here alive. And whenever I go, I want to be proud of myself."

I ask myself, "Where do we get such wonderful men? Where do they get their inner compass?" There is no flash of light, no blast of trumpets, no hum of meditation. There are only the familiar sights and sounds of soldiers moving from one place to the next.

Yet here at the turning point for Korea's future I realize that long-term success does not come from military might; on the road to Yongbyon, I realize that it comes from ideological superiority. As others have long known, winning all of your battles is not supreme excellence; the goal is to achieve order and satisfaction without fighting. The superior means is not the adversarial approach in which the goal is to neutralize any opponents, but rather to use any means necessary to maintain stability through equilibrium.

We walk over some low hills and see the road to Yongsan-dong. The command group joins me. I Company is more or less getting organized as they move along.

Near the tanks, we meet some men from regiment waiting to tell everyone that Yongsan-dong has been evacuated. We learn that the regimental command group, the artillery, and the First Battalion have moved from Yongsan-dong after midnight of 27–28 November to the east side of the Kur Yong River near the walled city of Yongbyon. I understand why I had been unable to get effective artillery support. We are told we should assemble at Yongbyon, and we do.

In recent years, Yongbyon has become well known for its nuclear processing plant.

In Yongbyon, the battalion is able to reorganize on 28–29 November. Survivors of K Company join us. I have no idea of how many of the battalion were killed or captured during these two days of being the "lost battalion."

The Battle for North Korea (24–28 November)

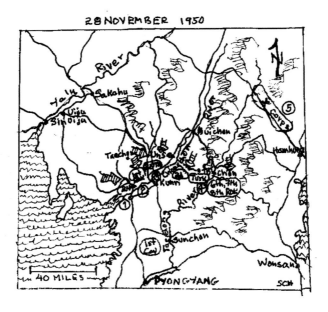

(1) Twenty-Fourth Division pulls back to defensive positions on the west (left) side of the bridgehead north of the Ch'ongch'on River and ties in with the First ROK

Division. (2) The First ROK Division is fighting just north of the Ch'ongch'on River, after a retreat of twelve miles from Taech'on. (3) Twenty-Fifth Division forms the east (right) side of the bridgehead north of the Ch'ongch'on River. (4) Turkish Brigade and ROK Divisions are under heavy attacks as the Chinese advance down the Taedong River valley. (5) X Corps is withdrawing from the Chosin Reservoir.

Another part of the main attack by the Chinese during 24–28 November is against the First ROK Division near Taech'on. The assaults start after dark on 25 November and continue all night. They attempt to drive a wedge between the First ROK and the Twenty-Fifth Division. Although the Twenty-Fifth Division holds its position, the First ROK Division falls back one mile during the night. During the daylight of 26 November, the First ROK Division recoils to advance three miles—to the outskirts of Taech'on—by dark.

On the night of 25–26 November, there are secondary attacks against the Twenty-Fourth Division on the left (west) of the First ROK Division, but they are not as strong as those against the First ROK, Twenty-Fifth, and Second Divisions. During daylight on 26 November, there are only patrols and probes against the Twenty-Fourth Division. Four horsemen are spotted by the Twenty-Seventh British Brigade, which gallop off when challenged.

The third part of the main attack is against the Second Division, ten miles from Kunu-ri. The Chinese drive down the Ch'ongch'on valley during the night of 25–26 November. They make frontal assaults against the frontline companies. At 0230 most of these attacks are stopped after heavy casualties. However, other Chinese units pass through gaps to attack units in the rear. During daylight on 26 November, the Second Division rebuilds its defenses.

Twenty-Ninth British and Turkish Brigades, from the Eighth Army reserve, are rushed forward to bolster the divisions under stress.

By noon of 26 November, the Chinese secondary attacks have inundated all of the South Korean divisions on the right (east) flank of the Eighth Army and have moved ten miles south to Tokch'on, blocking the ROK's supply route. The ROK Divisions fold, but by late afternoon they attempt to establish new defensive positions. Before 2100 hours, the Chinese control the Tokch'on area. The Turkish Brigade is to proceed to Tokch'on to protect the right flank of the Second Division from an attack down the Taedong River valley.[28]

The Turkish Brigade is in a defensive position on the east (right) flank, eight miles south of the Second Division. Just after midnight, the Chinese hit them with their full strength, and the men in long gray coats fight back with their bayonets, but in the end, what is left of the Turkish Brigade moves southwest to establish another blocking position.

The Seventh and Eighth ROK Divisions, to the right of the Second Division, retreat twenty miles to positions south of Tokch'on. The Sixth ROK Division moves up to give them support. The collapse of the ROK Divisions exposes the right flank of the Second Division, allowing the Chinese to start a flanking movement around the Eighth Army down the Taedong valley. Near Tokch'on, many CCF troops move south and southwest in small groups through gullies, down ridgelines, and over roads and trails.

In Tokyo, there is concern that the collapse of the ROK Divisions on the right flank of the Eighth Army might be exploited. The estimate of Chinese strength opposite the Eighth Army is raised from 54,000 to 101,000. On 26 November, Tokyo tells Washington, "Should the enemy elect to fight in the interior valleys, a slowing down of the United Nations offensive may result." This message makes it clear that Tokyo is unaware of the true situation along the Ch'ongch'on River.

The Chinese prepare to continue their second phase offensive of their main attack against the Eighth Army and to contain X Corps in the mountains so that it cannot influence the critical battle against the Eighth Army. The Eighth Army continues to retreat, but hopes to establish a defense north of Pyongyang.

---

[28] The Chinese Fortieth and Thirty-Eighth Armies continue their attack down the Ch'ongch'on River against the Second Division. The Ninth Regiment has to withdraw across the Ch'ongch'on River. The Thirty-Eighth Regiment fights off repeated assaults. In the afternoon they start to withdraw; the road north of Kunu-ri becomes bumper-to-bumper vehicles.

CHAPTER EIGHTEEN

DOWN TO PYONGYANG

29 November–6 December 1950

In the walled city of Yongbyon on 28–29 November, the Third Battalion, Thirty-Fifth Regiment is put back together. We have no idea that in future years this place will become well known as a nuclear processing plant for *Chosun Minjujui Inmun Kongwhakuk* (North Korean People's Republic). There is snow, and it is a bitter winter. But it seems that the Chinese, not us, are the "Divine Warriors." But now we know that warriors are not developed in ease and safety. Only through experience of suffering and trial with death ever present can duty be inspired, the inner compass be strengthened, and camaraderie be achieved.

All of those who escaped from the Pass of No Return have to cope with their near-death experiences.

These are brutal, bitter, nasty, hard times. As he rests in Yongbyon, Junior Long turns to thoughts of Sheryl Raburn to free his mind of the chaos, suffering, and death he had seen. He remembered Sheryl holding him tight, spreading her legs slightly while pushing her crotch toward him. As a good southern girl she considered sex a forbidden fruit and struggled against her feelings. Junior had to arouse her slowly. But after tasting that fruit, she became a violent storm of passion that would overwhelm him. It was not the reduction of tension that Junior remembered, but the union of fulfillment and the potential of life with Sheryl. Yet he did wonder if Sheryl could keep her desires in check until he returned or if she was enjoying the forbidden fruit with others. As he starts the march south, he wonders if he will ever see Sheryl again.

Going South

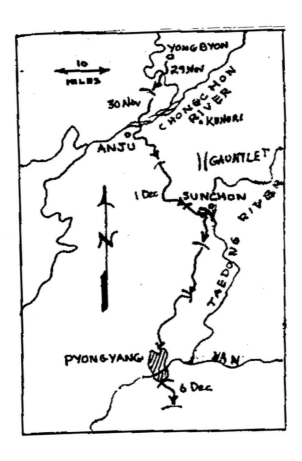

Late in the afternoon of 29 November, we leave Yongbyon and march toward the Ch'ongch'on River. Before midnight, the Third Battalion is in a defensive position a few miles north of where the Fifth Regimental Combat Team is holding a bridgehead on the north side of the river. Other units of the division are crossing. During the night of 29–30 November, Chinese patrols repeatedly fire at us. They know our every move. It is amazing how close they follow. We have to constantly be on guard. However, they are never able to launch an attack against us or to get behind us. For the next week, we are on the move. We march, ride trucks, dig in, get shot at, fight back, and are cold.

Near Anju, the road is packed with trucks. If the enemy has any aircraft, they will have a field day. It is a dry cold. With our winter clothing, it is not bad. After we cross the Ch'ongch'on River on 30 November, the Third Battalion is given the mission of providing the rear guard for the division. The Chinese are constantly probing us. We return fire. That is all that happens. They seem to be only interested in knowing our positions, not in actually attacking us. Fortunately the patrols only use rifles; rarely do we receive incoming artillery.

From Sunchon to Pyongyang, we continue as the rear guard. In our first position just south of Sunchon, we can see that city burning. Also, the buildings across the Taedong River are burning brightly. Men from the Turkish Brigade, the British Brigade, and the Second Division all pull back through our position immediately after going through what became known as "the Gauntlet": several miles of the road south of Kunu-ri.

We are able to hear firsthand about many of the events which are later recorded by S.L.A. Marshall in *The River and the Gauntlet: Defeat of the Eighth Army by the Chinese Communist Forces, November, 1950, in the Battle of the Chongchon River, Korea*. The Chinese trap many on this stretch of road and punish them. As they come through our position, they seem bewildered. Most are frightened, lonely individuals moving in a mob without equipment. Some talk about what had happened; others just stare and say nothing. Many learn that you have a better chance of surviving if you fight than if you are fleeing in panic.

Chinese Success

What happened north of the Ch'ongch'on River made the reasons for the Chinese success clear. First, they had been able to hide many men until they were ready to attack. Second, they had detailed and accurate intelligence on the units they faced. Third, they used the maneuver of inundation: finding soft spots, skipping through gaps, and taking up prepared positions behind units in order to destroy them as they withdrew. Fourth, they traveled light—which was a short-term advantage. Fifth, they moved at night on trails, not exclusively on roads.

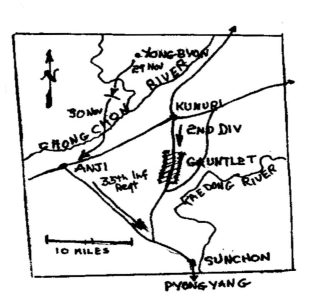

That the Chinese have won a major battle and that MacArthur's dream of a military victory has been lost cannot be denied. That some UN forces are no longer effective is true. Yet the magnitude of the success and failure is questionable. A good measure would be the number of casualties and equipment lost—yet this has never been established. Data is all over the landscape, but the losses are not trivial on either side.

In many US units—certainly in the Thirty-Fifth Regiment—there is confidence in their ability to prevail in combat, regardless of the odds against them. The retreats will continue, and with the X Corps useless on the east coast, there is no longer much hope that the Chinese can be stopped short of Seoul. The situation can be likened to the US 1943 defeat at Kasserine Pass in Tunisia. We know that defeat had been reversed within three months, and we expect to do the same.

We know the Chinese are excellent infantrymen and favor large-scale offensive operations but lack the logistical capability and firepower necessary to destroy the Eighth Army. On the other hand, the Chinese have their soldiers (and many people around the world) convinced they are the "good guys" fighting against imperialists. The Chinese are fighting, and winning, on the ideological battlefield. But on the military battlefield in Korea, superior firepower, airpower, logistics, and mobility allow the UN forces to regroup and rebuild.

The Battle near the Chosin Reservoir (27 November–6 December)

On the east coast, X Corps is having more trouble with the weather and terrain than with the enemy. There are sub-zero temperatures in the snowy mountains. The Taebaek Mountains prevent

X Corps from attacking the CCF moving down the Taedong River corridor to envelop the right flank of the Eighth Army. The Chinese plan is to contain X Corps so that it cannot influence its attempt to destroy the Eighth Army with its main attack.

Two task forces of the Seventh Division relieve the Fifth Marine Regiment on the eastern side of the Changjin (Chosin) Reservoir, but four miles separate the two[29] (#3 on map of 27–29 Nov 50). Most of the First Marine Division is still near Hagaru-ri, but units of the Seventh Marine Regiment are moving slowly up the western side of the reservoir toward Yudam-ni. Hagaru-ri is a village just south of the reservoir (#1 on map). Third Battalion, First Marine Regiment is south of Hagaru-ri in reserve. The reservoir is in the middle of a four-thousand-foot plateau. There is a steep and difficult sixty-four-mile road between Hagaru-ri and Hungnam (#2 on map). Since 16 November, engineers have been working to improve this road.

On 27 November, the two marine regiments continue their slow move toward Yudam-ni against light resistance. However, they receive some rifle fire most of the afternoon. At 2100 hours, the lead companies are attacked. During the night other Chinese bypass the lead units to attack marines on the road.

On hearing that the marines are under fire, Task Force Faith,[30] on the east side of the reservoir, goes into a tight defense for the night (#3 on map). It is planning to move forward the next day, but it is attacked at 2200. The platoon on a picket line is hit first, and there are no survivors. Then the whole task force is under attack until dawn, as is the other task force.[31]

On 28 November, the Chinese establish a roadblock on the MSR south of Hagaru-ri (#2 on map) and another roadblock behind TF Faith, which is then assaulted from three directions (#3 on map). They receive no support from the marines.

On 29 November, all forces in the reservoir area are placed under the command of the First Marine Division. The CG (Smith) is told to bring them together near Hagaru-ri and to secure twenty-two miles of the MSR south of Hagaru-ri. At 0630, the marines restore the Hagaru-ri perimeter after probes during the night. The two battalions the marines send to clear the roadblock on the MSR south of Hagaru-ri fail. The Hagaru-ri perimeter is surrounded, and the marines decide no other relief forces will be sent out. The marines commandeer units of the Thirty-First Regiment en route to the two task forces on the east side of the reservoir and incorporate them into the Hagaru-ri and the Koto-ri defensive perimeters.

South of Hagaru-ri, the British Marines are ambushed as they leave Koto-ri on the MSR (#2 on map on next page). Air strikes allow them to continue in the afternoon, yet they are stopped again before they reach Hagaru-ri. After dark, four hundred of them make it to Hagaru-ri, yet many are caught in "Hell Fire Valley."

For twelve hours, beginning at 1800 hours on 28 November, Chinese jab at the perimeter of TF Faith east of the reservoir. There are many casualties. By 0300 on the night of 29–30 November, TF Faith has used up most of its ammunition. There are twenty-one CCF Battalions attacking the Seventh Division units on the east side of the reservoir, yet they receive no support from the marines. TF Faith is ordered to move south. Cargo is taken out of trucks to make room for the one hundred plus wounded. The Chinese increase their fire as the task force assembles on the road. Starting at 0430 hours on 30 November, the flank security on either side of the road stumbles in the darkness over snow-covered ground. A Siberian tiger kills one soldier. They go three-quarters of the way to the other task force[32] without opposition. Then they hit a roadblock.

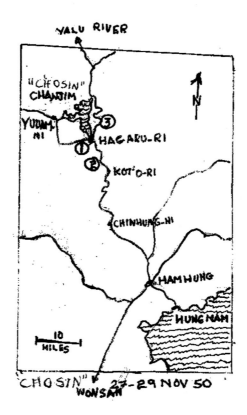

Chinese forces attack on both sides of the Changjin (Chosin) Reservoir. The marines on the west side withdraw from Yudam-ni toward Hagaru-ri. At daylight on 30 November, TF Faith takes intense fire. After a firefight, they get past the roadblock and at 1230 reach the other task force, which then becomes part of TF Faith. For these units of the Seventh Division to be saved, a relief force with tanks must break through with an attack from Hagaru-ri. However, that is not to be since the marines have decided all combat units should remain in the Hagaru-ri perimeter.

South of Hagaru-ri many of the British Marines are still surrounded in "Hell Fire Valley." Some are captured. Their casualties exceed three hundred, and they also lose seventy-five trucks. During the night of 30 November, the Chinese attack the Hagaru-ri perimeter, but they are beaten back before daylight.

Task Force Faith has been surrounded by thousands of Chinese for two days (#3 on map). The Corsairs fly cover during daylight and even at night by moonlight; they napalm, rocket, and machine-gun the enemy. It is very cold. There are many dead and wounded; the dead are stacked up in trucks. Many of the wounded go back into the fight. There is no hope of a relief force being sent from Hagaru-ri. Faith decides to break out of the perimeter and move to Hagaru-ri. As the column leaves their perimeter, they are attacked by the Chinese, and by mistake they are napalmed by an American plane. Two miles down the road, they are stopped at a destroyed bridge by intensive fire. They fight back, but the column falls apart, and the men scatter. Chinese snipers pick off soldiers. COL Faith is killed. Survivors straggle into Hagaru-ri for the next three days, almost all of them coming off the frozen reservoir. Of the 2,500 originally east of Chosin, less than 1,000 make it back to Hagaru-ri, and of those, only 385 are fit for duty.

After failing to take Hagaru-ri during the night of 30 November, the Chinese pull back, and there are no attacks for four days. The weather is hurting the Chinese more than the Americans. Because the supply road to Hamhung is cut, all supplies to the Americans at the reservoir must be delivered by airdrops from C-119s and C-47s. However, in the afternoon of 1 December, a C-47 lands successfully on a makeshift airstrip.

The role played by the Seventh Division east of the Chosin Reservoir is largely unknown. They[33] hold off twenty-one battalions advancing down the eastern side of the reservoir while the First Marine Division is fighting those on the western side. The army units receive limited air support, no artillery support, no logistical support, no medevac, and no relief force from Hagaru-ri. Overwhelming Chinese numbers finally destroy those army units. If the army units had not stopped those twenty-one battalions, the Chinese would have trapped the Fifth and Seventh Marine Regiments. Then the heroic story of Chosin, which has been told so often, would have been very different. Few marines are aware of what these army soldiers did for them, and those east of Chosin have never received the credit they deserve.

The Fifth and Seventh Marine Regiments move toward the Hagaru-ri perimeter through ice and snow. They must overcome roadblocks and rifle fire along the way, but the marines on the west side of Chosin are stronger than the enemy they face. The Chinese here are less aggressive than they had been. Many of the Chinese soldiers are now starving, sick, and freezing. Some are found huddled together in the snow, trying only to stay alive. The marines fight their way toward Hagaru-ri on a narrow winding road through the mountains. They are often shot at. They carry their wounded. It is very cold. For flank security, they have to often leave the road to walk on ridges through snow drifts. In the late afternoon, the men of the advance guard rejoice when they reach a pass from which they can see the Hagaru-ri airstrip, eleven miles away.

When the men of the marines reach the Hagaru-ri perimeter, they are dirty, hungry, and exhausted (#1 on map of 27–29 Nov 50). However, they march in as proud marines. There have been too many casualties—many from the freezing weather—at Hagaru-ri to be evacuated by helicopters and light aircraft. At night, the temperature drops to twenty-four degrees below zero. But after C-47s are able to land, some 1,300 casualties are evacuated, and 500 replacements arrive.

The withdrawal from Hagaru-ri begins. They must fight their way to Hamhung, but they have good close air support to help them. The route runs from Hagaru-ri to Koto-ri and then down to Chinhung-ni, where they are to meet the relief column coming up from Hamhung. As the marines and army survivors move down the MSR, they clear hills and ridges on each side of the road at the same time a tank-infantry team attacks down the road. On the sides of the road are piles of dead frozen Chinese soldiers, and in trucks are the frozen bodies of American drivers sitting behind the steering wheel where they were killed. By moving during the night of 6–7 December, the lead column reaches Koto-ri. By 1000 hours on 7 December, everyone clears Hagaru-ri except the rear guard, which follows after destroying all supplies. By midnight, fifteen thousand men are near Koto-ri (#2 on map).

There is still a sixteen-foot chasm in the road three miles south of Koto-ri. Because the CCF controls the road, trucks cannot bring the needed treadway bridge up from Hamhung. Army engineers and air force riggers are able to assemble, test, and air-drop eight sections of a treadway bridge into Koto-ri. As the column moves from Koto-ri toward Hamhung, there is vicious fighting for the peak controlling the Funchilin Pass. At 0800, a relief force of the First Battalion, First Marine Regiment moves north to the Funchilin Pass to meet the Seventh Marine Regiment and army units attacking south from Koto-ri. A snowstorm keeps close air support on the ground, and there is strong Chinese resistance. However, this pass must be taken. The sky clears. The marine and army units coming south on the MSR reach the bridge site at noon. CCF along the MSR fire on convoys but lack the strength to stop those moving toward the Funchilin Pass. The marines coming north take the mountain that overlooks the Funchilin Pass at 1500. The trucks with the treadway bridge sections arrive shortly after the site is cleared. Three hours later, the bridge is in place, and the trucks begin to cross.

The Seventh Marine Regiment, the trains, and the remainder of the Seventh Division—interspersed with refugees—pass the bridge site during the night of 9–10 December, and the following day, the Fifth Marine Regiment and the rear guard are attacked as they withdraw south. There are forty army and marine tanks in the rear guard, but all do not make it across the bridge.

The Battle for North Korea by the Eighth Army (27 November–6 December)

During the night of 28–29 November, those in the bridgehead north of the Ch'ongch'on River[34] start their withdrawal. All day, vehicles pack the roads, cross the river, and move toward Sunchon. It is cold, but dry. During the night of 29–30 November and the following day, the bridgehead is under constant attack. Refugees on the roads interfere with the troop movements and offer the enemy a way to infiltrate soldiers to the rear of UN positions. They are not allowed to use the bridges. Campfires flicker on the banks near the bridges; some attempt to wade across through the frigid water.

The Chinese attacks down the Ch'ongch'on valley cause the Second Division to retreat to Won-ni and Kunu-ri. The Chinese press their attacks toward Kunu-ri from the east and northeast and their envelopment around the right flank where the ROK Divisions had been. Three battalions of the Turkish Brigade are surrounded. Due to a lack of communication, the Turkish Brigade CO knows nothing of the attack. With tank support, the three battalions withdraw, but the Chinese follow them. This flanking movement then moves down the Taedong valley toward Sunchon. On the evening of 29 November, the Twenty-Third Regiment is north of Kunu-ri, and the Thirty-Eighth Regiment is authorized to withdraw from Kunu-ri to Sunchon—but the route is not specified. In the chilly moonlight, the Second Division starts to move from Kunu-ri into the unknown hell of the Gauntlet.

During the night of 28–29 November, the lead units of the Chinese flanking maneuver down the Taedong valley reach the main supply route (MSR) south of Kunu-ri and ambush some vehicles. Then they start to establish roadblocks. At daybreak, the Chinese ambush a supply convoy of the Turkish Brigade. MPs sent to investigate are killed. However, even though they hold positions covering one thousand yards of the MSR, the Chinese do not fire on tanks sent to clear the area. They wait in hiding for their prey.

The British Twenty-Ninth Brigade sets up a blocking position north of Sunchon and south of a pass on the road to Kunu-ri. During the night of 29–30 November, there are many burnt-out vehicles between Kunu-ri and Sunchon; the road is clogged.

During the night of 29–30, most of the Second Division begins its withdrawal from Kunu-ri to Sunchon. The lead battalion expects to reach a roadblock by 0700 and is prepared to clear it. However, they find a roadblock a mile north of where contact is expected. Actually, there are many roadblocks along the MSR to where the British have their blocking position south of the pass. The Second Division is unable to clear the MSR to the pass. In this one day, the division loses 3,758 men and most of its equipment. The losses would have been even greater if it had not been for close air support. All day aircraft fly up and down the road strafing enemy positions. When the planes are strafing, the Chinese stop firing and hide.

Southeast of Kunu-ri, the Turkish Brigade is surrounded twice, suffering many casualties as it fights its way back. Two battalions of the Second Division are sent to aid the Turks, but they never reach them. The Twenty-Third Regiment goes west from Kunu-ri to Anju rather than taking the MSR; it reaches Sunchon with few casualties.

Those in the bridgehead north of the Ch'ongch'on River are still being attacked, yet they are able to hold their positions. They continue to withdraw through Anju to Sunchon. After the last troops cross, the bridges are blown; thousands of shivering refugees are left stranded on the north side of the Ch'ongch'on River to soon again be in the hands of Kim Il-sung.

The Twenty-Fifth Division establishes a blocking position just north of Sunchon to allow the rest of the Eighth Army to move south toward Pyongyang. There is talk of a new defensive line being established north of Pyongyang.

Much of the Second Division is very badly mauled in the Gauntlet. As dazed soldiers stagger out, they tell us many stories of heroism, tragedy, and wasted lives. Repeatedly they tell of buddies being shot and dying as they look on. Some have glazed eyes and cannot speak. They keep coming; all are exhausted, and some are near death. We are told of those too wounded to move being run over by tanks. Many soldiers had an aura of frenzy, fear, and desperation. The Chinese have defeated them, and it shows. Most will never forget coming through the Gauntlet.

The Eighth Army delays the Chinese as best it can. For some units, it is orderly. They wait in blocking positions until the Chinese organize an attack, and then they move back using artillery to cover their withdrawal. However, for other units, it is a disorderly retreat. Some men lose their units to become frightened individuals in a mob of refugees and soldiers just trying to "get away." What is left of the Second Division and Turkish Brigade move to just north of Seoul to reorganize.

The Chinese have separated the Eighth Army in the west from X Corps on the east coast. The CCF is moving (a) down the Taedong River, (b) down the center of Korea, and (c) toward Wonsan. To keep from being flanked, the Eighth Army must continue to move south. X Corps is isolated.

I had never expected to see the disintegration of a US Army Division. On the Pusan perimeter, I saw men from the Twenty-Fourth Regiment run away when attacked. I know of units that have "bugged out." I have talked with many soldiers who had walked for days through the hills after their unit had been overrun. But these did not prepare me for the mob of frightened, lost bodies stumbling past me. It is true that the Twenty-Third Regiment made it out in good shape, and during the coming months, the Second Division will be reorganized into an effective fighting unit, yet here I see only distress, disorientation, and defeat.

It is decided that the Eighth Army is unable to establish a defense above Pyongyang and Wonsan, since the Chinese have enough troops to turn the flank of any such sea-to-sea line. A spokesman states: "We are trading space for time."

In Pyongyang, a city of three hundred thousand, the Communists distribute leaflets that proclaim: "You shall be free from the enemy soon." There is evidence of a strong "fifth column" in Pyongyang. Removing supplies from Pyongyang is hindered by the priority on locomotives for trains carrying casualties, by heavy demands on trucks for troop movements, and by damage caused during earlier air campaigns. From the port of Chinnamp'o LSTs, Japanese ships, US Navy transports, and Korean sailboats evacuate casualties, prisoners, and materiel sent from Pyongyang. They land either at Inch'on (port personnel, rations, and petroleum products) or Pusan (patients, prisoners, and supplies). Most of the materiel and supplies evacuated from Pyongyang are shipped to depots at Kaesong and around Seoul. Some are kept on railcars, which can be used to resupply combat divisions as needed. With air superiority, fighters and bombers continue to attack any enemy spotted moving toward Pyongyang.

Pyongyang echoes with the sound of demolition charges as the Eighth Army carries out its pledge to "destroy things of military value to the enemy." Fire and smoke billow over the city. Communist supporters are now active in Pyongyang. As the word gets out that Pyongyang will not be defended, refugees start to stream south. They are fear-stricken, and it is cold. Government officials have all vanished. Roads are choked. There is a light snow. As we move through this city, it is lifeless. Although we know there are people in most of the buildings, and there are the sounds of war in the distance, there is an awe-inspiring silence around us. We can hear the echo of our vehicles but hear no other sounds in the midst of so many buildings.

The Defeat

The last week of November has been a disaster for the Eighth Army and MacArthur. It is not just that the final drive for victory before Christmas is gone, nor even the men, materiel, and territory lost—it is the realization that there is no certainty that the Chinese can be stopped. The dark cloud is knowing that the US has strategic and tactical disadvantages in land battles on the Asian mainland. Nuclear weapons, both strategic and tactical, might offset these disadvantages, but do Americans have the will to use them?

The American idea of victory through the use of overwhelming firepower on the critical mass of the enemy's armed forces has its limitations. Poor intelligence plus skillful use of deception and concealment by the enemy puts UN units at risk. Reliance on technology and road-based mobility does not always mean superior tactical mobility. The failure to understand the maneuver of inundation causes many casualties and the loss of much equipment when units in the rear are assaulted. Having superior firepower is of little benefit if it cannot be used to kill the enemy. And the Americans fail to understand that the Chinese are thinking in terms of ideological conflict more than of conventional War.

A month earlier, the opportunity for stability and peace in Korea was within grasp. Then an agreement to divide North Korea and South Korea at the narrow neck of the Korean Peninsula was possible. That opportunity was lost in a quest for a conventional War victory. After the Chinese attack, in Washington a decision is made that it is no longer US policy to unify all of Korea; the US is willing to again have Korea divided at the 38th Parallel. In time, this decision will be recognized as a strategic error. A return to a divided Korea at the 38th Parallel will: (1) allow China to claim that it has defeated the US, (2) prevent stability on the Korean Peninsula, and (3) allow North Korea to rise again as a troublemaker.

In June 1951, UN forces will be strong enough to move back to the narrow neck of Korea, but the UN, the media, the American public, and the US political elite want an end to "the War." The enemy is never persons or armed forces, per se, but the ideals about good and bad, right and wrong, virtue and sin that guide individuals. Thus in ideological conflict it is will that determines if the outcome is success or failure. Peace and prosperity are not the norm; history's long record shows conflict, because of passions and desires, is the norm—and it is the violent conflict of Warfare and War that determines the direction history takes.

During the Withdrawal

During our rearguard action south of Sunchon, the ground is covered with snow, and more keeps falling. It is not unpleasant for a few hours, but night and day in it is different. It would be like staying outside for days in Wisconsin during January.

Living conditions in many ways are the best since the drive to the Yalu started on 24 November. Although we rarely have hot food, we still have plenty of C rations and water, and we are not hungry. Our clothing can handle the bitter cold.

Although we do not know it at the time, the Chinese suffer much more because they lack the boots and clothing we have. They have twice the number of casualties from frostbite as they have from UN weapons.

At night we can make some use of the native huts with the under-floor heating. Or we can sleep under piles of straw and hay. There are no trees; everything is bleak and brown. It certainly is not pleasant, but it isn't too bad. There is one improvement. No longer is there the smell of night soil—human excrement used as fertilizer. Only when close to the barrels in which it is stored is the smell noticeable. Also, we are able to move faster than the Chinese, so they are never able to assault our position or get behind us to set up roadblocks.

We have learned how to handle the Chinese. Our battalion is still an effective fighting unit, although others we see move in disarray and are incapable of stopping anyone. This is probably why we are the rear guard. When we are in a defense position during the daytime, we often see twelve soldiers trotting down the road toward us with a truck following them. At times the truck catches up with the soldiers, and others from the truck take their place. Whenever the trotters get close, we fire at them, and they disappear. The truck hides. In time, more Chinese appear on the road, and then patrols are sent against our position.

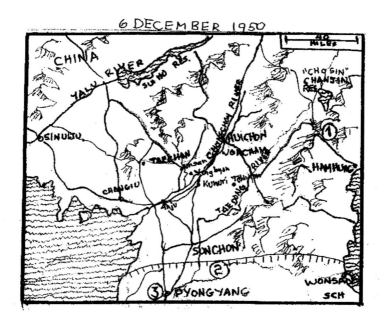

(1) Marines are trapped near Changjin (Chosin) River. (2) It is determined that the Eighth Army cannot successfully defend a line above Pyongyang and Wonsan. (3) Pyongyang is evacuated.

We no longer have a fire on a hill at night behind us to give us advance warning—there are no hills. However, we can tell from the intensity of the patrol action during the day and early evening when the Chinese are getting ready for an attack. We then pull back after dark to a prepared position a mile or so down the road. We leave some flashlights on our old position and have an outpost some two hundred yards away to tell us when it is attacked—which is usually around midnight. When this happens, we pound our old position with artillery. Sometimes we walk in the still of the night to waiting trucks. Then we travel some distance, passing marching Americans and Koreans until we establish a new defensive position and watch the disorderly and demoralized withdraw.

The Rest of the Winter

The largest ambush of American forces in history had taken place. The euphoria of the rapid move through North Korea in September and October had now turned into gloom and despair. As Homer Bigart wrote in the *New York Herald Tribune*: "UN forces are now paying the initial price for the unsound decision to launch an offensive north of the peninsula's narrow neck."

If we had been the "Divine Warriors," we would have established a defensive line on the Ch'ongch'on River and extended it across the neck of Korea to Hungnam. Then North Korea would have become a small, poor, mountainous buffer between China and a prosperous new Republic of Korea. But poor intelligence and a failure in strategic thinking prevented this.

General Ridgway blamed it on "MacArthur's eagerness to accomplish his assigned mission—a mission of which he had pleaded—the destruction of all hostile armed forces on the peninsula." And to "MacArthur's all-too-human weaknesses... Yet it should have been clear to anyone that his own refusal to accept the mounting evidence of massive Chinese intervention was largely responsible for the reckless scattering of our forces all over the map of Korea...But how could any man, not obsessed with his own reputation, have persisted in misinterpreting detailed intelligence reports and actual events on the battlefield?" (*The Korean War*, pages 74–75.)

Eros, Death, and Morality in War and Warfare

Again the mysterious linkage between Eros (unity) and Thanatos (death) became apparent as soldiers and civilians move south. Throughout history during the chaos of War and Warfare, when the customs, traditions, laws, and structures of a stable society have broken down, those with the ability to use force have taken women and girls—and sometimes boys—to satisfy their sexual desires. All of the carnage at the end of November 1950 demanded a means of escape from death; many of the soldiers used memories of the past, but sometimes it was done through chance encounters with females also fleeing south seeking to escape death. Having gone through days and nights of hell when death could come any moment, all of those that survive need some way to keep healthy and functioning minds. When sex is not possible, or is insufficient, Eros is the default solution.

But replacing sex with Eros is not easy because of the secretions of testosterone that intensify masculine characteristics of warriors such as physical energy, aggressiveness, and combat camaraderie. This fact has always established a fundamental dualism that has been reflected in arts, philosophies, and beliefs. This is the birth of conscience in the inner compass of individuals that allows them to make decisions on the basis of what is good or bad, right or wrong, virtuous or sinful. The combining of sex and Eros is one of the ways of achieving equilibrium within this dualism.

Humans and humans alone have the possibility of such choices to avoid unconscious cruelty and brutality to others. At the same time, they are warriors able to survive through being effective in both War and Warfare. This ability is usually called morality, but use of the term morality introduces a fundamental dispute. The morality for War and Warfare differs from that appropriate for Peace, yet many politicians, lawyers, and intellectuals want to apply peacetime morality to conditions of War and Warfare. They think of morality as being the same at all times and in all places. It cannot be. On the other hand, it is necessary to avoid moral relativism, which allows individuals to determine morality based on their personal experience or narrative, because morality must be based on absolutes. Yet these moral absolutes must differ for conditions of Peace, Warfare, and War. The ability to resolve this fundamental challenge is what distinguishes humans from other animals that also struggle against nature, the elements, fate, and enemies. Warriors are able to resolve this challenge and can be successful in ideological conflict. Those humans that are unable to establish appropriate moral absolutes for conditions of Peace, War, and Warfare do not survive in ideological conflict.

During the retreat toward Pyongyang, Dan Kelly replayed in his mind thoughts of Sandy. He remembered simple kisses from her and his caressing her soft skin. For Dan, to be wrapped in a full embrace by Sandy's warm, soft body was pure bliss. He remembered and savored their bond that put him in touch with eternity and immortality. It was a creative force allowing Dan to confront the finite human condition all around him with its weakness and capriciousness—thereby retaining his mental health.

The Military Profession

From a strictly military point of view, the withdrawal is no doubt the correct strategy. Because of its exposed right flank, the withdrawal is necessary to prevent the destruction of the Eighth Army. This gained the time needed to revive morale and to bring in much-needed artillery and armor. However, those setting policy for the UN forces never did address the ideological conflict successfully. Both Ridgway and MacArthur were conventional soldiers who thought of War and Peace in dichotomous terms. They both considered the military's goal to be achieving victory. They considered success in War[35] to be a military victory (i.e., the destruction of the opposing armed forces). However, success in Warfare[36] is not military victory, it is stability (i.e., a climate of order and satisfaction in which no one is able, or willing, to use force to achieve political goals).

MacArthur and Ridgway were two of the greatest military professionals our country has ever had. Their intelligence, brilliance, military judgment, military skills, and personal courage are beyond question. Yet they were products of a military profession in the West as it had developed for some three hundred years—since the birth of the nation-state. They did not appreciate what the Chinese had known for thousands of years.

During 1958–1961 while working with the Republic of China (Nationalist Chinese) on Taiwan, I had an opportunity to learn more about this. Some of the officers involved in providing information to the Americans in 1950 told me they had repeatedly stated that the Chinese Communists would come into Korea if the US forces moved toward the Yalu. They knew that Mao wanted the world to see Communist China as a world power; fighting the Americans in Korea would accomplish this.

Also, China's coming to the aid of North Korea would demonstrate that they could no longer be exploited by Western powers. Mao wanted to replace the Soviet Union as the big brother of North Korea and to challenge Russia's status as the leader of the entire communist world; going to the aid of North Korea, when the Soviet Union would not send troops, would accomplish this.

But the information provided by the Nationalist Chinese was rejected. The United States, and MacArthur specifically, ignored the fact that the Nationalist Chinese had excellent sources within the Chinese Communist armed forces. In fact, many of those to be deployed into Korea were former members of the Nationalist Army who had defected to the Communists in 1949.

Why was this ignored? MacArthur claimed to "understand the Oriental mind"; however, the truth is this was one of his weaknesses since he was convinced that he knew more than others about something that he did not fully understand.

In the end, the Communist leadership was able to have Americans destroy many of the Chinese they supported in World War II, but whose loyalty to Mao was questionable—an excellent example of Chinese strategic thinking. The Chinese were able to manipulate the US decision-making process and to take advantage of the antiwar feelings of the American people.

In 2007 David Halberstam reported in *The Coldest Winter* (334–391) what I learned about this in 1960.

While on Taiwan, I had an opportunity to study *The Art of War* by Sun Tzu, which was written in 500 BC, and how Sun Tzu's ideas were adapted and used by Mao Tse-tung to gain control of China. Moreover, I had a chance to discuss the long history of these ideas at length with many Chinese military

professionals and governmental officials. It became clear to me
that Sun Tzu and Mao were not only writing about what we call
war (i.e., conventional War between the symmetric armed forces
of rival political groups). Sun Tzu did discuss it and so did Mao,
referring to it as mobile warfare. But both were also concerned with
what is accurately called Warfare or Irregular Warfare—and what
Mao refers to as guerrilla warfare. As Sun Tzu said:

*All warfare is based on deception. Hence, when able to attack, we
must seem unable; when using our forces, we must seem inactive;
when we are near, we must make the enemy believe that we are
away; when far away, we must make him believe we are near.
Hold out baits to entice the enemy. Feign disorder, and crush him.*
(Part 1)

*In the practical art of war, the best thing of all is to take the
enemy's country whole and intact; to shatter and destroy it is not
so good...Hence to fight and conquer in all your battles is not
supreme excellence; supreme excellence consists in breaking the
enemy's resistance without fighting.* (Part 3)

Excursion into Pyongyang

By 6 December, we are in a defensive position a few miles south
of Pyongyang. We receive word that the northwestern part of the
city has been abandoned; the bridges over the Taedong River have
been destroyed.

A tank unit with the British Twenty-Ninth Brigade is holding
the southeast side of the Taedong River where their engineers have
destroyed the bridges and are now destroying warehouses. I drive
up to the southeast edge of the city where some US engineers are
preparing to blow up a bridge over a small stream.

"When do you plan to blow it?" I ask.

"Just as soon as the Brits come out. They are the only thing left. I wish they would quit dicking around."

On the other side of the bridge is a train track, with a string of boxcars and some flat cars loaded with new American tanks.

"What are tanks doing over there?" I ask.

"They're waiting for an engine. It's to take them out of here."

"How long have they been there?"

"Don't know. Maybe days." I look over and part of the city is burning.

Smoke rises in great pillars over the city. I decide to take a look around Pyongyang until the Centurion tanks of the Eighth Royal Irish Hussars come out. We cross the bridge. We have to detour around some exploding ammunition stocks. Then we come across the abandoned automotive repair shop of some US unit. We look around and pick up a few things we think the battalion might be able to use. Near it is a quartermaster food storage warehouse. It is burning. Most of the food has been destroyed. A few piles of cans are outside; Koreans are scampering all over the place. Any cans that have not burst open from the heat are quickly carried away.

The Koreans say there is a lot of stuff in the stadium. We drive over. Sure enough, there are row after row of boxes and cartons stacked around the track. Happily we drive in, only to be disappointed. Ammunition. Vast quantities of all types and kinds of ammunition. What would happen to it? Would it be used against us? Would our aircraft be sent to destroy it?

We can see our planes strafing on our side of the river. They are less than a mile away. Are they destroying valuable stocks, or had the Chinese crossed the river? I know it is time to get out of

Pyongyang. On the way back, we see a promising building; while inside, we hear tanks.

"The Brits are leaving. Drive back to the bridge," I say.

Before we reach the bridge where the engineers have their demolition ready, I see some men marching between that bridge and us. "What's this?" I think. I know all of our foot soldiers are to have been out several hours earlier. Is this a Chinese unit?

This is a time to be careful. We drive slowly toward the column of marching men. We have our weapons handy. I look carefully at them through my field glasses. They appear to be in American uniforms.

But it is still necessary to be cautious. The North Koreans have been known to wear captured uniforms during the daytime in order to achieve surprise. Perhaps the Chinese are doing the same. We drive closer.

I am now able to see their faces. They look like Americans, and I am relieved. We move closer, and I shout: "What unit?"

In a clear, unmistakable New Jersey twang came back, "Da Cav." I find out that this battalion of the First Cavalry Division had been forgotten. It never received the word to pull back. When they saw the British tanks leaving, they decided to get out. We drive beside the marching men to the bridge south of Pyongyang. Most of the tanks of the Irish Hussars have already crossed.

The engineers are eager to blow up the bridge and to head south. The train is now burning. The new tanks are still there. The engine never arrived. Will our aircraft be sent to destroy the tanks? One of the engineers says there is food in the boxcars. Since our trip into Pyongyang has been a bust, this is too much to pass up.

The first boxcar has stoves. The next is locked, and then we hit the jackpot: gallon cans of mixed nuts, mincemeat, and hard candy. This was all for Christmas dinners. Yet that car is burning. I climb in and throw down all we can carry in the jeep.

We drive triumphantly across the bridge as the last Americans to leave Pyongyang—careful to avoid the disgust in the eyes of the engineers. Pyongyang is burning. The last British Centurion crosses the bridge. The bridge explodes.

Several days later I go over to the British tankers who had been the last unit out of Pyongyang. Most of what they saw matched what I have seen; however, some of their stories are best forgotten. One lieutenant tells me of his attempt to save a South Korean hurt by one of his tanks. As he went to aid the man, a South Korean officer came up, took his pistol, and shot the helpless young soldier in the head. "Now we go," he said.

My Answer

Sometime during this retreat, I had time to answer my father's letter:

Dear Daddy,

I know your desire to get me out of danger is an expression of your love for me. This I will always cherish. But I do not want you to do anything to get me out of harm's way. It is my duty to serve until it is my turn to leave. If I should leave early someone else would have to take my place. That would not be right. Also I think I know how to do this better than most others. If I should leave early that advantage would be lost, and I believe that would result in unnecessary casualties.

I think I should stay as long as I am needed, even though I have no desire to be in harm's way. I do not think of it in terms of personal advantage—either through ensuring my personal safety or for career advancement. I consider what I am doing my duty. I will be happy to come back home, but only when it is my time without any influence being used on my behalf.

With all my love,

Sam Jr.

I received no reply. But my mother told me that my father— who was a lawyer and an ethicist but not a religious person— started to go to church with her and to pray every day.

After I returned, my parents gave me all of the correspondence. The final letter was to Uncle Bob:

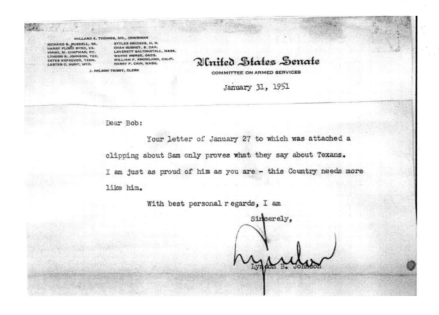

[29] First Battalion, Thirty-Second Regiment and Third Battalion, Thirty-First Regiment.

[30] First Battalion, Thirty-Second Regiment.

[31] Second Battalion, Thirty-First Regiment.

[32] Third Battalion, Thirty-First Regiment.

[33] The two battalions of the Seventh Division, Fifty-Second Field Artillery, and Fifteenth Anti-Aircraft Artillery (50 Quads).

[34] Twenty-Fourth, First ROK, and Twenty-Fifth Divisions.

[35] War is a condition in which the armed forces of states are engaged in conflict.

[36] Warfare, or Irregular Warfare, has many names; it is protracted conflict between non-state actors using all means possible to weaken or overthrow those in authority.

CHAPTER NINETEEN

DOWN TO SOUTH KOREA

7 December 1950–22 January 1951

The Chinese move into Pyongyang on 7 December. Three days later, the Eighth Army attempts to consolidate positions south of Pyongyang but north of Sariwon.

8 December 1950

(1) Eighth Army south of Pyongyang but north of Sariwon. (2) The marines move from Hagaru-ri to Hamhung. (3) The Seventh Division and South Koreans pull back to Iwon for evacuation.

There are no serious battles during the move back toward Seoul, but there is constant uncertainty and danger. There are always many refugees pouring through our positions. Are there any enemy fighters intermingled with these refugees? It is difficult to spot the well-trained Chinese sent at night through gaps in our positions. Yet it is possible to see signs if you keep your eyes open. What has changed? What are the refugees doing? Changes might be nothing. But, looking deeper, there might be empty, newly dug, camouflaged positions that look down on a road.

We learn there is a time to take counsel of your fears, but there are times to never listen to any fear. Will a roadblock be established in our rear? Will a sniper take out someone in a jeep? Will MPs at a crossroad directing traffic be killed? The unrecognized heroes in this retreat are the military police. Often placed in isolated spots to guide movement, they not only suffer from the bitter cold, but enemies hiding among the locals often kill them.

With each successful defense and withdrawal, the confidence of our soldiers—and unit cohesion—improves. Yet this is not true for others. Many of those we meet seem bewildered, and I am sure they would "bug out" rather than fight. Often I hear them say things like: "When are we going to get the hell out of this goddamn place?" British General Leslie Mansergh notes this defeatist attitude; after a visit to Korea, he reports:

They [Americans] have never studied or been taught defence. They appear only to have studied mechanized... advances at great speed. They do not understand locality defence in depth or all-around defence. Americans do not understand infiltration and feel very naked when anybody threatens their flank or rear. At night, headquarters blazed like gin palaces. Roadblocks, car parks, dumps, etc. were as crowded as Hampstead Heath on a bank holiday.

Nevertheless, the Chinese are able to repeatedly turn the Eighth Army's right flank with two divisions of Mongol cavalrymen and reconstituted North Korean units. By 19 December, the enemy is ready to attack down the traditional Ch'orwan-Yonch'on-Uijongbu route to Seoul. By the end of December 1950, UN forces finally establish defensive positions near the 38th Parallel.

This is to become the longest retreat in US military history. Yet this withdrawal does prevent the Chinese from destroying the UN forces. The farther we go south, the greater the number of refugees that pour through our positions and the more contact we have with the Koreans.

Eros and Death

As the units reorganize following dreadful days of fear, suffering, and death, the need to strengthen the warrior spirit is more important than equipment, supplies, and replacements. Leadership, discipline, training, and the inner strength of individuals are the answers. Yet at the most fundamental level, the fear of death has to be countered through the mysterious linkage between unity (Eros) and the death instinct (Thanatos). This linkage has been observed in all cultures. Although never mentioned by military historians, it cannot be denied or ignored during combat.

In ideological conflict, the Ethos of Eros is not as significant as belief, fear, desire, discipline, and training—yet it is not to be slighted. And it needs to be understood. It is Eros that gives the "breath of life to the clay forms" of humans—Eros gives life. Eros causes humans to hold off the tension of life, while lust provides a release of tension. The physical acts of sex apply to all animals, but Eros is a human quality of imagination, commitment, and belonging. Eros provides the motivation for a union with others seeking fulfillment. Lust is a need, but Eros is a desire. After the physical acts of sex, a person wants to sleep, but Eros causes a person to remember, savor, and look forward to repeating the many-splendored experience. It is possible to enjoy sex without any anxiety—just physical relief—but Eros requires a passion for belonging. It is the Ethos of Eros that creates the bond of "brotherly love" known as combat camaraderie. *Your "brothers" accept you for what you are. They would do anything for you, and love you no matter what.*

Eros is often translated as love, but love is a personal attachment that takes many forms. Eros is not sex or lust. Sex is the physical acts of libido that bring pleasure and relief, while Eros is the urge toward higher forms of being and relationship. In combat, warriors and soldiers take sex and Eros for granted, just as they take death for granted. As young males many do focus on the physical acts of sex, but in combat the focus must be the feelings and passions of Eros. *Being loved by someone gives you strength, while loving someone gives you courage.* Only Eros can provide an inner compass capable of facing death successfully. Thus the Ethos of Eros is an important component of ideological conflict during both Warfare and War.

Both Eros and Thanatos are related to creation and destruction; they are united in complex ways. Humans are unable to get away from the importance of love (unity) and death, and for warriors and soldiers they become critical. During Peace, love can be a personal matter, yet in War and Warfare it plays a role in the outcome as it helps develop the qualities warriors and soldiers need. Those not in the heat of combat—be they in the armed forces or not—can be passionless, rational planners, organizers, manipulators, and compromisers. Yet to strip fighters of their passion is to risk defeat. Warriors and soldiers must be principle driven, uncompromising, disciplined, masculine, and ruthless in order to cope with combat.

During this retreat it is impossible to know all that took place. How many elderly, infants, and handicapped are left behind to their fate? How many are too weak, or too slow, to complete the journey? How many of the soldiers find women among the refugees and together they are able to free their minds of fear and death as soldiers have done throughout the ages? How many innocents are killed by mistake or malice? No one will ever know.

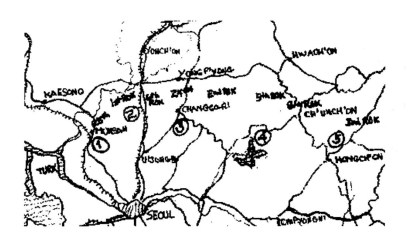

(1) Behind the Imjin River the Twenty-Fifth Division blocks the main road to Seoul. (2) First ROK and the Sixth ROK Divisions. (3) Twenty-Fourth Division is on the traditional

invasion route to Seoul. (4) In the center are the Second, Fifth, and Eighth ROK Divisions. (5) Third ROK Division is in the rugged mountains blocking the Hongch'on River valley.

In reserve are two British Brigades, 187th Airborne RCT, Second Division and First Cavalry Division.

On the Defensive around Seoul

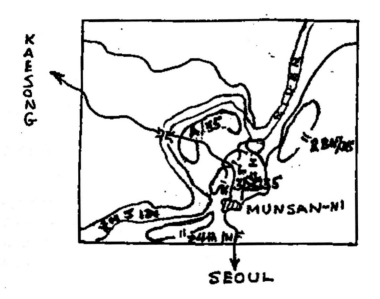

Spreading the ROK Division along the defense line has been frustrating. They are not fully manned, equipped, or trained and are needed to protect the people throughout South Korea. Nevertheless, they are moved to the 38th Parallel and police are given responsibility for handling insurgents. When the First Marine, Seventh, and Third Divisions arrive they are expected to replace some of those ROK Divisions, allowing them to return to internal security activities.

The Eighth Army establishes a defensive line south of the 38th Parallel with the Twenty-Fourth and Twenty-Fifth Divisions on the main routes to Seoul, six ROK Divisions defending Seoul, and other UN units in reserve. After weeks of delaying positions and retreating, we set up our first real defensive positions just south of the Imjin River. Since our battalion is astride the main road to Seoul, we expect to face a major attack. Among the buildings used by the American occupation forces before the war, we dig deep holes, build emplacements, string barbed wire, lay mines, and prepare for a tough fight. A Company, from the First Battalion, is deployed in outposts near the Imjin River, but is to pull back whenever an attack starts. Captain Sidney Berry, the commander, has 149 Americans and 36 Korean soldiers.

We improve our positions, fire in artillery, send out patrols, and check the refugees. The battalion command post is in a schoolhouse in Musan–ni. We are told the Eighth Army will make a determined stand to prevent the Chinese from taking Seoul.

On Christmas the Chinese cross the 38th Parallel at Kaesong. The South Korean National Assembly begins to move out of Seoul, as does much of the government. Many expect the Chinese to renew their offensive on Christmas day, but they do not. Troops celebrate Christmas as best they can with small trees decorated with colored paper. Chaplains move from unit to unit conducting simple services. Here we have a Christmas dinner with all of the trimmings. Music comes over the radio from Japan. Many think: "It is wonderful to hear 'Silent Night, Holy Night' under a full moon, even if we are far from home."

Ridgway meets with MacArthur as Walker's replacement. At the end of the meeting MacArthur says: "The Eighth Army is yours, Matt. Do what you think best." Ridgway begins a four-day inspection of all divisions. JCS sends a directive to MacArthur stating that Korea is not the place to fight a major war. They say no additional forces will be sent and that the UN is not to incur heavy losses. They remind MacArthur that the US and the UN are willing to accept a ceasefire on a line near the 38th Parallel. This is evidence that the ideological conflict has already been lost, since the leaders never consider shifting from War to Warfare, how to weaken the will of the enemy or strengthen the will of all backers of UN forces—they only consider how to end War with a ceasefire and a treaty.

When Ridgway gets back to Eighth Army headquarters in Taegu, he finds a lack of spirit: "I could read it in the faces of...leaders, from sergeants right on up to the top. They were unresponsive, reluctant to talk. I had to drag information out of them. There was a complete absence of that alertness, that aggressiveness, that you find in troops whose spirit is high." The soldiers he meets convince him that he is now the leader of a "bewildered army, not sure of itself or its leaders, not sure what they were doing there." Fear defeats more people than any other thing. The soldiers reflect "lost confidence and a lack of spirit." Everyone has the ability to do something well, and they let others down if they don't use that ability as best they can. After his four-day inspection of the Eighth Army, Ridgway concludes that his first task is to restore the morale and confidence of the Eighth Army, his second task is to improve leadership, and his third task is to get better intelligence at all levels.

To improve leadership at the upper level, Ridgway orders: "...division commanders to be up with their forward battalions, and...corps commanders up with the regiments that are in the hottest action." He moves his command post forward.

The Big Picture

We are unaware of all of the politics and operation disputes going on at corps, army, and Far East command levels discussed by David Halberstam in *The Coldest Winter*. Nor do we know of the policy and strategy disputes between GEN MacArthur and Washington.

We do know GEN Walton Walker had been killed on 23 December in a vehicle accident. We know that GEN Matthew Ridgway had taken command of the Eighth Army, and we know of his reputation as a fighter and leader. However, we know nothing of the political maneuvering, or the bewilderment and deep dismay that infects higher headquarters. We did not think the Eighth Army had collapsed. We know that some units had collapsed, but we know our regiment is now better than it was in November.

As the conflict moves back down to South Korea even those at the lower levels know:

- That the Chinese use strategy, tactics, and maneuvers more effectively, and they have better intelligence. They are an Asian army, without the firepower that a Western army considered essential, fighting like they had a few years earlier when they defeated the Nationalist Chinese.

- That the US has superior technology. The US has absolute control of the sea and air and the UN forces have superior medical care, transportation, and logistical support.

- That the UN and Chinese/North Koreans have an equal number of men committed, but the combat to support ratios gives the Chinese/North Koreans more front-line fighters.

- That the North Koreans are more ruthless than the Chinese, and that both the North Koreans and the Chinese are more disciplined and aggressive than the South Koreans and Americans.

- That many of the UN units are not sure of themselves or their leaders; much of the Eighth Army lacks confidence and spirit.

This is the situation Ridgway faces. He has to change it in order to prevent defeat. Without changes there is no hope of victory. His primary task is to restore the fighting spirit in all United Nations units.

In *This Kind of War*, T. R. Fehrenback noted:

Korea was the kind of war that since the dawn of history was fought by professionals, by legions. It was fought by men who soon knew they had small support or sympathy at home, who could read in the papers statements by prominent men that they should be withdrawn. It was fought by men whom the Army—at its own peril—had given neither training nor indoctrination, nor the hardness and bitter pride men must have to fight a war in which they do not in their hearts believe. The Army needed legions, but society didn't want them. It wanted citizen-soldiers.

US intellectuals, politicians, human right activists, and lawyers want armed forces restricted by the provision of the Geneva Conventions—regardless of the enemy or the conditions. This allows the Pacifist's Fallacy to trump common sense. Nothing can stop those with the right mental attitude from achieving their goal; nothing on earth can help those with the wrong mental attitude. The basic questions are:

- Is it possible for the West to win protracted conflict against ruthless, totalitarian, and ideologically motivated regimes?

- How is the will in pluralistic Western states maintained when many people do not support the foreign policy of their government?

In 1950 the US, the ROK, and the UN are not prepared to win an ideological conflict and most of their leaders did not understand its importance—they thought only of conventional War and Peace.

Chinese Offensive: 1–14 January 1950

After sending out patrols for weeks to locate weak spots in the defense around Seoul, the Chinese decide to attack on a bitterly cold New Year's Eve. At sunset on 31 December a few self-propelled guns fire on South Korean and American positions defending an area directly north of Seoul on the Imjin River; however, this is not on one of the traditional invasion routes. After dark, a company of Chinese troops cross the Imjin River and infiltrate into the rear of the Twenty-Fourth Division. By 2200, there is a battalion size attack. Also the Sixth ROK Division, to the west of the Twenty-Fourth Division, is being probed. Further to the west, the First ROK Division comes under attack.

MacArthur sends Washington proposals for expanding the conflict saying victory cannot be achieved if operations are limited to Korea. Fifteen F-86 jet fighters tangle with forty Russian-made jets over northwest Korea in the biggest air battle in Korea.

Seven Chinese Armies[37] and two North Korean Corps attack on New Year's Day, with the major attack down the Uijongbu corridor toward Seoul. An estimated 270,000 Chinese and North Korean troops are committed.[38] A spokesman says: "We don't know how many of the enemy are involved yet. There are a lot of them and they mean business." Chinese losses are heavy as they go through mine fields and barbed wire. The first wave has straw-filled sacks, which they throw on the barbed wire; they then lay down to form a living bridge for those who follow.

Because of the danger of being outflanked, there is a withdrawal to the outskirts of Seoul. Then on 3 January, Ridgway decides to give up the South Korean Capital and to move to positions south of the Han. The order to withdraw is given. As the trucks take the troops to the bridges they pass through the burning buildings, darkness, chaos, and despair of Seoul. When they go through '31 Circle' those who remember good times there years ago cheer loudly. They remember the Korean girls willing to please, competing for their dollars, and skilled at exciting. As they pass the circle there is no evidence of the bright lights, music, drinking, and sex that make this circle famous. They have no idea what the future will bring, but they take a final look at a place they remember for pleasure.

During the afternoon things are fluid northeast of Seoul. American tanks thrust seven miles north of Uijongbu and observe ten thousand enemy troops. Upon returning they direct artillery onto targets around Uijongbu.

Crossing the Han is complicated by thousands of refugees trying to get out of Seoul. It is a vision of a frozen hell. Only military traffic is to cross the bridges after 1500 on 3 January. It is very cold.

Huge pieces of ice come down the river to pile up against the pontoon bridges. Throughout the night of 3–4 January, the defenders of Seoul cross the Han to avoid being destroyed the next day. The refugees wait until the military cross. Before dark we cross the Han and immediately go into positions on the main road just south of Yongdungpo. There is a constant flow of refugees. We establish a checkpoint where a culvert had been destroyed. The refugees have to get off of the road, go down into a ditch, and then climb back up to the road. I tell our soldiers to pull over anyone who looked "suspicious." We actually do very little checking; since any such attempt would back up refugees for miles and cause many to go off through the rice paddies in order to bypass our checkpoint.

From time to time I go down to the checkpoint. I am there at about 2300 hours on the night of 3 January. With nothing better to do I help those refugees having difficulty climbing back up to the road. Today, in the era of suicide bombers, no one would do this. In the moonlight I see a vast mob of bodies trying to get to safety; they are no longer individuals. I see only an endless crowd pushing along in silence.

In the distance, fires are burning in Seoul. I know that the last units will move across the Han the next day, and then the last bridge will be destroyed. It is very sad to see these men, women, children, and babies trying to get away from the North Koreans who had controlled their city and killed so many during the past summer.

After many hours I pay little attention to those passing. Then I am brought back to reality by a woman's voice saying in perfect English: "Thank you, Captain." I look; in the moonlight I see a very beautiful young woman in a fur coat. I manage to say, "You are welcome."

"You are very kind. I need someone like you. How can I thank you?"

I reply: "By having a safe trip, and a happy life."

"But Captain, can't you protect me?"

"I'm sure everything will be okay."

"Maybe, I hope so," she says in almost a whisper. "Everything was so delightful. I hope we can have such a happy life again." She then joins the crowd and the fur coat vanishes in the darkness. Who is she? I have no idea. She is just one of thousands fleeing Seoul. But I would often wonder if she had a safe trip and a happy life. I also wonder what fatigue and moonlight might have done to me. In bright lights would she remain so young, beautiful, and willing?

At 1400 on 4 January the last bridge from Seoul goes into the Han River. The soldiers in Seoul then walk across the ice. The North Korean flag is hoisted over the city hall.

Map of 4 Jan 51:

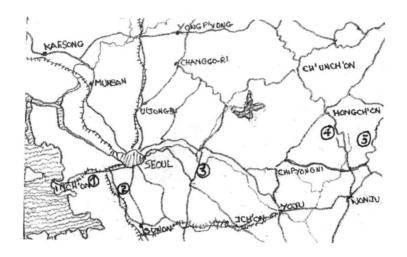

(1) Kimpo airport and the port of Inch'on are abandoned.
(2) Twenty-Fifth Division is in a blocking position north of
Anyang—eight miles south of the Han River. On this road
ROK soldiers are streaming south. Many are without
weapons and without leaders. They only want to get away
as fast as possible. (3) Several CCF Divisions have moved
down the Pakhan River corridor and are crossing the Han
River. (4) Seven NKPA divisions (over 180,000 soldiers)
advance from Ch'unch'on toward Wonju. (5) A NKPA
Division is moving down a valley in the western side of the
Taebaek Mountains toward Chech'on.

The Suffering, Agony, and Despair

The many refugees I see after the fall of Seoul are a vision of
tragedy and despair that is difficult to recognize as reality. It
would never be believed by anyone who has lived only in
conditions of Peace and thinks in terms of compassion, law,

justice, and civic virtues—as is true for most Americans. Repeatedly I am told of children and parents being lost in the frozen street of Seoul or the ice-filled waters of the Han, never to be seen again. It is a terrible time. The ice on the Han would break under the multitude seeking to cross; young and old would struggle and then sink helpless into the water. Others run hysterically past the dying. Only the strong and lucky survive.

Then for days small groups wander south without possessions or hope. They are cold, hungry, and often sick. There is always the fear of being overtaken by enemy or killed by someone for no apparent reason. All trappings of civility are missing and fate rules supreme. At times families crawl into an abandoned house to determine what to do. Often the decision is tragic—a teenage girl is to remain with the youngest children so that the others can continue. They promise to return. Only the strong have a chance of making it to safety and food. Those left have to beg and steal to survive: all know that the odds are against them, and that suffering will surely be their lot. Some find a soldier that will give them protection and food, and they are most grateful.

Those that I talk with do make it to the UN lines and long for the day they can return to where they left those they love.

Attacks in Central Korea

At the same time, the Chinese are attacking Seoul. The North Koreans are attacking in central Korea, as shown in this map of 7 January 1951.

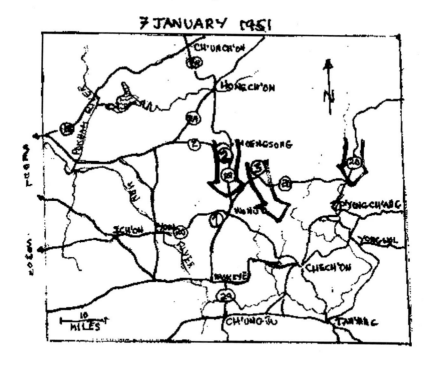

(1) Wonju, fifty miles east of Seoul, is at the bottom of a bowl with two regiments of the Second Division on the bowl's rim. At 0530 on 7 January 1951, four hundred NKPA (North Korean People's Army) troops disguised as civilians intermingle among the refugees and walk by outposts; they are not discovered until they open fire. Both regiments are then attacked. They finally abandon the town and its airfield and move south of Wonju. Then aircraft strafe and bomb Wonju. (2) Six NKPA divisions[39] continue the attack through Wonju toward Ch'ungju, twenty-seven miles to the south. Five thousand to seven thousand five hundred communist insurgents support these attacks. (3) Four NKPA divisions[40] move through the Taebaek Mountains toward Chech'on.

On 8 January, in an effort to motivate the Eighth Army, Ridgway issues this statement:

> *To me the issues are clear. It is not a question of this or that Korean town or village. Real estate is incidental. It is not restricted to the issue of freedom for our South Korean allies... though that freedom is a symbol of the wider issues, and included among them.*

> *The real issues are whether the power of Western civilization...shall defy and defeat communism; whether the rule of men who shoot their prisoners, enslave their citizens, and deride the dignity of man, shall displace the rule of those to whom the individual and his individual rights are sacred; whether we are to survive with God's hand to guide and lead us, or to perish in the dead existence of a Godless world.*

Map of 12 Jan 51:

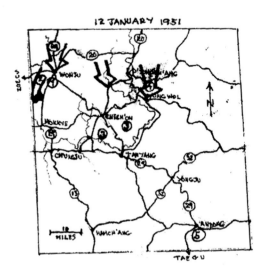

(1) Attacks continue near Wonju against the Second Division Task Force on Hill 247. Reinforcements by the French and Netherlands battalions help, as do air strikes. More than 1,100 of the enemy are killed. (2) Some of the enemy bypass Wonju and move southwest into the mountains; they are supported by local communist insurgents. (3) The 187th RCT and Seventh Division are assigned responsibility for patrolling a large area south of Chech'on. (4) East of Wonju, Ninth NK Division attacks Yongwol—in the high mountains thirty-eight miles, and two valleys, east of Wonju. (5) The 187th RCT moves up to Andong en route to the newly assigned patrolling area (3).

Peng's Problems and His Strategy

The CCF Third Campaign has been a great success, yet it brings new pressure on GEN Peng. He worries about his long supply lines and the enormous firepower of the Americans. Those in Beijing do not share these concerns. Huge victory rallies are held in China after Seoul is recaptured. The Chinese leaders think Peng is too cautious. Moreover, the Soviets are pressuring Mao to pursue the enemy. That the Russians think the Chinese are timid appalls Mao. Kim Il-sung visits Peng's headquarters and asks him to drive the Americans into the sea.

Peng has a more realistic view of the situation. He knows the Americans have not been defeated during the Third Campaign, and he realizes that UN units held together much better this time than they had in November. He does not know this new commander Ridgway. Peng is concerned that the Americans might be setting a trap for him.

Peng decides he can hold most of the Eighth Army south of the Han River and still have enough strength to attack down the central corridor, where he would have several advantages. He sets Wonju as his objective. He wants to build on the success the NKPA has had during their offensive.

From Wonju he could drive on south to Teague or turn west to envelop those units south of the Han River. He wants to move slowly so that he does not outrun his supply lines or expose his forces to the American firepower. Nevertheless, Mao cables Peng with directives for an aggressive next campaign. It is as if Mao had not heard anything Peng had said for several weeks. Mao, like MacArthur, is caught up in his own dreams.

UN Consolidate on 37th Parallel: 15–22 January 1951

The Eighth Army finally moves to defensive positions. On 14 January after the longest retreat in the history of the US Army, Ridgway creates a ten-mile deep defensive zone across Korea forty-five to fifty-five miles south of the 38th Parallel. It is very cold. There are many non-battle casualties from trench foot, frostbite, and respiratory diseases. The enemy slows its offensive operations in the center corridor because of casualties, plus a shortage of ammunition and other supplies.

Ridgway starts to change the Eighth Army. He makes cautious, coordinated, phased advances and he pounds the enemy with artillery and air attacks. He is using the technological and firepower superiority of the Eighth Army. The long supply lines of the Chinese are now a disadvantage. Ridgway is displeased with the withdrawal; he tells the Corps commanders: "Reports so far reaching me indicate your forces withdraw without evidence of having inflicted any substantial losses on enemy and without materiel delay. In fact, some major units are reported as having broken contact. I desire prompt confirming reports and if substantially correct, the reasons for non-compliance with my basic directives." This is but one of Ridgway's efforts to improve leadership.

The Fur Coat

We finally stop south of Osan and north of Sojong-ni. One afternoon I go to headquarters of the Twenty-Fifth Division to pick up some maps. This gives me an opportunity to see what is going on in the rear areas. I note many artillery units. Their condition suggests that they are new arrivals. There are many refugees, but they aren't moving south. It appears that they are somehow living in our area. On my return I have my driver stop in the town of Songhwan, which is ten miles behind our positions.

I sit down and lean back against the side of a house. My driver dozes off in the jeep. I look at the scene, watch the people, and think about what has happened during the past weeks.

A young woman comes down the street, but stops. She looks at the Captain on the side of the road, and then she starts to move on, but stops again. "Captain, why are you here?" she says in perfect English.

He thinks there is something familiar about her. "Oh, I am just resting. And you?"

"It is good to see you again, Captain. I thought it might be you, but in your uniforms many of you Americans look alike. I wasn't sure it was you. But I remember your voice. Do you remember me?"

"Where is your fur coat?" he asks with a smile.

"Oh, you do remember!" She jumps over and kisses him.

"I can show you my coat. That will prove I'm the one you wished a safe trip and a happy life that awful night. I'm staying with my aunt. She lives only a few blocks away."

He gets up and they walk together chatting. The house they stop at is not a thatch-covered hut, but one of the best houses in town. He is surprised that it is not damaged or taken over by the Americans. "A nice house," he says.

"Yes, my family has several businesses and many friends in the government."

They enter the house, which is attractively furnished. "Sit down. I'll get my fur coat." He looks around. Everything in the room is finer than anything he has seen in Korea. It is what you might find in an upper class Japanese home.

She stands in the doorway with the fur coat held tightly around her neck. "Remember me now?"

"When I saw you last you were walking away from me in that coat."

"Like this." She turns around so he sees only the back of the coat. After a few moments she adds, "But you deserve to see more." She slowly turns around to face him. This time she does not hold the coat tightly around her neck, but fully open. She is wearing nothing under the coat. The small breasts are soft to the touch and the origin of the world is before him.[41]

It is an hour later that she strokes his face. "Three times, that's the most I have ever had at one time. I am so happy."

"I didn't do much."

"That was enough," she says. "Have I thanked you enough?"

"All I can take, but maybe we can meet again."

"Anytime you want, Captain."

"Captain." It is the voice of my driver. I look up.

"Sir, don't you think we had better get back?" I stand up, get in the jeep, and we drive back to the battalion.

Years later as I learn of the dramatic development of South Korea after 1960, I often wonder how the life of the girl in the fur coat had changed. Had it indeed been a safe trip and a happy life to match that of her country? Of course, I never knew.

In the west 174,000 Chinese are south of the Han in front of us. But again they are hidden. We will surely fight again, but who will be the "Divine Warriors" this time?

North Korean Attacks Southeast of Wonju

Two North Koreans Corps continue their attacks near Wonju. They move undetected southeast of Wonju, past Chech'on and Tanyang with their lead units reaching Andong on 9 January, eighty miles southeast of Wonju. NKPA Second Division reaches Tanyang. NKPA Thirty-First Division also reaches Tanyang after moving on trails through the mountains. The Twenty-Seventh NKPA Division reaches Chech'on, twenty-two miles southeast of Wonju. The NKPA Tenth Division, after fights with Seventh Division patrols, changes its route and continues on trails until it reaches Andong.

Map of 14 Jan 51:

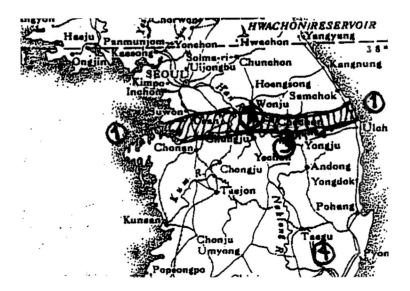

(1) The longest retreat in the history of the US Army is halted. The Eighth Army creates a ten-mile deep defensive zone across Korea (forty-five to fifty-five miles south of the 38th Parallel). (2) Second Division is given responsibility for both Wonju and twenty-two miles southeast to Chech'on. It is very cold. NKPA slow their offensive operations because of casualties and shortages of ammunition and other supplies. (3) Eighth ROK Division move to Tanyang to confront NKPA units there. (4) Third and Seventh Divisions are now in South Korea.

UN operations in the central corridor are best described as Hybrid War (a combination of conventional War and Warfare). UN forces go into defensive positions around villages and towns, and have artillery support. The NKPA are scattered with no artillery support. The NKPA units can move along snow-covered mountain trails for several days; the UN forces move on the roads and depend on their supply routes. The NKPA ambush vehicles, attack outposts and vulnerable locations in a wide area of the central corridor south of Wonju, yet there are few direct attacks on UN combat units—other than near Wonju.

However, by 16 January the NKPA divisions in the mountains southeast of Wonju have used up most of their supplies and have suffered casualties from artillery and air strikes. Also, they do not have the combat capability of the North Korean Divisions used in the summer of 1950 that invaded South Korea. They are unable to continue their offensive, so they just try to avoid UN forces.

Ridgway's Strategy and Limited View

Having established a defensive zone, in the third week of January 1951 GEN Ridgway turns his attention to: (1) restoring the fighting spirit, (2) encouraging all leaders to demonstrate greater energy and initiative, (3) obtaining better intelligence, and (4) improving planning in all headquarters. Ridgway is convinced that he can reinvigorate the Eighth Army through these improvements.

He knows he must stop any Chinese offensive that threatens to drive the UN from Korea; also he knows there are those thinking of using nuclear weapons. He knows he has to rebuild the will to fight in UN forces. He knows that the Americans have logistic, communication, and firepower advantages. He knows that the enemy has other advantages. What should be his strategy?

He decides that his best strategy is to inflict maximum casualties on the enemy so that each battle will cause staggering losses for the Chinese and North Koreans. The key to this kind of grinding strategy is artillery—and when possible close air support.

Although Ridgway speaks of defeating "Godless communism," he does not give much thought to the ideological struggle going on around the UN forces in Korea, since he sees himself fighting a conventional War. Thus, to him the insurgents are "guerrillas" which give support to the CCF and NKPA units—not insurgents attempting to take over South Korea. His rhetoric against communism is more a way to motivate his troops than it is an effort to win an ideological struggle. He does not think about local security, effective local authority, and building networks among the people throughout South Korea so that they are stronger than the networks of the communists. In other words, he does not recognize that the conflict is as much an ideological struggle of Warfare as it is a conventional War.

In the third week of January 1951 Ridgway prepares the Eighth Army to attack an enemy that is strong and determined.

---

[37] A Chinese army has about thirty thousand men, thus it is larger than a US Division, but smaller than a US Corps.

[38] One hundred thousand of the enemy make the initial attacks on the Twenty-Fourth, Twenty-Fifth, First ROK, Sixth ROK, and Second ROK Divisions defending Seoul.

[39] Sixth, Seventh, Twelfth, Twenty-Seventh, Twenty-Eighth, and Forty-Third Divisions. A NKPA division is a little larger than a US or South Korean regiment.

[40] Second, Ninth, Tenth, and Thirty-First.

[41] *Origin of the World* is the title of a painting by Gustave Courbet, in the Musee d'Orsay. It can be found online.

CHAPTER TWENTY

UP TO SEOUL

23 January–28 February 1951

Ridgway's first major offensive (Operation Thunderbolt) moves forward with the Turkish Brigade, Twenty-Fifth Division, Third Division, First Cavalry Division, supporting tanks, artillery, and close air support. The main attack is toward the Han River and Seoul. The goal is limited. There are only jabs with reconnaissance in force. It is a slow, cautious move up to the Han River to destroy as many of the enemy as possible with artillery and aircraft.

Initial Battlefield

On 25 January we are north of Osan, in the same place the 403 men of Task Force Smith had been the first American unit to fight in the Korean War. It is a ridge across the road which at its highest is two hundred feet above the road. There is a cold wind blowing as I look toward Suwon, as no doubt LTC Charles B Smith did on 5 July 1950. I know that it was rainy and overcast back then; now it is cold, dry, and overcast. Everything is now brown, while it must have been green back in the summer of 1950.

This map shows our movement north on 24, 25, and 26 January 1951.

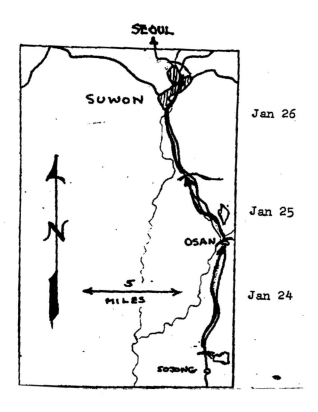

I can imagine what the young men of TF Smith on this ridge, fresh from garrison life in Japan, must have been thinking. A few days earlier their main interest was when they could get back to that special Japanese girl. But they have very different thoughts when at 0730 they see dark objects coming at them from Suwon, and then by 0830 when those objects become a column of thirty-three low-slung T-34 North Korean tanks firing on them with their 85-mm cannons and 7.62 coaxial machine guns. Each rifleman on this ridge has 120 rounds of ammunition and two days' C rations. A battery of 105 howitzers supports them.

I know the results of that battle and am happy that the enemy withdraws whenever we move forward in force. Whereas TF Smith had one battery of artillery, we have ample fire support.

Suwon According to the United Press

Throughout the United States on 26 Jan 1951 this United Press report appeared:

Captured Arms Found in Suwon
Officer Searches Cave Deserted by Reds

Suwon, Korea, Jan 26—(UP) When U.S. tanks and infantry moved into this old walled city today the natives warned that there were 200 Chinese Communists hiding in a cave inside the wall.

Tanks, 75-mm guns, and mortars were being moved into position to blast them out when a daring American officer volunteered to search the cave first.

He was Captain Sam C. Holliday, 24, of Houston, Tex. He said he didn't believe the natives and asked his unit commander for permission to go. Holliday drove his jeep up the hill and after 30 minutes the commander began to worry about him. When he finally came back, he had an armload of souvenirs, including a Chinese officer's coat, an American hand grenade, American tear gas grenade, American .50-caliber machine gun, and four sticks of dynamite made by a firm in Tacoma, Wash.

"I didn't think there were any Chinese there and there weren't," he told his commander. "They ran out to the north

during the night but left a lot of junk behind. As near as I can tell, they were the last Chinese in town."

Holliday said it did not take too much courage to investigate a cave that was supposed to be holding 200 Communists. "Actually, I knew they were not there even if a lot of Korean people said they were," Holliday said. "But I still had some doubts so I sent a bunch of kids up there to play outside the cave. They came back and told me there was nobody there and I believed them," he said.

The GIs found Suwon a ghost town. A few pitiful orphan children, ragged, dirty and hungry, roam among the American troops begging for food. A few refugees, their meager belongings strapped to their backs, wandered aimlessly.

Only a few homes remain standing and most of them are badly damaged. There are great piles of rubble and ashes and tangled telegraph and electric wires.

SOUTH GATE OF SUWON   SCH

What Actually Happened in Suwon

As is often the case, the media didn't report exactly what happened. Here is what happened in Suwon on 26 January 1951.

A week earlier a task force of the Twenty-Seventh "Wolf-hound" Regiment had come within a mile of Suwon and fired on the city, but when the Chinese confronted the task force, it returned to Osan.

On 26 January the Thirty-Fifth Regiment moves from the ridge where Task Force Smith had fought the initial battle of the war. It has orders to take Suwon. The Second Battalion is on the left side of the road and the Third Battalion is on the right side. The intelligence estimate we receive from higher headquarters says that a Chinese battalion is expected to fight a delaying action in Suwon. The estimate reasons that Suwon is the last built up area before Yongdungpo, and the Chinese want to avoid fighting in the open where our artillery and tanks would give us an advantage. They wanted a straight infantry fight inside the narrow streets of Suwon.

While I cannot argue with the logic of that estimate, my own information and observation tells me it is incorrect. As we move toward Suwon I pick up information from local Koreans that there had been many Chinese units in Suwon. However, I conclude that most of them had left on 22 February. They had gone into the hills north of Suwon but south of Anyang. My sources tell me that about two hundred Chinese had been left in Suwon, but they had departed on the night of 25–26 Feb.

This makes sense to me. It is logical that the Chinese would leave a unit behind when most of the troops withdrew to defensive positions in the hills. The unit left behind could send patrols out to see where we were and what we were doing. Two hundred seems about the right number for such a mission. They would know we were just south of Suwon during the night of 25–26 Feb. Then there would be no reason to remain in Suwon. However, I want to confirm this through personal observation.

On the morning of 26 January both battalions of the Thirty-Fifth Regiment move up to the hills overlooking Suwon. We have no enemy contact. I go to where I am able to examine the town through my field glasses. I lay flat on my belly, to make sure no one in Suwon can see me. I focus my binoculars on the town for twenty minutes. People are moving about with no sign of concern, and nothing suggests that the Chinese are there. I rise and move off of the hill. I am confident that my intelligence estimate, not that from higher headquarters, is correct. This is not the first time there had been such differences, and mine has always turned out to be correct.

I go over to the battalion command group on a bridge at the edge of the town. Of course they know of the intelligence estimate from regiment. Also, they have heard stories about the two hundred Chinese in the cave under the wall. LTC James H Lee (who had been promoted) was ready to launch an attack to clean the enemy out of Suwon.

I am very confident that using the whole battalion plus tanks to sweep the eastern side of Suwon would be a waste of time and effort. I assume the United Press reporter is listening while I state my opinion. LTC Lee is reluctant to accept my opinion because regiment's intelligence estimate had said we should expect to face an enemy battalion to fight a delaying action in Suwon. He does not want to ignore regiment's estimate.

I finally say, "Just let me go in there and take a look before we commit the whole battalion in an attack on the town."

"Okay, you have thirty minutes."

I then drive over to the entrance gate of the town with my driver, my interpreter, and one other man. Three of us get out of the jeep and walk through the center of Suwon while the jeep follows. We get conflicting stories from the Koreans. Some say all the Chinese have left during the night, but others say there are some Chinese still in a cave under part of the old city wall that surrounds the town.

We get in the jeep and drive to the location of the "cave." Cut in a chalk-colored cliff at the base of the wall are several openings. I have my interpreter tell several of the children, who are running after us, to go play around those openings to see if anyone is still there. They did this as we watch. The children return to say the "caves" are empty. We then move up slowly to the openings and find this to be true.

The whole cliff is honeycombed with tunnels connecting the many entrances. Within the tunnels are a variety of items the Chinese have left behind: mats, ammunition, explosives, and clothing. I drive back to the bridge and tell LTC Lee that the town is clear, and show him some of the things I found. The battalion then occupies the east side of Suwon.

General MacArthur's Visit

As we move out of Suwon on the morning of 28 January 1951 we are told a VIP will visit our battalion that afternoon. We are instructed to find an observation post that can be reached by jeeps. I assume our battalion is selected because we are on the main road north of the Suwon airport. By noon we have moved two miles up the road toward Seoul and our companies are in defensive positions. The enemy is three miles away in the hills south of Anyang. I select a small knoll just off of the road, which has a good view of our positions, but it also has a view of the road leading to Seoul with hills in the distance. Perhaps LTC Lee knows who the VIP is, but I do not.

Lee and I are waiting on the knoll when we get word that the VIP is on his way. We see a string of jeeps coming toward us, and Lee walks twenty yards over to where the jeeps are to stop. Then I see GEN MacArthur get out of a jeep, then GEN Ridgway out of another, and finally GEN Kean, our division commander, out of a third. Lee greets them and brings them up to where I am standing. MacArthur is not wearing his trademark dark glasses and he looks old. He is wearing his famous hat, and a winter coat with a fur collar. Ridgway is on the other side of Lee.

LTC Lee gets out his map and starts to explain where the companies are located. MacArthur looks off into the distance and says nothing. Several cameramen have moved in front of them and start taking pictures. GEN Kean and I stand in the back. There are a few questions, but certainly nothing new is learned from this visit. It lasts fifteen minutes. They go back to the jeeps and leave. Nevertheless, pictures from that visit are the most common images of MacArthur being in Korea "with the troops."

The Attack Continues Toward Seoul

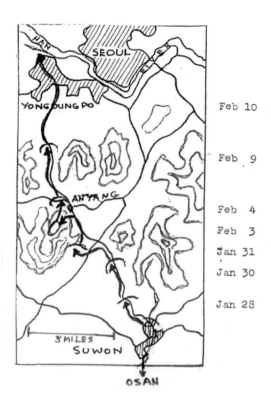

From 28 January until 10 February the Twenty-Fifth Division pushes the Chinese back toward the Han River while artillery and aircraft inflict great damage. The Thirty-Fifth Regiment advances up the main road to Yongdong Po and on 30 Jan 1951, we are facing the hills south of Anyang.

Western Front, Korea, Jan 30 (AP) "Fierce Fighting in UN Advance. They're firing on us from that hill," said Sergeant J. W. Hardin. That hill was a dust-covered mound 600 yards away. The men of King Company had just laboriously pried 150

Communists off the hill on which we were standing. Now they were to press forward to the next one.

We were eight miles north of Suwon. A spring like sun shone down on the grimy foot soldiers. The doughboys were slugging it out with a fanatical enemy. "They just get in their holes and die," said Lieutenant Arvine Eyer. "You have to go in and kill them."

On the hill a big recoilless rifle pounded the next ridge, trailing a fiery stream each time it sent more death across the small depression between the two hills. A machine gun hemstitched the ridge, its chatter echoing down the valley. Suddenly there was a high whining scream and a shell pounded into a dugout. Soon there was another. It was only 50 yards to the right of where Captain Sam C. Holliday and I watched the action.

An example of the fanatic resistance offered by the Chinese was told by Sergeant Arnold Missidine. "This guy was sitting in a beautifully camouflaged hole watching us walk down the road. He had only grenades, no rifle. When we began to position our men we put a South Korean soldier near that spot. He saw the Chinese soldier move and shot him. The wounded Chinaman pulled the pin of a grenade but before he could throw it the grenade went off and blew a big hunk out of him."

During February aircraft continually attack the supply routes in North Korea that bring supplies to the battlefield from China and the Soviet Union. Traffic only moves at night. From thirty thousand feet pilots can see long lines of headlights as trucks move on the main roads. However, when they fly low the trucks stop and the lights go out. Nevertheless air attacks destroy many trucks and damage to bridges reduces the use of trains. But supplies still get to the front lines, since these interdiction operations only reduce the supplies received.

On 1 February enemy resistance slackens south of Seoul. The temperature drops to twenty-five degrees below zero at night. Prisoners report that typhus and frostbite are widespread among Chinese troops. US units (Twenty-Fifth, Third, First Cavalry, and Twenty-Fourth Divisions) advance to within eight miles of Seoul. By 3 February the offensive Thunderbolt has gained twenty miles. For a second night the temperature drops to twenty-five below zero. Most of the combat units lack warming huts. Although they have good winter clothing, soldiers must huddle together to prevent cold weather injuries. A tank-infantry task force advances through thick fog to seven miles from Seoul. Another advances toward the port of Inch'on. Showing signs of life after two nights of quiet, the Chinese mount several probes and fire mortars from dusk until dawn. However, the artillery engage in counter-fire.

On 4 February the greatest exploitation of armor in Korea is launched toward Seoul on three routes. The main attack by the Twenty-Fifth Division is from Anyang, on the primary road[42] to Seoul. Four miles north of Anyang the Chinese put up "a hell of a battle." To the right, the Third Division and First Cavalry Division[43] make the other two attacks toward Seoul. Eighth Army estimates that the enemy has suffered 23,000 casualties in the first eleven days of the offensive. Ridgway has successfully revitalized the Eighth Army and the tide has turned against the Chinese. They have been defeated south of Seoul.

By 10 February, it is clear that the enemy is pulling back behind the Han River. They still hold Seoul, and are reported to be massing north of the Han River.

During the last three weeks of February there is little activity west of Seoul. US artillery fires across the bridgeless Han River at targets in Seoul. The Chinese return fire from cleverly camouflaged positions in Seoul. One shell sets a building containing sulfur on fire. The rotten egg smell causes some to think they are under a chemical attack. But calm returns with the explanation that sulfur dioxide is a gas released by volcanoes, but that it is not deadly. It is reported that the Chinese are bringing up Russian-made 120-mm guns. The amount of artillery fire from the Chinese suggests that the air strikes have not prevented resupply. South of the Han a brewery is found in Yongdong Po and soon many soldiers have all the beer they want. There are rumors of dead bodies in the vats. Finally, MPs are stationed at the brewery.

During the final week of January 1951, while the main attack of the Eighth Army is toward Seoul against the CCF, Ridgway plans a secondary thrust up Korea's central corridor along Route #29 from Wonju toward Hongch'on against the NKPA.

Fighting for the Central Corridor

The North Korean forces in the central corridor[44] are in bad shape and are instructed to move to the P'yongch'ang area (in high mountains forty miles, and two valleys, northeast of Wonju) to be reorganized. They reached their assembly areas by the end of January.

NK Tenth Division, which suffered heavy losses en route to Andong, is also told to withdraw to P'yongch'ang. If it cannot make it back it is to work with the local insurgents. For the next three weeks the First Marine Division conducts "anti-guerrilla" operations against the remnants of the Tenth Division. To support the main attack in the south of Seoul, UN forces in the central corridor push forward with a secondary attack. Knowing that the superior firepower of the attack south of Seoul will destroy his forces, Chinese General Peng plans to delay in the west and to fight his major battles in the mountains of the central corridor of Korea.

A motorized patrol of forty-five men from the Second Division is ambushed near a pair of railroad tunnels four miles south of Chip'yong-ni.[45] Air strikes cause the Chinese to withdraw, and a relief force arrives at 0330 the next morning.

Second Division takes up a position between the Han River and Wonju.[46]

Knowing that the enemy will try to either drive the Eighth Army out of Korea or destroy it, Ridgway rejects a static defense. Damaging the Chinese and North Koreans as much as possible, preserving his own forces, and improving the combat effectiveness of his divisions and brigades are his immediate goals.

Map of 31 Jan 51:

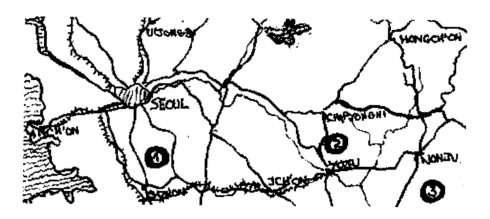

(1) Twenty-Fifth, Third, First Cavalry, and Twenty-Fourth Divisions prepare to advance to the south side of the Han River. Seoul, on the north side of the Han, is not an objective. (2) The Third Battalion, Twenty-Third Regiment, Second Division, and the French Battalion, with fire support from the Thirty-Seventh Field Artillery Battalion,

move to the Twin Tunnels area four miles south of Chip'yong-ni. (3) In the high mountains to the east of the Second Division there is patrol contact with the enemy in the vicinity of Wonju, Chech'on, Yongwol, and P'yongch'ang.

Mao sends General Peng this message: "Our forces must immediately prepare to launch the Fourth Campaign with the purpose of wiping out twenty to thirty thousand of the enemy and advancing to the Taejon-Andong line." The UN have plans to withdraw from Korea if pushed back to the Taejon-Andong line. Does Mao have intelligence on UN plans from British agents Donald Maclean, Harold Philby, and Guy Burgess? This order suggests that he does.

At dawn on 1 February the two battalions near Chip'yong-ni are attacked. After the bugles and horns the Chinese advance in heavy fog. While the first battle of the Twin Tunnels was limited, this is the start of a major battle against a much larger Chinese force. All day there is fierce fighting, heavy artillery fire, and eighty air strikes. Several times it seems that the Chinese will overrun the French and American soldiers. Finally, a French company commanded by Major Barthelemy charges the Chinese with fixed bayonets; the Chinese break and run. By dark the Chinese have suffered 1,300 KIA and an estimated 2,300 WIA.

Yet fighting on 2 February indicates the Chinese are determined to defend Chip'yong-ni, which is four miles away. The defenders of the Twin Tunnels have taken heavy casualties, are exhausted, and are low on ammo; the Chinese renew their attack. If the Chinese make another major assault all of the defenders of the Twin Tunnels expect to be killed. But a flight of Corsairs breaks through the clouds to pound the Chinese who are bunched up for an assault. The air force drops in ammo and a relief force arrives. The Twenty-Third Regiment has 225 casualties and has fought a major battle against a superior force, but it receives orders to move up to Chip'yong-ni after only a day to rest, resupply, and reorganize.

Map of 10 Feb 51:[47]

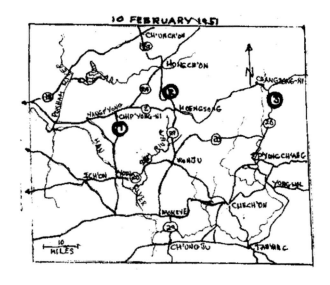

(1) Second Division (2) Fifth and Eighth ROK Divisions (3) Seventh and Third ROK Divisions

After dark on 11 February an attack is launched against the Eighth ROK Division, north of Hoengsong, from three directions. By midnight division headquarters loses contact with all regiments. No one knows the true situation. It is clear that a major attack is under way. But how many places will the Chinese attack? How strong will each be? Where will they go?

This attack catches the UN command by surprise since neither aerial reconnaissance nor radio intercepts have identified Chinese divisions[48] in the area. However, a few who accept information provided by a Chinese POW are not surprised. He is a captain and a former medical officer in the Chinese Nationalist Army. The information he provided proves to be very accurate, yet it is largely discounted because most Americans do not believe such a person could have such information. They do not realize that in the spirit of equalitarianism, and to motivate, the Chinese widely distribute information about future operations that Americans tightly hold on a "need to know" basis.

The surprise attack on 11 February destroys the Eighth ROK Division. Before daylight all units of that division and their support groups are surrounded with roadblocks on their withdrawal routes. Units become separated and divided, and then disintegrate. Small groups try to escape. Only a few make it out: 7,465 are killed or captured. The Third and Fifth ROK Divisions are engaged in heavy fighting on either side of Hoengsong. The attacks continue all day and through the night of 12–13 February. These two ROK Divisions withdraw toward Wonju.

On 13 February the Twenty-Third Regiment, Second Division is ordered back to Chip'yong-ni to prevent the Chinese from enveloping the right flank of the divisions at the Han opposite Seoul. Chip'yong-ni straddles a stream that is hugged on its northeast side by a mountain ridge. A perimeter defense is established around Chip'yong-ni.[49]

Artillery fires on enemy troops approaching Chip'yong-ni, but just after dark the Chinese are within a half mile of the perimeter. COL Freeman tells those at Chip'yong-ni: "We're going to stay here and fight it out." From 2300 until 0630 the next morning there are many assaults on the perimeter. The outcome of this battle is unclear.[50]

During the night of 13–14 February units of the three Chinese armies continue their attacks against the perimeter around Chip'yong-ni.[51] Flares soar, bugles blare, soldiers with satchel charges crawl forward, grenades blast, machine guns chatter, and there is unending rifle fire. It seems that dawn will never come. But when it does the fighting does not stop. During daylight the defenders have more air and artillery support, but their ammo is getting low. At first light the Twenty-Seventh British Brigade moves toward Chip'yong-ni.

Having taken Hoengsong, the Chinese move toward Wonju from the northwest and northeast. Units of the Second Division, 187th Brigade and the ROK Eighteenth Regiment go into defensive positions around Wonju from which they will fight for the next two days. The Chinese leaders are confident they will be able to capture Wonju and also force those units south of Seoul to pull back. In time they think they can reach the Taejon, Hamch'ang, Andong line—which their spies had said would trigger a withdrawal of UN forces from Korea.

At first light on 15 February the Fifth Cavalry Regiment renews its advance toward Chip'yong-ni, but by mid-afternoon has made limited progress. A task force of twenty-three tanks and an infantry company in armored personnel carriers is assembled to break through to Chip'yong-ni. At 1545 artillery fire and air strikes pound the hills as the task force moves forward.

During the first part of the advance there are many firefights in which many infantry soldiers are lost—but no tanks. At a road cut just south of their objective the task force must get through a strong roadblock; here a rocket knocks out one tank and two are damaged. At 1715 the lead tank enters Chip'yong-ni.

The tankers have only four KIA and three WIA, but the rifle company with the task force loses half of its soldiers. The heavy casualties among the infantry are the result of a decision by the task force commander (COL Crombez) to charge into Chip'yong-ni with the infantry riding on the tanks. The infantry Battalion CO (LTC Treacy) protests, and when ignored decides to go with his men. He is wounded, captured, and dies in a North Korean prison camp.

This event gives birth to one of the bitterest disputes in Korea. The surviving infantrymen of the task force collect statements and put Treacy in for the Congressional Medal of Honor. But when it gets to Crombez he says: "Medal of Honor, no, goddamn it, no." Crombez puts himself in for the Distinguished Service Cross. Many thought his recklessness and desire for personal glory resulted in unnecessary losses for the infantry-men. When his recommendation gets to the Eighth Army the chief of staff says: "No son of a bitch earns a DSC inspiring his troops buttoned up in a tank." Crombez appeals to Ridgway and he overrules his chief of staff, giving Crombez the DSC because Crombez brought the aid that Ridgway had promised Freeman if he held Chip'yong-ni.

As night falls a soft snow also falls on Chip'yong-ni. Thousands of Chinese bodies are covered—but there are American bodies among them. The next day the commanding officer (Captain Barrett) of the infantry company with the task force goes over the road by jeep in search of wounded infantrymen left by the tanks as they rushed to Chip'yong-ni.

The Chinese move away from Chip'yong-ni and Wonju. On 15 February there are attacks on the ROK Divisions, but the enemy appears to be exhausted since there are only probes for the next three days.[52]

Operation Killer

On 18 February Ridgway starts Operation Killer to keep pressure on the enemy by ordering an advance from Wonju north to Hoengsong. When the code name for Operation Killer (which Ridgway had personally selected for motivational reasons) reaches Washington there is a courteous protest. It is deemed politically insensitive. This incident illustrates the desire of many to ignore the reality of combat: killing is a fundamental. Neither conventional War[53] nor Warfare[54] are the give and take, the nonviolent cooperation and conflict of Peace.[55] Success (victory for War and stability for Warfare) depends on destroying the will to fight of your opponent. They are both ideological struggles. The outcome is determined by the inner strength of those in conflict. This is only accomplished when your adversaries convert, give up, or die. In both War and Warfare it is necessary to determine the most effective and efficient means, yet both involve killing your adversary. Those desiring Peace, but who are unwilling to pay the price to obtain Peace, do not understand this reality—they keep looking for a "soft" way. However, winning hearts and minds starts with ending the will to fight. Economic and political "development" accomplishes nothing unless local security is established and maintained.

Sam C. Holliday

Map of 28 Feb 51:

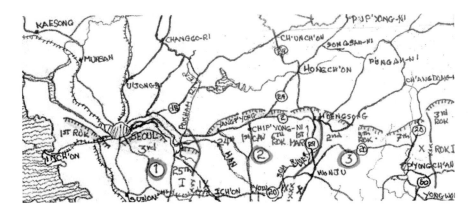

(1) Three divisions of I Corps hold the south bank of the Han River opposite Seoul. (2) Four divisions and a brigade of IX Corps hold a shallow arc north of the Han River and five miles above Chip'yong-ni to Hoengsong. (3) Four divisions and one brigade of X Corps are east of IX Corps. Three divisions of ROK III Corps are east of X Corps to the spine of the Taebaek Mountains.

UN troops start Operation Killer pushing slowly north. The goal is to destroy enemy forces and equipment and to disrupt any attempt to organize an offensive. Across the front, UN forces must first find the enemy, then fix them in place, and finally bring down artillery and air firepower to finish them. It is slow and difficult combat in below freezing weather.

The weather abruptly changes; it rises fifty degrees. There is rain for three days, the rivers rise, the fords are unusable, and the roads are quagmires, but at night there is still freezing. Operation Killer becomes a plodding affair. Resupply is a major problem, but frequent airdrops keep it from becoming critical.

There are forward area supply shortages, particularly in food, petroleum products, and ammunition, so the start date of Operation Ripper is in doubt. Stocks are expended during Operation Killer plus rains, melting ice, and snow have damaged roads, rail lines, bridges, and tunnels. In addition, Ridgway plans to cancel Ripper if there is clear evidence of an imminent attack, but intelligence is inadequate. He orders all units to patrol in front of their positions in order to identify enemy locations and strengths. Ridgway still sees his goal as "inflicting maximum losses on the enemy at minimum cost while maintaining major units intact."

By the end of February the Eighth Army has advanced only twenty miles in awful weather, and the terrain taken is of little importance. The success of Operation Killer is the number of Chinese and North Koreans killed, since this is how victory is usually achieved in War.

Peng Goes to Beijing

Peng recognizes the momentum of the November 1950 victories in North Korea has been lost. The great losses in February 1951 from American firepower, plus a vigorous new commander, cause him to fly to Beijing to talk personally with Mao. There has been tension between the two for several months, but now Peng decides he has to get Mao to realize there is not going to be a quick victory.

He arrives in mid-morning to find Mao still sleeping. Peng is told, "You can't go in."

Peng replies, "My men are dying on the battlefield. I can't wait for him to wake up."

Peng goes in, wakes up Mao, and tells him they are facing a new war—a long, difficult war. As comrades throughout their long civil war they discuss the situation in Korea. They agree on some rotation of troops, and that a united communist Korea is still the goal.

GEN Dehuai Peng has risen from being an impoverished peasant to being a trusted friend of Mao, and a hardened combat veteran who is admired as a soldier. On politics he has always deferred to Mao, who he considers an older brother.

Peng's early life was very harsh. The rich landowners he knew were cruel and mistreated the peasants. His mother died when he was young. His father was sick and unable to work. He dropped out of school. The youngest of his four brothers died of starvation. Peng went to live with his grandmother. Rather than beg for food he went into the forest to cut wood to sell. As a young boy (10–14) he did menial work to earn money, but would often be cheated out of what he had been promised to return home dirty and with bloody feet. As a teenager he saw landlords and merchants hoard food in order to drive up prices, which caused him to join protests. For this he had to leave his village. At seventeen he became a private in the Hunan Provincial Army.

He first supported Chiang Kai-shek because Peng thought he was a revolutionary who would change China so the peasants would have better lives. But he turned to the communists when he felt that Chiang was no longer going to "overthrow warlords, corrupt officials, local despots, and evil gentry and bring about a cut in land rent and interest."

In 1928 he became a member of the Communist party. In 1934 he helped develop the military strategies and tactics which would be used until 1949 to defeat the nationalists: nimble, irregular operations with dedicated, disciplined soldiers, never to challenge the enemy frontally, but to be able to move quickly and make decisive attacks when the enemy is vulnerable.

Several years after the Korean War, Peng challenged Mao on the direction he was taking China. Peng ended up being imprisoned, humiliated, and beaten to death.

South Korean Government

While the Eighth Army pushes forward in Operation Killer, and is planning Operation Ripper, the ROK government focuses on rebuilding the structures, processes, and procedures of governance. They know that long-term success depends on creation of a common sense of identity among all Koreans, i.e. building a nation. Yet their short-term challenge is the creation of effective and efficient governance at all levels for South Korea, i.e. building a state, and to do this the ROK government uses authoritarian means.

Ridgway's Evaluation of MacArthur

Twelve years later, I had the opportunity to discuss operations in Korea with General Mathew B. Ridgway. From August 1962 until December 1963 I was at the University of Pittsburgh earning a Master's in Public and International Affairs. General Ridgway lived next to the university and took an active interest in university affairs. In fact, the Matthew B. Ridgway Center for International Security Studies is at the University of Pittsburgh. In the living room of his home I had several one-on-one meetings with the General in which we discussed his views of the Korean War. He also asked me about my experiences.

In 1967 most of what we discussed was published in his book *The Korean War*. However, in our discussions he was more critical of General MacArthur and his staff than he was in his book. He thought the staff was too concerned with telling MacArthur what he wanted to hear and stroking his ego, thus not serving either MacArthur or his command well. He commented on MacArthur's taking credit for things he did not do and failing to acknowledge errors he did make. He thought the extravagant and grandiose statements made by MacArthur, and his challenging of the foreign policy of the president, were neither wise nor in the national interests. They were just a reflection of his ego. General Ridgway even suggested that MacArthur held delusions about what was going on in Korea and the use of nuclear weapons.

---

[42] Route number one.

[43] On routes nine and thirteen.

[44] Second, Ninth, Twenty-Seventh, and Thirty-First Divisions.

[45] The patrol suffers five KIA, twenty-nine WIA, and five MIA.

[46] The Twenty-Third Regiment sets up a patrol base in Wonju. The Eighth ROK Division is east of, and the Second Division north of, Chech'on. The Seventh Division is among the Taebaek Mountains north of Yongwol; it has pursued the NK Divisions to P'yongch'ang (twenty-five miles east of Wonju). It forms the east (right) flank of the Eighth Army.

[47]   1. Twenty-Third Regiment, Second Division, with the French Battalion, moves to Chip'yong-ni and establishes defensive positions. This is the first move of Operation Roundup, which also includes the advancing of the Second and Eighth ROK Divisions up Route #29 from Hoengsong to Hongch'on. Two tank-infantry teams of the Second Division are attached to the Eighth ROK Division for the attack toward Hongch'on, and a tank-infantry team from the 187th Regiment is organized as a reserve.

   2. The ROK Fifth and Eighth Divisions move on narrow roads and trails through the mountains parallel to Route #29. Physical contact between columns is rare. For three days the terrain is a greater obstacle than the enemy, but there are reports of enemy concentra-tion south of Hongch'on by 10 February 1951.

   After units of the Fortieth and Sixty-Sixth Chinese Armies move through Hongch'on they stay hidden during the day, unless there is a heavy cloud cover close to the ground. Vehicles are always hidden during the day. Anytime an airplane is heard all soldiers freeze in place. Thus UN forces do not know how many troops are south of Hongch'on, or where they are located. However, at night they move forward to positions from which they think they can attack the advancing ROK Divisions. The same is true of the Forty-Second Chinese Army north of Chip'yong-ni.

3. The Eighth and Third ROK Divisions advance slowly toward Hongch'on (thirty-three miles north of Wonju). The 198th, 120th, and 117th CCF Divisions have been waiting for days for just the right time to attack. The Seventh and Third ROK Divisions advance toward Ch'angdong-ni (Fifty miles and two valleys northeast of Wonju). The NK II Corps has been waiting for them.

[48] The 198th, 120th, and 117th CCF divisions had moved into position undetected.

[49] In the perimeter are: Twenty-Third Regiment; French Battalion; Ranger Company; FA Company, AAA Company; E Company.

[50] Third and Fifth ROK Divisions delay NKPA V Corps as they continue their withdrawal toward Wonju. To their east the Seventh and Ninth ROK Divisions withdraw while they hold back the NKPA II Corps. Remnants of the Eighth ROK Division move south in small groups.

[51] CCF Thirty-Ninth, Fortieth, and Forty-Second Armies.

[52] First Cavalry Division, Twenty-Seventh British Brigade, and Sixth ROK Division seize a rail line three miles northwest of Chip'yong-ni; this blocks any move into the Han River valley.

[53] War is symmetrical conflict between the armed forces of states.

[54] Warfare is asymmetrical conflict by non-state actors using all means possible to weaken or overthrow those in authority.

[55] Peace is a climate of order in which no one is willing to use violence for political ends.

CHAPTER TWENTY-ONE

COMMAND OF FOX COMPANY

1–23 March 1951

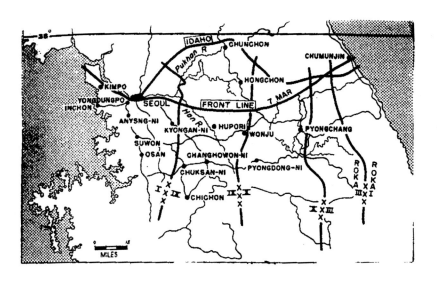

I commanded F (Fox) Company, Second Battalion, Thirty-Fifth "Cacti" Regiment, Twenty-Fifth "Tropic Lightning" Division, I Corps, Eighth Army during March, April, and May of 1951.

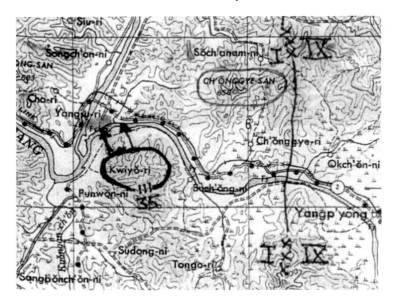

On 7 March the Thirty-Fifth Regiment makes an assault across the Han River at the junction of the Pukhan River east of Seoul. The temperature is fifteen degrees below zero. After the artillery preparation lifts at 0615, it takes twenty minutes for the assault boats to cross the river. They are unopposed. Tanks join the infantry. By 0800 the initial battalions had advanced one thousand yards in spite of mines, small arms, machine gun, and mortar fire. By the end of the day the regiment had gained more than a mile.

Twenty-Fifth Division troops fan out to increase the size of their bridgehead across the Han River. The enemy puts up a stubborn defense. It is estimated that during the first three days five thousand Chinese are killed, but more surrender than in the past. Aerial observers report many CCF troops moving out of Seoul.

Two days after crossing the Han the enemy still defends their positions, but withdraws when assaulted. Typical of such action is the capture, on 9 March, of Chonggye-san (658) the highest hill mass overlooking the bridgehead.

My first action as company commander is during the crossing of the Han River. The Second Battalion crosses during the afternoon of 7 March and initially takes a position behind the Third Battalion. On 8 March we move up to take a position on the Green Line. The next day F Company makes the assault on the enemy's position overlooking the bridgehead across the Han: Chonggye-San.

First Attack, 9 March 1951

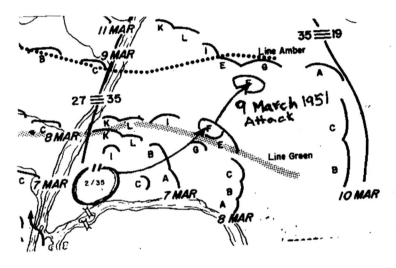

There are two ridges running to the top of Chonggye-San, the hill mass that dominated the bridgehead. The left ridge has a large knob about 150 yards from the top. Then there is a saddle over to the top. I plan to have the First Platoon and the Weapons Platoon move up the left ridge to establish their machine guns and the 57-mm recoilless rifle on the knob. They are to support the assault of the Second and Third Platoons as they advance up the right ridge. I am going to be on the right ridge with the two assaulting platoons.

We move up the ridges together. Artillery shells are landing on the top where the enemy is located. When the Second and Third Platoons are opposite the knob, I stop them until the Weapons Platoon can be set up and start firing at the top. As soon as they start firing I have the artillery shift forward of the two assault platoons. When we get within sixty yards of the top the enemy fires their final shots and withdraws. The two platoons continue to the top; I tell them not to walk around on the top but to immediately establish defensive positions. At the same time I tell the First Platoon and Weapons Platoon to move forward to join me on the top.

Unknown to me, the regimental commander COL Gerald C. Kelleher, who had been an outstanding commander during World War II, is with the First Platoon watching the attack. I guess he wants to see what his new company commander has. He walks across the saddle to the main ridge before I tell the First Platoon to move over.

"Fox Six, this is Cacti Six. I'm over here on your left flank and it is wide open. Where are you?"

He knew where I was, but I answered: "I'm getting the two assault platoons in a defensive position. I'll be over as soon as I finish."

"Hell, they're all gone. I'm here and nobody is shooting at me."

"Roger."

I walk over to where Colonel Kelleher is. "Good morning, sir."

"Holliday, what are you going to do?"

By then the First Platoon has joined us, so I said: "I'm going to take this platoon over and put it in a defensive position on our left flank."

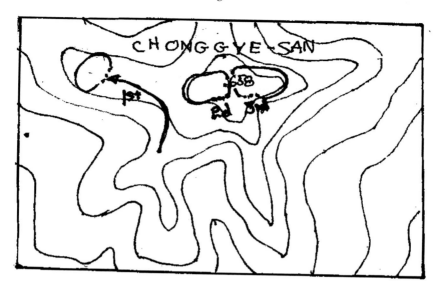

"I'm walking over there right now," he snaps.

"I'll go with you," I reply.

I signal with my hand for the platoon to follow. Without talking, the colonel and I walk over to the left side of the ridge top. He is not into small talk. I tell the platoon leader where to establish his defense.

The Colonel watches. He looks over at me: "Carry on, Holliday."

"Yes, sir." He leaves.

He is a hard-nosed, demanding, courageous, up-front combat leader. He had been a battalion commander in the 104th Division during World War II and because of his heroism had been promoted to full colonel and given command of the 414th Regiment.

He is big on discipline and expects his orders to be followed to the letter. Each soldier is to always carry his weapon and to wear all issued equipment—including helmets. Jeeps are always to be parked facing out (i.e., so they do not have to turn around). There are to be no lackadaisical soldiers in his regiment. It is always "Be prepared"; "Don't just stand there—do something." He is not loveable; he rarely smiles and is a contrast with his predecessor. Colonel Fisher had been stern, but friendly and fatherly. Under Kelleher the Thirty-Fifth Regiment was known as one of the best regiments in Korea.[56]

Eighth Army Offensive: 7 March–23 April 1951

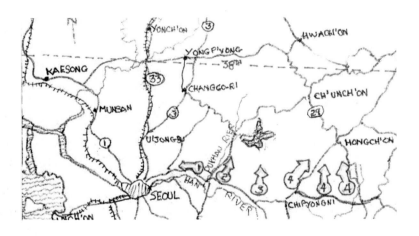

The crossing of the Han is the start of a general offensive involving the whole Eighth Army, which included Operations Ripper, Rugged, and Dauntless. In Operation Ripper, (1) Twenty-Seventh Regiment occupies the west side of the Pukhan River and moves west to a hill overlooking Seoul. Against moderate resistance, the Thirty-Fifth Regiment (2) expands the bridgehead across the Han ten miles up both sides of the Pukhan River. Against light resistance, Twenty-Fourth Division (3) advances toward the Chong'pyong Reservoir. The First Cavalry (4), Sixth

ROK, and First Marine Divisions (4) move toward Hongch'on and are in a position to out flank enemy forces in the center of Korea.

During this period the Twenty-Fifth Division is in the Uijongbu corridor that is the traditional invasion route to Seoul from the north. After crossing the Han we advance north up this corridor during March and then fight a delaying action over the same terrain during April.

Since 7 March delaying actions by NK forces in the center corridor had kept the gains short, but on 12 March they begin to withdraw, making advances easier. A recovery team finds more than 250 bodies of men from a US artillery support group that was attacked in mid-February. They also retrieve five 155-mm howitzers, six M-5 tractors, four tanks, and many damaged trucks.

In the mountains the ROK units make only minor adjustments because they are already ahead of the ROK units on the east coast, and the First Marine Division conducts anti-guerrilla operations.[57]

This is one of many times in Korea when conventional military units failed using traditional anti-guerrilla tactics. In War search and destroy missions to eliminate guerrillas in a specific area are often given to conventional War forces. However, these tactics are ineffective when the "guerrillas" can blend with the locals and have their support—either from agreement on ideology or from fear of being killed. Success goes to the side best able to provide local security and with the best intelligence networks, not to those with the most advanced technology and most firepower. This is a lesson that could have been learned in Korea, but was not. The error has been repeated in many places since the 1950s—with the same lack of success.

On the night of 12 March patrols from the Third Division cross the Han into Seoul and find shoreline positions vacant. ROK First Division crosses the Han during the afternoon of 13 March. On the night of 13 March units from the Third Division move more than a half mile north of the Han without making contact.[58]

On 14 March the ROK First and Third Divisions move through a devastated Seoul of ruins and corrugated iron. They move through the city seeing no enemy. First ROK Division raises a ROK flag on the capitol dome and reaches the north gate. On 15 March both divisions continue to search the city discovering a few North Korean deserters who have been away from their units too long to provide information of value. Aerial observers see no enemy activity immediately north of Seoul but they observe defensive preparations halfway between Seoul and Uijongbu.

The First Cavalry Division attacks Hongch'on from the west and the First Marine Division attacks Hongch'on from the east. They meet little resistance. The First Cavalry reaches Hongch'on and waits for the marines to move up and enter Hongch'on at noon on 15 March. The town is in ruins and undefended. There are small bombs dropped by the air force set to explode when disturbed.

The Chinese move six armies to just north of the 38th Parallel.[59]

F Company conducts sweeps, establishes defensive positions, and makes three attacks on significant objectives: Sori-Bong (25 March), Many Fingers Hill (30 March), and Triple Nickel Hill (4–5 April). At the end of this offensive the Eighth Army has liberated Seoul and established a new defensive line north of the 38th Parallel.[60]

Replacements

We are getting replacements which have been scheduled to go to the Twenty-Fourth Regiment, an all-black unit—except for some of the officers and senior NCOs. But it is being desegregated. Although they have been scheduled for the "Deuce Fo" because their records listed them as "Colored," some of these men are brown skinned and could easily pass as being from southern Europe or the Middle East. While PFC Sam D. Spain is jet black and clearly has African ancestors, with him came CPL Reginald Brown with his red hair and blue eyes; he could have been an Irishman with a good tan, and the medic Thomas is a "high yellow" with gray eyes and an appearance that only suggested African ancestors.

I make a special point of meeting with each of them to make certain they understand that I respect them, and expect as much from them as I do from anyone else in the company. I want them to know that I will make sure they are treated just like anyone else. If there are ever any racial problems, they are to come directly to me. I expect everyone in the company to do their best, to take care of others, and to live up to the traditions of brave warriors of all cultures.

I end our talk with, "There will be discrimination in this company—plenty of discrimination. But it won't be because of the color of your skin. It will be because of what you do, or don't do—just like everyone else. If you are careless, lazy, or cowardly you will be discriminated against, but if you are brave, strong, a skilled fighter, and a comrade to those with you, there will be discrimination in your favor with recognition, respect, and rewards."

Building a Combat-Ready Company

During March, I focus on improving the combat effectiveness of F Company. Fortunately, we have no stressful combat until 30 March. I know that combat camaraderie can only be created through shared stressful experiences; however, that same stress can destroy a unit. It cannot come from talk, it must be realized from experience in combat.

After I take command my initial goal is to convince the soldiers, the noncommissioned officers, and the platoon leaders of F Company that I am a capable commander they can trust. I think I have accomplished that with the 9 March attack, which was not only successful but also planned and executed with skill. Yet I know combat effectiveness will require more. It will require training and discipline, but most of all it will require strong inner compasses in each of my men. What they do in combat, and how they handle the traumatic experiences of combat, will primarily be ideological, i.e. the strength of their values, beliefs, and convictions. Combat effectiveness is dependent on combat camaraderie, and combat camaraderie depends on the strength of the inner compass of the warriors and soldiers involved. Men grow into warriors through experience if they meet combat honestly and courageously. Good judgment in combat comes from experience, but a lot of experience is the result of not being killed by bad judgment.

I have to prepare them to handle the stressful experiences that I know will come. The key to combat effectiveness is not new. As Sun Tzu said in *The Art of War*:

Regard your soldiers as your children and they will follow you into the deepest valleys; look on them as your own beloved sons, and they will stand by you even unto death.

If, however, you are indulgent, but unable to make your authority felt, kindhearted but unable to enforce your commands; and incapable, moreover, of quelling disorder, then your soldiers must be likened to spoiled children; they are useless for any practical purpose. (Part 10)

My aim is to convince all of those in F Company that they have to see themselves as a team if they are to survive. I am realistic, practical, and demanding on everything we have to do to prepare for the battles we will face in the coming weeks. I make sure that each day I talk with each squad. What I do varies; sometimes I gave instructions, sometimes I teach, sometimes I make corrections, but often I just ask questions and listen. I know that warriors and soldiers will forget what you say, they will even forget what you do, but they will never forget how you make them feel. I know that the secret to success for the company will be the leadership of the platoon and squad leaders.

I remind everyone in the company that they are infantrymen. It is the infantryman who is the point of the spear. There is never victory until infantrymen go the final yards, or hold firm. Being an infantryman is a dangerous job, but one of the most honorable, most selfless, and most demanding of callings. My aim is to shape the inner compass of each of the men in F Company so that under the stress of combat each will react as successful infantrymen always do.

There are a few things I often repeat:

"How ya doing? What do ya need?"

"Learn now. What you will learn in a firefight will be costly. More sweat now means less blood later."

"In an assault don't think—ACT! That will save your life."

"How much sleep hav'ya had today? Sleep whenever you can; but one of you must stay awake, and alert, whenever the enemy is near."

"Have you checked each other's weapons? If any of them fail you all will pay."

"Don't take the easy way in an attack since that is where the enemy's guns will be pointed. Always know who will cover you before you move. Move where you cannot be seen."

"If you take care of those with you, they will take care of you."

"What are your best skills? Which skills do you need to improve?"

"Those who live do the harder right rather than the easier wrong."

"If you see them, kill them. Forget about the innocent until proven guilty stuff. Would you rather feel bad because you killed someone, or be dead?"

"Forget about them being humans with families and friends—only remember that if you don't kill them, they will kill you."

"One of these days it might again be: Do unto others as you would have others do unto you. Now, however, it must be: Do unto others before they can do it to you."

Routine Activities and Standard Operating Procedures

Whenever possible I have a Korean hut in each platoon area so they can get out of the bad weather. But I also check to see that there are sentries to prevent surprise attacks while they are resting, cleaning up, sleeping, or just keeping warm.

Whenever we are in a defensive position I see that they have planned their fields of fire, know where others are, have established communication, and are dug in.

It normally takes me more than two hours to check defensive positions of the whole company. When I return to the company command post the first sergeant (Master Sergeant Bingham) always has a foxhole for both of us to share.

Ideological Preparedness

I often make reference to some well-known stories; I work them into our discussions. Many know these stories, but I have to use them with care. I cannot allow them to be just stories from the past. The lessons in these stories have to be relevant to them personally. The stories can be used to illustrate the timeless qualities of infantrymen and encourage them to identify with infantrymen of the past. I want them to feel this bond, and to see themselves as an extension of a noble tradition. I want them to have the moral confidence and certainty needed to act without hesitation. I want them to free themselves from uncertainties and doubts. I want them to act like Beowulf.

When appropriate, these are the stories I would use:

Horatius at the Bridge: One brave man doing the right thing can save many.

The Three Hundred Spartans at Thermopylae: Men of courage stand together.

Crossing the Rubicon: After an infantryman makes a daring decision there is no turning back.

William Tell: To be free, brave men must stand against tyranny and evil.

Travis's Message from the Alamo: Victory or Death.

Liberty or Death (Patrick Henry): Victory goes not only to the strong, it also goes to the vigilant, the active, and the brave. Is life so dear, or peace so sweet, as to be purchased at the price of chains and slavery?

I use these stories to remind each individual how as an infantrymen he differs from others:

- The infantryman is prepared to suffer, sacrifice, and die for others. Others often use words to describe a utopia of fairness, compassion, and love for which someone else is expected to suffer, sacrifice, and die to achieve.

- The infantryman is often unknown, looked down upon, or ignored. Others seek fame, adulation, and rewards. Yet it is the infantryman that is essential if any group is to grow and prosper.

- The infantryman lives in the reality of the present. Others are often creatures of an abstract fantasy future, or some mythical past.

I consider it an honor to be in the company of the infantrymen of F Company, and I did my best to let them know this. The next four chapters describe what the infantrymen of F Company did while I was in their company.

My Left Knee

It is a rainy day. But it is not nearly as cold as it had been. I am satisfied because I think F Company is battle ready. We are moving near a large hill mass east of Uijongbu called Sori-Bong—which we rename Easter Hill.

To get to our new location we have to cross some rice paddies, which are muddy with a few inches of water. The closest Chinese are several miles away. There is an occasional artillery shell, but they are being fired from such a great distance the chance of getting hit is very low. The company is in several columns walking on the small dikes between the rice paddies.

I hear the SWISH of incoming artillery. Instinctively I duck. The shell splashes harmlessly several hundred yards away. However, I slip off of the small muddy dike. I twist my left knee. This is to be a problem for the rest of my command of F Company. I try to straighten my leg, but can't. I know I will have to hobble along for several days.

That night I work to get the knee back in place and wrap it with an ACE bandage. In a few days it is better. From then on I keep it wrapped tight, and most of the time it is okay. However, I repeatedly hurt it and it gets worse and worse. I can still go up hills, but going down is very difficult and painful.[61]

The Advance to the 38th Parallel

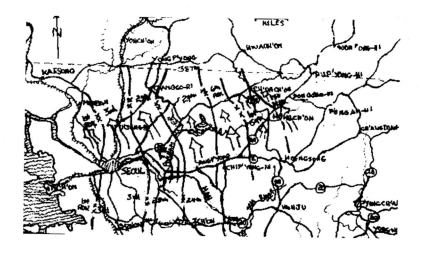

By 21 March all UN forces in western Korea are advancing to the 38th Parallel, yet the policy regarding advancing into North Korea again has not been resolved. In Washington it is decided that the commitments and risks associated with seeking a military victory in Korea are too great. The goal is set as a cease-fire and a negotiated settlement. It is agreed that how this is to be achieved should be made after the Eighth Army has driven the enemy north of the 38th Parallel. There are no plans of how to be successful in the Warfare that is sure to follow, or how to win the ideological conflict with China and North Korea.

Those of us at the lower levels have no knowledge of the struggles going on between MacArthur and Washington.

---

[56] Kelleher concluded his career as a brigadier general with two Distinguished Service Crosses and five Silver Stars. In retirement he was known as "The General." He died at ninety-five in Florida.

[57] In the rear of ROK I Corps, elements of the NKPA Tenth Division (which had been isolated since January) attempt to move north through UN positions. For the next ten days NKPA Tenth Division has a series of hide and seek skirmishes with the ROK Ninth and ROK Capital Divisions. Although the First Marine Division had been responsible for destroying the NKPA Tenth Division during February, the Tenth Division is still an effective, although smaller, unit.

[58] The three Divisions of I Corps advance abreast with the Second Division on the left (west), the Seventh Division following Route #20 on the right (east), and the ROK Fifth Division between the two US Divisions.

[59] The Sixty-Third, Sixty-Fourth, and Sixty-Fifth Chinese Armies and three artillery regiments have moved from China and the Twentieth, Twenty-Sixth, and Twenty-Seventh Chinese Armies have moved down from North Korea.

[60] After the Han crossing the Thirty-Fifth Regiment moved west into a staging area from which it could secure the hills overlooking the Pukham River Valley—the main route to Seoul from the northeast. By 24 March the Thirty-Fifth Regiment was in position to attack Sori-bong, a hill mass to the east of Uijongbu. Two roads used by the North Koreans when they captured Seoul in June 1950, and again by the Chinese when they captured Seoul in December 1950, were joined at Uijongbu—which is why that city was known as the gateway to Seoul.

[61] The fact I continue to climb up and down hills no doubt causes additional damage. The medial meniscus had been torn and a piece of cartilage kept getting where it should not be, causing the knee to "lock" and swell. It is operated on in 1952.

CHAPTER TWENTY-TWO

EASTER AND MANY FINGERS HILL

24–31 March 1951

On 23 March parachute troops of the 187th RCT land at Musan, on the Imjin River, against light resistance. There are only nineteen battle casualties. Some civilians try to carry away parachutes. The airborne operation fails to trap any units; the North Koreans have successfully pulled back behind the Imjin River. The tank task force links up with the 187th RCT at 1830. Another tank column of the Third Division moves from Seoul to Uijongbu. Units of the Chinese establish new positions north of Uijongbu.

On 24 March the Thirty-Fifth Regiment moves into position to attack Sori-Bong, a hill mass to the east of Uijongbu. Since our attack was on Easter Day, we call Sori-Bong Easter Hill.

Easter Hill: 25–26 March

In a thick fog and a steady drizzle on 25 March we start up Easter Hill. The Chinese have held this group of hills for several weeks and have well prepared defensive positions, so we are expecting some heavy fighting. We know that our goal is not to merely capture ground, but primarily to destroy the enemy.

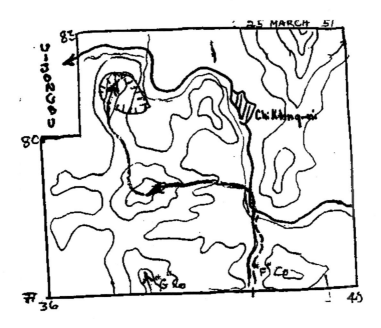

F Company is in a valley below, and east of, G Company. On 24 March G Company has a tough fight in capturing the south end of Easter Hill. That night they occupy that end of the ridge. G Company is to continue north along that ridge, while F Company is to envelop the Chinese positions by attacking, from the east, the last peaks of the ridge.

Before we start a drizzle sets in. The trail up the valley toward Chiktong-ni is so muddy the jeeps cannot be used. I move the company forward and over a low pass to a small stream where there is a road. Here I receive my final instructions. From the map I know that the hilltop I am to take is directly to our west, but we can only see a vague outline of the hill because of the rain and fog.

As we start our climb, the rain gets heavier. In spite of our raincoats, we are all soaked and cold. The slope is muddy. As we near the top, where I expect a fight, I jump the Third Platoon through the others. After several anxious minutes I see a white flare from the top of the hill—the signal that it has been taken. It turns out that the Chinese had left their positions during the night.

I am told that our position for the night of 25 March will be another hill to the north overlooking the road west of Chiktong-ni. This means we have to move another 1,200 yards along the ridge. This we do with no difficulty.

However, my left knee is giving me problems whenever I have to go down a steep slope. I put my arms around LT Smith, the forward observer, and Master Sergeant Paul A. Bingham, my first sergeant. This takes the weight off of the left leg. Then I hobble down the slope using only my right leg.

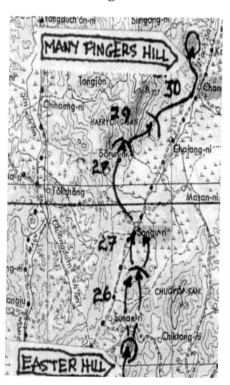

On 26 March we move off of Easter Hill to positions along the road north of Uijongbu. That night we are just southwest of Song-ri and eight miles northeast of Uijongbu.

27–29 March

Each day the Twenty-Fifth Division moves northeast along the road toward Kumhwa. The Chinese conduct delaying actions during the day and patrols around our defensive positions during the night. Eighth Army reports that three Chinese battalions have been captured, and there is heavy resistance in our area.

Frank Tribble watches his steps as he follows the squad leader across a narrow dike between rice paddies—as he has done so often. They reach a road and the SGT says: "We are to wait here."

Frank sits down, and soon he is thinking of Nancy as he so often does. He had spent his last year before being sent to Korea with her. He thought of their last night together. That night she held him tighter than ever before.

"Move out!" It is his platoon sergeant. Again there is the line of men moving together to some new hill. Frank knows he will soon be digging a foxhole. Perhaps the enemy will attack. Perhaps not. But surely there will be more moving and fighting and more thoughts of Nancy.

At Changgo-ri the road divides; the main road continues northeast to Kumhwa, and the other turns left and then north to Yongp'yong. The Chinese clearly intend to hold this location as long as possible because they have strong positions on the hills overlooking the road junction.

On 29 March the Second Battalion has a bloody fight capturing the hill west of Changgo-ri and south of the road to Yongp'yong. This is twenty-three miles from Seoul. The attack starts after breakfast, but as soon as the men start up a finger of the hill there are casualties from rifles, machine guns, and grenades. Some Chinese are fighting from a large cave. In taking the cave a platoon leader of G Company (LT Tilford Jones) is covered with blood. The fighting continues most of the day since the hill is well defended; there are many casualties—including the battalion CO (LTC Merritt). Finally the hill is taken and the enemy are dead, POWs, or have fled.

Many Fingers Hill: 30 March 1951

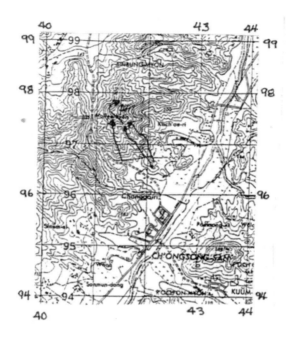

Two roads go north from Changgo-ri. The main road follows the river to the northeast. The other goes west from Changgo-ri over a low pass and then turns north into another valley. Between these two roads stands what we called "Many Fingers Hill." That hill overlooks Changgo-ri and controls both roads. It is the critical terrain in the area. It is the last defensive position south of the 38th Parallel.

On 30 March the First Battalion moves through Changgo-ri without opposition. At the same time G Company takes a hill directly west of Changgo-ri without opposition. However, the First Battalion starts to receive fire from the hill northwest of the town. B Company moves toward that hill, but by 1400 hours it is stopped by fire from one of the lower mounds near the main

road to Kumhwa. That is when I receive orders to take Many
Fingers Hill.

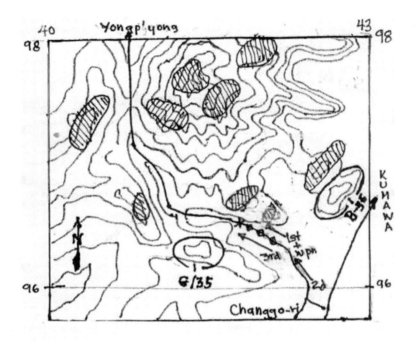

After looking over the hill, I decide a frontal attack on the hill is
not wise, and develop the following plan: F Company will move
up the west road, which is protected by G Company, and attack
Many Fingers Hill from the southwest using the high ground on
the west side of the pass as a base of fire. However, I am told there
is not sufficient daylight left for such envelopment and I will have
to attack the hill from the southeast. A platoon of half-tracks, with
multiple .50-caliber machine guns, is attached to me for this attack.

We start up the west road with the First Platoon and the
Weapons Platoon on the right side of the road. The Third Platoon
is on the left side of the road, with the half-tracks and Second
Platoon on the road. At the first knob we find a ditch across the

road that prevents the half-tracks from moving into firing positions. I leave LT Craig there with instructions to fill in the ditch and move up as soon as possible. The company moves on up. Against light opposition the First Platoon takes the first knob on the right with fire support from G Company, on a hill south of the road.

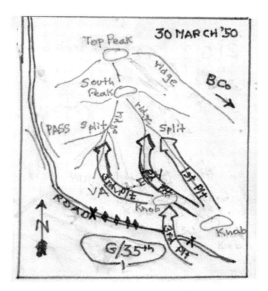

Just as we round a curve we find another—larger—ditch across the road, I move up to the edge of the ditch. *ZING*. The dirt on the left bank of the road kicks up. I jump behind the right bank. I am very glad the shooter is not a good marksman.

I cautiously look over the bank. I can see no movement, nor tell where the shot came from. However, this is the first time I get a good look at Many Fingers Hill, although I have an idea of what it is like from the map. Seventy-five yards in front of me a small ridge runs north from the road to the second knob on the right of the road; past that knob is a valley and after the valley the road turns north to the pass. I can see five fingers of the hill. One runs directly east from the top peak—forming the right skyline as I look at it. At the base of that finger B Company is attempting to take one of its lower mounds and has artillery firing further up that finger. The other four fingers do not actually come from the top peak, but from a second peak just south of it. From this second peak one ridge comes southeast about halfway down the hill and then splits into two ridges.

351

Another ridge from the southern peak comes south and splits about halfway down the hill into four smaller fingers—all of these smaller fingers end up in a valley to my left. The pass is on the far left side of the last of the fingers ending in the valley.

I order LT Whitner to cross the road with the Third Platoon and take the second knob on the right side of the road with fire support from Weapons Platoon on the first knob. As the Third Platoon nears the top of the second knob it draws fire from the enemy in front of B Company. However, this does not stop them; they take the second knob. The Third Platoon then overlooks the valley and can give fire support to the First and Second Platoons as they move up two of the ridges toward the southern peak from the southeast. The Weapons Platoon on the first knob can also provide fire support to the First and Second Platoons. Moreover, I move the artillery fire ahead of those two platoons.

I give instructions for Master Sergeant Lackner (First Platoon) and LT Toomy (Second Platoon) to cross the valley and move up two of the ridges to the south peak. Lackner is to be on the right ridge and Toomy is to be on the left. They are to join up about halfway to the top of the south peak where the two ridges come together. They are then to move on to take the south peak if they can. I give instructions to LT Smith, the artillery forward observer, to have the artillery fire prepared to move up

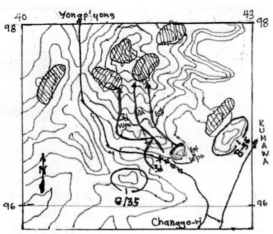

the ridges in advance of these two platoons. The Third Platoon on the second knob, and the Weapons Platoon on the first knob, are to give the First and Second Platoon fire support.

I have LT Smith start the artillery where the two ridges come together since I expect that location to be well defended. I tell Lackner and Toomey to move out. As soon as these platoons are in the valley they suffer casualties. The fire comes from their right—from the enemy in front of B Company.

Frank Tribble is one of the casualties. It feels like he has been kicked in the stomach as he falls to the ground. He pulls up his shirt to find a bullet hole with blood coming out. He feels around but can find no exit hole. There is a dull ache in his stomach, and some pain when he moves. But the pain is not as bad as the time he broke his arm.

Then he can only think of Nancy and the last time they were together. She held him tight, looked up with affection, and kissed him. When he tried to pull away, she pulled him back into her and wrapped her legs around him. He felt muscle contractions throughout her body and rhythmic movement of her pelvic muscles.

He hears rifle shots from up the ridge where the platoon has moved. Frank realizes he is on the ground where he has been shot. He is not going to let that bullet take him! He will be with Nancy once again!

Both platoons get across the valley and start up their ridges. They have no additional problems until they get to where the two ridges come together. There they meet the enemy that has survived the artillery. By now the half-tracks have gotten past the first ditch and are able to provide fire support; I instruct them to fire past where the two ridges join. However, some of the .50-caliber rounds fall on the two platoons. I stop the firing from the half-tracks and tell LT Craig to move them to where he can provide more effective fire support.

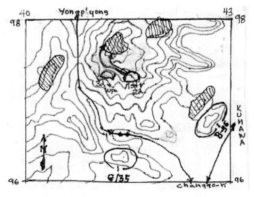

I decide to move the Third Platoon (LT Whitner) and the Weapons Platoon up one of the fingers running south from the south peak in order to relieve pressure on the First and Second Platoons. I move up with them. We are stopped by heavy fire just as we get even with the other two platoons.

"Fox Six," I hear on my radio from battalion. "We can see your men on top of the hill."

"They're not mine. We are still pinned down. I'm having fire placed on the top."

"Are you sure they aren't yours?"

"Yes, I'm in visual contact with all of my platoons."

I decide those on top are the Chinese fleeing from the First and Second Platoons. I then instruct LT Smith to place artillery on the top two peaks. And I tell LT Craig to do the same with the .50-caliber machine guns. I tell Lackner and Toomey that I think the enemy in front of them has moved out and for them to try to move forward in order to hit the flank of those holding up the Third Platoon. This they do; then all three platoons advance to the top two peaks. There we find many Chinese dugouts with clothing, ammunition, and other things indicating a rapid departure, but only dead and wounded Chinese.

Night is approaching and no one has moved up to tie in with us. We set up in a tight perimeter. We dig in, and as the 4.2-mm mortars are establishing defensive fire one of their rounds lands in our position. No one is killed, but several men are wounded.

Battalion calls as soon as a wire line is run to us to congratulate the company on a job well done. It is also said that the assistant division commander, Brigadier General John H. Michaelis, had watched the whole attack and said that it was the best attack he had seen in Korea. However, my guess is he is just trying to show his respect for the Thirty-Fifth Regiment. He was the commanding officer of the Twenty-Seventh "Wolfhound" Regiment, another regiment of the Twenty-Fifth Division. He and his regiment have received a great amount of publicity as the "fire brigade" of the Eighth Army. Michaelis himself has been touted in the press as the kind of officer the army needs and has been promoted to brigadier general. No doubt now as the assistant division commander he wants to show that he thinks the Thirty-Fifth Regiment is just as good as the Twenty-Seventh Regiment he had commanded.

There is no question about the excellence of the attack the company had made on Many Fingers Hill. I am very proud of them. They need to be complimented. I know it will have more meaning coming from a general than from me, so I make sure everyone knows what General Michaelis said.

That night (30 March) we have a searchlight shining on our hilltop; this allows us to eat a hot meal in full light. The Chinese are long gone, heading north toward the 38th Parallel.

On 31 March the Thirty-Fifth Regiment remains in the vicinity of Changgo-ri, establishing new defensive positions north of the pass on the road to Yongp'yong. Little did we know that we will return to these same positions in less than a month. The press reports: "Two armored patrols with tank guns blazing smashed across Korea's disputed 38th Parallel in pursuit of withdrawing enemy forces." This is a unit of the Twenty-Fifth Division moving north toward Kumhwa on the road from Changgo-ri—a move made possible by the capture of Many Fingers Hill.

Within five days F Company will conduct an attack on a dominant hill (555) just north of the 38th Parallel, which had been developed as a key stronghold before the start of the Korean War. It overlooks two of the roads from the north toward Uijongbu—and Seoul. It now seems that whenever there is a difficult hill to take, F Company is called upon. But, no doubt, this is how you always see things when you are a rifle company commander.

Crossing the 38th Parallel

As UN forces approach the 38th Parallel it is necessary to make a decision on crossing it. Washington has already decided on a ceasefire near the 38th. A military victory has been ruled out. But now it is necessary to determine how and when to seek a ceasefire.

During March, Washington concludes that the Chinese and North Koreans might realize they also cannot achieve a military victory, and might agree to a cease fire followed by peace negotiations. In order to explore this possibility Truman plans to make such a suggestion. MacArthur is informed of this on 20 March, and he is told not to make a major advance above the 38th Parallel until the reaction to Truman's proposal is known. It is still being debated if the Eighth Army should even cross the 38th Parallel, and MacArthur's recommendations are requested. On 21 March he points out that instructions from the JCS prevent any effort to defeat military forces in North Korea.

Ridgway plans to advance ten to twenty miles north of the 38th Parallel to the vicinity of the Hwach'on Reservoir. On 24 March

MacArthur offers to confer with his military counterpart about a possible ceasefire. He says he makes this offer "within the area of my authority as the military commander" and that he will use "any military means" to achieve this end. His previous remarks had suggested that China should be attacked if fighting continues. MacArthur's announcement angers Truman. He considers it an effort to sabotage his policy, since MacArthur has not cleared his statement with Washington as he had been directed. Truman decides MacArthur should be relieved.

Now there must be a decision on crossing the 38th Parallel, and if crossed how far the Eighth Army should go.

In MacArthur's usual visit to Korea before the start of a major offensive, he states that the pending operations will result in a "theoretical stalemate." He tells Ridgway that after he reaches his objectives to limit operations to patrolling with nothing larger than a battalion.

For some time MacArthur has been working for a military, not a diplomatic, solution. He has answered a letter from Congressman Martin, suggesting the use of Chiang Kai-shek's forces, by saying that this suggestion was in consonance with his view of "meeting force with maximum counter force." In the reply MacArthur adds that there is "no substitute for victory." MacArthur knows that Washington does not support his views on how to achieve a military solution, but he wants no further restrictions placed on his operations. The tragedy is that MacArthur's life of great accomplishments hides the fact that he does not think he should be involved with Warfare or ideological conflict. He does not consider them within the realm of the professional soldier.

MacArthur has the conventional soldier's view of success in War: victory with the destruction of the enemy's armed forces followed by a Peace settlement. He does not recognize Warfare as a concern of the military. He certainly does not consider stability a successful conclusion of War. If he understood Warfare, MacArthur would have recommended to Washington that a ceasefire after the Eighth Army reaches the narrow neck of Korea[62] would be more successful than stopping near the 38th Parallel. Then there would be only a small buffer state in the mountains of North Korea—incapable of influencing the geopolitical situation; this would bring stability to Korea. In time China might even agree to the unification of North and South Korea because of the economic advantages to all concerned. However, MacArthur is incapable of such a vision. He only wants a military victory.

---

[62] The narrow neck of Korea is just below the 40th Parallel. It is fifty miles north of P'yongch'ang and extends from Sinanju, in the west, to Hungnam, on the east coast.

CHAPTER TWENTY-THREE

TRIPLE NICKEL HILL

1–7 April 1951

1–3 April

The Thirty-Fifth Regiment moves up the road from Changgo-ri to the vicinity of Yongp'yong just north of the 38th Parallel. The press reports "little ground action" and "the UN line is virtually at the parallel all across Korea." GEN MacArthur's communiqué says the Chinese have stepped up movements of men and weapons for seven armies, so that there are now an estimated 250,000 soldiers in the vicinity of Ch'orwon (fifteen miles north of the Thirty-Fifth Regiment).

Orders for the Attack: 4 April

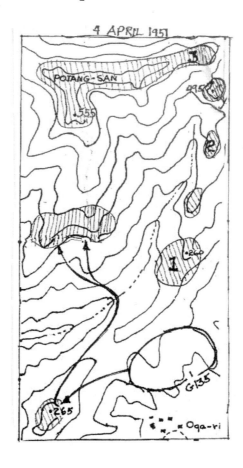

On 4 April the regiment consolidates its control of the Yongp'yong valley and the road west to the Imjin River. Overlooking this area is the Pojang-San hill mass with the highest elevation being 555 meters (therefore it is known as Triple Nickel Hill). It is the commanding piece of ground in the region. It overlooks two routes to Uijongbu. This has been one of the North Korean strong points prior to the war, and is now occupied by the Chinese. It is covered with bunkers able to withstand artillery fire, connecting tunnels, and prepared fields of fire. It is really a fortress.

G Company takes the first knob (265) on the left ridge after heavy fighting, and eighteen casualties. They then move up that ridge only to be stopped by machine gun fire from a group of bunkers less than halfway to the top. They spend the night opposite those bunkers. It is an uneventful night with only patrol action.

F Company is eating when I receive word that Major Cleves wants to see me on a small knoll our company is using as an outpost (126; see map on next page). The outpost offers an excellent view of Pojang-San (Triple Nickel Hill). Major Cleves, a burly, pleasant man, is acting battalion commander in the absence of LTC Hiram M. Merritt, who had been wounded on 29 March. I respect Cleves's administrative ability but wish LTC Merritt had been there to give me my orders, since we always have a productive exchange of ideas.

"Holliday, tomorrow morning you are going to take over the attack from Thompson. They are going to spend the night up there." He points to where I know G Company is, since I have been watching them all day.

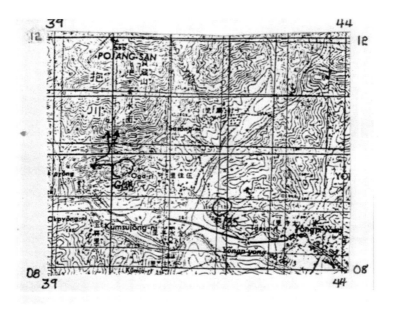

"Yes, sir."

"If you want you can attack through them. But I think it would be better to attack up that ridge. There are three objectives on it." He points to a ridge I had examined on the map and looked at during the day. It starts with knob 260 and then has several more knobs up the ridge. I am sure that each will be well prepared with bunkers. I know casualties will be high for anyone attacking up any ridge of Triple Nickel Hill.

"I don't think I want to attack through G Company."

"Good, when you get to the top, your third objective, you are to turn left to take the main ridge and finally 555 itself. I'll have Thompson join you in the final assault on the top of 555."

"Yes, sir."

"Any questions?"

"No sir. We will be off before daylight tomorrow."

"Good luck." I am delighted he has not been more specific.

What happened to G Company on 4 April convinced me that it is unwise to attack directly up any ridgeline of Triple Nickel. Surely the one starting with knob 260 will be better defended than the one used by G Company. The bunkers on each knob will probably cause any preparatory firing to be ineffective. Any attack from 260 up the ridgeline will face heavy machine gun fire from bunkers on each knob up to the top.

As I look over at Triple Nickel at dusk, and down at my map, I develop my plan for the next day. I have to keep both my mission and my men in mind. If I take care of both I will consider the attack on 555 a success. If I fail either I will consider it a failure. I also know I can explain any variation from what Major Cleves might have had in mind as the "fog of war."

The hill is heavily wooded and the eastern side, from 260, is steeper than the ridge used by G Company. I plan to use surprise. Moving up unseen on the right side of the ridge from 260 will place F Company on the right end of the top ridge of 555—which is actually my third objective as specified by Cleves. From there I can, if necessary, come down the ridge to take the second objective and then the first objective (260), or I can move along the top ridgeline to 555. I plan to let battalion make that decision after I take objective three.

We will have to go up the valley, to the right of the ridge Cleves had in mind, as far as possible before turning left for the climb to the top. I know that climb will be very steep and difficult; however, this will likely surprise the Chinese since they expect Americans to take the easiest route—and the one that allows direct fire from our tanks. With this plan I think I can achieve my mission with the fewest possible casualties. If anything goes wrong, I know I will be blamed. The easy, and self-serving, thing for me to do would be to attack up the ridge to objective one, and then objective two, and finally to objective three. But I decide to do it the way I think will fulfill my mission with the fewest casualties.

In my orders I tell the company to be prepared to be on our own for forty-eight hours. We will have to carry whatever we will need in food, water, and ammunitions for that time, since we will not be resupplied. Also I know we will be unable to evacuate our casualties.

The Surprise Attack: Morning 5 April

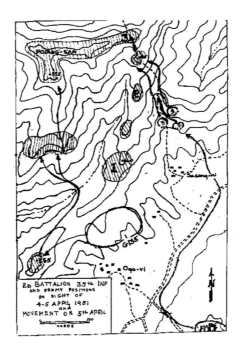

The next morning we are lucky. In addition to the "fog of war" there is some real fog. We start well before EMT (Early Morning Twilight) because I do not want anyone to know where the company is until we start our assault on the top of the ridge (third objective). I call battalion and tell them we are moving out; I hand the microphone back to my radio operator, James W. Grimes, and say: "Turn it off, and do not turn it on until I tell you to."

We pass a group of huts called Sasong-ni and then start up the valley to the right of the ridge with our three objectives. The First and Third Platoons are abreast, with the First on the right. Although I cannot see it I decide that we have passed the first objective on the ridge; then the same for the second objective. I tell LT Smith, my forward observer, to place artillery on the right end of the ridge top of 555 (our objective three).

When we are opposite where I think the third objective will be, I tell both platoons to turn left and to start climbing. As I had expected, it is very steep. We find several bunkers and foxholes, but no enemy. It is so steep that at times it is necessary to pull yourself from tree to tree. It is a very slow climb. The Third Platoon reaches the crest of the ridge without enemy contact, but as LT Leo C. Whitmer is bringing up his platoon he discovers some Chinese in a dugout twenty-five yards to his left down the ridge. Whitmer has those soldiers with him eliminate the Chinese in that dugout.

At the same time, SGT Emmons, the platoon sergeant of the Third Platoon, is caught with a squad in front of another dugout up the ridge to their right. The Chinese machine guns have them pinned down with several of the men wounded. The noise catches the attention of MSG Clarence Lackner, who has the First Platoon deployed farther to the right. With SGT First Class Clifford M. Cameron, his platoon sergeant, Lackner moves over to see what is going on. Seeing the situation he shouts:

"Stay down where you can't get hit. I'll come up on their blind side and get the bastards."

He tells one of his squad leaders to swing around and starts to move toward the bunker from the side.

Rat, tat, tat. The machine gun in the bunker again fires on MSG Emmons and his men. The squad making the attack hits the ground. Seeing this Lackner tells them: "Get up. We're going in. Line up and start firing!"

He marches them toward firing at the bunker. Since they are coming in from the side, the Chinese cannot use the machine gun on them. Those in the dugout start throwing grenades. Lackner takes a piece of a grenade in his right shoulder, but keeps his men moving toward the bunker. They kill all of the Chinese in that bunker.

The First Platoon then pushes up the ridge, but before they reach the top they come under machine gun fire from another hidden bunker and rifle fire from foxholes hidden in the woods. As Lackner is organizing his platoon for an assault, his shoulder begins to jerk and the bleeding increases. He turns the platoon over to SGT Cameron.

Moving Up the Ridge

While this is going on I contact the battalion by radio—the first time since we left before daylight: "I want to report that we are on the ridge between objective two and three."

"Roger, we heard the firing." Pause. "Did you say between two and three?"

"Roger," I reply.

"What happened to one and two?"

"I don't know. We bypassed them. They are no doubt waiting for us to come up the ridge. I have five wounded, but I'm going to attack objective three as soon as possible."

"You what? Oh!" Pause. "Okay. Roger. Out."

I send MSG Paul A. Bingham, my first sergeant, to take command of the First Platoon and to prepare them for another assault in conjunction with the Third Platoon. I send word for the Second Platoon, commanded by LT Wilber H. Toomy, to move up through the Third Platoon, to turn left and go down the ridge far enough to set up a defensive position to prevent a counterattack from the Chinese we had bypassed on the ridge below us. The Second Platoon moves down far enough to find some excellent positions which the Chinese had prepared expecting us to come up that ridge. The platoon moves in.

The Chinese launch a counterattack from a knob on the ridge above us, which I am to learn is 475, but the First Platoon stops it. I decide to attack that knob thinking it was our objective three, i.e. the right end of the top ridge.

The Third Platoon attempts to move up the ridge to that knob, but is stopped by machine gun fire from several positions and also rifle fire. SGT Yeikichi B. Hokazu, who speaks Japanese, works his way up close to the Chinese bunkers and foxholes. In Japanese, and a few words of Chinese, he tells the Chinese to surrender. A burst of machine gun fire is the answer. He ducks behind a larger rock. After a while he starts to talk to them again. This time a sniper knows where he is. We pass his body later during our assault.

Assault of Knob 475

I know we are too close to the enemy to use artillery. Moreover, I am not sure where we are. I have LT Smith place fire on the top ridge of 555, which was to our left front and walk it to the right. From where the rounds land I decide we probably face 475, which is the last knob on the ridge going up before the east-west top ridge of 555. However, I am still not sure.

I want tank fire on the enemy in front of us, but the tanks are so far away they do not know where we want them to shoot. Using the radio, air panels, and a few trial rounds we get them on target. I tell them to fire rounds for ten minutes: *WIZZZ, WHUMM*. The 76-mm shells come in. Also the slower: *ZOOOM, BANG* from 75-mm recoilless rifle shells dig into knob 475.

I tell the First and Third Platoons that after the tank shells stop, they are to assault the knob in front of the Third Platoon. I tell them to fix their bayonets. The Second Platoon and the 57-mm recoilless rifles are to support the other two platoons. The 60-mm mortars are also to support. I place LT James L. Ashworth, the Weapons Platoon leader, in charge of all fire support for the assault. The firing of the 57-mm recoilless rifle (RR) is to be the signal for the assault to start.

I take Ashworth with me as I go over to talk with CPL Elwood Ellens, the 57-mm RR squad leader. I want both of them to understand the critical role of direct fire in the success of the assault.

"You will have to move up so you can fire directly at any machine guns firing on us." CPL Ellens is a tall, jet-black soldier who moves in a slow, deliberate manner. He turns to his gunner and says: "This uns gonna be rough, ya better let me have that thing." Taking the weapon, he moves slowly up to where Hokazu had been killed. Ellens turns his head and nods that he is ready.

I call the tanks and 75-mm recoilless rifles and tell them to cease firing. I then tell Ellens to fire. The glare and blast from the 57-mm RR filled the air with dust and flame. I turn to Whitmer, the Third Platoon leader: "Let's go."

He gives a few short commands to his platoon, which is spread out among the trees. Everyone starts forward with bayonets fixed. I am reminded that victory is never achieved until infantrymen cross the final yards. All of our men start to fire. The crack of twigs over our heads tells me that all of the Chinese aren't in the bottom of their dugouts.

Master SGT Robert E. Lynch, the platoon sergeant of the Third Platoon, suddenly stops. He jumps back, and crouches down. He slowly removes his helmet. He just stares at a deep grove in the helmet, and then he places it back on his head. He looks over at Whitmer and me; then he starts forward again. I move forward a little more with the Third Platoon, and then I tell Whitmer I am going over to see what the First Platoon is doing.

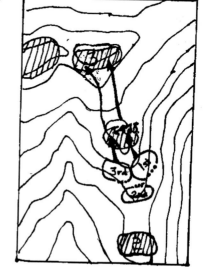

After pushing through some heavy brush, I find SGT Cameron and part of the First Platoon. They are moving forward slowly. To their right SGT Bingham is with the rest of the platoon. The foliage is so thick I can only see four or five men at a time. I move up the ridge with the First Platoon. The firing is now quite heavy. The rebel yells and shouts of my men fill the woods. The men of

F Company come through the woods shrieking wildly, with daring and firepower. Astonishment and uncertainty now grasps the Chinese defenders, in their holes they are torn by both shame and fear. There is not a line of advancing men; there are small groups converging on the enemy from all directions. Some of the Chinese try to run away, but they go only a few steps. The men of F Company are doing what all good infantrymen do: closing the last yards with vigor. The Chinese that stay in their emplacements have to stay low because of the volume of fire directed at them; some do throw grenades at us. Since they do not know where we are the grenades cause little damage. All of the enemy that remain are shot or bayoneted as they crouch in their holes hiding from the hail of bullets.

Capture of Objective Three: Afternoon 5 April

I move to the top of the knob and look across the saddle. The left side of the saddle is covered with grass but the right side has trees. The knob we just took is indeed 475 and the one across the saddle is our objective three (the right end of the top ridge of 555). To flank the enemy on 555 it will be necessary to take objective three.

Bingham comes through the trees to my right leading the First Platoon. I shout to him: "Keep going and take that hill." I point to the high ground on the other side of the saddle.

Things are now pretty disorganized. Going through the woods it had been impossible to keep a whole platoon together. I recognize the men with Bingham. They are the ones I had been with during the assault on 475. They move across the saddle using the woods as cover. I move along the crest of the saddle, with the grass to my left, hoping to see the Third Platoon as those men complete their assault of 475. I am about a third of the way across the saddle when I see Whitmer break through the brush on 475 at the head of the Third Platoon. I wave them forward. In true Fort Benning form I shout: "Follow me! Get to that hill as fast as you can."

The whole platoon starts across the clearing. They are firing, yelling, and shouting as loud as they can. Some of the men have whistles, which they are now blowing. The din of this rolling sound increases—and INCREASES—as the First and Third Platoons join together and assault objective three.

G Company, which is over one thousand yards away on the left ridge of 555, hear all of this noise and think the Chinese are staging a fanatic counterattack against us. The few Chinese that stay in their holes are shot or bayoneted. However, the vigor of our attack has the desired effect. Most of the enemy scamper away as we come toward them. A quick glance tells me that we have taken our objective three. I order a defense set up immediately. I place the machine guns on the left side of our position facing the top ridge of 555.

The firing of the 57-mm recoilless rifle, which was our signal to start the assault on 475, had also been a signal for our enemy. All of the time that the First and Third Platoons make their charge across the saddle the Chinese are dropping mortar shells where we had been. The Weapons Platoon and the headquarters personnel are in that area. They have to take cover, and often use the Chinese foxholes. LT Smith, my forward observer, is wounded; however, his sergeant continues the artillery fire on the top ridge as I had directed.

Defense of Objective Three: 5–6 April

It does not take the Chinese long to reorganize after we had taken their flank. Mortar shells start to fall on us. We have not been able to dig in, and the Chinese dugouts face in the wrong direction. We receive machine gun fire anytime someone moves. Some of our most exposed soldiers pull back for greater protection. This causes the enemy to push toward us. Our fire stops them before they can get close enough to make an assault.

On both 475 and objective three we find a lot of equipment, some of which had been captured from Americans. Both areas are cluttered with bodies. These Chinese appear to have been in very good physical condition and have ample weapons and ammunition.

MAJ Cleves calls on the radio to ask if I can push on to the other end of the top ridge of 555. I tell him no, and we are going to be lucky to hold where we are all night. I mention that we have already fought off one attack and we are under constant mortar and machine gun fire. It is beginning to get dark.

I expect patrols to be sent against us, and maybe an attack. I make my usual visit to each squad and congratulate everyone on a job well done. I tell all platoons to be sure to rotate the men in the forward positions so someone will always be awake. I tell them to follow all of our standard operating procedures (SOP) even though I know they are all tired. I specifically check the status of ammunition to ensure we can defend our position and I check on what is being done for our wounded since I know they cannot be evacuated. The Chinese send no patrols against us that night.

Over the radio I hear the battalion give G Company orders to move up from where they are, and where they had spent the previous night, as far as they can toward the top of 555. About 2300 hours Thompson reports that they are going into a perimeter on a knob just across from the left end of the top ridge of 555. They had no enemy contact as they moved up.

Just after midnight, we receive several bursts of machine gun fire from the enemy opposite us, and then silence. The next morning G Company moves over to 555 and then down the top ridge to us without firing a shot. The whole length of the top ridge is a maze of log and stone emplacements connected by trenches. Only scattered equipment, supplies and mangled corpses of Chinese soldiers remain on Triple Nickel Hill, where the day before five to eight hundred Chinese had been in excellent defensive positions. That was before our surprise attack on their flank.

Eighth Army reports "stubborn enemy opposition to the UN advance in the vicinity of Yongp'yong, two miles north of the parallel and thirty-three miles northeast of Seoul. Yongp'yong straddles a highway stretching northeast to the major Red supply and troop assembly hub of Kumhwa."

The capture of Triple Nickel Hill is the last major attack in this area prior to the Chinese Spring Offensive. The Twenty-Fifth Division goes from gaining and holding territory to reconnaissance in force in order to determine the enemy's location and plans. We are now north of the 38th Parallel and we know the Chinese are preparing for major attacks toward Uijongbu down the two routes on either side of Triple Nickel Hill. The Thirty-Fifth Regiment starts to prepare for a defense in depth on one of those two routes. Our defense is designed to inflict damage on the Chinese yet keep our units intact. The British Twenty-Ninth Brigade, to our west below the Imjin River, is to defend the other route to Uijongbu.

CHAPTER TWENTY-FOUR

CHINESE SPRING OFFENSIVE

7 April–18 May 1951

Prior to the Chinese Spring Offensive: 7–21 April 1951

After the capture of Triple Nickel the Twenty-Fifth Division consolidates its hold on the hill mass between the Yongp'yong River and Hanr'an River. This establishes control of the key terrain between two of the traditional invasion routes toward Uijongbu and Seoul.

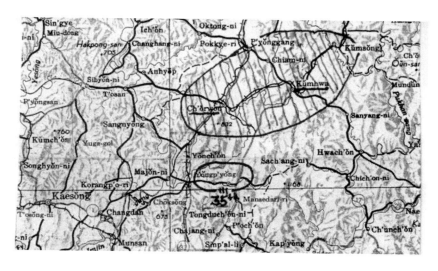

Enemy resistance stiffens whenever advances are made toward Ch'orwon or Kumhwa, where Chinese forces prepare for a new offensive and start brush fires to obscure their movements. It is reported that eighteen new divisions have arrived in an area five to fifteen miles northeast of the Thirty-Fifth Regiment (see map on previous page).

During 12–23 April there is be a lull before the storm along the 110-mile front. Enemy strength reaches 695,000 as they mass for a spring offensive. Smoke hides known assembly areas. Planning by US and ROK forces is not about holding specific ground; it is about killing the enemy, and weakening their will to fight.

Most UN units make limited objective attacks to determine where the enemy is located. Patrols are sent out daily. Administrative and support units are moved south of the road junction at Changgo-ri. Troops are placed where they can prevent the Chinese from establishing roadblocks on the MSR (Main Supply Route). Contact is made with the British Brigade on the Imjin River to our left. Twenty-Fifth Division advances toward Ch'orwon through steep ridges, and after crossing the Hant'an River, get to within five miles of Ch'orwon. Twenty-Fourth Division moves toward Kumhwa, but in the mountains they only advance a mile in three days, while on the road Sixth Tank Battalion moves to within seven miles of Kumhwa without contact.

The most visible enemy activity is smoke extending over ten miles north of the Eighth Army. Chinese and North Korean troops burn grass and brush and use smoke generators. Sometimes fog mixes with the smoke. In central Korea patrols from the ROK Sixth and First Marine divisions report a Chinese withdrawal. A captured document, dated 17 March, advocates action without regard for the loss or gain of ground which will "conserve our own power, deplete the enemy's strength, and secure for us more favorable conditions for future victory." As in the past, the Chinese and North Koreans conceal their locations until they move into forward assembly areas immediately before an attack. In fact, by 21 April the Chinese will be marching to forward assembly areas from which they plan to launch an attack with the goal of reaching Seoul by May Day.

The Reality of Combat

The first weeks of April are spent getting ready for the massive assaults, which we know are coming. I have many discussions with the men of F Company like this:

"Captain, what do you think will happen?"

"Some nights in the near future we are going to be hit with assaults like we have never seen before. They are going to come with everything they have. We will face hundreds of well-trained and disciplined Chinese soldiers. There will be bullets, flares, explosions, and chaos. There will be bugles, horns, and all kinds of sounds. You will see many men coming directly at you."

"Will they overwhelm us?"

"Not if I can help it. We should have plenty of artillery, but we are going to have to take care of each other. Survival will be up to all of us. Fear will grab each of us, but we cannot allow it to turn any of us into cowards. I do not expect anyone to take extraordinary risks, or be a hero, but I do expect each of us to do his duty. I will not allow any shirking. Each of us must remain a man among other men."

Then I add: "Protecting each other is our most important duty. You know, the Roman phalanx was the world's best fighting force not because each soldier was a skilled warrior, but because the shield of each soldier protected not himself but the man next to him. Then each warrior could use his sword to kill the enemy."

"But what do we do when they come to kill us?"

"Kill them first!" Then with a smile I say in half-hearted manner, "Besides, you know your odds of living are much better if you fight them. If you desert your comrades, you will never get past me."

Everyone in the company knows I am not kidding. While I will do everything possible to make sure everyone survives and that no one is captured, I will also make certain that no one "bugs out." They will fight with all their might when I say fight. They will move only when I tell them to move. Anyone deserting those depending on him should not have to worry about some future court.

I end with: "Death is something each of us has to face. A warrior is never afraid of death if it comes with honor, courage, bravery, and the bond of camaraderie. For those cowards that think only of themselves, approaching death brings with it a cloud of overwhelming fear, panic, and emotional devastation."

Deserting those depending on you in the heat of battle is not just cowardly—it is also the most insidious of crimes. Desertion has no counterpart during Peace. Justice as taught in law schools is for Peace, and is not relevant at the point of the spear. Camaraderie is the foundation upon which all success in War and Warfare is built. Destroy it and all is lost. In War and Warfare justice is accomplished when punishment fits the crime—not after following some tedious procedures written by lawyers far removed from where living or dying come with the speed of light. This is something that those who have never experienced real combat will probably never understand—or accept. But it is necessary for survival during combat.

Throughout history the leaders of the most capable military forces have considered it their duty to immediately destroy anyone who flees in the heat of battle. Yet in today's legalistic, politically correct, progressive, postmodern societies this would be unacceptable. But what is the cost? What does legalistic thinking, and also the introduction of women into combat, do to combat camaraderie and combat effectiveness?

What Infantrymen Do

Each time we move we dig in, establish interlocking fields of fire, run communication lines from each platoon, and call in defensive artillery and mortar fire. Stan J. Nikulsi, a wiry, young PFC from Illinois, runs the wires from each of the platoons to my company CP before he digs his own foxhole. Normally he walks through the ground that we hold; however, when we are spread out he has to go through gaps between platoons of several hundred yards.

On 12 April he is walking back with his reel of wire from the Second Platoon. He hears the *zing* of a rifle bullet next to his head. It is not a random shot—it is meant for him. He drops to the ground and starts to crawl with his rifle in one hand and the reel of wire in the other. Then he makes a short dash to a wall.

Against the wall is a GI. His rifle is on the ground beside him. He looks forward with a blank stare. Blood oozes from his shirt. Nikulsi finds that he is still breathing and has a pulse. Nikulsi tears

379

open his shirt and finds a large exit wound. The dark red blood moves across his white skin. A bullet had entered his back and gone through his body. "What can I do to save him? Or at least how can I help him?" The man collapses with his face in the ground. The pulse is gone. His hands are dark like all infantrymen who have been so close to dirt for weeks.

Nikulsi sees it all. The GI is still just a boy, like himself. He had a wonderful, long life ahead of him when he died. Who are those back home that will never know what he has just seen, but who will never forget what happened in this faraway place on this fateful day?

When Nikulsi brings the wire in to connect it to the company phone, I can tell he is shaken. "How are things going?" I ask.

"Bad, sir, very bad. There is a sniper out there," He then tells me what had happened.

I put my arm around him. "I am lucky to have you in my company. You are strong. Many others would not be able to handle what you have seen and come out whole. Don't think about the emotions that are tearing you apart. Think of how what you have experienced will make you stronger and better." I watch him closely the next few days, but say nothing more to him. As all infantrymen must, he is soon able to cope with the reality of combat. However, I'm sure he will never forget that young man he found against the wall.

On the night of 15 April PFC Ralph E. Dennison hears a soft, whispering hiss. There is no wind, so it must be someone. He holds his breath and motions for his foxhole mate to do the same. He holds his rifle tight. Twenty yards away something moves. It is a single Chinese soldier hidden in a tangle of brush. This is the point of a patrol. Others will be behind him.

Dennison sees and hears other movement. There is a moving shadow and then nothing. He holds his breath and looks. He knows SGT Paul has a machine gun team thirty yards to his right, and surely they also see the enemy crawling toward them. Dennison hears a metal click from the position of the machine gun, and he sees the eyes of the scout open wide. He fires at the scout. The machine gun opens up on the rest of the patrol. Other men in the platoon start to fire. Screams come from the enemy.

Then shouts from the platoon: "Let them have it! Kill the bastards!"

The machine gun stops. It is jammed. The gunner let the ammo belt get twisted.

Yet another patrol fails to make it back with information.

On 20 April CPL Henry W. Berry sees two enemy soldiers cross some rice paddies and go into a house. They are over three hundred yards away, and probably don't know we have an outpost in front of our positions. Berry wonders: "What should I do? My orders are to set up this outpost with three men and report any enemy activity."

Berry thinks he can get closer to the house without being seen. He knows he is to return to the company in about two hours when it gets dark.

"Spalding, come with me; I want to see what they are doing."

The building is in a small group of farmhouses we had come through before going into our defensive positions. Berry watches the house closely waiting for some sign that he and PFC Spalding have been seen. They move up and start to sweat even though it is not a hot day. When they are fifty yards from the house they see someone come to the door. The two Americans drop behind the dike of a rice paddy. The movement catches the attention of the soldier, and he says something in Chinese.

As the two Chinese soldiers come out of the house with their rifles, the two Americans fire at them. A bullet hits one and he topples to the ground, wriggling in agony. The other man stops in shock. He brings his rifle to a firing position. But he is shot before he can get off a round. Red blood flows from both men. They jerk and grunt. It took less than eight seconds.

The two Americans stand up, smile at each other and bump hands. "Great fun. Sure was."

Then Berry thinks about what they have just done. They have just killed two human beings, who have loved ones back in China. And here they are acting like they just won a ball game. He feels sick. But then he remembers the code of warriors: "If you do not kill them, they will kill you. Would you rather be alive and able to feel guilty, or dead because you were a caring, humane, compassionate person?"

The MacArthur Problem

There had been several times prior to December 1950 when MacArthur had ignored the policy prescribed by Washington, the most serious being the sending of American troops toward the Manchurian border in November 1950 when Washington had wanted only South Korean troops to be sent into the frontier area.[63]

On 3 December 1950 MacArthur sent a grim message to Washington. He reported that his troops were under strength, mentally fatigued, and physically battered while the Chinese had committed twenty-six divisions and had 200,000 fresh troops ready for battle. He suggested that direct action against

China itself might be the only way to prevent defeat in Korea. This started a foreign policy debate that lasted until MacArthur was removed from his command on 10 April 1951. On 13 February 1951 MacArthur declared that establishing "a line across Korea and entering into positional warfare is wholly unrealistic and illusory." MacArthur challenged the president's role as the nation's spokesman on foreign policy and openly opposed the decision to limit conflict to Korea. This went too far, and MacArthur was relieved.

On 11 April General Ridgway replaced General MacArthur. At the time those in Korea were unaware of the debates and politics that caused this change. With the departure of MacArthur, Syngman Rhee was left alone in his opposition to negotiations, and his advocacy for the reunification of Korea by force. At this time the UN command considered its mission to be "repel the aggression and restore international peace."

It is true that President Truman and General MacArthur had very different views on the enlargement of the war. It is true that MacArthur thought the only acceptable end was a military victory, or as he had expressed it in 1931: "Victory, immediate and complete!" Victory to MacArthur in this case is the defeat of Communism with "a blow from which it would never recover." On the other hand, Truman wanted a diplomatic solution.

MacArthur was willing to use whatever air power was necessary, but wanted to minimize the use of American ground forces on the Asian mainland. Truman did not want to use strategic bombing on China, and he did want UN agreement on any action taken in North Korea. Unfortunately, neither thought of pushing back up to the narrow neck of Korea and seeking a cease-fire agreement.

However, the real reason for MacArthur's dismissal is that he had publicly expressed his disagreement with policy decisions of the president repeatedly communicated to him by the JCS. Truman could not tolerate these challenges to his responsibilities as president.

The Chinese Spring Offensive: April 1951

The Chinese begin a general attack at 2200 hours on Sunday 22 April 1951 across a forty-mile front. At least 250,000 Chinese and North Korean soldiers are involved—some estimates place this number as high as 700,000. This offensive is called the CCF First Spring Offensive. It starts the last attempt by either side to achieve a military victory.

The major attack, with eight armies, is toward Seoul on three routes: from Yongp'yong, Youchon, and Kumhwa. The Thirty-Fifth Regiment conducts successful delaying actions on the route from Yongp'yong. The British Twenty-Ninth Brigade, Third Division and First ROK Division have great difficulty on the route from Youchon and the Twenty-Fourth Division has problems holding back the Chinese on the route from Kumhwa.

Initial Actions North of Uijongbu: 22–23 April

At midnight on 22 April, Chinese coming from Youchon probe the Twenty-Ninth British Brigade at the Korangp'o bend near the junction of the Imjin and Hant'an Rivers. Before dawn major assaults are made against the Belgian battalion and the Northumberland Fusiliers. Unfortunately, the British are not in well-prepared positions. They had expected this to be a short stop. They had set out no barbed wire or mines. The Chinese crossing the shallow Imjin River are pounded by artillery, but they keep moving forward. Four times the Chinese attack and four times they are thrown back, but they also find gaps and move through those gaps to attack rear units of the brigade.

From north of Yongp'yong three Chinese armies[64] attack on 22 April. After three hours of artillery fire, assaults by many waves of Chinese start at 2200 on the Turkish Brigade and Twenty-Fourth Regiment, and those assaults continue throughout the early hours of 23 April. Many men "bug out." The Twenty-Seventh Regiment holds its position and fights off all frontal attacks; but by dawn many units of the Twenty-Fifth Division and Turkish Brigade are surrounded in company perimeters. The Chinese have penetrated over a mile into the rear area of the Twenty-Fifth Division attacking the Thirty-Fifth Regiment, artillery units and support units with rifle fire. The Chinese taunt the Americans in English.

"GI you die."

"Hands up you live."

Infantry rifle companies, some artillery batteries, and tank platoons are told to hold their positions while the rest of the Twenty-Fifth Division withdraws to positions they had previously occupied south of the Hunt'an River. In the dark, and because of the many Chinese throughout the area, the infantry rifle company units are unable to withdraw intact; they move back as platoons, and at times even in squads. This results in many small unit battles north of the Hunt'an River from midnight until daylight.

As the Third Platoon, F Company moves back it comes upon one of our tanks that some Chinese are trying to capture. For some reason the tank is unable to move; the crew is attempting to get it started at the same time they use their .45-caliber M3 sub-machine gun (the grease gun) to shoot at the Chinese soldiers around them. The men of the Third Platoon attack the enemy and drive them away from the tank. But the shooting and grenade throwing then spreads to the sides of the road. Having fought for several hours, some of the men start to run out of ammunition. Led by their platoon sergeant, Cary J. Emmons, they use their rifles as clubs to kill some of the Chinese. PFC Sutton, a tough, no-nonsense soldier from Alabama, gets some ammunition to them as they continue their withdrawal.

Shortly after daylight on 23 April the Thirty-Fifth Regiment is ordered to take over from the Turks; the Turkish Brigade and the Twenty-Fourth Regiment go into reserve to reorganize. By 0900 on 23 April the Twenty-Fifth Division is in preplanned defensive positions south of the Hunt'an River.

All day on 23 April the British Twenty-Ninth Brigade is under heavy attack. They suffer heavy casualties. For artillery support for the Twenty-Ninth Brigade the British come from the Forty-Fifth Field Artillery Regiment, but it does not have access to the US medium and heavy artillery. In the afternoon the Twenty-Ninth Brigade command post is under attack. During the evening of 23 April the Belgian battalion withdraws across the river, and the Gloucester Battalion, in danger of being wiped out piecemeal, pulls back. During the night of 23–24 April there are cries and bugles as the Chinese again attack units throughout the zone of the British brigade.

From Kumhwa two Chinese armies[65] attack between the Twenty-Fifth and the Twenty-Fourth Divisions. A gap opens between the Nineteenth and Fifth Regiments of the Twenty-Fourth Division, and the Chinese advance three miles by dawn on 23 April.

Secondary Attacks 22–23 April

In addition to the three main attacks on 22–23 April 1951, there are secondary attacks on the flanks. On the west flank there is an attack from Munsan against the First ROK Division. On the east flank two North Korean armies attack the ROK Sixth Division; it suffers heavy casualties and disintegrates. The New Zealand Regiment supporting the South Koreans is in a desperate situation. The First Marine Division has two hours warning of the Chinese attack, and moves a reserve battalion to its left flank. At midnight that battalion meets retreating South Koreans, but is able to establish defensive positions before dawn of 23 April.

On 23 April the ROK Sixth Division attempts to reorganize fifteen miles south of its original positions.

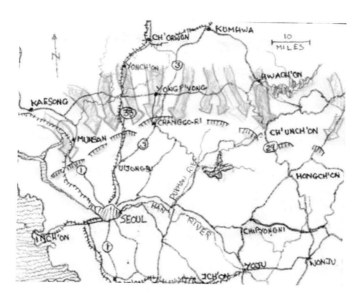

24–25 April for British Brigade

Early in the morning of 24 April a reserve battalion of the British Twenty-Ninth Brigade moves forward to support those units under heavy attack. A relief column of six Centurion tanks of the Eighth Hussars, four Filipino tanks, and Filipino infantry are sent forward to save the Gloucester battalion. It fails. A request by the brigade commander to withdraw is denied. However, an effort to save the Gloucester battalion with two battalions of the Sixty-Fifth Regiment and the Sixty-Fourth Tank Battalion is planned for 0630 on 25 April.

The Northumberland Battalion is ordered to pull back eight hundred yards. All day the Gloucester Battalion is under desperate pressure. Ammunition is short. After repeated Chinese assaults there is doubt of anyone getting out. At midnight the Twenty-Ninth British Brigade finally gets orders to withdraw; they have to run four miles of roadblocks since the Chinese are in their rear. At 0800 on 25 April the Twenty-Ninth British Brigade retreats in heavy fog. At first there are piecemeal scrambles as small groups fight Chinese along the road. Wounded cover the sides of the road. Finally, there is a chaotic struggle for survival as Chinese and British intermingle. The road south of the Imjin is strewn with wreckage as the survivors reach the safety of the Twenty-Fifth Division.

Withdrawal Tactics During 23–26 April

During 23–26 April the Twenty-Fourth and Twenty-Fifth Divisions conduct successful delaying actions back to positions north of Uijongbu on two routes northeast of Seoul.[66] During this time the Thirty-Fifth Regiment withdraws from the Hant'an River to Yongp'yong (Triple Nickel) and then to Changgo-ri (Many Fingers). We know the area and return to some of the positions we had used during the previous month. Not only do we establish our assigned defensive positions as usual, but we also plan withdrawal routes.

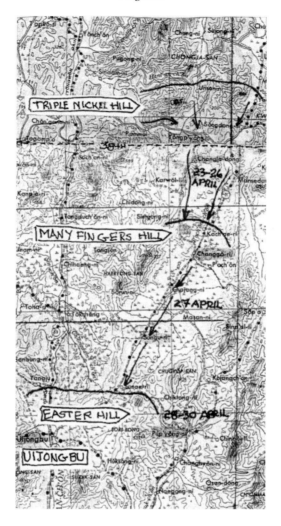

Our withdrawal routes are not on the road used by vehicles, but along foot trails parallel to roads. When we are in the front line I contact the commander of the company behind us and we discuss exactly how we will pull back. I make sure that we have a wire line between us so that I can keep him informed of our situation. Someone—usually the platoon sergeant but sometimes a squad leader—from each platoon walks the route during daylight so he will be able to guide his platoon in the dark if we withdraw. We expect ambush teams and snipers to infiltrate into our rear in order to attack us as we withdraw. Before dark each evening all vehicles move behind the unit to our rear. Then it is up to the Chinese. The key to this type of defense is for those in the front lines to be able to distinguish between a patrol, a local probing attack, and an assault. Between 22 and 26 April we fight off many patrols and several probing attacks by the Chinese. Making this distinction is my primary job. I have to use the sights and sounds I observe in front of our position and to our flanks, and from the reports of my platoon leaders, to make my decision. We fire at any patrols and bring artillery down on any probing attack. This is easy to do. We hold our position during these actions.

On 25 April using my binoculars I know the Chinese moving toward our position are larger than a patrol; they are probing to discover our defenses. I tell the machine gunners not to fire, and tell my forward observer to call in the artillery.

I hear the howling of a shell passing overhead. It hits behind the advancing enemy. The FO radios: "Drop fifty and fire for effect!"

The time-fused shells whizz over us and explode in midair, showering fragments across the enemy formation. There is a roaring, whooshing sound followed by high explosive shells hurling dirt and smoke into the air.

Then there is an explosion near us. Is it a short round? The answer comes quickly as there are several more explosions even closer. "Incoming. Take cover." *WHAAAMM!* The Chinese have mortars to support this probe. The men of F Company go deep into their foxholes, only to pop up to shoot at any of the Chinese still moving forward. It is soon clear that our artillery is more effective than their mortars. The noise fades. Within twenty minutes the enemy has withdrawn, taking their wounded with them. We check on all of our soldiers and have no casualties. Later we move forward to find five bodies.

It is more difficult to know when the Chinese are getting ready to make an assault. We know that any assault will come in the dark and that they will try to go around our flanks at the same time they send several waves against the front of our position. When I determine they are moving soldiers into positions from which they can make an assault I send one platoon back to selected positions along our withdrawal route. This is to ensure that we will not be ambushed. If there is no assault, that platoon returns at daylight. Then I keep the other platoons in their positions as long as possible, using artillery as much as possible.

When I determine the Chinese are moving up for an assault I order the platoons to withdraw one at a time. I come out with the last platoon. I did this successfully each time we were in the front line—except once. We would be at least a hundred yards back of our defensive position when we hear the bugles and whistles of the Chinese assaulting. Then I bring artillery down on our old position.

These are hectic and confusing nights and everyone has amazing stories to tell. At times we are intermingled with Chinese, and confusion reigns. Sometimes it is difficult to tell friend from foe. I am told one time a BAR man shouted, "All you GI SOBs hit the ground." Then he shot everyone still standing.

Between 22 and 26 April, F Company is able to avoid all assaults. Thus our withdrawals are routine, and we do not experience the repeated waves of the enemy that others report during this period. We use ammunition, brains, and discipline while they are using discipline and bodies. We are trading space for blood. The Thirty-Fifth Regiment is able to keep out of serious trouble while killing many Chinese with artillery fire. By 26 April we are back to Many Fingers Hill.

My Failure to Identify an Assault

One night I delay too long. I decide it is going to be an assault and send most of the company back along the evacuation route.

At midnight I am waiting with the last platoon for signs of an imminent assault on our front, when I realize that large numbers of the enemy are moving around our flanks. What should I do? How do I protect my men?

If I take the platoon back from our defensive position, as planned, there is a good chance the enemy will be waiting for us. I decide that the best thing to do is to move as rapidly as possible through the enemy on our left flank. It is not only the closest way to our withdrawal route, but I think there are fewer Chinese on that flank. I shout to those on my right, "Assemble around me." Although they probably cannot see me, I made a fist with my hand and pumped it up and down over my head. They come to me in a slow trot. I then walk to my left telling my men to follow me. In less than three minutes I have the whole platoon around me.

"Fix your bayonets. We're going through them as fast as we can. Stay close. Shoot any of them you see."

I'm sure the Chinese will never expect a tight phalanx of Americans charging at them. They expect us to be in our foxholes. We know the ground better than they do and we have surprise on our side—also, my men are disciplined and they trust me.

"Let's go." We move into the unknown.

It is dark and I have no idea of how many Chinese are in front of us, but I do expect them to be moving to our rear. I do not have to give any orders as we move. We meet many groups of the enemy walking slowly in the dark; they are surprised; they scatter when we fire at them. We get no return fire.

After moving some four hundred yards through many Chinese, I turn the platoon to the left to make our way to our withdrawal route. I order artillery fire on our old position. We find the platoon guarding our withdrawal route, and together we move to the company behind us.

I'm not sure if any of my men used their bayonets that night. However, I do know we suffer no casualties. The next morning the whole company is very happy telling each other what they did.

On 26 April the regiment still holds strong defensive positions north of the road junction at Changgo-ri—where the battle for Many Fingers Hill had been fought on 30 March.

27–30 April 1951: Move to No Name Line

On 27 April the Thirty-Fifth Regiment makes a major move back to defensive positions north of Uijongbu near Easter Hill, and eleven miles north of Seoul. Here we take up positions to block both the main road from Kumhwa to Seoul and the road on which the British Twenty-Ninth Brigade had withdrawn.

There is some evidence that the main attack toward Seoul is beginning to falter. Van Fleet establishes a new defense line—it becomes known as No Name Line. Van Fleet believes that giving up the ROK capital a third time will "ruin the spirit of the nation."

On 28 and 29 April the Thirty-Fifth Regiment fights several times to hold Uijongbu. The press reports, "The pressure of the Chinese horde was felt in terrific fighting around Uijongbu. An entire enemy battalion was destroyed northeast of Uijongbu by artillery and rifle fire." The infantry hold the Chinese in place so that the artillery can kill them. The weather is now warmer. The howitzers and Long Tom rifles are hurling hundreds of thousands of shells. Mortars are also active when the Chinese get close.

However, things are not holding up as well northwest of Seoul on the route from Munsan-ni. There the Chinese drive to within four miles of Seoul. They even reach the Han River and a move down the north bank would have doomed the Korean capital again. Nevertheless, the Chinese are having very heavy casualties—an estimated forty-five thousand in the first week of their offensive. Their frontline troops went into battle with eight days' supply of rice and ammunition, and have to resupply before attempting to take Seoul. The Chinese Spring Offensive comes to a halt.

The advance of the enemy along the route from the northwest toward Seoul outflanked the positions held by the Twenty-Fifth Division on the route toward Seoul from Uijongbu. Therefore, without a fight the Thirty-Fifth Regiment withdraws from Uijongbu to defensive positions just north of Seoul in order to tie in with those defending the northwest approach to that city on the No Name Line. To defend Seoul, six regiments are north of the city and the same number assemble in and on the edges of the city. The British Twenty-Ninth Brigade, the Turkish Brigade, and ROK Marines are south of the Han River. UN forces establish defensive positions from north of Seoul across Korea to the east coast just south of the 38th Parallel. Along No Name Line probing attacks are thrown back; the First Spring Offensive stops. The press reported, "The big Red spring offensive bogged down Tuesday (1 May) short of Seoul—the May Day goal."

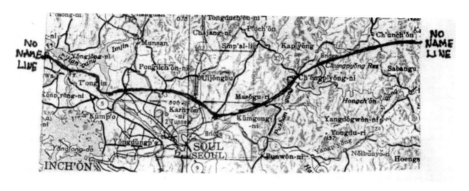

Stalemate: 1–15 May 1951

After 1 May the Chinese pull back out of artillery range to regroup. This is the high-water mark for the Chinese on the military battlefield in Korea. The Eighth Army improves its defensive position, sends out reconnaissance patrols, and uses air attacks to weaken the enemy. Until 18 May the area near Uijongbu is a no man's land. Bitter fights are fought throughout this area. Yet on the ideological and strategic communication battlefields the Chinese are having great success, with support eroding in New York at the UN while an antiwar movement grows throughout the US.

Tactically and strategically the conflict in Korea is remarkably devoid in interest after 1 May 1951—compared to the dramatic moves up and down Korea during the previous year. Those battles had molded hardened soldiers on both sides; so two capable armies face each other in May 1951. In military terms, the main strengths of the North Koreans and Chinese are the skill and dedication of their infantry soldiers, and the main strength of the Americans is their technological superiority. The Chinese are no longer capable of mounting the kind of offensive they did on 27 November 1950 and 22 April 1951, yet they are more than capable of being a tough defender. And the US has displayed only ineptness in the ideological conflict and in strategic communication.

The Twenty-Fifth Division sends tank-infantry task forces back to Uijongbu, destroying enemy outposts en route and killing as many of the Chinese as possible. The Thirty-Fifth Regiment is on the western part of the No Name Line about which it is reported: "The Reds were building up strength massively in four main sectors—north and east of Uijongbu, and north and west of Ch'unch'on. They tried to hide their movements under smoke screens created by smudge pots and burning brush. The Eighth Army braced for the attack—with barbed wire, minefields, and massed artillery. Any night the Chinese might blow their bugles and whistles, set off their green flares, and attack."

During my daily visits to each squad I usually talk with several men at a time, but now and then I single out one of the men to see if I can get a more accurate picture of just how things are going. On 10 May I sit down with Tom Jensen, a bright, blond PFC from Iowa. After the usual chit-chat I say: "I see that Sergeant Emmons is keeping all of you busy."

"He sure is. He is a great platoon sergeant. He looks after all of us and is always a square shooter."

"I'm sure glad to hear that."

"And sir, he is also a great fighter. You should have seen him the other night. He had just checked on Roller and me and was walking away when I saw two Chinks rise up behind him and try to grab him. They sure picked the wrong guy. He kicked one in the groin and hit the other with his rifle. Then as they were coming back at him he shot both of them. Then he just walked over, kicked them, and shot them again to make sure they didn't bother anyone else. Then he went off to check on the rest of the platoon."

I am surprised because I have not heard of this, but I only reply, "That sure must have been something to see."

It did not make sense to me, but Jensen told it in such a matter-of-fact way I had to believe it. They might have been part of a patrol sent to capture someone to interrogate. If they got close enough to try to grab him, they could have easily shot him. I ask SGT Paul about it, and he says he had heard about it. I conclude that during the previous weeks we have been in so much fighting and seen so much killing that this incident was nothing out of ordinary—so no one had bothered to tell me about it.

Chinese Attack in the Center: 15–20 May 1951

During 13–15 May POWs say that the main attack will be in the center.[67] They claim that the initial goal of the attack is to sever the six ROK Divisions on the eastern front from the remainder of the Eighth Army. The final goal is to destroy the ROK Divisions and the Second Division. Yet many have serious doubts about this information, because they wonder how ordinary soldiers could have learned about such plans.

Reports from agents say Chinese forces are shifting eastward. Rain and fog hinder air observation, and the Eighth Army has no technical information to corroborate these movements east of the Pukhan River. Many doubt there is any shift east of Ch'unch'on because of supply problems in the mountains. Also there are doubts about these reports since there are other reports of troops massing north of Uijongbu. What is real and what is disinformation designed to deceive?

If the enemy attacks, Van Fleet plans to use five times a normal day's artillery ammunition. At that rate there are seven days of ammunition on hand and he is prepared to move it to wherever the enemy attacks. Aircraft are prepared to attack any troop concentrations found. Actually, Peng is moving five armies[68] at night and under cover of smoke screens. They practice the strictest possible camouflage discipline. They are going into the area east of Ch'unch'on, and north of the Soyang River, behind screening forces. Peng plans to attack in the higher Taebaek Mountains despite the logistical problems there. He thinks that only if the UN's superior mobility, firepower, and air power is offset can he defeat them with greater numbers. He thinks this is possible in the mountains east of Ch'unch'on where there are few good roads. In keeping with the Oriental way of conflict Peng is betting on deception and surprise.

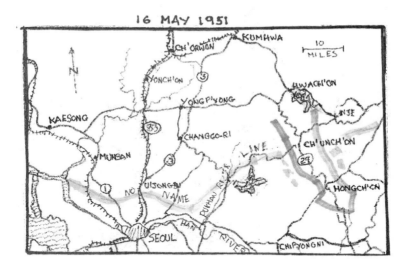

On 16 May 1951 in central Korea 137,000 Chinese and 38,000 North Koreans attack UN forces that are north of the eastern part of the No Name Line. Their main attacks are against ROK (Republic of Korea) units and the US Second Division down Route 29 through Ch'unch'on to Hongch'on. This is called the Second Spring Offensive, and in it the enemy suffers probably their greatest casualties of the entire war.

On 16 May the sky is overcast so aerial reconnaissance is ineffective, and without targets artillery and aircraft are unable to halt the waves of coffee-colored uniforms. The Chinese have little respect for the ROK troops since they have beaten them several times. Also they know they have defeated the Second Division before. On the night of 16–17 May the Thirty-Eighth Regiment holds firm. Artillery takes a terrific toll on the attackers. The division history states: "The groans of the wounded, screams of the attackers, and the blast of bugles mingled with the clattering roar of battle as waves of Chinese pushed against the line."

The Chinese continue their attack on the ROK Fifth, Seventh, Third, and Ninth Divisions south of the Soyang River. The South Koreans fight, but are overwhelmed by superior numbers. They fall back, and are authorized to move back to the No Name Line. However, they are not only outnumbered, they are also outgunned and poorly led. Many of their units are scattered and when they attempt to disengage they divide into small groups retreating in disorder. The artillery of the ROK Fifth and Seventh Divisions withdraw into the Second Division area.

The Second Division is also under attack, but holds. Infantry units defend their hilltops in bunkers they had prepared, and tanks roam in the valleys. The French Battalion is sent forward to plug a gap. Artillerymen are exhausted from loading shells. During the night of 17–18 May the Chinese assault the wire barriers on Hill 800, a key defensive position. Chinese and Americans wander around on Hill 800 in confusion; after much close-in fighting in the dark the Chinese are driven off the hill by dawn.

The division holds its positions during all of 18 May and pounds the enemy with artillery. However, two hundred Chinese are in the bunkers the Americans had built attack again in the dark. Two thousand artillery shells fall in ten minutes. Fighting goes on all night. By dawn on 19 May the Chinese retreat; they stream north without their dead. It is estimated that since the start of the attack in the center of Korea on 16 May the attacking units have thirty-five thousand casualties. East of the Second Division, the ROK Divisions give up much ground and lose much equipment. This causes friction between the ROK government and Washington. The South Koreans claim they have many new divisions, but need supplies; Washington claims that political interference and poor leadership has caused much equipment to be abandoned.

Meanwhile north of Seoul near Uijongbu on the western part of the No Name Line (see map on page 395), the enemy masses and steps up its patrolling, but does not make a major attack. The UN forces on the western part of the No Name Line make probes north to find the enemy. But no UN units move from No Name Line.

By 19 May the enemy action in the center of Korea slackens, and on the night of 19–20 May the probes stop. B-29s drop 170 tons of proximity-fused bombs. Many of the ROK Divisions remain tangled, and scattered groups trickle into collecting points.

F Company

The members of F Company have shared many stressful experiences since the end of February. They have proven themselves in stubborn defenses, smooth withdrawals, aggressive patrolling, and on tank-infantry teams.

The company has lost many of its most experienced men, but has absorbed replacements. The men have experienced the stress of combat with its boredom, bad weather, monotony, hardship, fatigue, excitement, and horror. They have seen, smelt, heard, and touched combat. They have demonstrated their skills and competence in the world's most dangerous job—that of an infantryman. On 18 May 1951 I am confident that they are as good as any rifle company in Korea—maybe ever.

However, on 21 May 1951 F Company is to be seriously challenged on Skeleton Hill.

---

[63] From 1962 to 1964 at the US Army Command and General Staff College and at the University of Pittsburgh I was able to study the Truman-MacArthur controversy.

[64] In III Army Group down both sides of Route #33.

[65] Of the IX Army Group centered on Route #3.

66 Yongp'yong-Changgo-ri and Kumhwa-Changgo-ri.

67 With the CCF Fifteenth, Twelfth, and Twenty-Seventh Armies.

68 Sixtieth, Fifteenth, Twelfth, Twenty-Seventh, and Twentieth.

CHAPTER TWENTY-FIVE

THE BATTLE OF SKELETON HILL

19–24 May 1951

To relieve pressure on those in the center of Korea, an attack north of Seoul starts on 20 May. Near Uijongbu the Second and Third Battalions of the Thirty-Fifth Regiment meet stiff resistance on Sukak-san, but by the end of the day hold the southern portion of that hill mass. The Turkish Brigade, to the east of the Thirty-Fifth Regiment, is also heavily engaged, but is unable to move the enemy from a long ridge with hill 329 (which will become Skeleton Hill) at its northern end.

Attacking Hill 329

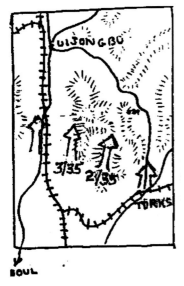

There has been a slow rain all morning on 21 May; now at noon the sky is dark and the air is filled with mist. I am in a small Korean shrine (myo) with the headquarters group. The Third Battalion is on a hill mass (Surak-San) to our west. It is possible to pick out small black dots as they move along the skyline. They do not seem to be fighting. The Turks are fighting 1,500 yards south of us.

F Company is spread out in a few huts. We hope we will be forgotten. On the far side of the valley in front of us there is an extension of the ridge on which the Turks are fighting. The last knob on that ridge is higher than the rest of the ridge; on the map I note that it is 329 meters high.

All morning I watch that ridge through my field glasses, since I am sure it will have to be cleared. There are men on each knob of the ridge, yet there is more movement on hill 329—which was to

become known as Skeleton Hill—than any other knob. It is a good rule that there are ten times as many people in a defensive position as you can see. I conclude that three or four hundred Chinese must be on hill 329. It is easy to see them going in and out of foxholes on the near side, but also the movement suggests that foxholes are also on the reverse side.

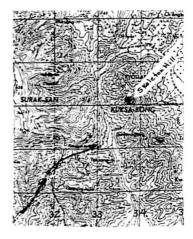

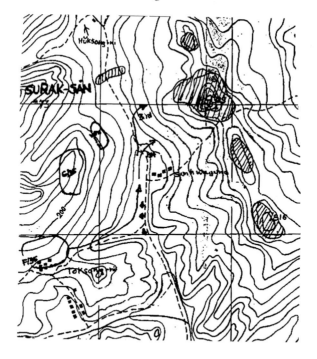

"Battalion wants you, sir." It is James W. Grimes, my radio operator. Maybe they'll have us button up for the night, I hope. The order from LTC Hiram M. Merritt is clear and simple: "Take hill 329. A tank platoon and G Company will support you."

I know what is coming and have no desire for it. After an unsuccessful attempt to delay until the Turks have cleared up their end of the ridge, I tell the platoons to prepare to move and for the platoon leaders to join me.

New Platoon Leaders

This is the first real action for three new platoon leaders. All had been civilians only a few weeks ago. They had joined the Inactive Reserve in 1946. Now they are about to lead a platoon in combat. I have placed them with LT Lackner (he has been awarded a battle field commission) for several days to help them get adjusted. I move LT Clarence Lackner, my most experienced and most capable officer, from a rifle platoon—where he has been since arriving in Korea—to the Weapons Platoon. The new officers are all willing and eager, but have never faced the drama of leading men in an assault. LT English, a cautious, quiet ROTC graduate, has the Second Platoon. LT Jackson, an energetic, serious man from Tennessee, has the Third Platoon.

LT Paul E. Clawson, an open, friendly, fun-loving OCS graduate who had come to the company after the Battle for Triple Nickel Hill, is the First Platoon leader. My artillery forward observer is now LT Joseph Shankle, a 1950 graduate of West Point. However, how a person looks and talks, where he is from, where he is educated or trained, and his personality are never good predictors of how he will respond to close combat in which death is just around the corner. Some become so paralyzed by fear they are unable to think clearly or act. For others the reality of violence, blood, and breathing men motionless next to corpses brings clarity to the mind and certainty to action. The difference lies hidden in the inner compass of each individual—what does he consider good, right, virtuous, and heroic or bad, wrong, sinful, and cowardly. This is the final test in ideological conflict.

When all of the platoon leaders arrive I tell them: "See that hill?" I point to hill 329. "That is our objective. Look at the two ridges going up from the valley." I make sure each of them see them. "The Third Platoon will go up the left ridge. The First Platoon will go up the right ridge. I will start off with the First. The Second will follow the First and will be used as needed. Weapons, a platoon of tanks, and G Company will support." I then explain the details and answer all of their questions. I make sure each understands what we are going to do. I end with:

"When we get to the top I do not want to see anyone standing on the top celebrating."

I move down to talk with the tank platoon leader. I have Clawson (First Platoon) and Jackson (Third Platoon) with me. I tell the tanker what we are going to do and discuss how the tanks should give us fire support. I can see G Company moving into position on the hill to my left. I know Lackner will place the Weapons Platoon into position on the same hill. The Turks are still fighting far back to our right on the other end of the ridge.

Start of the Attack

I call battalion: "We are moving out." LT Shankle starts artillery firing on our objective. Bursts of black puffs from VT shells cover the hill, and the whine and crash of 155 shells cause dirt and smoke to cover the top of the hill. It looks like no one could be alive there, but previous experience has taught me how wrong this can be.

The First Platoon comes up the valley to where the tanks are located, and we walk down to where the right ridge starts. Clawson starts up that ridge. The First is to move up until they hit resistance, and then to set up a position from which it can support the movement of the Third. I plan to follow the First so I can bring the Second into action whenever needed, but I decide to continue down the valley with the Third until they start up the left ridge.

As Jackson and I continue up the valley with the Third we hear *ZINGGG*—a rifle bullet. Soon there are more. I call the tanks and tell them to move up the valley with us to see if they can stop the rifle fire. The roars of tank engines start, and shortly thereafter there is the heavy chatter of their .50 cal. machine guns and the *BOOM-THUM* of their guns.

The grass is knee high as we move up the valley. My right foot is blue and cold, as I am wearing only a native Korean grass sandal. I had injured my Achilles tendon several days earlier and I can't walk with a regular combat boot on that foot. My left knee is still swollen from a series of injuries over several months. I cannot straighten my left leg, I can only step down on my toe, and I have to be helped whenever I want to go down a hill. When I hear the *ZINGGG* of a rifle bullet I hop into some water and I am now both cold and wet.

G Company calls: "We can see about fifty bad guys in an ambush just ahead of you." They give me the coordinates. I stop and quickly spot the point on the map. If everything is correct I know that the Third Platoon will move up the left ridge before they reach the ambush. I ask CPT Thompson, CO of G Company, to direct mortar fire on the enemy ambush. From the mortar bursts and the comments over the radio, I know that all has not gone well for the would-be ambushers.

The men of the First on the right ridge are still walking upright so I know they have not met any resistance. I note that the artillery fire has increased on the top of 329. I talk with Clawson over the hand radio; he says everything is all right and sounds upbeat and eager. He has been the platoon leader for over three weeks but this is his first attack. I cannot see the Third and I cannot reach its leader, Jackson, on the hand radio. Nor can I reach English with the Second. The hand radios are often useless. I send a messenger back to tell LT English to follow as close as possible behind the First.

I tell Shankle to stop all artillery fire, and I start to climb the right ridge, with the company command group, after the First. At the first clearing I stop to see what the Third is doing. They are moving up the left ridge, but are keeping off of the crest, so I assume they have received some fire from their left flank.

The *rat-tat-tat* of a machine gun and a flurry of rifle shots tell me the First has run into something. I glance back into the valley. The tanks are firing, but the Second has not left the valley. The familiar whine/thud of incoming artillery stops even before Shankle notifies me that all batteries had ceased fire on 329 (a.k.a. Skeleton Hill). Our mortars, our 57-mm recoilless rifles, G Company, and the tanks are all firing ahead of our platoons. All is going well, but I know it will not last.

"Friendly Fire"

To my left I hear machine gun fire; then rifles—the Third has hit something. An enemy mortar shell lands near. I continue to move up.

Just before I reach the First Platoon a volley of artillery hits to my right. From the whine of the shells I can tell they are our artillery. I call battalion and tell them to get the artillery halted. Shankle does the same over his radio directly to the artillery.

Another volley. This time it is closer. Shankle says it looks like a battery of 105s is "traversing left." Whatever it is I decide we should hit the ground. I yell: "Get down! Take cover!" I then dive into a small ditch with the command group.

With my face to the ground I count the seconds as each volley moves closer and closer. The ground shakes as the shells land to our right. The loud blasts are bad enough, but the incoming *WHIZZ* is even worse because you do not know where it will land. The ground shakes again, and branches of the bushes above me are torn apart by shrapnel. The volleys move across to our left. The smell of cordite fills the air. There is silence. I wait for the scream of "MEDIC!" Only silence. No one in the command group is hit.

Battalion calls: "Are you okay?"

"By some miracle we aren't all dead," I answer angrily. "I don't know who's hit yet. That could have finished off most of the company. I'm moving up to the First Platoon. I'll try to get them moving."

I start to move, but grab the radio hand set again, "Find out who in hell is responsible for that firing! Damn it, after that I don't know if I can get my men moving again. OUT!"

First and Second Platoons

I am not happy as I move through the men of the First Platoon. All are still flat on the ground. "Where's your Lieutenant?" I keep getting, "Up front."

Finally, I reach Sergeant Arnold who is the acting platoon sergeant, but less than two weeks before he had been an assistant squad leader. He had been sent to us from the artillery. Casualties, a lack of NCO replacements, and rotation had cut deeply. The regular platoon sergeant of the First Platoon is in Japan on R&R. "Where is the Lieutenant?" He points.

On his knees, slumped forward with blood-covered brains down the back of his head and neck, is LT Paul E. Clawson.

I turn to Sergeant Arnold; he is on his right knee, his eyes are blank with a frozen stare. His mouth is open. "Arnold!"

"Yes, sir." He seems to come back.

"I want you to get this platoon up and ready to charge this hill. I'm going to get the Second. I'll bring them up to your right and then all of us will charge the top. Understand?"

"Yes, sir. But we have also lost one of our squad leaders."

"Okay," I reply. I move over to CPL Darell T. Dorsett, the only black man in the platoon. "Dorsett, you are now the squad leader. Help Arnold get the men ready to take that hill." From what I have seen of Dorsett I know he has the ability and courage to lead men in combat.

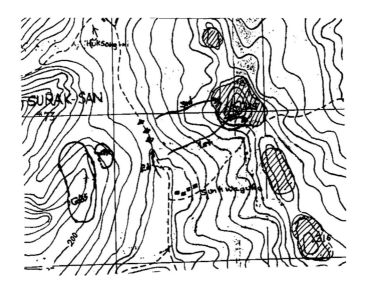

I watch for a few minutes. Arnold goes about reorganizing the platoon as if he has done it all of his life. Dorsett is talking with his squad. I talk with Frank E. Korn, Robert V. Lewis, and David K. Lindsey. They tell me of LT Clawson killing three of the Chinese and carrying a wounded soldier to safety. I am determined that Clawson's heroism will be recognized.

I look down the ridge for the Second Platoon. It is not there. It did not follow the First. I look through my field glasses and see some men sitting down near the tanks. I try to reach the Second by hand radio. No success. Maybe it is the batteries. Maybe English did not understand my orders. Maybe my messenger got lost. Maybe it is the rain. Maybe it is the damn hand radios. At this time, the reason is of no importance. How do I make the assault on the top of the hills as soon as possible?

I get the tank platoon leader on my 300 radio and tell him to relay a message to English to bring the Second Platoon up as soon as possible. We are getting fire from the top of the hill. What should I do? What can I do?

Changes for the Third Platoon

I know it will take the Second too long to reach us, so I know I will have to use the two platoons I have. I can see the Third on their ridge less than one hundred yards to my left. I try the hand radio again. I get a faint reply—the first contact since we moved out. I learn that the artillery did not reach them, but they are drawing heavy rifle fire from their left. Also, several machine guns block the way up the ridge they are on.

I order Jackson to bring the Third over to where the First is and tell him I will give him instructions when he arrives. I tell Sergeant Arnold it will not be the Second on his right, but Third.

LT Jackson comes up holding his M1911 Colt .45 automatic in one hand while the other is covered with blood, and two of his fingers seem to be barely attached to his hand. His face combines anger and shock. "Don't you think you had better get that hand taken care of?" I ask.

"No sir, I want to get those dirty bastards!" This is not the same man I had talked with a short time ago. Looking back down the slope I see MSGT Gary J. Emmons moving among the soldiers of the Third. I recognize that Jackson needs some help. He is now a brave individual gripped by pain, anger, and pride. I think it best to let him go with the platoon for he can lead by example, yet I know SGT Emmons will be needed. I have worked with Emmons on several assaults. I tell Jackson to swing the platoon over to the right of the First. Then I walk over to Emmons and tell him where I think there is a gap in the Chinese positions. He understands the situation. "Don't worry, sir. I'll take care of everything. The Lieutenant is a good infantryman. It's too bad we did not have more time together. We will miss him."

First Assault

Occasionally, enemy mortar shells drop near us, and there is the *zip* of a rifle bullet now and then. Nevertheless, the First is now reorganized and the Third is on line with it and has moved over to where I had seen a weak spot. I look around. Most of the men are crouched low, holding tightly to their weapons. They are all looking toward me.

So that all of the men could see me, I stand up. I shout as loud as I can: "All right, LET'S GO! TOGETHER. KEEP FIRING. Stay in line."

I see them start to move, and again I shout: "FIRE! FIRE! FIRE! Everyone move together." A few glances tell me they are following me slowly.

"COME ON, YELL!"

The firing picks up and the shouts grow louder. Not words; just yells of all kinds. I know both platoons are moving.

I let them pass me, but I continue to yell for them to keep moving and firing. I have to confront some of the laggards and order them to get up with the other men. From time to time in the past I had joked with them that their odds would always be better assaulting the enemy rather than trying to run back past me. I think I might have to put those words to the test—but I do not.

I cannot see most of the Third, but from the firing and yells from their direction I know that Jackson and Emmons are taking care of things.

On the top and around the sides of the hill, men in Chinese uniforms begin to appear as they dart from their holes. Most soon stumble to the ground. The yelling and shooting seems to increase. All of the men are captured by that feeling which only comes to infantrymen who are going the final yards and are now killing those who moments ago had been trying to kill them. Rifles fire. Eyes stare. Adrenaline flows. Bodies lunge forward. We are one. No thoughts of girls or mother. Life and death dance together. A second never ends. Do not fail. Be a man. Forward! Kill! Live!

The First Platoon charges up the hill with PFC William P. McCraney leading his squad. He throws a grenade to silence a machine gun and then, although he is wounded, takes his squad to the top. The squad continues firing until all of the Chinese throwing grenades are killed and they are on the top of the hill.

I still cannot see most of the Third, but from the firing and yells from their direction I know they are also moving up. I hope they have found an opening to the top. I later learn that LT Jackson charged forward, wrestling a Chinese soldier's own weapon from him and beating him to death.

To my left I see a man rise from a camouflaged hole some fifteen yards away; he aims his rifle at me. Hardly had he fired when two of my men turn their rifles on him and he slumps back into his hole.

I feel a sharp sting on my right wrist. I look down. My .45 is gone. My field jacket is ripped. The back of my hand is raw flesh and red blood. I try to move my fingers, and they all move. I pick up my .45.

On the very top of the hill, where an enemy machine gun had been firing at us, I can see two or three of my men waving their hands and yelling for joy. I am both happy and concerned. Happy because they have reached the top, but worried because I know they are targets for those in any reserve slope defense. A few of the men remain on the top of the hill but most take up positions near the top. No one is able to move over to find positions on the other side. I know we will have to make another assault.

Second Assault

Sticks start to float through the air, landing on our side of the hill. Most fall among our men on or near the top. But some are thrown so hard they land near me. They are not sticks. They are grenades with wooden throwing handles. They are exploding all around us. One lands three feet to my left. I fall to the ground and it explodes. I feel nothing except the force of the blast. For some ten minutes my men are tossing grenades over to the other side, and a constant stream of Chinese grenades come over to our side. There is almost no rifle firing now.

CHINESE HAND GRENADE

There is no longer a line, only individuals crouched down below the crest. Someway we have to get to the enemy on the other side, if we are to capture this hill.

Again I jump up and scream: "EVERYONE UP. FIRE. OVER TO THE OTHER SIDE."

The rifles start to crack again. Again my warriors advance. Some drop into holes. Some grenades also land in those holes. One man crawled by: "I'm hit in both legs."

I come upon the body of CPL Henry W. Berry. Death is always wrenching. Each of the men that crawl back from the crest have grenade wounds. PFC McCraney hops by with a smile on his face: "I got a good one, sir. Japan here I come."

I think: "He earned it with the red badge of courage." I tell him and another wounded soldier to go to the aid station.

Third Assault

No one is still on the top—at least no one fighting. We are getting thinned out, but we will have to get over to the other side in another assault or wait until the Second comes up. However, the time lost will give the Chinese time to regroup and that will surely increase our casualties. We need to try again while they are off balance.

Again I stand up, yell, and start forward. Again they yell back, start firing, and move forward. I have just started when something hit my left elbow so hard it spins me halfway around. My arm goes dead. I drop to my knees to check what has happened. I feel no pain, but I cannot move the fingers of my left hand, and my forearm is numb. I am dizzy. I hear Shankle, my forward observer, who had been by my side from the beginning, yell: "They've got the captain. Let's get them. Over the top for the captain!" He ran among the men of the First and then he ran over toward the Third ordering them over the top.

When I get to my feet, everyone is moving, yelling, and firing. The first men move over and I follow them. On the other side of the ridge, Chinese are running away. My warriors are firing at them. As more of my soldiers come over the top they move down far enough to have some protection. They keep firing at those running. Many Chinese stumble and fall.

Only a few yards from the crest other Chinese are crawling down the hill through the brush and rocks. It is more like target shooting than fighting. I see one crawling between two rocks just thirty-five yards away from me. I point my .45 at him and fire more in keeping with the spirit of the occasion than in any hope of hitting him. He stops and does not move. Later I check and he is dead.

Holding the Top of Skeleton Hill

I then move among my men giving instruction on the zone each platoon is to defend; I expect some kind of counterattack. I look for the Second Platoon. They are still moving up the ridge toward us. When they finally arrive I give LT English his zone.

During the next hour there is an occasional crack from a rifle as one of my men spot an enemy trying to sneak down the hill. But now there is a strange silence. No one is talking. No doubt they are thinking of many things. Maybe of a buddy just wounded or killed; maybe of the human he just killed; maybe of a wife, son, daughter, mother, or father far away; maybe of the tranquility of a boyhood day, or maybe of some girl. Around them is the cloak that infantrymen have worn forever.

I become aware of a slow drizzle. Five prisoners are brought in and several men with wounds come over to where I have the command group. LT Jackson comes over to report his platoon is in position. The wild look is now gone. He looks very tired, and I can tell his hand is giving him great pain. I tell him to take the other wounded and the prisoners down the hill to battalion.

Then I walk around our defensive positions. In several of the foxholes we find human bones with bits of clothing attached. We wonder what battle they were from. We think it appropriate to rename this: Skeleton Hill. Some of the foxholes have bodies of Chinese in them. Other Chinese bodies are scattered here and there. Abandoned equipment covers the hill: one large mortar, two heavy machine guns, six light machine guns, many rifles, and many boxes of grenades. Everyone in the First and Third are wet and exhausted—those in the Second are just wet.

While I am with the men of the Third Platoon they tell me of the single-handed conquests of LT Jackson. I then go over to where this had taken place and find the limp bodies of Chinese over their guns. I could visualize the grim fighting that had taken place there.

It now begins to rain. MSGT Paul A. Bingham, my first sergeant, has selected a pit which is larger than the other holes on the hill, where he, CPL Edmund F. McCartney, and I will be. They have removed two bodies from that pit. The bottom is covered with water. In the pit we find a pouch full of maps and papers, which indicates that this had been the command post of the regiment fighting the Turks, and that the reserve battalion of that regiment had defended Skeleton Hill.

The Turks move down the ridge to make contact with us. Battalion tells us that the artillery fire on us during the first part of our attack was the predatory fire for the Turks. The Turks did not know that we were attacking the other end of the ridge they were attacking.

The company settles in for the night. There are enough foxholes so we do not have to do any digging—just removal of the bodies of Chinese from today's fight and then to settle in with the skeletal remains of some previous fight for that hill. Communication is set up and defensive fire is called in. We have a hot meal. The three of us curl up in the pit to spend the night in the mud and water. I have no feeling in my left forearm. My right ankle and left knee hurt. My right hand looks bad, but it works. But none of this keeps me from sleeping.

The Morning After

The next morning (22 May) I go to the battalion aid station to have my wounds dressed. I also start the paperwork to get my soldiers (including Clawson, Jackson, and McCraney) recognized for their heroism. The medic says I am lucky that the bullet that hit my right hand had only torn up a lot of skin and flesh, but there is nothing that will prevent it from functioning. My left forearm has a number of small puncture wounds from parts of a Chinese hand grenade, but they cannot tell me why my arm is paralyzed. I tell them I will come back when my company comes off of the hill. I do think I am very lucky—lucky to be alive and to have the honor of commanding such wonderful men.

I go back up Skeleton Hill to F Company. I am told that sixty-eight enemy bodies have been found, and that in addition to LT Clawson and CPL Berry two other men were killed: PFC Ralph E. Dennison and PFC George Roller.

Van Fleet reports to Ridgway, "The enemy's initial punch in the eastern and central eastern section is shot." Fighting declines across the front.

I remain with F Company until the battalion goes into reserve on 24 May. My left arm is paralyzed, the wound on my right hand is bandaged, I am still wearing the Korean sandal on my right foot, and my left knee prevents me from going downhill without help. Yet I think I should remain. We make some minor adjustment in our defensive positions on 22 May—where we remain through 23 May.

CHAPTER TWENTY-SIX

WHILE IN JAPAN

25 May–21 June 1951

On 24 May I go back to the battalion aid station to see what they can do for my wounds. They again change the bandages on my right hand, but can do nothing for the paralyzed left arm, my left knee, or right Achilles tendon. They send me to the division clearing station. The doctors there decide to evacuate me to Japan.

Medical Evacuation

I remember very little of that trip. Perhaps they gave me a sedative, or perhaps I just slept, and nurses come in and out. I think I am on a train at one point. I do remember transferring to a ship. The ship takes me to somewhere in Japan and finally I end up in a hospital in Kobe.

In the Kobe hospital I am given a complete examination.[69]

The doctor's orders are simple: rest, hot tubs, and physical therapy. That sounds good to me. They remove all of the metal fragments in my left arm—except the one causing the paralysis—

and my bandages are changed daily until everything heals. In a few days some feeling comes back to the fingers of my left hand, and in time the paralysis fades.

While I am healing I have time to reflect on what I learned from my experience in Korea. While in the hot tubs repairing my body, while walking to strengthen my muscles, and while relaxing in the tranquility of Japanese gardens I develop some ideas about conflict and cooperation and how to establish a climate of order and satisfaction among people. During my time in Japan I come to realize that what I have experienced and observed is not only battles between armed forces but also an ideological conflict in which there is a struggle over the inner compass of individuals.

My most vivid recollections concern how people react to combat. There were those in infantry, tank, artillery and engineer combat units, and there were those in various support units. There were those at lower organic levels (team, squad, platoon, company and battalion) and those in the specialized staffs of higher headquarters. There were the fighters (warriors, soldiers, infantrymen and tankers) who see combat as a challenge, a test of their manhood; also there were those who have none of the military virtues and do all they can to avoid combat, i.e., the military in name only.

I recognize, vaguely, that I have seen various kinds of ideological conflict. I realize it has three parts. One is the moral and ethical beliefs of individuals. This part concerns the inner compass that determines behavior since it shapes what individuals consider right, wrong, good, bad, heroic, cowardly, virtuous, and sinful; the ancient Greeks called it Sacred Authority.[70] The second part is what people consider the best way to structure government—which is called Secular Authority. This part is what people normally call ideology, i.e., the doctrine of political/ economic movements (Capitalism, Socialism, Fascism, Communism, etc.) that determine the rules, regulations, and laws of government. The third part of ideological conflict concerns how the will of "we" is kept strong, while the will of "they" is weakened through strategic communication.[71]

I begin to wonder how the Oriental way of conflict differed from the Western way of war. I wonder why some can cope with the fear of death, but others cannot, and why Eros is so often associated with the warrior ethos.

It will take me many years to evaluate how history supports or refutes these ideas. In the end I conclude that ideological conflict and strategic communication are not understood by most Americans, and are therefore neglected, by the policymakers of the United States.

The Samurai

If I had been on the banks of the Rhine, Loire, or Thames I might have explored the middle ages with its feudalism, chivalry, and a moral code shared by all honorable knights. But I was in Japan so I looked back at the time of the samurai and Bushido (thirteenth to sixteenth centuries) to get some perspective on the ideology, which shaped the inner compass of the samurai.

The samurai need common inner compasses to guide their behavior as warriors with great responsibilities. These responsibilities require honor, and in return, the samurai are given privileges. The ethos of the samurai, like the ethos of all great warriors, is never realized completely, but it still provides the inner compass for such warriors. It is not any written code that is important; it cannot be recorded in abstract, legal terms. It is best kept as a few words passed down by word of mouth. It is the unuttered and the unwritten that is important—its importance rests in how well it guides the actions of the warrior. For warriors of the United States, a similar code is built around Duty, Honor, and Country, providing the same ethos, until these ideals were transformed into legal terms so they could be defended in courts.

To be effective, any such code must have four aspects: it places identity in something larger than self, it requires freedom for independent action, it depends on a belief in absolutes, and it includes a sense of honor. The code must support vigorous initiative, quick reaction, a capacity to take decisive action, and a willingness to suffer. Also, it must encourage the manly virtues— honesty, courage, vigor, valor, compassion, composure, decisiveness, sympathy, steadfastness, aggressiveness, and magnanimity— and above all, duty.

The position of women in the thinking of the samurai is somewhat contradictory to the Western mind. On the one hand, the samurai idealize a woman who has the heroic fortitude of the bravest of men, who is willing to go to extreme measures to defend her chastity, or a daughter's sacrifice for her father, a wife for her husband, and a mother for her sons. On the other hand, one of the privileges granted the samurai is the freedom to enjoy all the pleasures women can provide. Sex is considered as essential for the life of the samurai as food, water, and shelter—without modesty, guilt, or regret. If a man does not enjoy sex, he cannot be a good samurai.

Warriors, Soldiers, Supporters, and MINOs

In the armed forces there are warriors and soldiers who have personal contact with the enemy in the realm of killing and being killed. Without supporters, who have no direct contact with the enemy, the warriors and soldiers could never be successful. Also many supporters have all of the military virtues and are as brave as anyone. However, also in the armed forces there are those who look and talk like fighters but who lack the military virtues and flee whenever danger, suffering, and hardship come their way — these are the MINOs, the military in name only.

Warriors display courage and bravery in combat during both War and Warfare. Warriors might be tribal fighters or members of large military organizations. Their bravery and a disregard of death might come from pain, hatred, fear, envy, self-interest, anger, or frenzy — or from a deep sense of combat camaraderie. Warriors are usually brutish men — not the timid kind; relish action — not words; value unity — not diversity; are comfortable with myth, legend, custom, and tradition — not with legality and political correctness; are simple and direct — not clever and devious; favor merit and obedience — not equality and license.

Success in conflict requires warriors who are self-motivated risk takers. They are willing and eager to do what is needed to achieve victory in War and stability in Warfare or Peace. Warriors are men of action. Reputations are made through action. Action can result in either success or failure, and it is this fact that produces a high. But the high through action is short lived — it lasts no longer than the action. Such exhilaration is only possible when there is stress — the higher the stress the greater the high. The action of warriors is bright, dramatic, chaotic, and exciting. However, action alone can be tragic, and when carried to the extreme it leads to self-destruction and death during fighting.

Warriors must feel responsible for their actions. In the past "will power" made warriors honest, brave, and courageous. A strong inner compass does the same. Without a strong, firm inner compass individuals lack the ability to make rapid, decisive decisions—they become flotsam moved by determinism. Of course, taking anything to the extreme is likely to produce a bad outcome. Thus the correct behavior should not be determined by nineteenth century "will power." Nineteenth century "will power" attempted to repress any irrational tendencies. On the other hand, the inner compass of an individual includes instincts, drives, customs, and traditions. Sacred Authority provides guides so that a person can make judgments about right behavior.

The goal is to combine free will, personal responsibility, duty, and discipline—to have Sacred Authority and Secular Authority be equally strong but parts of a dynamic whole. Combat requires warriors who take orders and have a sense of duty, yet are imaginative, thinking, self-motivated individuals. Warriors become heroes because they are examples of loyalty, dedication, and patriotism. Their behavior demonstrates honor, discipline, duty, and a sense of purpose. Their demeanor is stern and severe. They are usually motivated by God's will and the ecstasy of belief. They enjoy a high degree of individual freedom because a strong internal compass provides self-control of their behavior—thus the actions of a warrior are ideological.

Acts of personal bravery by warriors and organization bravery by soldiers differ, and the bravery of warriors does not last as long as the bravery of soldiers.

The soldier is judged by his contribution to the combat effectiveness of the unit, by how he supports his comrades, and by how he maintains order. Leaders use discipline and training combined with self-interest to achieve combat effectiveness. A soldier is not brave because he is ordered to be brave by a legal superior, but because his inner compass directs him to be brave—thus at its foundation soldiers actions are ideological.

Organizational bravery of soldiers is the result of discipline, training, and a sense of common identity. The training for soldiers stresses courage within a cohesive unit, in obedience to leaders—over the rash, bold acts of individuals. Organizational courage requires soldiers to fight together in both War and Warfare even when they know the odds are against them. They will not desert their comrade, they will do their duty in an honorable way, and they will obey their leaders.

Soldiers fight together for a reason, at the same time the courageous acts of warriors are recognized and appreciated. As a result, the courage of soldiers is both emotion and reason based—it comes from the inner compass and is, therefore, ideological. The soldier must hold his own life dear, not cheap, yet be willing to give up his life for those fighting with him to achieve their common goal.

Discipline during training is how to introduce into the inner compass of soldiers the courage they will need. Drill instills the psychological effect of keeping together. When a soldier enters a Western military organization he is separated from his class, race, sex, and political loyalties to become a part of an identically appearing body of men. Marching and chanting together accomplishes this. Each man occupies a space equidistant from others. They are in step—again and again. To become separated means high casualties. A few well-trained and disciplined soldiers can easily defeat a mob.

In combat, be it in War or Warfare, the greatest weakness is giving up, for success always requires just one more time after something goes wrong. Warriors and soldiers both build on failure; they use experience as a stepping-stone. They don't forget mistakes, but they don't let them sap their vigor. Victory in War and success in the protracted conflict of Warfare is judged by the obstacles overcome. Whether a person thinks that he can, or thinks he can't, he is usually correct.

Warriors and soldiers think it is a disgrace to run away from comrades during a fight and they choose duty, honor, and death over seeking safety through flight. At times the courage, audacity, and heroism of warriors and the training, discipline, and steadfastness of soldiers are overcome by technology, corruption, poor leadership, poor intelligence, and the number of enemy fighters, politicians, and intellectuals engaging in factional quarrels. Regardless of the odds against them, warriors and soldiers do not flee from any enemy; rather, they stay with their comrades, or they perish.

Warriors and soldiers don't ask what the world needs. They ask what those with them need. What the world needs are individuals who struggle together to do what is right, and act as what they do makes a difference—and it does.

Supporters of warriors and soldiers are in most ways no different from those they support. They are just in a different location and have different duties.

On the other hand, those in the armed forces who are military in name only (MINOs, pronounced minnows), rely on the strength of others for protection; they often desert those fighting with them as soon as they fear death more than dishonor. They can be found in both combat and support units. When they are exposed to combat and death they usually show signs of combat fatigue, which might be brief or long lasting.

MINOs think, hesitate, contemplate, evaluate, and think again before they act; they are often clever, devious, timid, arrogant, and flamboyant; they often excel in the use of words; they value diversity over unity, and stress legality and political correctness. MINOs merely tolerate the military virtues since they favor ease, comfort, and sophistication. They place feelings, intentions, and legality over doing what is right. They look to Secular Authority for guidance rather than to Sacred Authority (shared moral, ethical, and religious beliefs), and for MINOs even Secular Authority is "flexible."

Killing and being killed is the realm of the warrior and soldier. Most of the "military" never have personal contact with the enemy and thus do not know the realm of the warrior and soldier. Since the 1950s it has been rare for more than 30% of the armed forces in a "combat theater" to be warriors and soldiers, yet they determine the outcome. Therefore, combat effectiveness, victory in War, and success in Warfare all require warriors and soldiers to be elevated and rewarded above all others. To treat all of those who have served in the armed forces—all veterans—the same is in the interests of politicians, but it is not right or in the best interest of the nation. Those who have actually placed their lives in danger for the nation should be respected more than others if the nation is to have future protection from threats.

Action in Korea from 24 May to 21 June

During the time I am in Japan events in Korea are not as dramatic as those I had experienced in going up and down that country. The US is seeking a ceasefire.

Shortly after I left Korea (24 May) the Eighth Army pushes forward against melting resistance. Attacks in the center are cautious, and the division commanders are reprimanded for not breaking through the covering force to reach the enemy's main force. Peng is unable to make effective attacks in the mountains, and this endangers his forces in the high mountains. He has fresh reserves, yet the casualties in his assault units are exceptionally high from artillery and air attacks. Rapid movement allows most of the enemy's units to withdraw out of the reach of Van Fleet's counterattack. Peng orders a withdrawal with the covering forces only fighting to protect their withdrawal. The Hwach'on Reservoir again divides the Chinese and North Korean forces.

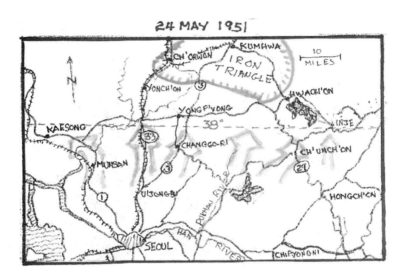

24 MAY 1951

On 24 May there is an incident in which GEN Almond decides to take direct control of a tank company. The Second Division attacks with the Seventy-Second Tank Battalion to seize a bridge site near Inje. LT Tom Fife is the platoon leader of the lead unit, and his company commander, CPT Bill Ross, is getting the plans for the move to Inje, when GEN Almond lands his helicopter near the tank company's assembly area. He is unhappy with the speed of the advance. He tells Fife to move the entire company to an objective he shows him on his map. The tanks are to travel at twenty mph, and to "keep going until you hit a mine." Fife cranks up the company and starts moving—also radioing CPT Ross. Ross orders Fife to halt and wait for him.

He was on the MATH DEPARTMENT AT WEST POINT WITH ME!

Almond, from above, sees the tanks stop and immediately lands and confronts LT Fife. When told that he is waiting for the company commander, Almond gets on Fife's radio (CPT Al Haig and Fife have to boost him up onto the back deck of the tank) and radios the battalion commander. In no uncertain language Almond orders the battalion commander to get the tanks moving to the objective he has selected.

Soon all of the company is on the move. It goes through groups of Chinese rattled by the appearance of tanks. It comes up on the rear of four thousand Chinese scrambling north under punishing air attacks. By 1630 the tankers are nine miles from Inje and take positions at the bridge site. They continue firing on enemy groups scurrying for safety near the river. However the Chinese set up a roadblock behind them. They have to be resupplied by airdrops until the Second Division arrives.

By 28 May Beijing's dream of a military victory has vanished, yet they are determined to hold the Iron Triangle as long as possible. Their real goal is part of the ideological conflict: to be able to claim they defeated the Americans by negotiating a settlement that keeps North Korea intact. To do this they will have to influence the American decision-making process as well as hold back the UN forces.

In the west the First ROK Division advances to Munsan on the Imjin River. First Cavalry Division also reaches the Imjin River and continues up Route 33 until it reaches Ch'orwon (the west corner of the Iron Triangle). Third Division moves directly to Ch'orwon. Twenty-Fifth Division moves toward Kumhwa (the northern corner of the Iron Triangle).

On 30 May drenching rains turn roads into boggy tracks and, along with low clouds and fog, limit close air support and observation. Ridgway instructs Van Fleet to prepare plans for the next sixty days. Van Fleet directs the Corps commanders to fortify positions when they reach the Iron Triangle, and thereafter to conduct limited objective attacks, reconnaissance in force, and patrolling. No new attacks into North Korea are planned.[72]

The US Eighth Army initiates Operation Pile-Driver to gain control of the Iron Triangle. This is expected to take two weeks, but bad weather delays its start. By 15 June UN forces control the Iron Triangle and prepare defensive positions on, or north of, the Kansas line.

Negotiations

After weeks of debate, the JCS sends Ridgway a new policy statement that is a major redefinition of his mission. He is to continue to inflict losses on the Chinese and North Korean armed forces, but also to terminate hostilities under appropriate armistice arrangements. The JCS retains the authority it had assumed over general Eighth Army advances. The UN and allied leaders decide that a cease-fire will be satisfactory and that UN forces need not seek a military victory over North Korea. UN Secretary General Trygve Lie states, "If a cease-fire could be arranged approximately along the 38th Parallel then the main purpose of the security council resolutions will be fulfilled, provided that a cease-fire is followed by the restoration of peace and security in the area." Secretary of State Dean Acheson states the US position is a cease-fire at or near the 38th Parallel. Seeking a response to these statements, State Department officials "cast about like a pack of hounds searching for a scent."

Through agents in New York, Washington, and London, the Chinese know all of the arguments made behind decisions at the UN and in Washington and can plan their strategy accordingly. If they can retain a viable North Korea they know they can claim they have defeated the United States, which in November 1950 was advancing toward their border. They think that during any armistice talks they can achieve their goal through deception, misdirection, strategic communication, psychology, and patience.

Diplomats in Washington, New York, Beijing, and Moscow discuss the US cease-fire proposals. Representatives of countries with forces in Korea meet in Washington. They are concerned by the lack of response. They consider another cease-fire proposal, but decide to make the US position known to Premier Mao Tse-tung and Foreign Minister Chou En-lai through neutral diplomats. Mao repeats a 1937 statement that "a true revolutionary leader must be adept at making himself and his followers advance and change their views according to changing circumstances." But the Chinese do nothing, with Chou En-lai only making a statement about the weather. The diplomats of the West are confused by the Chinese response since it is not in keeping with their view of negotiations, i.e., a clear statement of positions followed by give and take until an agreement is reached. The Chinese know how Americans think, they know the arguments among the American decision makers, they know about the antiwar movement in the US, and they know how to manipulate the media.

The Americans think they are negotiating a cease-fire agreement, but the Chinese are engaged in ideological conflict. The British diplomat Ernest Satow has stated the Western view of negotiations between states: "Diplomacy is the application of intelligence and tact to the conduct of official relations." And Harold Nicolson, a well-known author on diplomacy, explains it: "The worst kind of diplomats are missionaries, fanatics, and lawyers; the best kind are the reasonable and humane skeptics." However, that is not how the Chinese see negotiations. They see them as "conflict by another means." They are not seeking a solution; they want to get as much as they can, they are in no rush, and they have no intention of being reasonable, agreeable, or diplomatic.

On 1 June 1951 the secretary-general of the United Nations (Trygve Lie) says that he thinks a cease-fire close to the 38th Parallel will satisfy the Security Council's resolutions. On 7 June Secretary of State Dean Acheson tells a senate committee that the UN forces should accept an armistice. Thus instead of an advance to the narrow neck of the Korean peninsula there is a stalemate on the existing front and negotiations—and there will be vicious fighting and many deaths for several years without purpose.

On 17 June the front line divisions reach the limits of the general advance authorized by the JCS in support of efforts to open cease-fire negotiations. As yet there are no signs that Chinese and North Korean authorities favor cease-fire negotiations—perhaps because the Chinese know what the UN and US are willing to do as a result of reports from agents in Washington, New York, and London. The Chinese think they can get what they want through patience and strategic communication superiority. It is like playing poker with someone who knows the cards you hold. Nevertheless, there are repeated efforts on many levels by UN and US officials to open armistice talks.

Return to Korea

By 21 June 1951, eleven months after I left Okinawa for Korea and a month after I was wounded, I am ready to be returned to duty. I ask to be sent back to the Thirty-Fifth Regiment so that I can complete my normal tour there. I do not know what my assignment will be or what the future might hold.

[69] During the examination the doctors tell me:

1. The bullet that hit the right hand tore up the skin and flesh but ricocheted off of a bone so it did no permanent damage. After it heals it should be as good as new.

2. The Achilles tendon of the right foot is only strained and inflamed. It would have to be wrapped for several weeks to prevent additional damage, but with heat and time it will be okay; however, I will have to be careful not to hurt it again.

3. The left knee has torn cartilage (medial meniscus) and will have to be operated on some-day. However, recovery from such an operation will require several weeks in a cast fol-lowed by several months of therapy. After the operation I should be able to walk normally; however, I will always have to exercise to keep the knee tight in order to prevent another injury. Until such an operation I will have to keep the knee wrapped and try not to twist it. If it does "lock up" I should try to get it back in place, and use ice packs so that it does not swell and cause additional damage.

4. The left forearm has many pieces of metal from a Chinese grenade in it. All are small. Most are in the flesh and can be removed. However, one piece that has entered the back of the elbow is causing the forearm to be paralyzed. Only time will tell if the nerve has been cut or just injured. In a few weeks that piece of metal should be covered with scar tissue and the nerve should repair itself—if it is not cut. They decide against attempting to remove that part of the grenade for fear of doing more damage to the nerve. Therefore, for the time being the doctors decide on heat therapy and waiting to see what happens.

[70] Sacred Authority is the moral and ethical belief that shapes the inner compass of individuals. It is that which must not be violated or disregarded, and is expressed in custom and tradition. Although it often is a reflection in religions, it is not necessarily sacred in the sense of being holy or given by God. Sacred Authority is contrasted with Secular Authority, i.e., the rules, regulations, laws, pro-cesses, and procedures of government.

[71] Ideology does refer to a body of doctrine, opinions, and assertions of a political or cultural move-ment (Capitalism, Socialism, Fascism, Communism, etc.) along with the devices for establishing that doctrine in the rules, regulations, and laws of government. However, here ideological conflict is used to describe something broader, i.e., the struggle to shape the inner compass and point of view of individuals regarding what is right or wrong, good or bad, and virtuous or evil. It does include the efforts to advance political or cultural doctrine, opinions and assertions that determine Secular Au-thority (i.e., the rules, regulations, and laws of government) but it also includes Sacred Authority (i.e., that which is considered moral and ethical).

[72] In the center there are plans to capture Hwach'on (the eastern corner of the Iron Triangle) with an attack on 5 June. The Second and Seventh ROK Divisions are to move to positions between Kum-hwa (the northern corner of the Iron Triangle) and the Hwach'on Reservoir. The Sixth ROK Division is to advance to the Hwach'on Reservoir. Rain and heavy low clouds limit flights by air observers. Seven thousand North Korean soldiers are reported to be moving ahead of the Second Division, but blocking positions and minefields covered by fire slow the division. Nevertheless, a task force enters Inje at 1430. It is evening before the division clears the town.

CHAPTER TWENTY-SEVEN

S-2, THIRTY-FIFTH
INFANTRY REGIMENT

22 June–25 July 1951

On 23 June 1951 I return to the Thirty-Fifth Regiment, and I am made the regimental S-2 (intelligence officer). Also I am asked to extend my normal one-year tour.

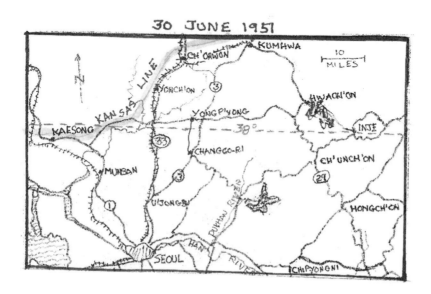

Eighth Army Operations after 22 June 1951

The objective of the operations of the Eighth Army after 22 June 1951 is to establish stability on the Korean Peninsula. The goal is no longer victory. The conflict is no longer a conventional War; it had changed from War to Warfare, even though there would be intensive combat between armed forces for two more years. The ideological struggle will be more important than the battles between military forces.

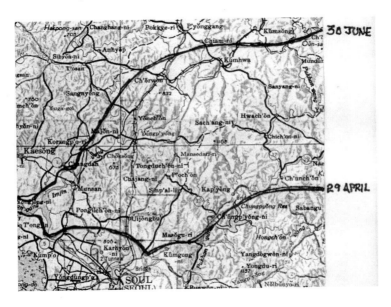

On 22 June the JCS asks Ridgway how an advance into North Korea would affect UN operations. He defers commenting on any offensive until Van Fleet completes plans for advancing to the Pyongyang-Wonsan line. It is clear that the revitalized Eighth Army could move to the Pyongyang-Wonsan line, or on to the narrow neck, if there was the will in Washington. Beijing's dream of a military victory over the United States, which was justified in the winter of 1950, has now vanished. Their hope of unifying Korea has been crushed by the determination to defend South Korea,

regardless of the costs in blood and treasure. The Chinese forces in Korea are exhausted and unable to stop the Eighth Army.

It would have been possible for UN forces to advance to the narrowest part of the Korean peninsula, fifty miles north of the Pyongyang-Wonsan line, in order to establish a border on the Ch'ongch'on River in the west and include Hamhung and Hungnam in the east. This would have established a weak buffer state between The Republic of Korea and China. The future of Korea and the world would have been much different if that had been done. Yet there is neither the will in Washington, or the American people, nor support from allies for such a course. On the other hand, Syngman Rhee wants the UN forces to advance to the Yalu River in order to unify Korea as the Republic of Korea.

At the UN, Malik announces that the Soviets believe the conflict could be settled and that the belligerents should start discussions to arrange a cease-fire and an armistice that provides for the mutual withdrawal of forces from the 38th Parallel. Ridgway thinks the proposal might be an attempt to get UN armed forces away from the 38th Parallel. He states: "the well-earned reputation for duplicity and dishonesty possessed by the USSR" and "the slowness with which deliberative bodies such as the Security Council produce positive action" requires the Eighth Army to remain alert.

MacArthur made a strategic error in November 1950 by advancing toward the Yalu River, an action that was considered a threat by China. In June 1951 the US government, and the American people, made the opposite strategic error by not having the Eighth Army advance as far as it could. With adequate intelligence it could have been determined that in June 1951 China is prepared to accept a weakened North Korea as a buffer state in the mountains between an enlarged Republic of Korea and its Yalu

River border. China would not have considered an advance to the Ch'ongch'on River a threat requiring additional military forces in Korea. Yet this opportunity is not seized.

Observations and Conclusions

Through visits to the headquarters of the Twenty-Fifth Division and I Corps, I am able to compare and contrast the attitudes and interests of those in these headquarters with those I experienced at the company and battalion levels.

To me the military staffs focus too much on reports, data, maps, and abstract thinking. The lower levels are more organic; there the focus is on common interests and on how to solve concrete problems in order to achieve something together. At the higher levels, it seems to me, the staff officers focus on narrow concerns. I observe turf battles, manipulation, and "one-upmanship." All of those on the staffs have accomplished careers, of which each is justly proud. The atmosphere is different from what I have observed in a rifle company and in an infantry battalion. However, as a twenty-five-year-old who has never been at the upper levels of any large organization, I realize there might be reasons for these differences that I do not understand.

Discussions about where the representatives of the UN forces and the commander of the Communist forces in Korea might meet to arrange an armistice are under way during June 1951. The last large-scale operations are completed and a new battle line is established. It is clear to me that the battle lines will solidify and forces will be in a situation much like that of World War I, except that units will be dug in on isolated hilltops rather than in trenches facing each other. I cannot see much need for my skills as a regimental S-2 so I consider when to leave Korea.[73]

Should I Extend My Tour in Korea?

On 6 July 1951 I tell COL Kelleher I have decided to leave as soon as he can get a replacement for me. He asks me to reconsider. He tells me he does not think he can get a better regimental S-2, and that he thinks I will be a valuable asset for the regiment. However, he makes it clear that the decision is mine to make. He asks me to think it over for a few days and then to tell the regimental S-1 my decision.

On 8 July 1951 the military leaders of both sides meet at a teahouse in Kaesong. Plenary sessions for the armistice talks start on 10 July. I conclude that intelligence will now become routine: the analysis of reports and the confirmation of data. I am sure that I will be no better than many others at such staff work. The dynamic situations that I have experienced will be no more, and the need for my strengths will be unlikely. The next day (11 July) I tell the S-1 I am not going to extend. I start back

on 21 July, and leave Inch'on by ship on 24 July—one year after my arrival in Korea.

After I Leave Korea

Negotiations on the armistice are slow, and break down in August. On 25 August plenary sessions are resumed at Panmnjom. There are many battles, with much suffering and many casualties, to reestablish the defensive line and to secure specific hills: Bloody Ridge, Heartbreak Ridge, Old Baldy, Pork Chop, White Horse, Triangle Hill, Pike's Peak, Jane Russell Hill, Sandy Hill, and T-Bone Hill. Finally there is the signing of an armistice agreement on 27 July 1953.

Afterword

The Korean War differs from all others—as is always true of any conflict. Conflict/Cooperation is always time and place specific. War, Warfare, and Peace are all distinctive conditions, each with their own strategies, tactics, processes, and procedures. Yet in reality Conflict/Cooperation is always time and place specific.

We should remember what General Douglas MacArthur said in his 1951 farewell address to congress:

Once war is forced upon us, there is no other alternative than to apply every available means to bring it to a swift end. War's very object is victory, not prolonged indecision. In war, there is no substitute for victory.

But there is a distinction between War and Warfare. That distinction needs to be recognized. MacArthur is correct about

War, but not about Warfare. The failure to understand this distinction caused MacArthur to make the strategic error of moving past the narrow neck of Korea toward the Yalu in an attempt to "achieve victory." While the objective in War is victory, the objective in Warfare is stability, i.e., a climate of order and satisfaction. The Korean War lasted from June 1950 until May 1951, and the fighting and dying continued until 1953. It should have lasted only until Thanksgiving 1950. MacArthur's failure to shift to Warfare at that time—from seeking victory to establishing stability—was very costly in blood, treasure, and the future of Korea. This was a strategic error of being too aggressive in seeking "victory." MacArthur should have realized that stability could be achieved with a division of Korea at the Ch'ongch'on River on the west and including Hamhung on the east.

After May 1951 there was a shift from War to Warfare—the objective was no longer victory, it was stability. Unfortunately, this was a strategic error in the opposite direction. Rather than exploiting the military advantage of the Eighth Army, a misjudgment by the foreign policy establishment, and a lack of will, resulted in negotiations for a cease-fire line near the 38th Parallel. More lasting stability, at lower costs, would have been achieved by pushing the battle lines to the Ch'ongch'on River before starting armistice talks.

Also, the United States failed to learn from the Korean War that Warfare must be fought in the human domain—it is ideological conflict. Overwhelming force and technological superiority is not enough. Strategic communication, i.e., maintaining the will on your side while weakening the will of your opponents, is the critical mass in Warfare.

Lessons Learned and Often Forgotten

I learned many things in Korea, yet the most important for me was the bond infantrymen and tankers have from experiencing combat together. It is an extreme version of the bond of a family who has shared stressful experiences together. The bond is combat camaraderie, and it comes from the Ethos of Eros. Perhaps a sports team, a group of missionaries, and a cell of political revolutionaries can also know these same feelings to some extent.

Infantrymen and tankers are not martyrs. Martyrs die for a cause as individuals. They are both warriors and soldiers. They kill and are killed. The goal of infantrymen and tankers is to live, not to die; when they do die it is with others while attempting to achieve something together. Infantrymen and tankers know they are the ones who must go the final yards together. When the debates, discussions, compromises, and concessions are over and when the support has—or has not—been provided, it is necessary for some to go the final yards. This is when the actions of infantrymen and tankers determine the outcome. This is what makes infantryman and tankers unique. This can be expressed like this: At some point infantryman and tankers write a blank check made payable to "Those going the final yards with me for any amount up to and including my life."

It is the infantrymen and tankers who wear the boots that stand on a piece of ground, and when they stand on that piece of ground there is no doubt about who has won. As long as they hold that piece of ground day and night it is won. If they do not hold that piece of ground it has not been won. That is the test that counts.

Most of those in the armed forces do not share the bond infantrymen and tankers feel. They do not understand these feelings since they have never "seen, felt, heard, and touched" combat as infantrymen and tankers do; for others combat is made up of abstractions they know about, rather than reality they have lived and emotions they can never forget. Combat is not just being near where there is fighting, or being in danger of being killed by a sniper or an IED; it is being united with your "brothers" in life or death struggles against an "enemy." Also, this feeling, this bond, cannot be achieved in the higher levels of any larger organization. It can only be achieved at the point of the spear.

Many lessons could have been learned from what happened in Korea: the role of the infantrymen and tankers, the importance of intelligence, the maneuver of inundation, the use of torture, the importance of leadership, the nature of aggressive interrogation, the importance of the inner compass of individuals, how to cope with the fear of death, the appeal and limitations of socialism, the advantages of fire/air support in War, significance of combat camaraderie, and the importance of the human domain in Warfare.

The most important lessons that could have been learned in Korea are:

- That Warfare differs from both Peace and War.
- That being either too aggressive or too cautious can be a strategic error.
- That strategic communication is the critical mass during ideological conflict.

All of these lessons, and more, can be learned from knowledge of what actually happened during the Unknown War—during 1950 and 1951 when we went up and down Korea. Hopefully *Forgotten: Ideological Conflicts in Korea, Vietnam, Iraq, and Afghanistan* will now contribute to greater awareness of what could have been learned.

On leaving Korea I looked forward to seeing Joan and starting the next phase of my life.

---

[73] I discuss the situation with two classmates who have to make the same decision: would we extend in order to get another promotion? All of us have been in Korea since June 1950. We are captains in positions that called for a major; Sid Berry is S-3 of the First Battalion, Don McGraw is S-3 of the Third Battalion, and I am S-2 of the regiment. We have already received one battlefield promotion, we have been company commanders, have been wounded, have received several awards, and know we will get a second battlefield promotion to major if we stay. At different times I discuss the options with Sid and Don. Neither of us tries to convince the other what the decision should be, nor do we ever say what our decision will be. We are just friends evaluating an important decision each of us would have to make.

CHAPTER TWENTY-EIGHT

VIETNAM REVISITED

1944–1975

Conflict in Vietnam is like an elephant described by blind men who only touch one part of it. This summary of what took place from 1944 to 1975 is an attempt to describe the whole elephant.

After Vietnam, just like after Korea, lessons were forgotten and then many of the same mistakes were repeated in the Balkans, Iraq, Afghanistan, and the Middle East. If the USA continues to forget these lessons they will be repeated in the future. What did the USA forget about Vietnam?

- Warfare differs from both War and Peace.

- The Western way of war differs from the Oriental way of conflict.

- Only members of groups (i.e., those who consider themselves "we") can accomplish lasting economic and political change—"foreigners" cannot do it.

- Long-term stability requires economic and political conditions that reinforce a climate of order and satisfaction at the local level, and it is a mistake to attempt to persuade rival groups prepared to use force to eliminate each other to form a central coalition government.

- The inner compass of individuals, strategic communication, a sense of common (including national) identity, and the strength of wills are the battlefields of ideological conflict.

- Success in Warfare, i.e., stability, requires equilibrium between Secular Authority and Sacred Authority, which can be achieved by either authoritarian means or representative governance.

The East is east and the West is west and the twain have often met. In the past three hundred years the East has taken much from the West, yet the West still has much to learn from the East.

The Origin of US Vietnam Policy (1944–1954)

Unquestioned preconceptions about the creation and decline of nation-states were forged during World War II. The horrors of that war were blamed on nationalism.

After World War II, three contending ideologies struggled for acceptance as the replacement of nationalism: capitalism, communism, and internationalism. Vietnam was caught up in this struggle. The French wanted to retain control of Indo-China. The US wanted to contain Communism, spread American ways, and change underdeveloped countries. The Soviet Union wanted to expand Communism. China wanted to regain its place as the "central kingdom." Internationalists wanted to weaken nationalism, spread human rights and social justice, and change underdeveloped countries so that there is greater equality among all people.

These ideological struggles all came together in the small, far away country of Vietnam. Yet none of the three ideologies were able to create the vigor, sense of identity, order, innovation, satisfaction, and patriotism to rival nationalism.

France colonized Vietnam in 1885 calling it French Indochina. During World War II, the Japanese occupied it. In 1941, a Marxist-Leninist named Ho Chi Minh began the Vietminh movement to expel the Japanese and then to win independence from the French. At the end of World War II five US OSS teams (mainly NY lawyers) were operating with the Vietminh in North Vietnam, after having gotten Ho Chi Minh released on 16 September 1943 from a Chinese prison. "Decolonization" was one aspect of the ideology of internationalism. For a short time the US was allied with the Vietminh, but that ended when the French returned to Indochina in 1945.

For many years prior to 1954 the US was deeply involved with Vietnam. The State Department repeatedly asked for increased military aid for the French. This was motivated in part by the fear that if Communists controlled Vietnam all of Southeast Asia might topple "like dominoes." During the 1950s there were three preconceptions on the role of the military in foreign policy: (1) the military profession should be limited to how to achieve victory in conventional War, (2) the military must improve their ability to fight guerrilla warfare, and (3) the military has to be an active participant in the projection of "soft power." The "soft power" concept was a virus some caught while doing graduate studies at prestigious universities. "Soft power" challenges the warrior ethos of self-confidence, courage, massive firepower, and aggressiveness that is associated with "hard power," that has always been the hallmark of a military victory in War.

The US foreign policy establishment not only looked at nationalism as an evil to be eliminated, but they looked at Vietnam through these three preconceptions on the role of the military. Since the US policy makers after 1944 failed to grasp the scope and complexity of Warfare they were never able to adopt effective strategies for Vietnam. Then in the 1970s after there was no military victory those that wanted to limit the military to conventional War said "never again!" Those that focused on guerrilla warfare were never able to recognize that counterinsurgency is just one aspect of Warfare. And those that wanted the military to be agents of "soft power" argued that the military had failed to adapt.

Truth should always be the goal—not the defense of preconceptions. The history of conflict is a bizarre mixture of facts, incomplete recollections, misunderstandings, fiction, and omissions. Thus seeking the truth is an endless and frustrating task. But the truth about Warfare that could have been found in Vietnam was forgotten after the USA left Vietnam.

In 1953, US Army Chief of Staff General Matthew B. Ridgway discouraged President Dwight D. Eisenhower from taking a greater role in Vietnam. Ridgway thought the US should not support colonialism on principle and that the costs of a victory in Vietnam would be too high.

In late 1953 the French established an airbase at Dienbienphu to stop movement through Laos and Cambodia into southern Vietnam. The North Vietnamese moved four divisions into the hills overlooking Dienbienphu and started a siege of the ten thousand French soldiers there. The goal was to create a psychological sense of defeat. A fierce battle ended with the French defeat on 7 May 1954. In Geneva on 12 July 1954 a cease-fire agreement was signed, ending an eight-year colonial war and French hegemony in Indochina.

Vietnam was divided at the 17th Parallel between North Vietnam and South Vietnam. The French tricolor came down in Hanoi after seven decades. The wealthy tried to bribe their way out but most Vietnamese had to face an uncertain future. Hanoi's buildings were covered with "May President Ho Chi Minh Live a Thousand Years."

French influence in Southeast Asia ended on 29 September 1954 when the French were told the US would no longer finance French forces in Indochina and that training of the ARVN and VNAF would be the responsibility of the US MAAG-Vietnam. The last French military base in Vietnam was closed on 26 April 1956.

In the south the French departure started a struggle between Premier Ngo Dinh Diem and Bao Dai. On 23 October 1955 Diem won an election and proclaimed himself president of the Republic of Vietnam. He then cancelled elections set for 1956 to unite Vietnam. For the next year Diem built a functioning state and put down insurgents. But Diem's weaknesses were visible by 1957. He was never able to appeal to Vietnamese nationalism, and his regime showed signs of incompetence and corruption. Diem put his family members in power and his opponents in jail. By 1959 80% of Vietnamese villages were under Communist control.

US Actions in Vietnam 1954–1964

After the French left Vietnam in 1954 the immediate goal should have been stability at the local level. How to accomplish local stability is actually a continuum. At one end is a strong authoritarian central government, i.e., a ruthless police state willing and capable of eliminating all opposition. At the other end of the continuum is a decentralized confederacy of self-governing provinces, districts, towns, and villages. Between these polar extremes are a variety of ways to establish stability used by Chiang Kai-shek in Taiwan, Syngman Rhee in South Korea, Lee Kuan Yew in Singapore, Tito in Yugoslavia, Ataturk in Turkey, Augusto Pinochet in Chile, the Malaysian Federation, the United Arab Emirates, and the eighteenth century thirteen sovereign states of America.

The immediate goal should not have been a single Vietnam nation-state—that could evolve in time. The model of the new Vietnam in 1954, of both the north and the south, should have been that of nineteenth century Switzerland. There should have been some central state authority however; its power should have been limited regarding how it affects the daily life of individuals, thus allowing various ideologies to exist. The central authority should have been in the ancient capital of Hue, rather than in either Hanoi or Saigon.

Vietnam in 1954 was a country of many factions, but the Annamese people living along the coast, in the Red River Valley of Tonking and in the Mekong Delta did have a common identity; this could be the basis for a future nation. After all, the Annamese people had struggled for four hundred years to build their country. However, any attempt to establish a strong centralized government for the whole country was a recipe for failure. In addition to the Annamese there were Caoaistes, Hoa Hao, Chinese, and Cambodians. Some of those living in Vietnam had been Westernized, but others retained their old ways and shared little love for the "butter-eaters"—those who had adopted French ways.

There were Catholics, Buddhists, and a variety of other belief systems. Each faction had its own identity, and it would be impossible to create a single nation in 1954. Therefore, any central state government had to be some form of confederation—something like that in Switzerland in the nineteenth century. Communists would dominate some of those provinces, nationalists would dominate others, and anti-Communists would dominate others. But each province would have many factions. In time Vietnam might become a nation-state, but they must do so at their own pace.

US policy should have been to help create a very high degree of decentralization of authority, and a reliance on custom and tradition rather than law. It is possible to build a state with a strong centralized government, authoritarian means, ruthless leaders, and strict compliance with rules, regulations, and laws. It can also be done with a confederation while still maintaining a high degree of individual freedom. In other words, the US should not have focused on ideology; instead it should have advocated a Vietnam state, including both the north and the south, which was a confederation of many self-governing provinces.

Would Ho Chi Minh have agreed? He would probably accept a confederation because he knew that he could appeal to the nationalistic feelings of the Vietnamese better than could Ngo Dinh Diem. Thus he probably thought he would eventually rule all of Vietnam. But the US would have had to bet on being able to separate him from China and the Soviet Union.

The Vietnamese are a practical and commercially oriented people who would find capitalism and a better standard of living more appealing than Communist ideology. Vietnam could easily have taken its own path, as did Taiwan, South Korea, Yugoslavia, Malaysia, and Chile. Each had a strong sense of common identity, each had checks and balances between centralization and decentralization as appropriate for a specific place and time, each had strong leaders able to stand up to foreigners at the same time they benefited from foreigners, each had people with a good work ethic, and each was able to have economic change through the effort of individuals.

The lives of the Vietnam people should have been controlled, as much as possible, by local customs and traditions—not by any single ideology. The country should have been divided into self-governing provinces. Although each province would have its own police and territorial forces, the central government would have armed forces capable of preventing any province from disturbing another province. Yet this was not done because of several misconceptions regarding nation building.

The US viewed the Geneva settlement in 1954 as a loss in prestige for the US and as giving the Communists an "advance salient" for pressures against non-Communist states in Southeast Asia. Therefore, the US sought to contain North Vietnam.

As early as 1961, Vietcong[74] insurgents were active in most provinces of South Vietnam. Maxwell Taylor said that the increase in Vietcong activity required US troops for logistical support and to reassure Diem of US willingness to help the ARVN stop the Vietcong. Foreshadowing future problems Taylor was thinking in terms of conventional War.[75]

On the other hand, there were those who had studied Warfare[76], who recognized that the Vietcong was part of a political movement. They knew of the conflicts in the Philippines, Malaysia, and Indochina. They knew that for years men had come out of the jungle to kill in order to make certain that the people knew the government could not provide them security. They knew that the incompetent, corrupt Diem regime was incapable of appealing to

Vietnam nationalism. They knew that the Communist networks were expanding into all factions of the people living in Vietnam. They knew that the key to Warfare is 24-7 security for individuals. But the American political elite did not want to encourage nationalism and they were thinking of conventional War to stop the Communists in North Vietnam from invading South Vietnam. They wanted to encourage internationalism, and economic and political development in accordance with the ideals expressed in the UN Charter—and to contain Communism.

General Paul D. Harkins commanded the Military Assistance Command Vietnam from February 1962 to June 1964. Harkins, like most Americans when they arrived in Vietnam, knew little about Vietnam's past, about the Vietcong's relationship with the north, about the various factions within Vietnam, or about Warfare. He thought the role of the military professional was to achieve victory in War and to conduct counter-guerrilla operations.

As an example of the thinking of the time, Harkins's key staff officer BGEN Gerald Kelleher dismissed the importance of Warfare by saying, "The job of the US military is to kill Vietcong." When it was pointed out that the French had killed a lot of Vietcong, but they had been defeated, Kelleher replied: "Didn't kill enough Vietcong." [77]

From 1954 to 1963 there was often tension and many disagreements between the US and the government of South Vietnam regarding US support and the possibility of the South Vietnam reaching an agreement with Hanoi to become a "neutralist" regarding Communism. Many Americans were in South Vietnam, and other countries in Southeast Asia, trying to advance economic and political development in keeping with American ideas on capitalism and democracy. While they talked of freedom, the American Declaration of Independence, and the evils of Communism, they were in fact supporting the Diem regime and the Catholic Church, which most of the Vietnamese did not support. Those in Saigon and Washington never understood the importance of "building up" after establishing security and authority at the local level. They attempted "building down" with and through the central government in Saigon.

During this time the US MAAG organized and trained the South Vietnamese Army (ARVN) and the Vietnamese Air Force (VNAF) to be capable of stopping an invasion by the North Vietnam Army. Logistical support and tactical air control centers were established. Those trained and supported had none of the capabilities of territorial forces to live among the people in hamlets, villages, and districts to provide local security. There was no training in Warfare since the US officers training the ARVN and VNAF only understood conventional War. However, a few military officers did observe what was going on in the countryside, they had studied past Warfare, and they realized that something else had to be done. But what?

US military leaders in Vietnam were unable to see what was going on in Vietnam, because it was not in their eyes "external aggression"; it was just "crime" and thus a police not a military matter. They ignored those who wanted to use what they had learned from the successes and failures in Greece (1944–1949), Spain (1944–1952), China (1945–1949), Iran (1945–1946), Indochina (1945–1954), Philippines (1946–1954), Madagascar (1947–1949), Korea (1948–1953), Malaysia (1948–1960), Burma (1947–1962), Kenya (1952–1955), the Cameroons (1953–1961), and Cuba (1956–1958).

On 17 April 1959 the Deputy MAAG-Vietnam (MG Samuel Myers) told the US Senate: "The Vietminh guerrillas...were gradually nibbled away until they cease to be a major menace to the government. They are now able to maintain internal security and have reached the point where that responsibility could be turned over to the civilian agencies." Yet at that time the Vietcong and Vietminh had extended their networks throughout South Vietnam. Most Americans did not recognize the threat because they did not understand Warfare. The truth is that Warfare had not changed for thousands of years. But for three hundred years the professional soldiers of the West wanted to ignore it because it was not "military," i.e., within the realm of conventional War during which the armed forces of states use firepower to destroy each other.

However, it should be noted that there were soldiers in the West who did not have this narrow view of what was "military." For example, Napoleon said that morale is to material as ten is to one. In other words, the attitudes and convictions are ten times more important than weapons of destruction. He also used strategic communication to weaken his enemies before he marched with his troops, and much of his actions were designed to exploit psychological weaknesses.

In 1958 the Vietminh from the north had begun to intimidate villagers, to assassinate local officials, and to control the countryside. Saigon countered with the fortified hamlet program and a buildup of the ARVN. By July 1963 the Communists controlled most of the countryside. The government controlled the district towns.

In the 1960s when the US found those in authority in Saigon unwilling or unable to perform their own internal security and "winning hearts, minds, and stomachs" functions, the US tried to do it for them—with disastrous consequences for both the RVN and for us. This error was repeated in Iran, the Balkans, Iraq, Afghanistan, and the Middle East. In August 1963 the possibility of a coup against Diem resulted in a top-level meeting and debate over US policy. At this meeting a critical and long-reaching strategic error was made. Having a mercurial family as the main instrument of US policy did not seem to be a sound course. Secretary of State Dean Rusk, Secretary of Defense Robert McNamara, General Maxwell Taylor, National Security Advisor McGeorge Bundy, and their staff were willing to see an end of the Diem family, but they wanted to reopen communication with those in the Diem regime in order to find some way to keep a pro-US democratic government in South Vietnam. These men were the best of the foreign policy establishment — they were products of an elite education. All were internationalists seeking to expand the rule of law, interventionists committed to the spread of democratic values and ideas, and liberal idealists dedicated to social justice and human rights for all people. However, their experience and knowledge were primarily in European history and the Western way of war. None of them understood how to be successful in ideological conflict, although all of them had spent much of their lives trying to halt the spread of Communism.

Paul Kattenburg, a foreign service officer who had worked in Vietnam for many years in the fifties, was the only person at this meeting with in depth knowledge of Vietnam and the Far East. He came to the US at seventeen to escape the Nazis and was dedicated to advancing US interests at the lowest possible cost. He held the Vietnam desk in the State Department, and carried the case against the Diem regime.

Kattenburg knew that the whole Diem regime — not just the Diem family — did not have the support of the people living in Vietnam. Their Catholicism and acceptance of French culture alienated many Vietnamese who were Mahayana Buddhist. Most Vietnamese saw Ho Chi Minh, and those with him, as more nationalistic—even though they were hardline Leninists—than those in the Diem regime. The Vietnamese people knew that Ho Chi Minh considered China an enemy, but that the American backers of Diem had supported China. Kattenburg did not think the US using conventional armed forces to win a military victory was practical, since it would be very costly in time, blood, and treasure—and perhaps a failure. Also he did not think the American public would support protracted warfare in which there would be no clear victory—only stability. He thought the Diem family was hopeless and the wise policy was for the US to cut its losses and get out of Vietnam honorably.

Taylor, McNamara, and Rusk dismissed Kattenburg's arguments saying the US would not be defeated. Bundy said nothing. Kattenburg thought, but did not say: "None of these men know what they are talking about." After this meeting Kattenburg was removed from the Vietnam desk and assigned non-Vietnam positions in the State Department.[78]

In October 1963, nationalist generals—with the backing of Ambassador Lodge—conducted a successful coup against the feudal regime headed by the Diem family. It has been said that Diem was "separated from the people by cardinals, police cars, and foreign advisors when he should have been walking in the rice fields unprotected, learning the hard way how to be both loved and obeyed." The problem was that no Diem successor was able to inspire Vietnamese nationalism—and the US foreign policy establishment favored internationalism over nationalism. Between November 1963 and September 1965 Saigon had nine different administrations.

On 21 November Lodge was en route to tell Kennedy that the war in Vietnam was going badly. On that day Kennedy was killed in Dallas, so he told President Lyndon B. Johnson. Johnson replied: "I am not going to lose Vietnam." Nevertheless, he gave priority to his Great Society programs and consistently downplayed the Vietnam War.

In December 1963 McNamara reported that the situation was deteriorating so fast that within a few months he expected Vietnam to be neutral or taken over by the Communists. He talked of covert operations against the North.

Decisions during 1954 to 1964 regarding Vietnam appear to have been made upon feelings, preconceptions, and politics. All policy makers had similar preconceptions, which prevented in-depth debate. There is no evidence that the goals, interests, and fears of the North Vietnamese leaders were understood or that careful analysis of intelligence carried much weight. There is no evidence that the policy makers understood how the Western way of war differs from the Oriental way of conflict.

There is no evidence that a careful evaluation of national interests determined decisions. Where is the evidence that the following questions were ever answered: What is our goal? How should we accomplish that goal? What are we willing to pay in treasure and blood to achieve that goal?

US Actions in Vietnam 1964–1967

In 1964 events in Vietnam called for decisions, but the political elite wanted to avoid making difficult decisions during an election year. In January the JCS moved to expand the war. By the spring of 1964 Vietnam became a sensitive and dangerous subject. Washington wanted to keep Vietnam quiet. In June 1964 Westmoreland replaced Harkins. In August the Tonkin incidents occurred. In October the US Air Force base at Bien Hoa was attacked and five B-57s were destroyed. The Vietcong attacked an officer's quarters in Saigon and the base at Pleiku. However, such efforts against Americans in South Vietnam did not upset the apple cart.

On 13 February 1965, after Johnson had won reelection, it was decided to bomb North Vietnam into submission. However, in a few months it became clear that Hanoi was willing to take great damage and would never capitulate from the bombing alone. Hanoi knew that Vietcong successes and Saigon failures had deep roots, and the Americans were seeking a quick victory. Perhaps there was not sufficient damage in, and around, Hanoi because of limitations imposed or a failure of intelligence to reveal the proper targets. Yet the four most important factors allowing Hanoi to withstand the bombing were: (1) the ability of Hanoi to play the role of the defender of Vietnam from foreigners, (2) the need to combine airpower with ground power, (3) the failure to use strategic bombing, (4) US being ineffective in strategic communication in order to keep Americans will strong and to weaken the will of the enemy.

In March 1965 the JCS proposed that US combat units be used to fight in South Vietnam. The struggle over sending combat troops began. On 1 April Taylor made the argument against American soldiers fighting on the mainland of Asia and against the use of "search and destroy" tactics. Rusk agreed, but the president decided to send two additional marine battalions to operate in a fifty-mile radius. Then on 6 April President Johnson approved an increase of eighteen to twenty thousand men. On 15 April McNamara approved a brigade being sent into combat. Taylor realized that he had lost the policy argument. Westmoreland's argument that an escalation of US combat troops would bring a quick victory had won. President Johnson established a special team to direct how the war was to be fought—this caused many problems.

US forces streamed into Vietnam. Westmoreland was getting everything he wanted, and he thought only of conventional War. And he knew that the conventional ARVN units could not defeat the unconventional Vietcong forces. He visualized an attrition strategy that killed so many of the enemy that they would lose the "will to fight." To carry out his strategy Westmoreland used large-unit "search and destroy" tactics, firepower, and airpower. But this is like using a tractor to crush a beetle. He did not try to provide local security or effective local authority. His strategy had no lasting effect. The enemy just faded away into the jungle or across the borders into Laos or Cambodia. They replaced their losses and extended their networks throughout South Vietnam.

The "search and destroy" tactics evolved in the summer of 1965. The Vietcong changed tactics from ambushes to attacks by battalions; now they showed a willingness to stand and fight. It was clear that the original estimate of 175,000 for 1965 would go as high as 210,000. B-52s would fly from Guam. Then in 1966 another 100,000 would be needed.

Most of the Americans arriving in 1965–1966 were prepared to fight a conventional War in a foreign country against an enemy that was fighting Warfare in their own country. Among the policy makers the conflict in Vietnam was seen as a conventional War that required overwhelming firepower against the critical mass of the enemy. To those in Hanoi it was an ideological and psychological struggle with strategic communication being the critical "battlefield." This was the Oriental way of conflict meeting the Western way of war.

Hanoi saw the conflict as interlocking actions—political, psychological, economic, military, overt, covert, violent, nonviolent, local, regional, and international. To achieve their goal Hanoi had to exploit the tensions within South Vietnam.

They had to have the support—from either conviction or fear—of the people. In this conflict conventional War armed forces no longer enjoyed their decisive role. Saigon was not up against just bands of guerrillas, but rather against networks seeking to impose their will upon the people of South Vietnam. This is why outposts, raids, ambushes, and large-scale sweeps rarely achieved the desired results. Saigon could only achieve stability by neutralizing the networks that supported the insurgents—which they were unable to do.

There were continual debates over what airpower could, and should, do. Pinpoint, tactical bombing was used rather than strategic bombing. The only strategic target in North Vietnam was Hanoi, and strategic bombing required it to be totally destroyed—like Dresden, Mainz, Hamburg, Tokyo, and Hiroshima. Anything less would only be feel-good publicity, at the cost of the lives of many airmen. However, those making decisions were unwilling to use strategic bombing—it was too brutal, awful, immoral, and "uncivilized" for those who advocated internationalism.

Hanoi countered the build-up of US combat forces by sending units of the North Vietnamese Army into South Vietnam. Protest against the Vietnam War in the United States increased. The ground situation deteriorated. The fortified hamlet program failed to provide 24-7 security; soldiers with rescue units to their villages often found the bodies of their children wrapped neatly in a straw mat, tagged for burial, and with a note condemning "traitors of the people." In the fall of 1964, the Buddhists demonstrated in Saigon and explosions were set off in Saigon. The Vietcong became more aggressive in the fertile Mekong delta. In the summer of 1965, the ARVN fought gallantly against the Vietcong at Dong Xoai.

In November 1965, NVA regiments fought a ferocious battle with the helicopter-transported US First Cavalry Division in the

Ia Drang Valley. This battle has been portrayed in the book and movie *We Were Soldiers*. Its favorable outcome reinforced Westmorland's notion that he could win a war of attrition—and a quick victory. It is typical of how conventional thinking generals see War—campaigns ending in decisive head-to-head battles with the use of overwhelming firepower to annihilate the critical mass of the enemy forces.

Also in November 1965 the JCS proposed military action which they thought would bring a quick victory: massive use of air power to destroy Hanoi and close North Vietnam's harbors with mines. This was the Western way of war carried to the extreme. President Johnson not only rejected their proposals but, in coarse and degrading language those present were unable to forget, the President accused the JCS of trying to pass to him the buck for World War III. In December McNamara pushed for a bombing pause.

During 1965 those in Saigon talked about poor security, infiltration of enemy agents, terrorism, lack of economic development, and corruption. At the same time the Vietcong leaders talked of taxation, the military draft, and land tenure—which were the concerns of rice paddy farmers. The Vietcong knew how to co-opt and articulate the grievances of the target group. They were fighting ideological and psychological struggles on the strategic communication battlefield of protracted conflict.

American civilians thought they had the solution in economic aid, i.e., the "soft power" approach. Yet they failed to understand that economic aid, and large-scale projects, only benefit the insurgents until local security is established and the enemy networks used to control and manipulate the people are destroyed. Words, intentions, and good deeds mean nothing as long as fear fills the air. On the other hand, wherever there is stability, humanitarian assistance and local economic development can play a significant role in returning order and satisfaction to a people disoriented by military operations they have observed, but for which they do not understand the underlying reasons. Winning stomachs, hearts, and minds is important, but it can only be done through economic development after there is stability.

During 1966 the Vietcong became increasingly confident they could cause all Americans to leave Vietnam. As the Vietcong leader Huynh Tan Phat said: "Our men can live off the land; they can move freely. The Americans don't know the terrain, the language, or the people. Soon half the Vietnamese with the Americans will be National Liberation Front agents." The Vietcong and Hanoi were winning the strategic communication campaign as those in the US and around the world turned against US actions in Vietnam. They understood the Oriental way of conflict, but the Americans did not.

In February 1967 the president was told: "the adverse military tide has been reversed, and General Westmoreland now has the initiative. The enemy can no longer hope to win the war in South Vietnam. We can win the war if we apply pressure upon the enemy relentlessly in the North and in the South." In April 1967 there were 470,000 men in Vietnam. By July 1967 McNamara tried to halt the war, particularly the bombing. He did not challenge past bombing, but he argued that bombing is not a way to achieve victory. The president did not agree, so bombing continued.

During 1966 and 1967 US forces defeated North Vietnam Army units many times only to see them withdraw into Laos, Cambodia, or North Vietnam. This prompted a debate over invading North Vietnam to achieve a military victory on the ground. But the memories of the Chinese coming into Korea in November 1950 when US forces moved toward the Yalu River were too vivid, so it was decided that US ground forces would remain in South Vietnam. This ensured that the outcome would be determined by the Oriental way of conflict, rather than the Western way of war. There would be no overwhelming application of force destroying the enemy's armed forces giving a quick victory. The outcome would be determined by strategic communication in ideological conflicts over common identity, dedication, determination, patriotism, and the inner compass of individuals. Which side has strong warriors and which side has wobbly compromisers? Those in Saigon were still confident a military victory was possible, but those in Washington were not.

There had been many who questioned the "search and destroy" tactics and the attrition strategy of Westmoreland. They had studied Warfare and knew that success was stability with security at the local level—not military victory, or even killing many of the enemy. They knew how the views of Clausewitz and Sun Tzu differ. They knew that the Western way of war stresses destruction, firepower, direct action, and speed, while the Oriental way of conflict stresses psychology, deception, surprise, and patience.

They knew that small is better than large. They knew that ponderous sweeps with battalions is less effective than small hunter-killer teams and targeted killings by covert operators. They knew that correct analysis and diagnosis of the situation is better than anything taught on counterinsurgency (COIN) or nation building. They knew that COIN operations by "foreigners" are costly and ineffective in the long run. They knew that at the local level those controlling the central government who do not share a common identity with the people can be seen as "foreigners" just as much as those from another country. Yet those with such knowledge were never able to overcome the Western conventional wisdom about war gained in European wars and the American Civil War.

Warfare as fought by the Vietcong and the Vietminh was invisible: they would hit and fade away, they could not hold ground, their successes never showed. But the Tet offensives of 1968, which started on 31 January 1968 and lasted several weeks, changed this.

The Tet Offensive, 1968

Early in the morning of 31 January 1968 a thirty-six-hour truce, in effect to observe the lunar New Year with the Tet Nguyen Dan celebrations, is broken by attacks across South Vietnam. After the introduction of conventional War forces in Vietnam in 1964 the US had been using its technological superiority. To counter this overwhelming firepower the Communists would attack weak points at night. In this surprise attack the North Vietnamese and the Vietcong attacked throughout South Vietnam but mainly in Saigon, which was considered invincible. The South Vietnamese had been willing to fight with the Americans, and for the regime of Nguyen Van Thieu, only if security could be provided at the local level 24 hours per day, 7 days a week. This attack on Tet raised doubts in the minds of most South Vietnamese.

For three years the Communists had been fighting from the shadows of the jungle or from Laos, Cambodia, and North Vietnam. They used surprise, deception, terror, and raids into villages. They avoided strong points to attack weak targets as they established networks within all factions in South Vietnam. The Tet offensive changed this, but the Communists were all beaten back within three weeks with great losses. However, those in the US saw different pictures—they saw dying American soldiers in the capital and corrupt South Vietnamese officers killing unarmed civilians. TV allows people to see soldiers in the heat of combat. Tet is when misconception about what was taking place in Vietnam snatched defeat from the jaws of victory.

Tet was a military defeat for the attackers since US and ARVN stopped attacks all over Vietnam and killed 162,000. In the end the enemy held no new territory. However, the goal had been to create a psychological sense of defeat in keeping with the Oriental way of conflict. In fact, the credibility of the attrition strategy and Westmoreland's reputation were destroyed by how the Tet offensives were reported in the US and around the world. The enemy had demonstrated a will and capability, which Americans thought had been destroyed, and thus created a feeling that the US had lost the war. Americans failed to understand that in Warfare strategic communications is the critical campaign. The light at the end of the tunnel went out.

Americans wanted the protests on US streets to stop and the killing in Vietnam to end. "Make Love, Not War" had won. By June 1968 some 680,000 Americans were in Vietnam, but no military victory was in sight. Units were behind barbed wire in firebases, made large sweeps, sprayed Agent Orange on the sides of roads, and bombed any enemy located.

It can be accurately claimed that in Vietnam the communists were soundly defeated in the Tet offensive, but in the ideological conflict it was the turning point that resulted in success for the communists. Vocal antiwar critics and the media were the decisive factor—not the armed forces in Vietnam. The costs in lives and dollars were too great for most Americans. The number of communists killed meant very little, and the US could not win a decisive victory with technology.

US Actions Regarding Vietnam 1970–1975

Limited success did finally come to Vietnam in late 1970, after the Cambodian incursion and some of those with an understanding of Warfare and the Oriental way of conflict were finally heard.

By 1971 there was stability in most of South Vietnam. There were four million members of the People's Self-Defense Forces and Regional Forces to provide security at the local level. US ground combat forces were leaving, but the US was still providing logistical and financial support. The US military had won every battle. The ARVN was able to defeat NVA forces sent into South Vietnam. Abrams even questioned the need for any US combat forces.

But by then it was too late—Vietnam had already been lost back in the United States. Unable to win on the military battlefield, the North Vietnamese knew they could win the ideological conflict on the strategic communication battlefield by using deception, patience, and steadfastness. That fact played out in the Paris negotiations. The Americans were decisively defeated in getting their views accepted. This was primarily because much of the media was more interested in exposing US shortcomings and appealing to antiwar factions than in supporting what the US was doing in Vietnam. The ideological struggle in Vietnam would determine the outcome. In the end military success on the battlefield in Vietnam was not the decisive factor. The costs in blood and treasure in Vietnam were wasted in Paris and the United States. Those who had fought in Vietnam returned home to the condemnation and verbal abuse of many Americans.

On 31 May 1971 Kissinger offered to withdraw US troops in return for the release of all US prisoners. On 26 June 1971 the

North Vietnamese agreed if the US also stopped supporting the Saigon government, there was a new "peace" government in Saigon, and North Vietnamese forces were allowed in South Vietnam to "monitor compliance" with any agreement. Negotiations continued in Paris and Warfare continued in South Vietnam.

In 1973 when the last US Army combat units left, the Vietcong was destroyed and the ARVN was stronger than the NVA. However, three years later NVA divisions invaded South Vietnam in a conventional War and won a military victory.

The Saigon government was dependent on the US for financial and logistical support, thus when that support was taken away Saigon was doomed, since those in Hanoi were seen as more nationalistic. Those Vietnamese in Hanoi were able to portray themselves as protecting the poor Vietnamese people from foreigners and their puppets in Saigon. Actually, Hanoi was supported by both China and the Soviet Union. The Paris Peace Accords of January 1973 allowed NVA units to move into South Vietnam, which ensured a military victory for Hanoi. Saigon fell on 30 April 1975. After that millions of people in Southeast Asia died.

My Experience

I was deeply involved with what took place in Vietnam from 1960 until 1970. Based on what I had learned in Korea and Taiwan, in 1959 I started to worry about what was being done in Vietnam. As I learned more about past successes and failures in Warfare I became even more concerned. In 1962 a French officer and I wrote *Irregular Warfare in a Nutshell* in an effort to change actions in Vietnam. As far as I know, our effort had little if any impact on events in Vietnam, although it did sow seeds that have influenced others in the 1990s and 2000s as they researched Warfare.[79]

While in the Pentagon, from 1964 to 1966 I was awarded a Legion of Merit for my work in force planning, including the deployment of forces to Vietnam.[80] In 1967 the chief of staff of the army had the Army War College create a new position to study actions in Vietnam and I was selected for that position. For my work there I was awarded a second Legion of Merit;[81] however, during this time I, and those who agreed with me, were never able to change what was being done in Vietnam. Out of frustration, I decided to retire from the army and do something where I could see the results of my efforts.

However, first I thought I should go to Vietnam to try to put into practice what I had learned. I requested an assignment in Vietnam. In 1970, I was deputy director of training of the Army of South Vietnam and then the commanding officer of the Second Brigade, Twenty-Fifth Division. Nevertheless, it was clear to me that I was expected to use the "search and destroy" tactics of conventional War which I opposed, and not use what I knew to be effective in Warfare. Rather than continuing my quest for an impossible dream, I put in for retirement and got a PhD at the University of South Carolina so I could have a second career.

I also decided not to find fault with those "in the arena" by writing about what was done wrong in Vietnam or what should have been done—a decision I kept for thirty-eight years. However, I did use my knowledge of Warfare to comment on what should be done in Iran, the Balkans, Afghanistan, Iraq, and the Middle East—with the same lack of success that I had regarding actions in Vietnam.

74 Vietcong, or Viet Cong, are those who live in the south of Vietnam and want to weaken or overthrow the government (i.e., those who hold Secular Authority at the various levels of government). The Vietminh, or Viet Minh, are members of a political movement that started in 1941 to fight Japanese occupation, then gained control of some of northern Vietnam in 1945, and after the French withdrew attempted to unite Vietnam under its control.

75 Conventional War, as seen in the West for over three hundred years, is conflict between the acknowledged armed forces of states, each attempting to destroy the symmetrical armed forces of the other or to gain territory. War is diplomacy by other means, with victory going to one side. In total war there is unlimited use of force.

76 Warfare is asymmetrical conflict; it is between sovereign states and insurgents willing to use force to bring about the destruction or overthrow of those in authority. Warfare is politics by other means, with the outcome being stability—not victory. It is protracted, incremental, unceasing, and without a definitive end. Stability, i.e., success in Warfare, is realized when there is a climate of order and satisfaction and no one is willing to use force to achieve political ends. Although the single word Warfare is better, in this chapter I will at times use irregular Warfare for clarity. In the past Warfare has gone by many names: irregular warfare, unconventional war, internal war, subversive war, revolution, civil war, guerrilla war, intrastate war, insurrection, rebellion, imperialism, political development, economic development, internal security, stability, law and order, nation building, and peacekeeping. Yet the terminology remains confusing, and the perspective most often narrow. To correct this the single word Warfare is used for conflict that is neither Peace nor conventional War.

77 I knew Kelleher well. In Korea I commanded a rifle company in his regiment, and he selected me as his S-2.

78 Paul Kattenburg was my PhD advisor at the University of South Carolina and we spent many hours discussing Vietnam.

79 See *Irregular Warfare in a Nutshell* at:
http://cgsc.cdmhost.com/cdm/ref/collection/p124201coll2/id/581.

80 Legion of Merit for January 1964 to July 1966 while in the Force and Mobilization Planning Branch of the Department of the Army: "During the development of the Army Buildup Plans, which provided the foundation for a major increase in Army units and strength, he played a foremost role in the timely completion of the planning effort through his foresight and objectivity. He also made full use of his extensive background experiences and professional skill in developing this large scale planning."

81 Legion of Merit for June 1967 to February 1970 while a member of the faculty of the Army War College: "He personally organized, developed, and implemented a new course on Stability Operations and other innovations to the War College curriculum. His contributions were of marked educational significance relative to the role of the United States military in Internal Defense and Development Operations."

CHAPTER TWENTY-NINE

LESSONS FROM KOREA AND VIETNAM

What lessons could, and should, we have learned from Korea and Vietnam? If our political elite had learned the correct lessons in the 1950s and 1960s would the outcomes in Iraq and Afghanistan have been better? The answer is clearly: YES. Also, such lessons could improve the outcomes in future foreign policy decisions. There are at least six lessons that could have been learned.

- First, stop thinking of the common terms of peace and war, and start thinking in terms of Peace, Warfare, and War.

- Second, understand how the Oriental way of conflict differs from the Western way of war.

- Third, understand that ideological conflict, strategic communication, and covert operations are as important as diplomacy, economic changes, political changes, and operations by conventional armed forces.

- Fourth, identify the misconceptions about nation building among the political elite.

- Fifth, develop a realistic conceptual framework to guide sociopolitical changes.

- Sixth, recognize that dedication, honor, duty, discipline, principles, Ethos of Eros, and camaraderie are essential if we are to have warriors and soldiers effective in War and Warfare.

Cooperation/Conflict (Peace-Warfare-War)

Peace and war are not dichotomous conditions—as most in the West have assumed for over three hundred years.

Conflict/Cooperation is actually various combinations of conflict and cooperation continually interacting within a whole. However, when it is visualized as a spectrum, or continuum, it extends from unlimited use of force to no use of force. At one end of the spectrum is War and at the other end is Peace. In the middle is Warfare.

As a continuum Peace-Warfare-War has three distinctive conditions with unique strategies, tactics, procedures, methods, and techniques, yet there is no clear break between these conditions. They intermingle, overlap, and are often conducted simultaneously. When War and Warfare occur at the same place and time they can be referred to as Mid-Intensity Conflict (hybrid war). When Peace and Warfare occur at the same place and time they can be referred to as Low-Intensity Conflict (containment).

Politics is Conflict/Cooperation, without the use of force, within a state during Peace to determine who gets what, when, and how. Any violence is personal or criminal—not political.

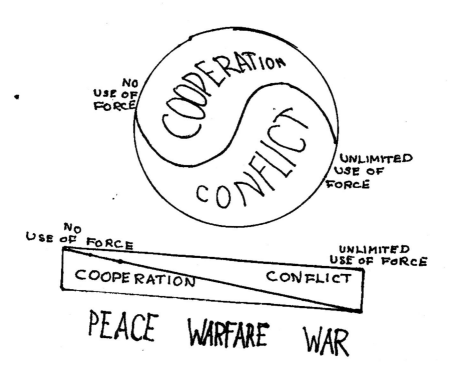

Diplomacy is Conflict/Cooperation, without the use of force, between states during Peace. Politics and diplomacy use the same means: common identity, argument, spin, propaganda, manipulation, coalition formation, group loyalty, ideological commitment, "horse trading," bribery, and intimidation.

War is conflict between the acknowledged armed forces of states, each attempting to destroy the armed forces of the other. War is diplomacy by other means, with victory going to one side. In total war, at the very end of the spectrum, there is unlimited use of force, which today means nuclear war.

Warfare (often referred to as Irregular Warfare and many other names) is asymmetrical conflict; it is between sovereign states and non-state actors seeking to bring about the destruction of or overthrow those in authority. Warfare is politics by other means, with the outcome being stability—not victory. It is protracted, incremental, unceasing, and without a definitive end. Stability, i.e., success in Warfare, is realized when there is a climate of order and satisfaction and no one is willing to use force to achieve political ends.

To sever Conflict/Cooperation (i.e., conflict and cooperation interacting within a whole) contradicts reality, at best; separations are a convenience used to classify similar conditions. But the fact that Conflict/Cooperation is always protracted, asymmetric, and ideological should always be remembered.

While any division of Conflict/Cooperation is artificial, words must be assigned to portions of it if we are to communicate or conduct effective and efficient operations. Many small, abstract categories are impractical, even though useful for academic research. The most useful categories are: Peace, Warfare, and War. Using these three categories it is possible to have individuals with distinctive identity, training, and equipment for units capable of operations in all aspects of Conflict/ Cooperation.

Warfare in Korea and Vietnam

For many the conflict in Korea from 1950 to 1951 was a conventional War of combat by UN armed forces against those of North Korea and China. They argued about why it should be a total war or a limited war but rarely about how to achieve stability at the lowest possible costs. They focused on personalities and foreign affairs issues. They paid little attention to the struggle going on in most villages, towns, and cities of Korea as Warfare raged between the supporters of Kim Il-sung and Syngman Rhee.

Others did realize that the struggle throughout Korea was over shaping the minds and controlling the bodies of the Korean people, i.e., an ideological conflict.[82] It was between those willing to use violence to destroy those that do not agree with them. It was Warfare to be won by whomever maintained the will of those on their side and weakened the will of their opponents. The same was true in Vietnam. Stability is realized when there is a climate of order and no one is willing to use force to achieve political ends. There was no stability in either Korea or Vietnam after 1945; therefore, there was no peace.

In Warfare each side attempts to expand its networks and its authority. The goal is local security with order and predictability; each side wants to provide security on its terms. Each side is attempting to neutralize the other side and to eliminate all opposing leaders—and potential leaders.

Unfortunately, most Americans do not understand Warfare. They see such struggles through their understanding of peacetime political debates within a system of representative government. But the conflicts in Korea and Vietnam did not conform to progressive ideas about politics, compromise, and the rule of law. Those conflicts can only be understood through the lens of convert, submit, or die.

Most Americans think of political and economic change during Peace. Yet without stability there can be no Peace. Stability at the local level (with a climate of order and satisfaction) must come before there can be any lasting improvement in living conditions. Most Americans incorrectly think that "economic and political development by a central government" will bring stability. Yet it is just the opposite. With the bottom up (phoenix) approach there can be change with a minimum of force, but the top down (neocolonial) approach through centralized governance requires a great deal of force—and the killing of many people.

In Korea and Vietnam much could have been learned about how to fight and succeed in Warfare, and how to achieve stability. Yet Americans did not learn those lessons. Operations in Vietnam, Bosnia, Afghanistan, and Iraq would have been very different if Americans had learned how to fight Warfare effectively and efficiently in the 1950s and the 1960s.

End of Conventional War in Korea

Although few realize it, the conventional War in Korea came to an end in May of 1951. UN operations were never a "police action" as some politicians called it because they did not want to use the word war—or recognize the idea of "limited war." However, after May 1951 neither side was looking forward to a military victory. The Chinese were incapable of sustaining an attack against UN forces, and Washington was unwilling to push north. Therefore, the outcome was destined to be a cease-fire; the only questions being when, how, and where?

Yes, the armed forces of the UN continued to battle with the armed forces of China and North Korea, and there was heroism by individuals and suffering by many, yet no future military action would significantly alter the situation. However, the UN armed forces were involved in holding the de facto cease-fire line that eventually was formalized north of the 38th Parallel. The US never got involved in the counterinsurgency operation in South Korea, although they became a major concern of the governments of both North and South Korea—as they were for the governments of North and South Vietnam.

From May 1951 Warfare was the norm until the 1980s. Yes, there was some hybrid war (a combination of conventional War and Warfare) until 1953 but the conventional armed forces became less and less important. During the same time local security, local authority, psychology, building and maintaining networks, gaining support of the people (winning stomachs, hearts, and minds), assassination, targeted killing, neutralization, and strategic communication all increased in importance.

In Korea the UN won and lost various battles, but ended up with a draw because it lost on the strategic communication and ideological conflict battlefields. Even though the Chinese and North Koreans suffered much greater casualties, their wills remained strong longer than those of the American people and their leaders.

After 1953 the authoritarian regimes of Rhee and Pak were willing to use the ROK Army, as well as national police, to suppress any political opposition or protests, whether or not they were in fact North Korean inspired or directed. The US had very little to do in this. Ultimately, it is the responsibility of those with Secular Authority to win the hearts, minds, and stomachs of the people living in that territory by first and foremost providing 24-hour security. The people must be protected.

After security was established at the local level it was necessary to provide what is generally perceived as honest and fair governance (including policing and courts) at all levels and encourage economic development (infrastructure improvements, basic education, stable currency, encouragement of savings and investment).

In Korea after May 1951, armed forces were no longer the critical mass to be destroyed. The networks of the insurgent organizations, hiding among the people, had to be neutralized, leaders that had to be killed, and it was on the ideological, psychological, and strategic communication battlefields that success or failure was achieved. North Korea has no problem with insurgent networks; since they were a centralized police state they just eliminated anyone that did not give unquestioning loyalty. In South Korea achieving stability was much more difficult.

Events in Korea from 1950 to 1953 obviously required a change in how Americans viewed war. The terms "cold war" and "limited war" were invented for this purpose. Yet most Americans, and certainly not the foreign policy establishment, were unwilling to make the changes necessary to be successful in Warfare. This failure foreshadowed what took place in Vietnam and many other places after Vietnam. In protracted conflict there is no declaration of war, the conflict lacks clear objectives, the nature and scope of operations often change, and there is no victory. Americans—both those fighting and those at home—did not understand and disliked such ambiguity. But such is the very nature of ideological conflict.

South Korea After 1951

The South Koreans realized that change could only be achieved after stability has been established. They knew that actions by foreigners to achieve "economic and political development" couldn't provide stability until security was established. They knew the "soft power approach" would not work since they were in an ideological struggle with the communists. Thus the authoritarian ways of Rhee during the 1950s were not only useful, they were necessary.

However, the South Koreans knew that stability, as a climate of order and satisfaction, is only possible when people go beyond security. This realization was reflected by the removal of Syngman Rhee in 1960. After that representative governments, dominated by the military, ruled the Republic of Korea during a period of achievement, competitiveness, prosperity, and fulfillment. The success after 1960 was largely due to the balancing of two contradictions: hierarchy and personal freedom—in keeping with Yin/Yang.

Ultimately there was success in South Korea because the political elite were ready and willing to create stability—albeit not as "democratically" as many Americans would have preferred. It took the ROK a generation and a half to prepare for the representative governance that did occur at the end of the 1980s—after twenty-five years. A similar pattern ultimately brought a climate of order and satisfaction to the people of Taiwan, the Philippines, and Thailand. Americans need to recognize and appreciate this pattern.

Korea from 1960 to 2010 has become a model for others in the developing world. But it had to have the foundation created in the 1950s, when South Korea was one of the poorest countries in the world and was fighting a determined enemy. The Republic of Korea has been able to have economic growth because of its own balance of authoritarian rule and personal freedom.

It is true that money from America and production to support the Vietnam War gave the Koreans a unique opportunity for economic development. Yet it was their patriotism, belief system, energy, nationalism, determination, and organization that allowed the South Koreans to use the phoenix (bottom up) approach to achieve an economic miracle. Chinese and Japanese had long looked down on the Korean people, so they seized the opportunity to prove that perception false. Fortunately they were able to escape the paternalistic neocolonial (top down) approach by foreigners, which some in US advocated. This was because Rhee was such a determined, arrogant, self-centered nationalist. Progressives fail to give him the credit he deserves.

There are many ways to achieve stability, and South Korea was able to muddle through with what was appropriate for it. It got its start under the iron rule of the military led by Park Chung-hee. However, it is important to realize that the '60s, '70s, '80s, and '90s would have been impossible without what happened in the 1950s. Economic development is much more complex than most people realize. It requires an understanding of how first to achieve stability and then to maintain equilibrium among many contradictions.

Korea had a long history of innovation and openness to new ideas prior to the 1950s. It had developed moveable types long before Gutenberg. It stressed stability through checks and balances in governance before the Chinese. The Koreans thought of opposites and interacting parts of a whole in harmony, rather than as the ideological ends of a spectrum fighting each other. This fact is recognized by the Yin-Yang symbol in their flag. This heritage was a great advantage for it provided an ideological foundation upon which South Korea was able to rise like a phoenix.

The economic development of South Korea was based on:

1. Ancient customs and traditions that molded the discipline and work ethic of the Korean people.
2. Strong social cohesion forged during the suffering and combat of 1950 and 1951.

3. Powerful big conglomerates (Chaebol), unusually successful at applying technological change to prove that Koreans are not inferior to the Chinese and Japanese.

The Koreans knew they could not adopt the American form of governance as long as they were in an ideological struggle with the communists. Thus the authoritarian ways of Rhee during the 1950s had much in common with how Ataturk was able to reform Turkey following the collapse of the Ottoman Empire.

After Syngman Rhee was removed in 1960 South Korea had representative government, dominated by the military that provided security and order, during a period of remarkable achievement, competitiveness, prosperity, and fulfillment. The Koreans were successful because they were ready and willing to govern themselves their own way — while they built ties with US corporations.

The success after 1960 was largely due to the balancing of two contradictions: hierarchy and personal freedom. This is Yin/Yang in action, something that would benefit any country wanting economic growth.

Oriental Way of Conflict and the Western Way of War

The rich and varied military history of the Central Kingdom — as China calls itself — was largely unknown to American military leaders when they were in Korea and Vietnam. They would recognize Sun Tsu as the author of *The Art of War*, but lack any understanding of the strategies and tactics behind his words. Zheng Chenggong who defeated the Dutch was unknown.

Over 350 years ago the West fought its first conventional War with China. In the seventeenth century the Dutch were famous in Europe for their weapons, tactics, and logistics, but the Chinese easily defeated them in February 1662. Generalissimo Zheng Chenggong swept the Dutch off of Taiwan.

Chinese military traditions provide lessons for the future as China seeks to expand its influence. Among the factors that have enabled the Chinese to succeed in conflict since 101 BC, when Chinese armies conquered a string of oases as far as the Jaxartes (Syr Darya) River and established the "Silk Road," were their military traditions. These traditions are a rich and effective collection of strategic ideas and tactics that stress deception, misdirection, surprise, strategic communication, and patience. Since military leaders in China today are still deeply imbued with their traditional view of conflict, the West should study it. How are the Western and Oriental ways of fighting similar, and how do they differ?

Westerners still tend to underestimate Chinese military prowess, viewing China as a historically peaceful giant frequently invaded by bellicose neighbors: Huns, Mongols, Manchus, and, of course, Japanese. During World War II, US and British propaganda strengthened this image by depicting China as a hapless victim of a modern, assertive, and Westernized Japan. In Korea Westerners were continually surprised by the tactics of North Koreans and Chinese, and during the long armistice negotiations most Westerners failed to understand that for the Chinese this was just another form of conflict.

Most Westerners know that the Chinese invented gunpowder but think they only used it for fireworks. In fact, the first guns were developed in China, as were the first cannons, rockets, grenades, and land mines. The Chinese eagerly studied foreigners' weapons, such as Japanese muskets and English cannons. In many ways Oriental armed forces are very much like those of the West. Yet there are differences that need to be understood. During World War II the US attempted to develop a Western army in China only to see it defeated in Warfare by communists using traditional Chinese ways.

Chinese have many advantages in their indirect ways. Chinese military commanders are able to draw on two millennia of careful thinking on both War and Warfare. Most Westerners know that Sun Tzu is read by corporate CEOs from Germany to California, but most Westerners have no idea how many brilliant strategists, tacticians, and logistics experts succeeded Sun Tzu, building a rich body of thought for the many interactions of cooperation and conflict. The Chinese blend the psychological and material in ways rarely matched in the West—except by Napoleon, Cromwell, Francis Marion, and T. E. Lawrence. But after Borodino even Napoleon forgot this blending; he waited in Moscow to be defeated by the weather, a decline in morale and discipline among his troops, and a lack of food.

Zheng Chenggong reduced complex ways to a few words, much as Westerners use the terms "Trojan Horse" and "Blitzkrieg." In 1662 he outwitted the Dutch at nearly every turn, luring them into traps and combining naval and land forces in unexpected ways.

Yet Americans rarely study how to use these ideas. Chinese leaders are aware of China's military traditions. They know about Sun Tzu, Zhuge Liang, and Qi Jiguang. But they also know Western military traditions. They are following Sun Tzu's advice: "Know your enemy and know yourself."

Western culture stresses rational analysis, dissemination of knowledge, timing, and initiative. When it is without the constraint of religion, Western culture depends on amoral science and technology. The ideals of representative governance, religious tolerance, and compassion are not allowed to hinder the pursuit of combat effectiveness in war. Western culture stresses rational analysis without constrains of politics, philosophy, ideology, or religion; this results in weapons and transportation capable of bringing great destructive power on their enemies. The Western culture gives an advantage in war, but luck, numbers of combat troops, courage, cowardice, brilliance, inexperience, and initiative can tilt the advantage in any direction.

The Western way of war depends on technology, logistics, firepower, organization, tactical adaptation, personal freedom, soldiers fighting together, and a military strategy of annihilating, direct confrontation, driving the enemy from the battlefield; courageous warriors and soldiers anxious for brief, clear-cut, decisive battles to achieve victory; conflict by a united people intent on destroying the enemy's will with a series of battles; a quick resolution. The Western way of war is to use overwhelming firepower, to annihilate the critical mass of the enemy, and to obliterate—not to punish, check, or humiliate.

The Oriental way of conflict is a rich and effective collection of strategic ideas and tactics that stress deception, misdirection, erosion strategy, deception, ruse, ambush, raiding, surprise, terrorism, the warrior ethos, encirclement, inundation, the execution of prisoners, concealment, surprise, psychology, human skills, strategic communication, converting your enemies, patience, and long-term control. The Oriental way of conflict gives an advantage in Warfare.

Since the seventeenth century the Chinese have learned much from the West, but the West has learned much less from the Chinese. Western leaders could learn how to deal with things outside of the military battlefield, and how to cope with the unexpected. The Chinese know that the most brilliant commander cannot have a contingency plan for everything. The Chinese commander wants to know how his opponent thinks and what he can do to cause misperceptions. In War the Chinese are as concerned with the psychological and strategic communication battlefields as they are with the battlefield on which armed forces meet. They would prefer for their enemy to change sides rather than to have to destroy them with overwhelming force. In both War and Warfare their strategic goals are to deceive and to fight only when success is certain, yet their tactics stress spontaneity.

Mao Zedong was correct when he asserted that foreigners cannot win another peoples' revolution for them; people must fight and win their own revolution. That is true whether the revolution is a fascist, Leninist, Islamist, progressive, postmodern, or American. All revolutions must be bottom up—not top down.

Today, as Americans take a new look at the Pacific, they ignore China's military traditions of conflict at their peril. The goal should be to combine the Oriental way of conflict and the Western way of war.

How Things Might Have Been Different in Vietnam

In Vietnam the USA decisively defeated the North Vietnamese and the Vietcong in every conventional War battle, yet the North Vietnamese finally gained control of Vietnam because of their superiority in ideological conflict and strategic communication. The wills of the communists remained firm as the USA withdrew from Vietnam—thus snatching defeat from the jaws of victory.

In Vietnam from 1965, when US combat forces arrived in large numbers until the spring of 1970 there was little evidence that any lessons from Korea were applied in Vietnam. It is true that conventional War and Warfare were combined but that was probably a continuation of tactics used by the French and British in Southeast Asia. The Americans used large conventional War forces in search and destroy sweeps. But victory in War would only be possible if the north was conquered or at least there was a regime change in the north. And the US would not support the actions that were required. This was a strategic error of being too cautious.

In Vietnam Warfare was addressed with the activities of CORDS, the Phoenix program, and the CIA Counter Terror Teams. However, there were not the capable nationalistic leaders and grassroots support to make these successful. These activities were unable to combine tasks to achieve local security, effective local authority, and weld the people together with a common national identity. This was largely a failure to understand the importance of strategic communication and how local leaders must integrate into a nation-state.

In the spring of 1970, under General Abrams, the emphasis shifted to Warfare; by 1971 stability was at hand. During 1971 and 1972 the ARVN (the Army of South Vietnam) successfully handled the conventional War in the South. By 1972 the pacification program had eliminated insurgents in South Vietnam, yet North Vietnamese armed forces remained in the South. The Paris Agreement said nothing about this. Anyone familiar with the ideological conflict in Korea would know this meant the North Vietnamese would eventfully win. This was a failure to understand that in Warfare strategic communication and networks among the people are the critical mass—not enemy armed forces. Those who are able to maintain the will of those on their side and to weaken the will of those who oppose them will be successful in Warfare.

On 27 January 1973 the "Agreement on Ending the War and Restoring Peace in Vietnam" was signed in Paris, and during 1974 North Vietnam built up their forces in the South. In 1974 deep cuts in US assistance to South Vietnam ensured victory for the North, plus over a million deaths and over two million refugees.

There were voices—including General Harold K. Johnson— suggesting how to apply the lessons from Korea to Vietnam. However, those voices lost out to the conventional soldiers and the foreign policy establishment.

How Things Might Have Been Different in Iran

In January 1979 the Shah of Iran was overthrown. Within a year Iran was a centralized theocracy that had neutralized all opposition and was committed to removing the United States from the Middle East. Any comparison with Syngman Rhee would favor the Shah. As the dominant state in the Middle East, Iran had greater geopolitical value to the United States than Korea. While the Shah regime was authoritarian it was no more so than Rhee's, and the Shah was more lenient with his ideological enemies. The Shah had done much to modernize Iran economically, wanted to Westernize the country, and saw himself as Iran's Kemal Ataturk.

Anyone who had learned the lessons from Korea and Vietnam would have recognized that Ayatollah Khomeini headed a major ideological threat to US interests, and would have done much more than the Carter administration did to prevent him from coming to power. While the Shah might have had to leave Iran, the US was capable of preventing Khomeini from becoming Iran's leader—if it had the will. However, the foreign policy establishment did not favor such a course since it would require extensive use of covert and strategic communication means—and they naively thought diplomatic means could do the job.

How Things Might Have Been Different in the Balkans

During 1994–1999 our political leaders attempted to blame all of the problems in the Balkans on a diabolical Milosevic and to generate public support with images of suffering and tales of atrocities. Such spinning and rationalization would be understandable in a political campaign, but it is destructive in foreign relations. Lessons from Korea and Vietnam would have revealed that the problem was not Milosevic and Serb nationalism but the problem was an ideological struggle resulting from the penetration of Islam into Europe. For centuries Serbia had been the front line in this conflict. Yet our policy makers did not see that Serbia was only performing its traditional role of protecting Western culture—they wanted to blame nationalism and the Serbs.

Why did our policy makers get it so wrong? They were not thinking in terms of ideological conflict. Those who lived through Korea and Vietnam should have recognized the ideological threat and given it greater importance. But our policy makers were concerned with other matters. They thought:

1. Nationalism is an anachronism of the nineteenth century, and anyone espousing nationalism is backward, uneducated, dangerous, and perhaps deranged.

490

2. The nation-state, and sovereignty, should no longer be the foundations of the international system.

3. Since the mission of NATO, as stated in its charter, is no longer relevant, they must create new missions for NATO.

With regard to the ideological struggle between Islam and Western culture the results in Bosnia have been costly and highly questionable. In Kosovo the results have been disastrous. This is an example of the tragic outcome when the enemy is improperly defined because of a failure to understand that Warfare is primarily an ideological struggle. Also this was an error of being too aggressive in the use of conventional War forces.

How Things Might Have Been Different in Iraq

After twenty-one days of very successful war fighting in Iraq, the policy makers failed to transition to Warfare. Instead the United States and the coalition followed an approach that is best described as neocolonial. The overriding goal of this approach was establishing a sovereign central government for Iraq that duplicates Western ideas about democracy and elections. The focus was on the centralization of authority in Baghdad in order to create and maintain legitimacy, the rule of law, and administrative capability to govern all of Iraq.

The neocolonial orientation prevented a rapid move to a stable Iraq state. The Iraqi Army and police were demobilized, rather than being used for local security. The de-Ba'athification was done in a way that prevented a smooth transition to new governmental structures and procedures. Tribal leaders were ignored. It should have been recognized that immediately after the war fighting campaign there was not Peace—there was Warfare. And actions should have reflected that reality.

Rather than impose Western ideals of democracy on Iraq, the aim should have been to build on the non-Western ideas of democracy. Starting in Greece, Western democracy was built on individualism and supremacy of state authority through the rule of law. However, there is a long tradition of non-Western democracy in China, India, and Iraq that is built on groups of individuals (families, tribes, clans, guilds, or villages). The regulation of most social, cultural, and economic activities in Iraq should be left to the myriad of local groups and assemblies. Those who had learned lessons from Korea and Vietnam would have recognized that the neo-colonial approach is both costly and ineffective.

After expending vast amounts of blood and treasure in Iraq, the USA retains very little influence after the conventional War forces left. It was never seen and fought as an ideological conflict.

How Things Might Have Been Different in Afghanistan

In Afghanistan the USA, with its local allies, defeated the Taliban and established an Afghanistan government, yet was never successful in establishing stability during the Warfare that followed. USA attempted to use the neocolonial—top down—approach rather than the bottom up (phoenix) approach and was unable to create a climate of order and satisfaction in which insurgents are neutralized.

State building in Afghanistan should never have focused on the creation of a strong central authority in Kabul, but on establishing thirty-four self-governing provinces. Tribal, religious, and secular leaders in provinces should have established provincial, district, and local governmental structures and processes, as each province deemed appropriate. Customs and traditions of the Afghans would determine the leaders—not Western political thought on democracy or elections.

Whereas Korea and Vietnam have long histories and some common identity, those living in the area called Afghanistan have no basis for an effective central government—even one that is authoritarian and oppressive. This difference should have been obvious to anyone who had learned lessons about Warfare from Korea and Vietnam.

The Blinders of Preconceptions

Bureaucracies of large organizations (military, business, education, government, not-for-profit, or religious) usually wear their preconceptions as blinders, and are slow to adjust to reality. This has certainly been true of the military establishment regarding Warfare being a concern of the military. Nevertheless it is disturbing to find out that during, and after Korea and Vietnam, many of those in staff and command positions at the higher levels still want to limit the military to War as seen in the West for the past three hundred years.

Conventional War is the struggle between armed forces each championing its state and each attempting to weaken the will of its enemy and the destruction of their armed forces. War fighting, force development, logistics, and technology for conventional War have been the focus of military professionals in the nation states of the West since the Treaty of Westphalia (1648). This is the conflict visualized by the Geneva Conventions and the rules of War. Conventional War has established principles regarding strategies and tactics for achieving victory. Among those principles are: (1) identify the critical mass of the enemy and attack it with overwhelming forces, (2) find them, fix them, fight them, and finish them, (3) use battlefield tactics that best integrate firepower and maneuvers, and (4) gain an advantage with technological superiority. In Korea the conventional soldiers assumed that technological advances had made millennia-old realities of conflict obsolete, that machines could replace human beings, and that costly systems and weapons could ensure victory.

Military professionals must know all of the principles for success in conventional War, yet in Korea and Vietnam limiting their thinking to such principles was a mistake. Efforts to communicate this mistake were merely tolerated. This was evidence that what had happened in Korea and Vietnam was unknown even to many of those who were, or had been, there.

Most military professionals are convinced that superiority in materiel and firepower can achieve victory. In other words, the biggest dog in town could dominate not only all the other dogs, but also the cats, snakes, insects, and bacteria. The advantages of massive concentrations of technologically superior air, land, and sea forces are obvious, yet they also have vulnerabilities. The tactics of lightly armed hit-and-run forces, covert operations, and targeted killings, which the Chinese had perfected during their civil war, also have their own advantages—and vulnerabilities.

Also, many policy makers did not even consider strategic communication and ideological conflict. While it was under-standable that those at the lower levels in the military would only be concerned with their immediate tasks, the upper levels of the military should recognize the critical importance of keeping the will of those in government, and the American people, strong. This failure was an outcome of how many defined a military professional. They thought it was unprofessional to focus on anything other than finding, fixing, fighting, and finishing the Chinese, North Korean, and North Vietnamese armed forces.

In time the conflict in Korea would become the Unknown War because few people knew or cared about what happened there. But a greater tragedy is that the lessons that could have been learned from the conflict in Korea were never learned—or were forgotten. Many of the errors made in Korea were repeated in Vietnam from 1965 until 1970, in Iraq after 9 April 2003 (following twenty-one days of successful war fighting) until 2005, and in Afghanistan.

Why were the same mistakes made in Vietnam, Iraq, and Afghanistan? There are four reasons:

- The glory days of World War II.

- Most people in the West think of War and Peace in dichotomous terms and do not recognize Warfare, which is neither Peace nor War.

- Americans lack the patience needed for protracted conflict.

- Most people do not learn from their mistakes—they just keep trying to do the same things better.

It is clear that air power and technologically superior land forces, used with skill by Matthew B. Ridgway, changed the course of events in Korea. He committed superior firepower and technology to destroy enemy forces—not to take terrain. General Ridgway demonstrated how to achieve victory in conventional War. This was the lesson conventional military leaders learned from Korea. If there had been the will, the same tactics could have been used to push the Chinese and North Koreans back to the narrow neck of the Korean Peninsula in June 1951.

Yet Ridgway's solution has limitations, and these limitations were not learned. Our enemies learned that they had to make our machines, techniques, procedures, and tactics ineffective. They learned that they had to fight in ways to offset our technological superiority. They learned that they must fight us in the human domain. They learned the importance of strategic communication. They learned how to win in ideological conflicts. Most of those in the United States and Europe did not learn these lessons.

As negotiations regarding both Korea and Vietnam demonstrate, the greatest weakness of the United States, and the West in general, is strategic communication in ideological conflict, i.e., to maintain the will of your side while you weaken the will of your opponent. Our enemies around the world learned from Korea and Vietnam that impatience, and a media that thinks its primary role is to expose errors made by its own government, are America's Achilles' heel. Apathy, disinterest, and impatience of those living in the US and Europe makes them ineffective in Warfare because it has no end. This handicap will continue until they become more effective in strategic communication during ideological conflict.

Also Americans must always honor those at the point of the spear more than those who stand on the sidelines or find fault with those in the arena doing the fighting. Debates on foreign policy should never be allowed to diminish the honor due those who risk their lives for their country. Traditional military professionals are frustrated by the fact Warfare is protracted without a definitive ending—and hopefully victory. This is what they seek in conventional War. Stability (how success is judged in Warfare) does not give the traditional military professional the emotional lift of "mission accomplished" with victory in War. Therefore, the scope of the military profession has to be expanded to include Warfare as well as War, or a new profession has to be created to focus on Warfare and how to achieve stability. In general it is necessary to recognize the trilogy of War-Warfare-Peace as three distinctive conditions within Conflict/Cooperation.

Four Misconceptions About Building Social-Political Structures

Four misconceptions about nation building have dominated the thinking of Americans since 1944:

First, those identifying with social-political structures being built must provide the leadership, dedication, vision, and energy. Others can only help.

There are several critical differences between building a nation and the creation of a state, or the expansion of an empire, or the formation of a federation. A state is based on power enhancement—by either force or law—and administration. Expanding an empire, i.e., creating hegemony, requires a desire to dominate, superiority of armed forces that control territory, and ruthlessness. A federation requires agreement among subunits. A confederation is a state with considerable decentralization of authority to smaller self-governing units—which are often called provinces.

US policy makers should determine what social-political structures those living in a specific location desire and then assist them in achieving the needed change. The US should not attempt to impose any specific ideology. Minimum foreign involvement will always produce maximum benefits at the lowest possible cost.

Second, nation-state building is not attempting to persuade rival groups prepared to use force to eliminate each other to form a coalition government. It is naive to treat factions, each of whom demand control of the same territory, as parties in a system of parliamentary government. The United States made that mistake from 1944 to 1947 in its policy toward China. It repeated this mistake in Vietnam—and many other places.

This mistake is the outcome of Americans' obsession with (1) authority of the central government, (2) "rule of law" to replace custom and tradition, and (3) "democracy" defined as universal suffrage and elections. This obsession shaped US policy toward South Vietnam, and it has caused this same error to be repeated again and again in other places. Ideological tunnel vision of the American political elite, who wanted others to have the benefits of the "American Way," has often hindered state building—and squandered billions of dollars. America has been the kid who others use every day, but still shows up to fork over his lunch money assuming at some point everyone will like him because he's so good hearted and generous.

Third, local security must come before social, political, and economic change. In other words, efforts at political and economic development do not provide a climate of order and satisfaction. It is just the opposite; stability is a prerequisite for any political and economic development. So-called "soft power" can always be defeated by "hard power," although many hold dearly to the illusion that this is not true. One uneducated insurgent with a knife, that he is willing to use to kill, is more powerful than a contingent of humanitarians, development experts, politicians, and soldiers who will not kill. People have to be kept alive before anyone can win their stomachs, hearts, and minds.

Fourth, the creation of a nation is a long—several generations at least—process; the maintenance of a nation is a never-ending process. This is at odds with the American desire for a quick fix. A Vietnam nation-state in 1954 was a bridge too far.

Today there are many examples of how long it takes to build a nation, even under favorable conditions. Spain after five hundred years is still trying to absorb the Basques and the Catalans. After three hundred years as the British Isles, Ireland broke away in 1922; both Wales and Scotland still have separatist movements. Although some countries in South America and Asia seem to have developed national identities, it is difficult to find any true nation in Africa. Will Canada break up? After extreme efforts in Germany and Italy to build nations around common languages, the primary identification of many of the citizens in those states is something other than a nation.

Both building and preventing the decline of a nation-state are arts requiring the balancing of many factors. It is not something that can be done quickly or by following a specific recipe, and foreigners certainly cannot do it. It was foolhardy for the US to attempt to build a Vietnam nation-state in 1954: although, it would have been possible to establish a confederation, in Hue, with many self-governing provinces throughout Vietnam.

Nine Lessons That Could Have Been Learned from Korea and Vietnam

1. Warfare differs from both War and Peace. The goal of conventional War is the elimination of your enemy's will to fight and the neutralization of your enemy's armed forces. Success in conventional War is victory, followed by an agreement on the new order. The goal of Warfare is a climate of order and reduction of dissatisfaction to the point that no one is willing to use violence for political ends. Success in Warfare is stability, i.e., a climate of order and satisfaction. The goal of Peace is

freedom from fear and the opportunity for individuals to pursue their own bliss. Success in Peace is no one willing to use violence for political ends.

2. Success in both War and Warfare requires a comprehensive, competent intelligence and covert capabilities. If anyone thinks they will be left twisting in the wind— or in jail—it will be impossible to get the intelligence needed or to take the action required. Laws and procedures designed to collect evidence for a trial in peacetime, or to punish criminals, are inadequate for Warfare.

3. For success in Warfare it is necessary to recognize and accept attitudes and convictions, as well as the laws, rules, and regulations, which are inappropriate during Peace.

4. In Warfare it is necessary to eliminate the networks within many factions that give aid and comfort to those who want to weaken or destroy your side. It is necessary to recognize that many of the insurgents hide within legitimate organizations advocating peace, understanding, and equality. It requires actions which will weaken the will of leaders, alter the decision-making processes, and change the attitudes and opinions of those who give the insurgent leaders power.

5. Success or failure on the battlefields of ideological conflict is essentially a question of marketing—which is well known to many Americans.

6. The degree of decentralization depends on the level of dissatisfaction and the degree of authoritarianism that is acceptable. A prerequisite for Warfare is to determine the form of governance capable of providing stability. When the people lack a common sense of identity they

do not see themselves as "we," and are often willing to use violence against those they consider "they." In such situations stability might require a strong, coercive, ruthless regime, a confederacy of self-governing provinces, or something between these extremes.

7. The members of a country must accomplish any real change—only those who consider themselves "we" can do it. Others (i.e., "foreigners") can assist, but the leadership, dedication, vision, and energy must come from within. But when there are deep divisions in a country the "foreigners" might be the elite in control of the central government, or those in another province or those with another ideology. Success is easier and cheaper when contributions by "foreigners" are small and unseen.

8. Long-term stability requires economic conditions that reinforce a climate of order and satisfaction at the local level. Such changes should be through encouraging the entrepreneurial spirit of the people to solve their everyday economic problems, rather than through foreign financed large-scale infrastructure projects.

9. It is a mistake to attempt to persuade rival groups prepared to use force to eliminate each other to form a central coalition government.

---

[82] Ideology does refer to a body of doctrine, opinions, and assertions of a political or cultural movement (Capitalism, Socialism, Fascism, Communism, etc.) along with the devices for establishing that doctrine in the rules, regulations, and laws of government. However, here ideological conflict is used to describe something broader, i.e., the struggle to shape the inner compass and point of view of individuals regarding what is right or wrong, good or bad, and virtuous or evil. It does include the efforts to advance political or cultural doctrine, opinions and assertions that determine Secular Authority (i.e., the rules, regulations, and laws of government) but it also includes Sacred Authority (i.e., that which is considered moral and ethical).

CHAPTER THIRTY

HOW TO BE EFFECTIVE IN IDEOLOGICAL CONFLICT

Korea and Vietnam show that success in Warfare cannot be achieved in the same way that victory is achieved in conventional War. Yet this is not recognized by many because they only consider ideological conflict during Peace; they think war should be resolved by overwhelming force.[83] However, success in ideological conflict during Warfare requires recognition that:

1. The phoenix approach, not the neocolonial approach, is needed (i.e., stability is achieved from the bottom up, not from the top down).

2. War fighting forces alone cannot achieve stability.

3. Economic and political change is only possible after stability has been achieved.

4. Those unable to provide security at the local level twenty-four hours a day, seven days a week will fail.

5. Those with the most effective networks among the people will be successful.

6. The four tasks for achieving stability are:

- Achieve local security.
- Provide effective local authority.
- Organize and motivate the people.
- Satisfy aspirations of the people.

The Need for Policy Clarity

US policy must be clear and specific, not based on feelings and preconceptions. Policy cannot be a political position or a desire. Policy must state what is to be done, how it is to be accomplished, and what it is worth in both blood and treasure.

US policy needs to address all three aspects of ideological conflict: (1) what individuals consider good or bad, right or wrong, (2) the political, economic, and cultural doctrines considered best, and (3) communication to influence wills. It needs to enhance stability at the local level at the lowest possible costs, and this is best done by influencing how people think and what they believe. Until all three aspects of ideological conflict are addressed the US might win all of the military battles, at great cost in lives and treasure, but end up with its national interests worse off than they were before conventional War forces were introduced. This is a most important policy lesson that should have been learned from both Korea and Vietnam, but it was not.

The overriding foreign policy concern for the US should always be to make sure no one willing and able to threaten US interests is allowed to survive. Policy makers must consider the use of covert means to convince leaders in other countries that their survival depends on their making sure that no one within their territory threatens US interests. Since fear is the greatest motivator, often this will require targeted killing by planes, missiles, drones, or covert assassination. How this is to be accomplished will no doubt be hotly debated. Nevertheless, it is essential that those ordered to carry out any such action always be supported and protected so they will not be charged at some future time with "human rights violations" or "war crimes."

It should be US policy that funds go to the local level and not to central governments. Central governments must support themselves from their own taxes, not with US aid. And the economy situation should be such that more revenue flows back to the US than from the US.

Policy makers must have access to, and be willing to listen to, those who do not share the conventional wisdom on foreign policy. Those voices that challenge the conventional wisdom of the foreign policy establishment (military and civilian) must be heard and evaluated. Our country needs individuals who see a need, and without consulting with higher authority, simply go ahead and try to solve that need. Such innovative individuals are inclined to disrupt the status quo. This runs counter to the way traditional organizations function. All large bureaucracies reward those who conform—if US policy is to be effective, this needs to be modified.

US policy makers need to agree on a simple conceptual framework of how the people of any country can have lasting social-political change. There will always be debates on economic, political, social, and moral issues, but there must be agreement among policy makers on the process by which these issues are resolved.

US policy makers must understand how the Western way of war differs from the Oriental way of conflict. In Peace, Warfare, and conventional War the Oriental way of conflict stresses deception, misdirection, concealment, inundation, psychology, strategic communication, conversion of your enemies, human skills, surprise, patience, and long-term control. In contrast, the Western way of war stresses destruction, firepower, overwhelming force, technology, machines, penetration, elimination of your enemies, logic, science, speed, and swift victory. US policy needs to understand erosion strategy and know how to use strategic communications to keep Americans united and their will strong, while causing all enemies to fragment and their will to be weakened.

The Constraints of Peacetime Laws and International Law

In Korea and Vietnam the military was constrained by rules created by lawyers, diplomats, and politicians for those engaged in War, i.e., conflict between the armed forces of states attempting to destroy each other. US armed forces were required to follow the constraints of "civilized conduct in time of war" as specified in the Geneva Conventions. This is following the path of great powers of the past as they became soft and limp in their decline. In Korea and Vietnam warriors and soldiers would have been punished if they did what they thought necessary when it did not comply with international law. This naive faith in international law is one of the reasons we have been unsuccessful in Warfare.

In Korea and Vietnam warriors and soldiers were faced with situations that lawyers, diplomats, politicians, and human rights activists never considered, could never understand, and would never have to face themselves. In Warfare there are situations alien to civil society during Peace in which political theory regarding justice, the rule of law, and law enforcement are not appropriate. In Warfare there are situations alien to the symmetrical conflict of War between the armed forces of states, i.e., those for which diplomats, politicians, and lawyers write the rules.

Roles, rules, and standards specifically for Warfare need to be developed and stated.

What does Duty and Honor require? What should a patriot do to prevent the decline and decay of his or her country? Does each individual have an adequate inner compass to allow him to make the correct judgments between right and wrong, between good and bad? Who is willing to recognize the truth? Who has the courage to do the harder right rather than the self-serving wrong? In order to make such judgments it is necessary to reject moral relativism in which no view is any more valid than any other but to have moral absolutes that recognize the situations that will be faced during Warfare.

How do patriots keep the military instrument of their nation hard, ruthless, and strong?

The Need for Ideological Certainty

Moral relativism is the surest way to be defeated in ideological conflict. After all of the debates, discussions, compromises, and concessions have taken place there is a need for warriors to defeat the "others." This can be done by military means or by other means. In any ideological conflict if one side is certain about their convictions and the other is not, it is only a question of time until the side with moral certainty wins. Currently the US needs moral certainty about decentralization over centralization, individual responsibility over dependency, free will over indoctrination, equality of opportunity over equality of outcomes, religion of personal redemption over sociopolitical ideology of submission, and capitalism over socialism. Diversity on these is a weakness, not a strength.

On Socialism/Capitalism

In the *Chosun Minjujui Inmun Kongwhakuk* (North Korean People's Republic) it was possible to see the results of socialism, to reflect on its strengths and weaknesses, and come to some conclusions regarding it. Here it is possible to consider those aspects of ideological conflict that deal with ideology as a body of doctrines, opinions, and assertions of a political or cultural movement (Capitalism, Socialism, Fascism, Communism, etc.) along with the devices for establishing that doctrine in the rules, regulations, and laws of government. This is the ideological conflict over which Secular Authority (the rules, regulations, laws, processes, and procedures of government) is best.

First, socialism of the left, as illustrated in North Korea, North Vietnam, and China, contrasted with the vision of the Founders of the United States. Second, there are similarities between socialism of the left (communism) and socialism of the right (that of Mussolini and Hitler, which is often called fascism). Both require the centralization of power. Third, there are several different meanings given to the terms "democracy," "equality," and "the people."[84]

It is difficult to get a handle on socialism. Most people think of socialism in economic terms and contrast socialism with capitalism. However, socialism has several dimensions (economic, political, and cultural); there is considerable emotional commitment to contending views regarding socialism, and the terminology is inconsistent

and confusing. Yet the critical distinction is that all socialism depends on the centralization of power while Americanism depends on power not being centralized.

Socialism advocates centralized economic control, or at least planning, by government. The degree of state ownership of the means of production is of no real importance; under socialism of the left (communism) it is all owned by the state, while under socialism of the right (fascism) it is only controlled by the state. Under both there is no market. The economic aspect of socialism is reflected in the historical struggle between the concentration and dispersion of wealth.

Capitalism permits, and motivates, people to invest their savings in productive enterprises and promises dividends in return. Socialism claims that such free enterprise results in inequality and injustice because of greed and abuses, which only government can correct. Americanism favors decentralization and private ownership of the means of production, which benefits society as a whole. Americanism seeks to avoid the corruption, incompetence, inefficiency, and ineffectiveness which always occur with centralization and control of the means of production by government. Rewards are what motivate people to make great efforts. However, when government takes all rewards away no one will want, or try, to achieve.

The fear of the seductive appeal of the "stuff" provided under socialism (of either the left or the right) has caused capitalists to seek greater equality of outcomes, and the fear of the economic successes of capitalism has caused socialists to seek greater freedom for individuals and some decentralization. Yet capitalism is the natural ordering of human relations since it does not interfere with the way people relate in their own self-interests. As a result, self-improvement and innovation of individuals are the foundations of capitalism—this creates jobs and improves the lot of everyone.

Politically socialists value equality of outcomes more than freedom and equality of opportunity. They expect government to take from the rich and to give to the poor, and socialists claim they do this. They think in terms of a collective rather in terms of individuals. Socialists expect government to give them protection from economic, social, and psychological distress. Their concept of "the people" is a collective with the leaders exercising the authority of a sovereign. This results in the concentration of power in the hands of the elite who claim they seek a utopia of equality and fairness. This is the opposite of individuals having free will yet uniting for the common good. Politically, socialism centralizes authority and Americanism decentralizes authority. Another way of explaining the difference is: socialism centralizes both Secular and Sacred Authority, while Americanism keeps Secular Authority and Sacred Authority in balance with neither dominating the other.[85]

Culturally socialists think capitalism exploits the poor for the benefit of the rich. They think governmental authority should be used to reward or punish in order to progress toward a utopian goal of equality and fairness. Americans believe in rewards based on merit, and that punishment should be given for antisocial deeds. Thus there is a clear contrast between free individuals united for the common good under Americanism, but with the opportunity for success or failure on their own merits, and socialism that is a collective in which government ensures "fairness" and equality of outcomes for everyone.

The foundation of Americanism is a culture in which each citizen needs an inner compass that guides behavior to do right rather than wrong, and good rather than bad. Socialism has no need for individuals to have an inner compass since the rules, regulations, and laws are established and enforced by an elite that controls government, thus specifying what is right or wrong and what is good or bad. Americanism values individual responsibility and freedom while socialism values collective responsibility to ensure fairness and economic, political, and emotional protection for all.

The Hegelian dialectic, Marxism, and Western liberalism all assume that contradictions eventually lead to unity as the result of struggle. For many this process of continual conflict is considered "progress." And it is also a convenient excuse for the centralization of power in government under some elite. Many consider this view progress. The older idea of balancing opposites, as expressed in the Chinese yin-yang, is not only more realistic but also a way to achieve the decentralization of power.

The Hegelian dialectic is based on the concept that one assertible proposition (thesis) is necessarily opposed by an equally assertible and mutually contradictory proposition (antithesis), the mutual contradiction being reconciled in a higher level of truth by a third proposition (synthesis). Regardless of the outcome, many consider the process itself "progress." Therefore, all "progressives" (Marxists, Socialists, Fascists, Liberals, and Postmodernists) see themselves as caring, compassionate humans on a noble quest to achieve a utopia of equality and fairness among people.

The adversarial approach pits those who seek truth in faith and duty against those who seek truth in law and empirical evidence. A better way is to balance subjectivism and objectivism, rather than domination by either. This view is compatible not only with yin-yang, but also with Aristotle's golden mean, the stable state of physics, the homeostatic equilibrium of systems theory, and the checks and balances of the Founders of America.

Regardless of how it is expressed, most people recognize that human affairs involve so many changing interdependent variables that they can never be understood fully, nor that all of the consequences can be precisely predicted. To overcome this limitation, the adversarial approach always results in the centralization of authority—and power. However, a climate of order and satisfaction is best achieved through the balancing of both Secular Authority and Sacred Authority and the decentralization of power.

Ideas about how best to understand human affairs is at the core the debate about the relationship of reason to reality. Subjectivism means that reality is based on feelings and empathy—not reason. On the other hand, objectivism is based on reality being independent of the human mind since it requires knowledge from facts outside of consciousness.

Stability, i.e., a climate of order and satisfaction, is most likely to be achieved by the equilibrium of opposites. This would mean that Sacred Authority and Secular Authority should be balanced so that neither dominates the other. It would mean the same for the subject and the object. Thus this is exactly what the Founders of America attempted to create with checks and balances which can be more accurately called Stability through Equilibrium (StE).

On Decentralization/Centralization

Korea has provided ample evidence that centralization of authority does provide efficiency to accomplish a specific agenda. Yet in the long run decentralization is a better way to achieve a climate of order and satisfaction.

At the company level in the military, the advantages of decentralization have some practical applications regarding small unit leadership. A platoon, and even a squad, is a very effective fighting unit if it has good leadership. It is not equipment that is most important; it is the ability to move quickly and to surprise your enemy. This is only possible when those at the lowest level are willing and able to make decisions. It is true that any infantryman needs certain equipment: weapons, ammunition, and water. However, the  small unit leader must think in terms of stealth and cunning and must have the motivation, will, and determination to close those final yards and to kill. Although small unit leadership is important in conventional War, it is even more important in Warfare.

Any successful country needs to balance Sacred Authority and Secular Authority, rather than allow either to dominate the other. In other words the inner compass of individuals is as important as the "rule of law." This is also why capitalism is better than socialism (of either the left or the right). It is decentralization that provides best for the common good.

When the Founders of America used the eighteenth century political term "free State," they were referring to decentralized governance in which just power, i.e., Secular Authority, is carried out for the good of all Americans. They were contrasting a tyrannical, despotic, authoritarian, totalitarian regime with a representative republic of, by, and for citizens who have accepted a social contract that recognizes unalienable rights, endowed by the Creator, in return for the acceptance of responsibilities. They were making a distinction between collective rights determined by government for the welfare of all and individual rights of life,

513

freedom, and the pursuit of happiness earned by the citizens of the American nation.

The idea of collective rights is the cornerstone of post-modern (progressive) thought that seeks to weaken the principles and ideals embodied in the Declaration of Independence, Constitution, and other documents of the Founders. The small, limited government envisioned by the Founders existed for the purpose of securing the rights of individual citizens of the American nation. Each person who earns American citizenship enjoys the equal protection of his life, freedom, and the pursuit of happiness, while accepting the obligation to protect the rights of all other American citizens. In contrast progressive utopia is a centralized administrative state to protect the "disadvantaged" and to ensure "welfare social justice for the people" as determined by the experts controlled by the political elite.

It is important to note that in the American system, in contrast with those of other countries, American citizens are to be moral and informed individuals governed by the Constitution and thus Secular Authority, established by the Founders. Also, Americans, in contrast to those living in other countries, have a social contract among moral individuals forming one indivisible nation. Then those Americans execute a second political contract in which power to govern for the benefit of all is delegated to certain governmental structures and processes (as specified in the Constitution).

A Conceptual Framework for Social-Political Change

A realistic conceptual framework of change would have been a useful tool during our efforts in Vietnam. Yet the US political elite had no agreement on any conceptual framework. In fact, they had many different views on how it should be done. This lack of agreement is a sure sign of failure.

A key lesson from both Korea and Vietnam is the need for a practical conceptual framework for how to have lasting social-political change, which is an essential part of ideological conflict. Such a concept would have reduced the cost, in both blood and treasure, of US actions in Vietnam. However, no conceptual framework can guarantee success since each situation is different. Analysis and appropriate modification is essential because each place and time is a unique challenge.

Social-political change requires continual attention to four interrelated tasks:

1. Achieve local security.
2. Provide effective local authority.
3. Organize and motivate the people.
4. Satisfy aspirations of the people.

The first task, achieving local security, is a prerequisite for the other three tasks. However, local security cannot be seen as an end in itself. It is merely a means to the end of change and building. However, when the focus is on the creation of a state, actions to control the territory of that state by the central government can be carried to the extreme. Such actions actually hinder lasting social-political change since those actions do not produce a self-regulating equilibrium. Often many people are at odds with the political elite of the central government, in which case it is necessary to rely on local authorities or to rely on a ruthless, authoritarian regime.

Local security is achieved when governmental authority at the local level can provide personal protection for the people 24-7 and no group can use violence for political ends. Any group committed to the use of force to weaken or overthrow the governmental authority (i.e., insurgents) must be neutralized. There are many ways this can be done with varying degrees of centralization of power. This should be accomplished by local police and territorial forces of the provinces; however, these should have been integrated into an alliance coordinated by a central government. Small is always better than large. In addition the confederation should have had armed forces stronger than any of the provinces.

Local security requires an effective intelligence system that will allow rapid response to any attempt at intimidation by the insurgent group, or payment to it. When terrorism becomes a tool of the insurgent group, a capability greater than that appropriate for policing ordinary crime must be added. This will usually require some temporary limitations on civil rights and the legal system. Finally, if the insurgent group gains control of a part of the state's territory, control must be regained, with armed forces if necessary, and the leaders of any guerilla groups must be neutralized. Unfortunately these are the only operations that some military professionals consider the role of the military.

The second task needed for lasting change is to provide effective local authority. Each individual lives in a concrete, human, face-to-face world of clear and specific events and situations. Aspirations and an unseen environment may shape an individual's spiritual and material life, but he knows through what he sees, hears, smells, and feels. This task provides local leadership. Leadership which is: alert for signs of problems, inequalities, and injustices; able to use initiative and flexibility to win loyalty and produce results; capable of countering acts of intimidation, violence, and destruction; able to see that everyone can earn a decent living; loyal to the established institutions; capable of educating each individual with values which blend freedom, ambition, duty, and responsibility in accordance with the customs and traditions of his nation.

The third task to achieve lasting change is to organize and motivate the people. A nation is no more than people welded together by a common destiny that binds together tomorrow, today, and yesterday into an active whole. This task creates and maintains shared values, attitudes, habits, and goals which shape the institutions through which a nation lives and grows: patterns of cooperation and conflict; the fabric of sanctioned relationship; the unseen lines of magnetic strength which link, join, and confine; the elusive cultural environment; an economic system that works. This task creates kinship.

It is necessary to remember that all four of the tasks are interrelated. For example, the satisfaction each individual achieves through the first and second task must be retained by the third task. Also, the organizing and motivating of the third task must recognize and accommodate differences in wealth, land, resources, markets, and convictions of those living in the various provinces.

Within the third and fourth tasks is economic improvement, which is essential for long-term satisfaction. However, such changes should be through encouraging the entrepreneurial spirit of the people to solve their everyday economic problems, rather than through foreign financed large-scale infrastructure projects. The focus should be on providing a better life for most of the people within their own districts and provinces, not on projects that increase the power of the central government. Success can only be determined by the training, attitude, and effort of individuals, not on the dollars spent, the schools built, the roads improved, or projects completed. Economic projects usually end up increasing the wealth of a few and propping up corrupt and chaotic officials and their friends. Self-help brings a better life and greater satisfaction.

The fourth task is to satisfy aspirations of a people who see themselves as "we." The fuel of progress is the never-ending attempt to satisfy aspirations. Aspirations can unite people in common effort; yet, aspirations can set one against another, preventing progress. Satisfying aspirations is an elusive, two-faced task of building. Sole concern with satisfying aspirations can only result in turmoil, frustration, and bitterness; as past aspirations are approached new and more demanding ones are invented. This task means that each nation has its own unique customs and traditions. This task, just like the first task of achieving security, will actually hinder sociopolitical change when it is carried to an extreme.

If this conceptual framework is to be useful, actions to accomplish these four tasks of sociopolitical change must be interrelated, and the building and maintenance of a nation-state must be seen as a never-ending process. Perhaps what Jefferson said in 1806 should be remembered: "Our duty is, therefore, to act upon things as they are, and to make a reasonable provision for whatever they may be."

The bottom line, no conceptual framework is any good if it is not applied to a specific situation with knowledge, understanding, and skill. How long does it take to make social-political change? It is wrong to think in terms of months or years. Decades or centuries are more realistic. For example, the Chinese Communists needed from 1900 to the 1990s to establish a new value system. Even today in China with all of the apparent stability there are still many millions of Chinese who endorse astrology and guanshi.

Reflections on Morality

Both Korea and Vietnam provide evidence that morality—including ethics and law—needed to be reexamined and revised if we are ever to be successful in ideological conflict.

Many people have their ideas of morality shaped by an ideal utopian society and world. The same is true for ethics and law. They seek the ideals of peace and love offered by religion, or the peace, cooperation, and justice presented by Western liberalism. They want to ignore the fighting, killing, brutality, and dying that are basic realities of the amoral world in which we live. The morality for Peace (when no one is willing or able to use forces to achieve a political goal) should not be transferred as the morality for either War or Warfare.

There also is a fundamental difference between War and Warfare. One is conflict between the armed forces of states that agree to certain rules of war, and attempt to enforce those rules on their armed forces. War requires a military instrument composed of war fighting forces. The other involves those who recognize the authority of no state, or those states which make no attempt to enforce shared rules. Warfare requires a military instrument composed of both war fighting forces and stability forces. Therefore the morality for Warfare must differ from that for conventional War.

The morality for Peace is not appropriate for the conditions of either War or Warfare. Such morality would make the military instrument soft, sophisticated, and weak. Yet "situational ethics," in which each individual defines his or her own morality based on personal feelings, must also be avoided. Those that use modern technology must be able to kill those they cannot see—both enemy military and civilians. The warrior must be able to do what infantrymen and tankers have always done—kill before being

519

killed. Interrogators must be able to do what interrogators have always done—obtain information in time to prevent death. Those engaged in the ideological conflict and strategic communication must be able to do what patriots have always done—to spin, deceive, mislead, exaggerate, and lie for their country.

How can these differences, and contradictions, be resolved? That is the challenge of the new moralities for Peace, Warfare, and War. The first step is to recognize that each of these three conditions is distinctive. The second step is to recognize that universal (natural) law or morality cannot apply for all three conditions. The third step is to establish the three new moralities.

What needs to be done? The Geneva Conventions should be considered only treaties between states that agree on what is appropriate conduct for members of their armed forces during conventional War. They should not be considered law. Each state should be responsible for the conduct of the members of its own armed forces. The Geneva Conventions do not apply—although many lawyers claim they do—in conflict with those states which have not signed those treaties, and certainly they do not apply during conflict with insurgents who are not under the authority of any state, and place no constraints on their own conduct, i.e., during Warfare. To do otherwise is detrimental to security, order, and a climate of satisfaction. It also places members of the armed forces in untenable situations, and it makes the job of the warriors and soldiers even more dangerous.

Each state should determine what it considers appropriate conduct during Warfare and how that differs from what is considered appropriate during conventional War or Peace. No military should be constrained by any universal law administered by some world body. Even more important, what is appropriate in Warfare should be determined by those who have, or will participate, in such conflict. Lawyers, diplomats, politicians, or human rights activists who seek to impose rules on others, which conform to their own political or ideological convictions, should not determine what is appropriate in Warfare.

It is time for anyone who believes in Duty, Honor, and Country to work to achieve a proper understanding of Peace-Warfare-War.

The Pacifist's Fallacy and Torture

In 1951 as the conventional War forces settled in on the proposed cease-fire line in Korea, Warfare became the more common form of conflict, and the Pacifist's Fallacy became more apparent. Throughout South Korea the ROK government is in a deadly struggle with Communist insurgents, but many Americans think only those means appropriate for Peace should be used.

Is it compassionate to do unto others, as you would have others do unto you? This Golden Rule is a teaching of many religions. It provides order and stability during Peace when those involved share moral and ethical convictions and are unwilling to use force to achieve their political goals. However, in Warfare it is naive to think that others will do unto you as you do unto them. This is the Pacifist's Fallacy. During Warfare those who follow the Golden Rule will probably be the victims of their own compassion before their enemies change their ways. This is one of the reasons to make a clear distinction between Peace and Warfare. However, those who have accepted the Pacifist's Fallacy do not make that distinction.

What is torture? Politicians, lawyers and human rights activists have given us several definitions—many based on the Pacifist's Fallacy. But these definitions are only expressions of how idealists would like things to be. They ignore reality. They are idealized visions of what their authors think civilized conduct should be; they are an expression of the Utopian goal of universal "rule of law." They fail to realistically describe torture.

Torture Causes Permanent Physical Damage to a Person

Real torture can be sadism, but in Warfare it is likely an effort to have a psychological impact on others. The Chinese—and Koreans—have long considered defeating your enemy without fighting to be supreme excellence. This is not only true at the strategic level, but it is true for all levels of conflict. This requires the weakening of the will of an opponent.

Fear is one of the ways to erode an opponent's will, and fear can be caused in many ways. On the other hand, there are many actions that are not torture that make someone fearful or uncomfortable; many of these are appropriate techniques used to collect intelligence or as psychological techniques to weaken wills.

Too often those with unrealistic views of torture confuse aggressive interrogation techniques with torture. Those with experience in interrogation should make the decisions on which techniques are effective with a specific person and which are not. Some things work and others do not. Experienced interrogators know best what to use. Politicians, lawyers, and human rights activists should never be allowed to determine which interrogation techniques are appropriate. To do this will result in an inability to counter threats and in unnecessary deaths.

Those who dream of a utopian world of love, peace, and harmony never understand real torture, since they have accepted the Pacifist's Fallacy. Torture, for them, is a horror to be avoided, ignored, and outlawed. They refuse to recognize that torture has long been one aspect of the human condition that has often been used by evil ones to achieve some goals or desires. They are unable to distinguish interrogation by those with knowledge, skills, and compassion from the actions of evil ones. They are unable to distinguish interrogation techniques that cause no permanent physical harm from actions that do cause permanent physical harm. Those who have accepted the Pacifist's Fallacy see anything that makes someone uncomfortable as "torture."

During Warfare evil ones use pain and fear as a tactic in order to weaken the will of an opponent. Children are killed not because they are a threat, but to cause pain and fear in others. They often use propaganda, torture, and public execution for the same reason. However, such actions by evil ones should never be confused with interrogation techniques seeking information to save lives.

To think that if everyone on your side is kind, caring, and compassionate others will be the same is the Pacifist's Fallacy. There are evil people in the world—as the North Koreans demonstrated in 1950 and others did in Vietnam. While there is evil, this fact should not be an excuse to expand the meaning of "torture" so as it prevents actions necessary to save lives. To do this would be immoral.

Psychology of Warriors and Soldiers

Who are infantrymen and tankers? They are warriors and soldiers. A person becomes an infantryman or a tanker whenever he enters combat where failure means death: when he must impose his will on an enemy, when no quarter is asked and none is given, when he must use whatever he has to destroy an enemy. The name of his organization is of no importance; it makes no difference how he arrived at the scene of battle; if makes no difference what others might call him. What turns a person into a warrior or soldier is the reality of being with other infantrymen or tankers after fire support has been lifted, in a life or death struggle against an enemy that wants to destroy him and those with him. The importance of fighters in conventional War is recognized; unfortunately, the importance of fighters in ideological conflict and strategic communication is not recognized.

The infantryman and tanker are "alive" because death can come at any moment. Few others can be so fascinated by human existence. In moments of danger the infantryman or tanker is absorbed into the reality he "sees." The awe and astonishment of those fleeting moments will live a lifetime. For the infantryman and tanker there are long periods of boredom and monotony, interrupted by excitement and the fascination of horror and drama. Others in the military and in civilian life never experience these highs and lows, this insecurity or this variety. The reality of combat can be both sublime and ridiculous, it can combine beauty and the grotesque, and it can have both harmony and havoc. It is this whole that warriors and soldiers "see" and "know," but that is missing in life of those in the military removed from combat and in the lives of civilians. It is also what discourages many warriors and soldiers from talking about what they have experienced in combat.

Infantrymen and tankers cannot be understood in terms of abstract notions; they can only be understood in terms of the concrete feelings and emotions that are the reality of combat. The abstractions of academe (be it philosophy, psychology, political science, law, or sociology) are not merely false but they are distortions of reality by intellectuals. So are the abstractions of politicians, lawyers, generals, admirals, staff officers in bureaucracies, and political activists who have a specific agenda to advance. Infantrymen live in the present—the concrete reality that they can see, touch, smell, and hear—not the past or the future. Others can use the past to create abstractions with which they can plan for the future. The presence of fighters in teams, squads, platoons, companies, and battalions has a powerful fascination, which creates hate, love, fear, and belief. For such men duty and honor carry a specific obligation to those individuals who depend on them, and on whom they depend.

Reality can be ugly but it can also be an aesthetic delight, which needs neither education nor intellect to appreciate.

The feeling of belonging together with those who have shared the stress of combat is what makes warriors and soldiers unique— it is the bedrock of the Ethos of Eros. This feeling might also be found through religion or political ideology, but it is more common in the heat of battle. It is not the cause that is important; it is the sharing of a stressful experience. It is not the abstract good that is the essence of morale; it is loyalty among those with shared experiences. It comes from the spontaneity of belonging; it is combat camaraderie. It gives meaning to life.

Only camaraderie, and loyalty to the group, can provide fighting morale. This can only be learned through experience in stressful situations—it is not in the realm of formal education or abstract thought. Duty and honor have unique meanings for the infantryman and tanker, but those meanings are very different from that of those held captive by the notions and attitudes of abstract thought. This is why combat-experienced sergeants, captains, and colonels should have final authority on correct behavior in combat, rather than generals, staff officers, lawyers, and politicians. It should be a question of what is right and combat effective, not a question of what is legal and politically correct. It is a matter of Sacred Authority—not Secular Authority.

For most of those in the military, duty and honor are abstractions just as rights, responsibility, legality, and morality. However, in combat the infantryman and tanker live in the here and now. The concrete absorbs him. He is awed by the spectacle, by the unusual that his senses bring to him. Others live in the routine, the established, and the known of conventional wisdom—but not an infantryman or a tanker.

The love and hate of "we" and "they" for infantrymen and tankers in combat is distinctive. The closer you are to the enemy the less you are likely to hate him. Those in military headquarters will be more rigid, hateful, and self-serving than the fighters at the point of the spear—unless the fighter happens to be a psychopath. The generals, staff officers, politicians, and civilians far removed from the reality of combat are likely to be even more bloodthirsty. Pacifists, lawyers, and rights activists who consider notions and emotions of War and Warfare abstractions will mistake killing of an enemy with murder, interrogation to ensure self-preservation with torture, or heroism with sadism.

While we can observe the Ethos of Eros of the warrior during conventional War, we need to recognize that the same warrior ethos is needed for ideological conflict and strategic communication during Warfare.

The Camaraderie of Warriors and Soldiers

Camaraderie is built on stress and shared stressful experiences. Nothing is more stressful than real combat, in which life hangs by a thin thread. Those that face life and death together often form a bond that lasts a lifetime. In addition there is "combat camaraderie" which all of those with experience in real combat feel—the hallmark of warriors and soldiers.

The feelings that create "combat camaraderie" are something that can be recognized, but which are difficult to explain. Those who have not experienced real combat—even those in the armed forces—rarely understand these feelings. Any explanation is inadequate, but what happened in Korea and Vietnam might at least give an impression.

Shared stressful experiences and the randomness of life are known, to some degree, by many people at many times. But it reaches its zenith in infantrymen or tankers who have been in combat where life might end at any moment. At those moments things must be done and only a person's inner compass can determine what is right and necessary. At such times the infantryman and tanker learn that luck, fate, proximity, and position all have their part in shaping reality; this creates "combat camaraderie."

The basis is the realization of the randomness of life. In the past it was called fate. Some might see it as the hand of the divine. Or perhaps just luck. Why were some killed or captured? What is the difference between life and death? What did those who died in Korea and Vietnam do? Why did they die in such a faraway place? What did others do? Why were some able to find their way back to their units, but others were captured or killed? Why were some able to do heroic deeds but think they were only doing what was right and necessary? Why did some collapse when faced with uncertainty, chaos, death, and horror, and others will never be able to be free of the trauma of that experience?

Are those things that were done, but never known, as important as those that are known, praised, and rewarded? And finally each person asks: Why did I live?

In Korea and Vietnam many no doubt did many worthy, brave, and heroic things that will never be known or noted. Others surely did things that they would like to forget and hope no one knows. All of those who have experienced combat understand this. It is the fact they share this understanding that provides the bond of "combat camaraderie." No one needs to defer to anyone else who survives as having "had it worse" or "done more." Such is the human condition, which is magnified in combat.

No one knows what actually happened. Each person will remember things differently; each remembers only part of the whole. And what is remembered will change over time. Those that say the least will probably know that which is closest to what actually happened—they do not want to relive that experience. Those that say the most might not have even been there, or at least their memories are shaped by their concerns. Some of what is "remembered" is only partially true, and much of what was done will never be known. Most of those who have never experienced real combat cannot understand this. Infantrymen or tankers who have experienced real combat will.

It is important that the experience of combat be understood and given value. To ignore this turns some of the most important decisions over to intellectuals, idealists, politicians, pacifists, engineers, managers, lawyers, political activists, scientists, analysts, and technicians. Yet no group can survive and grow if its warriors and soldiers are ignored. Others often look down on infantrymen and tankers, finding them lacking in civility, intellect, or morality. However, throughout history it has been infantrymen at the critical place and time who have made the difference between success and failure, between victory and defeat, between freedom and servility. After discussions and after support someone must take the final action. It is infantrymen who go the final yards. Infantrymen play a critical role in the rising stages of any group.

The qualities of infantrymen and tankers are always the same, be it Horatius at the bridge, Cortez confronting an empire, a teenager charging with Pickett at Gettysburg, a member of a staff pressing the harder right even when it is a career ender, or a ranger running to the side of a fallen brother. Going the final yards is never easy, but it is essential. Warriors and soldiers all have shared stressful experiences and they feel the randomness of life; they share the bond of "combat camaraderie." When any group casts its fighters aside, when it forgets the Ethos of Eros, it is in its declining stages.

Sex, Eros, and Death in Combat

In combat it is the absence of Eros that causes the fear of death—and uncontrolled stress that can result in mental disability, which in the past was known as combat fatigue. Death is the ultimate symbol of impotence—the lack of life—and sex is an easy way to counter this inner dread. Sex can prove vitality; it can show individuals that they are alive. The Ethos of Eros is a more difficult, yet more lasting, way to counter the fear of death.

This raises the question of what the outcome will be if women are integrated into combat units. Because of the relationship of Eros and death, such integration is very different from the integration of religions, races, or cultures. The obsession of politicians for advancing policies appropriate for Peace, in the name of equality, fairness, and justice, can destroy combat effectiveness if the realities of War and Warfare are not taken into consideration.

The critical symptom in the decline and decay of all great powers is for those in their armed forces to be transformed from masculine, principle-driven, uncompromising, disciplined, ruthless warriors with a common sense of identity into feminine, compromising, soft individuals lacking common identity, honor, purpose, and dedication. During such decline, the concern is on the performance in sexual acts, rather than on bridging the gap between being and becoming; they are thinking of themselves, rather than of those that have survived through unity. These changes during decline result in worthless and empty psyches easily damaged by stress and chaos. Combat effectiveness requires more than having members of armed forces that look and talk "military," shuffle paper and data with skill, make others feel good, are technical experts, are a cross section of the country, and are intelligent, caring, humane, and civilized individuals.

Success in both War and Warfare requires masculine, self-confident, courageous, risk-taking, and aggressive warriors and soldiers with strong Ethos of Eros. Thus the weakening of the qualities fighters need to face death has always been a sure sign of the fall of a great power.

The Bedrock of All Conflict and Cooperation Is Ideological

Ideological conflict needs clear images of "we" and "they" or "us" and "them" in both War and Warfare; in both ideological conflict requires a distinction between murder and killing—one being wrong, sinful, and illegal, and the other being right, honorable, and legal. Peace requires less extreme versions of "we" and "they" than War. In the Western way of war the enemy "they" often embodies undifferentiated evil; this inspires hatred and thus allows the use of any means to achieve a military victory. "They" are converted into sub-human, cold-blooded beasts with demonic powers that can be abhorred. This deionization permits the use of artillery, aerial bombardment, and nuclear weapons. The Oriental way of conflict allows greater flexibility—the goal is the same yet the focus is on deception, erosion of will, and conquest without fighting does not require "them" to be demon-possessed, sub-human creatures. While the Western way is more effective in War, the Oriental way is more effective in Warfare. In Warfare there is contact between "we" and "they" and the goal is to establish and maintain stability during protracted conflict, so "they" and "them" are often seen as those to be converted. Of course, in Peace there is a need to create a common identity so there must be efforts to lessen any "we–they" distinctions—diversity is more acceptable and desirable.

Success in ideological conflict requires an understanding of and the skillful use of the imaging of both "we" and "they." The legal and moral requirements of Peace, Warfare, and War are all unique; therefore the requirements appropriate for one should not be expected in the other two. This is probably the most difficult thing anyone making policy decisions must do; it is much easier to think of absolutes that apply in all situations or to have no absolutes. Yet the traps of moral relativism, universal morality, lawlessness, and universal laws all must be avoided.

Moral relativism, which allows each individual to determine what is right, correct, and appropriate based on his or her own experience and personal narrative, is disastrous in combat. Yet moral absolutism, i.e., the same Sacred Authority for all under all conditions, is equally disastrous. In combat the Pacifist's Fallacy of universal morality and universal laws is dysfunctional. Each group must have its rules, regulations, and laws, i.e., its own Secular Authority; lawlessness permits chaos and makes effective action impossible. Yet the supremacy of Secular Authority, without being checked and balanced by Sacred Authority, is also dysfunctional. Secular Authority must be checked to prevent soldiers from claiming they are not responsible for acts of murderous ecstasy because they are "only doing their duty as ordered." This was the issue addressed in the war trials following World War II. Although those trials might not have hit the correct equilibrium, they at least came to grips with this perplexing problem. Also, Sacred Authority must also be checked and balanced so that true believers do not think it is their duty to kill all nonbelievers.

In all combat, the crucial moment comes when a person is ordered to do something that his inner compass tells him is wrong, illegal, immoral, or sinful. He is torn and helpless. Is he free to violate the orders of his legal superior? Can he void his bond with his "brothers," his convictions, and his nation? Can he act on his own free will or must he be an instrument of others' wills? These are decisions that all humans must make, but they are most difficult in combat—be it War or Warfare. When a person takes on the responsibility to make such a decision on his own in accordance with his own inner compass he abandons group security and protection. This is like jumping from a cliff unto darkness not knowing what the consequences will be. The need to repeatedly make such decisions is the main cause of combat fatigue.[86]

---

[83] In 1962 I published *Irregular Warfare in a Nutshell*, which discussed how to fight both the defensive and offensive aspects of Irregular Warfare (which I later decided should be called just Warfare). While Director of Stability Studies at the US Army War College from 1967 until 1970, I wrote and argued about how to be successful in Vietnam, i.e., how to achieve a climate of order and satisfaction through a bottom-up approach. From 2002 to 2005 at the Armiger Cromwell Center I did the same regarding Iraq and Afghanistan.

[84] Modern Western democracy was fashioned by eighteenth- and nineteenth-century liberals; advocating universal suffrage, social equality, civil rights, rule of law, limited government, and a democratic political process. In the twentieth century Western democracy was further transformed to an ideology that postulates a "best" society based on social concern, human dignity, and international law to be provided by centralized governance. However, democracy actually grew out of families, clans, village communities, and guilds in many parts of the world before 500 BC. It has had many forms and characteristics, demonstrating many strengths and weaknesses. Democratic theory rests on the assumption that all citizens of a state are, at least for political purposes, equal. While there have always been disputes over the meaning of "democracy," it is generally agreed that a democracy must be some form of representative governance with accountability, a social contract, protection of the well-being of the individual, and policy determined by the principle of majority rule.

[85] Sacred Authority provided an inner compass so that individuals can make judgments between right and wrong; it is the result of custom, tradition, and civic virtue; it is based on shared moral, ethical, and religious beliefs. As such it allowed the expression of free will and provided protection from authoritarian government. However, when taken to the extreme Sacred Authority can result in individuals becoming a repressive collective with hostility toward "others" because it must not be violated or disregarded. As is so often the case, when something good is taken to the extreme it becomes something bad. This is certainly true for the inner compass of individuals.

Secular Authority (rules, regulations, and laws established and administered by government) provides the stability essential for a climate of order and satisfaction of any country. Without the enforcement of laws there is anarchy. With the enforcement of laws there can be either order and satisfaction or tyranny. It is recognized that cultural values, attitudes, customs, and traditions come before law—thus all law is not the same. Lawyers, with a very few exceptions, see social, political, economic, and foreign affairs in terms of legality, i.e., they seek to resolve conflict through the rules, regulations, laws, processes, and procedures of Secular Authority. Thus they see law as the final, and supreme, authority. Today most of our politicians and judges are lawyers, and many of those in the media and other influential positions are influenced by the legal mind set.

[86] Since Vietnam, this is often called Post-Traumatic Stress Disorder or PTSD.

CHAPTER THIRTY-ONE

FUTURE POLICY

Can the lessons from Korea and Vietnam be useful in the future? I think they can. *Forgotten: Ideological Conflicts in Korea, Vietnam, Iraq, and Afghanistan* is an attempt to describe and explain the lessons that should have been learned so they might be used in the future. This will require the US political elite and the military establishment to no longer think of War and Peace in dichotomous terms. Warriors and soldiers will be needed for success in Warfare, ideological conflict, and strategic communication. Achieving stability, with order and satisfaction in which no one is willing or able to use force to achieve political goals, will have to be considered just as important as victory in War. Whereas Peace can cope with diversity, War and Warfare require unity, with diversity being a handicap and possibly even the difference between success and failure.

The Building of a Nation-State

Since 1945 there have been many examples of success and failure in building nation-states. Nevertheless, efforts by the US foreign policy establishment have produced many costly failures since World War II.

There are four things that must be done to achieve stability, and then to maintain it while building a nation-state. Stability is a homeostatic equilibrium. Authoritarian and oppressive methods can achieve stability, but stability can also be achieved through a balancing of order and freedom. The four things that must be done are overlapping and in practice can't be separated. They must be used as appropriate for each specific situation.

Security is the first thing that must be accomplished, but it is merely a means to achieve stability. When the focus is solely on security, actions often actually hinder the realization of a climate of order and satisfaction since they do not produce self-regulating equilibrium. Achieving security has three parts:

- Destruction of Insurgent Units. This is often the only task accepted as "military" by many people. Operations are no different from anti-guerrilla operations in conventional War. The goal should be to make these operations unnecessary.

- Local Security. A climate of order at the local level is critical. It requires a combination of: (a) neighborhood watch groups, (b) police activities, and (c) local security operations by stability forces organized and trained for internal security.

- Neutralization of the Insurgent Organization. The third part needed to achieve security requires a latticework of information flow, followed by rapid reaction to any intimidation or propaganda by the insurgents. It is the parallel hierarchy of the insurgent organization that provides control over the people, and allows the insurgency to bloom again after repeated setbacks. It also requires targeted killing of enemy leaders.

Effective local authority is the second thing that must be accomplished. After security is established, local leaders must preserve stability by being alert for signs of problems, inequalities, and injustices. They must out-organize the insurgents.

A common identity is the third thing that must be accomplished. The people must be welded together by a common destiny. They must be cohesive. How the people are welded together, and the principles, values, and ideals they share will vary depending on the degree of decentralization of power.

Finally the never-ending attempt to fulfill aspirations is the fuel of change; it can unite people in a common effort. Yet aspirations can also set one against another. Satisfying aspirations is an elusive, two-faced—yet essential—part of maintaining stability. However, fulfilling aspirations, just like the three parts of achieving security, will actually hinder stability when it is carried too far.

It is useful to compare the model for building a nation-state presented here with that advocated since 1945 by the US foreign policy establishment. The outcome of repeated attempts to use "soft power" have been costly failures. These failures are the result of five realities:

1. Economic and political change is ineffective and inefficient if there is not security. Security must come first even if the government is authoritarian.

2. Those identifying with the nation being built must accomplish the nation building. Others can assist, but the leadership, dedication, vision, and energy must come from within.

3. Nation-building is not attempting to persuade rival groups to form a coalition government or to have elections.

4. Governance must be based on the customs and traditions; i.e., what the people think is right rather than want the government says is legal. The building must be from the bottom up, not from the top down.

5. Large-scale economic projects often hinder more than they contribute to nation building. Economic development should focus on providing a better life for the people, rather than on economic output or integration into international trade.

The creation of a nation-state is a long—several generations at least—process; the maintenance of a nation-state is a never-ending process.

Economic development must start small on a solid foundation, rather than trying to start large on a weak foundation. In each village, town, and district, successful local leaders encourage people to:

- Find what needs to be done and then do it, rather than waiting for some government official to say what should be done, how it should be done, and when it should be done.

- Create a new product or service for those living nearby, rather than being concerned about economic theory.

- Solve any economic problem with what is available.

- Do something that saves time, simplifies a process, or improves living conditions.

- Encourage greater production and then make good use of any surplus created.

The phoenix (bottom-up) approach to economic development recognizes that the action of filling a need comes first. It contrasts with the neocolonial (top-down) approach, which uses economic theory for large-scale production, infrastructure, and projects financed by foreign capital. The top-down approach often hinders economic improvements. It can:

- Prop up corrupt and chaotic governments.

- Damage the environment with dams and highway projects.

- Increase the country's debt.

- Leave a trail of destruction and poverty.

When "economic development" is controlled by the central government, its true goal is often to increase the state's power and the wealth of those with political connections rather than to provide a better life for the people.

Growth in each village, town, district, city, and country is a function of productivity, i.e., all of the goods and services produced by that political group. If any one of these groups consumes more than it produces it becomes dependent—and beholden—on others. When any one of these groups produces more than it consumes it has a surplus (called profit) which can be used for trade to improve the living standards or to influence the actions of others. When the reward is great, the effort to succeed is great. But if there is to be growth some portion must be used to purchase tools that further improve productivity.

This relationship between economics, politics, and growth is simple, yet it is filled with many problems in practice because there is always a struggle to determine: Who says how the profits are to be spent?

People want stuff, people want what others have, people want a good life without effort, and they are willing to trade their surplus stuff for others' surplus stuff. And politicians use this to their advantage. Politicians want power and control, politicians want support from those who will give them power. To get that support politicians promise, in the name of fairness or some utopian goal, to spread the profits from those with more stuff to those with less stuff.

Therefore, politicians willingly spend not only any surpluses of over-producers—collected through taxes—but also incur debt from outside sources in order to buy "fair" outcomes for everyone. This reduces the incentives for under-producers to do better. This problem can occur at any level, but it increases with the centralization of power, which expands the tax base, the tax level, and the source of outside money (debt).

After there is security 24-7 at the local level and there is a reasonable degree of stability, it is possible to create an economic culture that lays the foundation for social-political change—and in time nation-building. With stability it is possible to have laws, rules, and regulations under which contracts can be entered into with a reasonable expectation of enforcement. Profits can then be exported and a rational business climate can encourage foreign investment. However, if this arrangement is to work there must first be security and then stability plus indigenous decisions at the lower levels. This is why the bottom-up (phoenix) approach works, but the top-down (neo-colonial) approach does not.

Building of States and Nations

From Korea and Vietnam lessons should have been learned about how to build states and nations and who should, and who cannot, do such building. First the difference between state building and nation building must be recognized. Unfortunately many in the US military and the US foreign policy establishment failed to make these distinctions.

State building concerns how to establish and maintain Secular Authority (the rule of law) throughout a specific territory. It is primarily a top-down process and requires centralized control what uses force to eliminate opposition to the political elite that controls the central government. It is appropriately referred to as the neocolonial approach, and it is usually authoritarian.

Nation building concerns how to create and maintain a common identity among people through equilibrium between Secular Authority (governmental rules, regulations, and laws) and customs and traditions as expressed in Sacred Authority (how individuals get an inner compass that allows them to make judgments). Building a nation is primarily a bottom-up process and requires a high degree of decentralized control. It is appropriately referred to as the phoenix approach.

Foreigners cannot build a nation; only those who share a common identity and consider themselves "we" can.

Future Ideological Threats

In the future, existential threats to America are more likely to be ideological than they are to be from the armed forces of other states. There will be no doubt that conventional armed forces need often to counter actions by others. Thus the military instrument needs to be strong and ready. Yet the most probable existential threats to America are likely to be from the Third Jihad and postmodern thought.

The erosion strategy of the Islamists primarily uses covert actions. It seeks to weaken the unity and will of Americans and increase the number of people that submit to Allah. They will use strategic communications to present Islam as a religion of peace and to convince Americans that those who oppose the spread of Islam not only lie but engage in immoral and sinful behavior. They will claim that anyone who does not accept the way of Allah is a bigot. Of course, all Muslims are not Islamists who support the Third Jihad. Therefore, it should be the future policy of the USA to eliminate the Islamists and also to support the modern Muslims who accept and respect American principles and ideals—those Muslims who want better lives rather than spiritual purity in the eyes of Allah.

The other existential threat to America comes from postmodern (progressive) thought. It seeks to deconstruct the concepts, institutions, roles, rules, and standards associated with traditional Western culture. It visualizes "progress" toward a utopia that is nonjudgmental, nondiscriminatory, and resolves all disagreement through compromise. In 2014, postmodern thought shapes the views of most intellectuals, academics, and the media in Europe and the USA. It seeks to fundamentally transform the America established by our Founders. Unless this threat is successfully countered, America will decline and decay.

Ideological Conflict Is the Oldest Form of Conflict/ Cooperation

In the mythology of the ancient Greeks, the connection between combat and wisdom was recognized. Apollo is the god of thinking, but he carries the bow and arrow. Athena is the goddess of wisdom, yet she has a helmet and shield. The Greeks had no military caste since to be a citizen you had to be a soldier. All citizens were aware of the suffering and disasters caused by conflict, yet they also recognized the noble character and greatness of common effort that evolved from conflict. They sought the Golden Mean that keeps these opposites balanced. Western leaders can learn much from the Greek view of the need to keep conflict and cooperation in equilibrium.

Among the most refined, most intellectual, and most civilized there is an illusion that good is achieved only through compassion, compromise, and cooperation. But good is also achieved through conflict. Sensuality, selfishness, materialism, and exploitation of the weak are all common during peace. Vices flourish during peace. During conflict people learn what is true, they clarify strength of thought, and they test their unity. The civic virtues of courage, fidelity, and sacrifice are cultivated. They are nourished by conflict, and they waste what they have built during times of comfort and ease; they are built during struggle and they expire during peace. Creativity, restlessness, respect of merit, nobleness, honesty, patriotism, and the elimination of evil are encouraged during conflict. Struggle brings human energies to their highest level and define that which is noble, right, and good.

Conflict provides the spiritual sustenance upon which the forebears of Western culture were raised up before postmodern thought began to infect those influenced by science. As those in the West have lost the will to practice its Christian birthright, they can find merit in the civic virtues of Greece, Rome, China, Korea, Japan, and Scandinavia. Such civic virtues are jewels created in blood, steel, horror, suffering, unity, and determination. But this does not mean that conflict is to be worshiped because it gave birth to civic virtues. All things that are good turn into something bad when taken to the extreme.

Civilized warriors and soldiers are expected to have composure and subdued strength; unchecked violence should never be praised as it is among barbarians. Conflict, be it War or Warfare, should be approached with a high and noble disposition, which rejects the extremes of brute force. In War destruction of an enemy should end with victory, and rebuilding should begin. In Warfare violence should be kept to a minimum at the same time achieving stability should be the primary concern.

Today when we speak of conflict it is more often an ideological, or spiritual, struggle than it is the overwhelming violence of conventional War between the armed forces of states. Conflict and cooperation have been transferred from an outward to an inward battlefield on which the inner compasses of individuals are shaped. Though we walk in the flesh, we live or die in the soul. Conventional War requires the production of expensive weapons systems and large organizations. Warfare requires neither. Therefore, it can be expected that there will be support for conventional War from manufacturers who want to make money and from those in the military who want more positions for high-ranking officers. There will be many who want to apply values and attitudes appropriate for Peace when they are both costly and ineffective. Yet what we need most is knowledge on how to be successful in Warfare at the lowest possible cost—and the skill, will, and courage to turn that knowledge into action.

Perhaps Kipling was only partly correct when he wrote:

> *Oh, East is East, and West is West, and never the two shall meet,*
>
> *Till Earth and Sky stand presently at God's great Judgment Seat;*
>
> *But there is neither East nor West, Border, nor Breed, nor Birth,*
>
> *When two strong men stand face to face, tho' they come from the ends of the earth.*

Nevertheless, policy makers need to remember: The East is east and the West is west and they have often met. In the past three hundred years, the East has taken much from the West; it is time for the West to again take more from the East.

APPENDIX ONE

ORIGIN OF THE KOREAN WAR

At the lower levels, we understood that the attack by North Korea on 25 June 1950 was unprovoked aggression to united Korea under a communist regime. We had no idea that one day there would be a debate about the origin of the Korean War.

Two years later in *The Hidden History of the Korean War*, I. F. Stone would advance the argument that the attack was not a surprise, but that those who wanted to expand the American empire and preserve the power of America's puppets staged it. This argument was largely ignored because Stone was known to have ties to the Soviet Union. Since the 1960s many progressives, who claim America's war-based imperialism is the cause of the world's problems and who support world governance as a replacement for the nation-state system, have continued to argue that America was largely responsible for the Korean War, and the deaths and destruction of that war. In 2010 this view again appeared in *The Korean War: A History* by Bruce Cumings.

The evidence does not support such revisionist history. The Truman administration had twice decided that Korea was of little strategic interest. Documents of the Soviet Union and the People's Republic of China, released in the 1990s, showed that Kim Il-sung convinced the Soviet leadership that he could defeat South Korea with minimal risk of US intervention. He received Soviet approval for a military effort to unify Korea. Also, China sent all of their ethnic Korean soldiers back to North Korea prior to the attack. Although the origin of the Korean War is murky and there were many policy debates, it is clear that the attack on 25 June 1950 was unprovoked aggression. It was this surprise that caused Washington to reverse its policy.

At the Potsdam Conference of July 1945, the US was concerned about the invasion of Japan. After the atomic bombs on 6 and 9 August 1945, the rapid occupation of Manchuria by the Soviet Army caused a new concern. On 10 August 1945 it was decided that the US would participate in the occupation of Korea. Since the US was unable to deploy any forces to Korea, two Army colonels—one being Dean Rush, a future Secretary of State and the other "Tic" Bonesteel, who became the Commanding General in Korea—selected the 38th Parallel to limit the advance of the Soviet Army. When Americans did arrive in Korea, they made common cause with the orderly Japanese and showed contempt for the unruly Koreans who were divided by old rivalries—the Americans seemed to be unaware of the ruthless behavior of the Japanese during their occupation of Korea. As H. Merell Benninghoff, the State Department's representative in Korea, reported: "There are no qualified Koreans for other than the low-ranking positions, either in government or in public utilities and communications." This early failure to establish common cause with the Koreans was a tragic mistake.

Also the Americans thought that since the War was over, i.e., victory over the Japanese had been achieved, there would be Peace and it was only necessary to bring economic and political development to Korea. The ideological struggles among Korean communists, socialists, nationalists, and capitalists were never fully understood. The importance of local authority and the dangers of centralized power were not recognized. The American conceptual framework lacked the strategies, tactics, and procedures for conflict that was neither Peace nor War.

On 20 October 1945, Syngman Rhee returned to Korea after thirty-five years in exile to form a new government. Rhee was a prickly, anti-communist, uncompromising Korean nationalist whom the State Department opposed because they considered him a mischief-maker. This was the start of the ideological struggle between the conservative Korean Democratic Party (KDP) and the socialist/communist Korean People's Republic (KPR) to establish an authoritarian centralized government for South Korea. The bitter ideological differences and hatred from a tragic history made it impossible to move to a representative democracy of, by, and for the individual citizens with liberty and justice for all.

By the fall of 1946, the Communists had consolidated their control of North Korea, so the Americans decided to create an anti-communist South Korea that would provide a counter-balance to North Korea. However, the 38th Parallel was an impractical border. In 1946, China was still involved in a bitter civil war, but success by the communists was increasingly likely. After the departure of the Red Army from North Korea, the United States should have moved rapidly north, under the threat of using nuclear weapons, with enough armed forces to expand the Republic of Korea (South Korea). A practical border could have been established at the narrow neck of Korea below the 40th Parallel so that the ROK would include both Anju and Hungnam. This would have made North Korea a mountainous buffer state having a long border with China. This would have ensured future stability not only on the Korean peninsula, but also in the region.

However, such action was not considered because the focus of the Truman administration was on peace, preventing the Soviet Union from controlling Europe and the reconstruction of Europe and Japan. The US armed forces had demobilized and those in Korea and Japan were now occupation troops—not war fighters.

On 24 July 1948 Syngman Rhee became the first elected leader of the Republic of Korea. On 14 August 1948, General MacArthur told the Koreans, "An artificial barrier has divided your land. This barrier must and shall be torn down." The Democratic People's Republic of Korea (DPRK) was established on 9 September 1948. During the next two years, Rhee established an authoritarian government which created a market-oriented country with some degree of personal freedom and corruption. No doubt his regime killed thousands of Koreans who actively sided—overtly or covertly—with the ruthlessly disciplined totalitarian collective of the north. If this had not been done, South Korea would probably have fallen to the communists.

The US did not provide the South Koreans with the means for armed aggression to unite Korea. Rhee's requests to replace his secondhand infantry weapons and outmoded artillery were repeatedly denied. The military advisory group remained small, and Rhee was given no tanks or effective anti-tank weapons. On the other hand, the Soviet Union provided the North Koreans with the tanks, artillery, aircraft, and training needed for an attempt to unite Korea through aggression.

There was intelligence of a buildup of North Korean forces during the spring of 1950 and there was talk of a North Korean attack. However, the lack of preparedness of both the South Korean and American forces is convincing evidence that the attack by the North Koreans was a surprise and they were responsible for the four million deaths and the destruction that followed. Debates on the origin of the Korean War continue to this day. However, more important is the critical lesson that armed forces can never be allowed to become soft and hollow. Armed forces must always be kept ready with well-trained, disciplined, war-hardened fighters.

APPENDIX TWO

THE ETHOS OF EROS

Before science surpassed religion as the linchpin of Western culture, the Ethos of Eros was a significant factor in combat success. And it still should be. Eros is often translated as love, but its original meaning was unity. Therefore, Ethos of Eros as presented here does not describe romantic love or sex—it describes the bond of mutual dependency and expectations. It is the basis of combat camaraderie and provides protection from combat fatigue.

Eros has a long history and several meanings. The oldest usage of Eros is the closest to the unity of combat camaraderie. The earliest Greek thinkers (including Hesiod) considered Eros one of the three primordial gods at the time of the creation of the cosmos. The Greeks from 2,000 to 600 BC worshiped the three primordial gods: Earth (nature and living things), Chaos (conflict, disaster, tragedy, and hate), and Eros (unity, cooperation, and love). Eros and Chaos engaged in endless struggles to control and use Earth. Eros was the power capable of uniting people in a common bond. For them it was "life energy" that challenged reason, allowing humans to survive. For Sophocles, Eros was the god who caused Antigone's tragedy. In all cases Eros united people so they were able to control Chaos. Empedocles introduced the idea of cycles with love and conflict interacting with each other, and unfortunately he gave it a link to sexual love by using Aphrodite as the name for love. For some this changed Eros from life-preserving instincts to protect into erotic sex. That interpretation continues today through the works of Schopenhauer and Freud. This needs to be corrected.

The meaning of Eros was further confused by the Greeks of the fifth century BC. They called brotherly love without sexual passion *phileo* love, and it was what sustained military units in combat. But *phileo* love is not combat camaraderie for several reasons. At that time the Greeks had words for many different types of love: parental, filial, conjugal affection, fraternal feelings, friendship, heterosexual passion, homosexual passion, love of country, love of wisdom, and love of the gods. Each of these words had narrow and specific meanings—which makes them useful for scientific analysis. Yet combat camaraderie is not narrow or specific; it requires a concept that unites and combines many aspects of love that support the bond of mutual dependency and expectations. *Phileo* did not have the philosophic history of Eros that overlaps and interacts with other forms of love. Also *phileo* love was considered less noble than *agape* love, but combat camaraderie is selfless, self-sacrificing love and should be considered the noblest form of love.

Eros, as an overarching word for unity, cooperation, and love, comes from belief that the origin of the world is an act of creation, mutual dependency, and building. Love in all of its forms is also one of the most powerful of human impulses. In *Phaedrus* Plato represented Eros as a charioteer trying to control two horses, one passion and the other togetherness. In keeping with the Platonic tradition, based on Plato's *Symposium*, love has a unique metaphysical status—being part of both the material and the ideal world. Before and after Plato, Eros has been interpreted as unity and love in general and also as erotic sex. There have been interpretations by Aristotle, Augustine, Dante, Marsilio Ficino, Leone Ebreo, Spinoza, Schopenhauer, and many others. Kant saw Eros as the power to release a person from the prison of the self. In *Forgotten* an interpretation of Eros is presented that can be useful today and in the future to improve combat effectiveness and to reduce combat fatigue.

The Ethos of Eros lacks scientific credibility because it cannot be measured and is difficult to describe in a way that will allow scientific research. The Ethos of Eros is one of the factors that shapes the inner compass of individuals that allows them to make judgments on the basis of what is good or bad, right or wrong, virtuous or sinful. Humans, and humans alone, have the possibility of choices to avoid unconscious cruelty and brutality to others. Therefore, Ethos of Eros is an accurate name for that which generates combat camaraderie as it allows warriors and soldiers to be effective and to survive in both War and Warfare.

The mysterious linkage between Eros and Thanatos (death) has never been adequately explained, even though it often appears in history and literature. We do know that after death there is no Eros. Eros is the life-preserving instinct that seeks to protect those that are loved. If there is an absence of Eros during combat, the fear of death takes control of the mind—and such uncontrolled stress can result in mental disability. Death is the ultimate symbol of impotence—the lack of life—and Eros is a way to counter this inner dread. Sex only shows individuals they are alive. But it is Eros that is able to preserve a clear, strong, purposeful mind under the most stressful of situations.

Psychologists and psychiatrists focus on diagnosis and treatment of disorders (therefore they address PTSD), but even more important are ways to improve combat effectiveness and prevent combat fatigue. This has been forgotten. Although it has gone by many names, combat fatigue has always been a part of combat. In the past the Ethos of Eros was seen as something that gave warriors and soldiers a sense of common identity, will, courage, and spirit that produced success in combat and reduced combat fatigue. Eros causes humans to hold off the tension of life. Eros is a human quality of imagination, commitment, and belonging. Eros provides the motivation for a union with others seeking fulfillment. Eros causes a person to remember, savor, and look forward to repeating experiences of significance.

It is the Ethos of Eros that creates the bond of brotherhood known as combat camaraderie, and builds a "Band of Brothers." Your "brothers" accept you for what you are; they would do anything for you, and love you no matter what. Being loved by someone gives you strength, while loving others gives you courage.

ABOUT THE AUTHOR

Sam C. Holliday was born in a Model T Ford on Seymour Highway en route to Wichita Falls, Texas, in 1926. He graduated from Lamar High School, Houston, Texas, in 1943. He received his BS from the United States Military Academy, West Point, New York, in 1948 and his Masters in Public and International Affairs from the University of Pittsburgh in 1964. He received his PhD in International Relations and Management from the University of South Carolina (1974). He has been married to Joan A. Holliday since 1951, and they have two sons, Mark and Lee. In the US Army he was awarded a Silver Star, two Bronze Stars for valor, a Purple Heart, two Legions of Merit, and a Combat Infantryman Badge. He is author of *Irregular Warfare in a Nutshell*, with Pierre C. Dabezies (1962 and 1968), *The Tao of Thor* (1968), *USAWC Stability Operations Readings* (1969), and numerous articles on subjects related to the themes of this book. He is currently Director of Armiger Cromwell Center, LLC.

For more information, please contact:

Armiger Cromwell Center, LLC
3750 Peachtree Road, NE, Suite 374
Atlanta, Georgia 30319-1322